Lahiri Mahasaya of The Kriya Lineage

THE SPIRITUAL SCIENCE
OF KRIYA YOGA

Goswami Kriyananda

The Temple of Kriya Yoga
• Chicago •

Cover photograph copyright © Dominique Levin
Cover art copyright © Rebecca Romanoff
Illustrations by Eric Klein and Lynn Wallace-Mills

First Edition, March 1976
Second Edition, August, 1985
Third Edition, March, 1988
Fourth Edition, Revised, March, 1992
Fifth Edition, October, 1998

Library of Congress Card Catalog Number: 85-051501
ISBN: 0-9613099-1-1

Published by The Temple of Kriya Yoga
2414 N. Kedzie, Chicago, IL. 60647

Printed in the United States of America

Books and Home Study Courses
By Goswami Kriyananda

Books

Spiritual Science of Kriya Yoga
Beginner's Guide to Meditation
Intermediate Guide to Meditation
The Wisdom & Way of Astrology
The Bhagavad Gita
The Laws of Karma: Deeper Insight
      to the Esoteric Teaching of Kriya Yoga
Extraordinary Spiritual Potential
The Kriya Yoga Upanishad and the
      Ten Mystical Yoga Upanishads
Pathway to God-Consciousness
A Yoga Dictionary of Basic Sanskirt Terms
A Yoga Dictionary of Basic Astrological Terms
Beginner's Guide to Meditation with 2 audio tapes
Beginner's Guide to Meditation- A Talking Book

Home Study Courses

The Chakras: The Garden of God
The Sacred Apprenticeship: The Guru/Disciple Relationship
The Philosophy & Methodology of Kriya Yoga
Establishing a Firm Foundation for Your Spiritual Life
The Yoga Sutras of Patanjali

In French

La Science Spirituelle du Kriya Yoga
Guide Pratique de Méditation

In Spanish

Su Primer Guía de Meditación

In Italian

La Scienza Spirituale Dello Yoga di Kriya
E.S.P.: Tuoi Eccezionali Poteri Spirituali
Astrologi: Via e Saggezza

In Dutch

Kriya Yoga: Werk en Oefenboek

DEDICATION

Sri Lahiri Mahasaya and my guru have shown by their personal life that every person can attain God-Realization while being a householder. In them, we find perfect examples of the Truth ... Illumination.

I was initiated into kriya yoga by my guru, Sri Shelliji. Shelliji was initiated by Paramahansa Yogananda. Yoganandaji was initiated by Sri Yukteswarji, who in turn received kriya yoga initiation from Lahiri Mahasaya, who was initiated by Sri Sri Babaji: the spiritual fountainhead of the Kriya Lineage.

This volume is a striving to demonstrate that the spiritual science of kriya yoga is a meaningful esoteric pathway to Reality.

This textbook is dedicated to my beloved disciples and students who have shared in its production. May the good karma which they have accumulated through their unselfish and untiring devotion bring to them the greatest of rewards ... to share afresh the bread of Truth to those who hunger spiritually.

PREFACE

In recent times we have seen an increasing interest in eastern philosophy, most particularly yoga. Yoga, a philosophy of happiness through spiritual wisdom, has captured the imagination and interest of the western world. Yoga is a way to find happiness on all levels of your being: physically, mentally, and spiritually. Yoga is a way to achieve serenity and calmness. There is no mystery or magic in yoga. It simply is an accomplishment through time-tested mental and physical techniques. With the west turning to eastern thought, the elusive and mysterious achievements of self-control through harmonious living become more understandable.

Despite the fantastic unfoldment and inroads yoga has made on the western mind, there are westerners who are prejudiced toward yoga. These prejudices are based on misconceptions of its nature and function. It is my hope that some of these misconceptions will be cleared up.

Many prejudices are based upon two misconceptions: 1) that yoga does not possess a systematic approach to its goal, and 2) that it is not a scientifically-based philosophy. Neither of these is true. It is my goal to show that yoga is scientific and logical, and that it does possess an ancient systematic approach to the problems of everyday living.

Yoga is based upon the noble and spiritual experiences of the Indian mind. What one person has experienced, all are capable of experiencing. The search for Truth is not a cultural prerogative. The understanding, the grasping, and the experience of Truth is the birthright of all mankind.

There is an inversion taking place today. The eastern world is busy learning all it can about western technology and economics, while we in the west are busy learning all we can about their sublime, spiritual philosophy. Let us move forward in knowledge, and also in the mystical experience of our everyday happiness.

If I have gained something of benefit from yoga, so you can also. One of the purposes of this book is to help you solve your everyday problems, help you become more beautiful, and to realize your innate dignity.

If you give a person a fish, he will eat but for a day ... but if you teach him to fish he will eat forever! I offer this book at the feet of the Lord which dwells in the hearts of all souls.

Many decades ago, I came to spend an afternoon with a great sage who became my spiritual preceptor. I came to lunch, but I stayed for life. It is my hope that you will partake of this spiritual food, and that you will stay for life....

TABLE OF CONTENTS

INTRODUCTION

This text has been written to give you a deeper understanding of the basic why's and wherefore's of the philosophy and disciplines of yoga.

The Vishnu Purana, one of the ancient spiritual texts of India, points out that each and every person will know when mankind has entered the Dark Age (kali yuga): 'When society reaches the stage that property confers rank, where wealth becomes the only source of virtue, where passion is the sole bond between man and woman, and where falsehood is the source of success.'

The purpose of this text is to assist you in searching out the inner way. The inner way is the release from externalized values that have only mechanized and brutalized man's mind, causing him to destroy that which is beautiful and meaningful. This text is a spiritual map for the conquest of the inner life and the exploration of the cosmic universe that dwells within. Some of the more closely guarded secrets or techniques that will help you to walk the pathway are given. This, therefore, is a manual for mystics. The underlying philosophical foundation for this manual can be summarized as follows:

1. This universe and every individual thing in this universe is permeated with a single energy called light. This universe and every individual thing in this universe is an emanation from a single source, called the great light. Some philosophies refer to this light or source of energy as prana, kriya, or kundalini.

2. This energy, although definitely single, manifests in four worlds, and on seven planes.

3. This energy, although single in nature, manifests itself on the seven sub-planes in three distinctive ways.

       a. Inertia or resistance,
       b. Passionate activity,
       c. Compassionate activity.

Inertia is related to material substance, or matter (prakriti). It is the unconscious substance. Matter takes on three forms: gross, subtle and super-subtle.

Passionate activity is related to mind, which is a form of super-subtle matter. Mind has many levels of expression, including the memory storage banks called soul. It is conscious substance ... or, at least mirrored matter.

Finally, the material substance reacts with the mind substance to produce a harmonious reaction called life. The interaction of these two opposites produces a compassionate activity called self-consciousness.

4. For mankind, and all other cerebral-spinal beings, our existence has a dual nature of an external cosmos or macrocosm, and an inner universe or microcosm. This seemingly external universe is composed of both mind-stuff and matter-stuff; the internal universe is also composed of mind-stuff and matter-substance. The external universe seems to have a predominance of matter-stuff, whereas the internal universe seems to have a predominance of mind-stuff. The macrocosm is an exact duplicate of the microcosm. Others, inaccurately, would say the microcosm is an exact duplicate of the macrocosm.

5. The mystic seeks, by various means, to identify the corresponding mind-stuff centers (chakras) in the body with those matter-stuff centers of the macrocosm. Through the great science of yoga, the mystic seeks to find this correspondence in order to merge the individual self with the cosmic self. This is done by balancing the inner universe so that one can slip into the outer universe. In short, the function of the mystic is to find the doctrine of correspondence which will reveal the absolute law of his own being, and, therefore, the physical laws of this universe. He aligns the forces, wherein he moves from more complex and emotional states of consciousness to simpler, non-emotional states of consciousness. The unfoldment of his spiritual evolution is caused by the interaction of unconscious matter with conscious matter to produce self-conscious awareness.

This points out that liberation, illumination, and emancipation come about only through experience. This should give you an idea of the importance of the earth, your body, and your mind. These experiences are not a punishment, but gifts of Life by which you find your evolutionary, spiritual destiny.

6. This evolution occurs through the interplay and balancing of the forces called qualities (gunas). No state of consciousness can be transcended until it is balanced. This means on whatever rung of life you find yourself, unless that particular rung is balanced, you will be unable to transcend it and

return to a more fundamental state. When this transpires, you have attained a higher illuminative stage, ever closer to the ultimate illumination of cosmic consciousness.

7. This process takes an infinite period of time and consequently all beings reincarnate again and again into the world of existence until these four worlds and seven planes are balanced. Each of these seven planes is linked to a basic law of kriya: a law of creation. At each of the seven stages there is a given technique of kriya. Thus, there are seven major initiations into kriya yoga.

The purpose of this manual for mystics is to move you from the realms of secondary and tertiary thought back to the mainstream of primary cosmic consciousness. You can establish in a given lifetime perfect health, perfect happiness, or perfect knowledge. You can improve the karma of this lifetime!

This idea was eloquently expressed by a holy man in India. We were sitting in a railroad station. I asked him if the train was on time. He answered my question, adding,

> 'Few souls are as noble as the locomotive,
> having the capacity to move in and of itself,
> and having the power to move others.'

Chapter 1

THE LAW OF ABSTENTION
(YAMA)

There is a prescribed order in the study and practice of yoga. What is the first step? The first step consists of understanding and practicing the eight stages of yoga. Before considering these steps, there are a few things that need be said.

Yoga is a school of theological philosophy that is not aimed at self-denial, but rather at the extinction of negative emotionalities and physical-spiritual imbalances. Balance is the word that symbolizes kriya yoga. The balance of all things, and the balance in all things. Modern man might best understand this as moderation in all things.

The key ideology of kriya yoga is: He who knows a drop of water knows all water, whenever or wherever it is found. In the selfsame manner, when you realize the truth of the temple of your own body, so will you know the truth of the total universe. This principle is really the understanding of the unification of the two opposite forces within the universe: matter and Spirit. These two forces bring about an interaction of self-conscious awareness which produces illumination. For some people, the union of opposites is difficult to understand because one of the Indian philosophies (as well as western fundamentalism) claims the universe to be illusion (maya). However, according to the Sankhya Yoga philosophy, the world is not an illusion; the world is real and eternal. The world is made for real experiences through which we gain real knowledge of our real being. Thus, the yogis say that Truth is not a matter of intellectualization. Truth must be lived and thus experienced.

There are eight essential stages in the study and practice of yoga. These are:

1. Abstentions (yama)
2. Observances (niyama)
3. Postures (asan)
4. Life-force control (pranayama)
5. Sense-withdrawal (pratyahara)
6. Concentration (dharana)
7. Meditation (dhyana)
8. Contemplation (samadhi)

1

The first four stages are called the outer or gross steps, while the last four stages are called the inner or subtle steps.

Abstentions and observances are worked at together.

Postures and life-force control are worked at together, etc.

The objective of the first four stages of yoga is to cleanse the mental and physical body of physical and mental phlegm. In yoga, the cleansing of the mind is called the cleansing of the astral channels (nadis). This cleansing takes place so the life-force can flow through these astral channels, activating greater consciousness, greater self-consciousness, and greater balanced, self-conscious awareness within ourselves.

The astral channels correspond to the physical nerves, the nerves being the only part of your physical body that are never re-generated during your lifetime. The astral channels are super pre-mental channels by which consciousness reaches out into infinity. Just as we make physical contact, and know we have touched something because of the current flowing through the physical nerves, so, in the same way, we know we have made contact with the spiritual life-forms by the pranic energy flowing through our astral channels.

Abstentions-observances cleanse the mind-states, the subtler astral channels, whereas posture and life-energy control tend to cleanse the physical-astral channels. These two, working together, cleanse the total vehicle of your mind/body, so that the energies can flow through the astral channels to the opposite end reaching into the causal plane of God-consciousness. These outer stages reach their perfection in the fourth stage called pranayama, which is the control of the pranic life force, predominantly through breathing procedures.

What is prana? Prana is cosmic energy; the primal force of this universe which interacts upon mind and body to make us aware of the spiritual nature of existence. The spiritual nature of existence, when realized, brings into our mental and physical being a balanced and harmonious life, bringing about happiness, bliss, ecstasy, joy, and wisdom. This pranic energy exists in all life-forms. It manifests most predominantly in cerebral-spinal beings through their breathing. It is for this reason that many people call pranayama, breath control. That is to say, through the control of the breathing we gain control of prana. As we gain control of prana, we intensify the activation of the astral channels, producing an increased awareness.

Having cleansed or cleared these subtle astral passages, we can then direct the life-current through them, healing the body and stimulating unfolding awareness. As we gain control over the prana, we can balance or neutralize the energies that cause restlessness of the mind. This produces a calm, serene, harmonious being. When this happens, we recognize everyday experience was a vague and blurred state of consciousness. This is realized as we become more vividly aware. Consequently, there is a focusing on enlivened consciousness.

Wherever you look in nature, you will find a rhythm. This simply points out that there is not only a basic series of stages in the accomplishment of yoga, but each of these stages needs to be worked at rhythmically and harmoniously, not only within themselves, but in relationship to each other.

The first of the eight stages in the rhythmic unfoldment of cosmic consciousness is abstinences. These are to abstain from:

1. Injury
2. Lying
3. Stealing
4. Sensuality
5. Greed

These abstinences are usually listed in their positive psychological forms:

1. Non-violence (ahimsa)
2. Truthfulness (satya)
3. Non-stealing (asteya)
4. Celibacy (brahmacharya)
5. Non-greed (aparigraha)

It is extremely important for modern man to recognize that the basis of the abstinences is psychological. The purpose of the abstinences is to:

1. Cleanse the astral channels,
2. Gather the life-force,
3. Direct the life-force for health and spiritual utilization.

If a person is lying, injuring, or stealing, his life-force will be scattered. Through the psychological self-disciplining of these abstinences, he gathers the life-force as in a magnifying glass, in order to produce spiritual warmth to kindle the spiritual fire (kriya-kundalini).

On a spiritual level, and according to the law of karma, the practice of non-violence guarantees that violence will not interfere with one's own spiritual search. Physical violence, which would tend to impede spiritual progress, will not come to one's own body nor mind. By the practice of truthfulness, the law of karma allows the truth to come into one's life, mind, heart, and soul. It is through this sort of spiritual logic regarding the law of karma that you ascend closer to the ultimate apex of cosmic consciousness.

Each of the abstinences are in turn sub-divided into three groups:
1. Intellectual
2. Verbal
3. Physical

For example, there are three divisions of non-violence: intellectual non-violence, verbal non-violence, and physical non-violence. Intellectual non-violence is called baudhika ahimsa; verbal non-violence is called vachika ahimsa; and physical non-violence is called sharirik ahimsa. Let us examine non-violence on these three levels.

I. NON-VIOLENCE
(Ahimsa)

Intellectual Non-Violence
(Baudhika Ahimsa)

The main source of non-violence is within our intellects. Our intellects ascertain harmonious or inharmonious energies of the mind, which sooner or later must manifest harmoniously or inharmoniously. Later it manifests into harmonious or inharmonious action. Therefore, complete non-violence is renunciation of violence in body, speech, and especially thought.

The practice of non-violence produces a number of effects:
1. It brings about the accumulation of good karma in this lifetime, as well as in succeeding lifetimes.
2. It brings about non-agitation of the mind so that concentration is possible. It is only with concentration that meditation is possible. It is only with meditation that illumination is possible.
3. It magnetically and mystically draws into your life non-violent people and events. Your social exchange becomes filled with happiness and pleasure, and there is an effortless intellectual exchange and exploration of human consciousness.

The more you realize that everything is Spirit (atma), the more easily and more fully you become established in non-violence. When your life is permeated by ahimsa, your intellect is not disturbed, even when you become hurt or insulted. This brings about the attainment of a non-scattered mind. This attainment enables you to concentrate which in turn enables you to meditate. This rapidly brings you into full cosmic consciousness.

Verbal Non-Violence
(Vachika Ahimsa)

As you master intellectual non-violence, non-violence of speech becomes perfected. Verbal violence manifests itself in various ways, such as:
1. Abusive words,
2. Insulting statements,
3. Angry speech, and
4. Bad advice!

Needless to say, verbal non-violence arises by acquiring the verbal habits of:
1. Speaking softly,
2. Speaking gently, and
3. Speaking wisely.

Non-violence is to be observed on all levels, not just the physical level with which most people identify it. There is a saying in the Mahabharata: A wound caused by an arrow or axe heals swiftly, but a wound caused by violent speech heals very slowly. In becoming established in non-violence, it is important to understand, intellectually and spiritually, that the Spirit that pervades your life is the Spirit that pervades all of life. The dignity of your being is the dignity of every soul. The spirit is the same in each and every living form. We should come to understand that the spirit in a bacterium is not small, and the spirit in an elephant is not large.

Physical Non-Violence
(Sharirik Ahimsa)

As you become established in intellectual and verbal non-violence, physical non-violence is also established. The observance of physical non-violence means not cutting, slashing, wounding, or bruising another's body and/or one's own body. Quite often we do violence to our own bodies through improper diet and mode of living.

According to the Yoga Sutras, when a person becomes completely established in non-violence, violence cannot touch him. One faithful Hindu pointed out that ahimsa is a great and noble state which few are capable of attaining. Some great religious leaders were not fully established in non-violence; otherwise, they would not have come to violent ends.

It is important to note that the rules laid down for abstinences and observances must be according to:

1. Class,
2. Time,
3. Place,
4. Circumstance.

A person must understand these four conditions in order to spiritually live in this world. An example will be helpful: According to the yogic position one should not kill in order to satisfy his craving for meat, yet it is quite proper under certain circumstances to defend a child against a wild animal. If one does not understand these rules of class, time, place, and circumstance, he will find it impossible to function spiritually in this physical world. This would defeat the purpose of yoga, which is the attainment of wisdom.

To the renunciate in a monastery, ashram, or cave, the vows of abstinences and observances are to be taken without consideration of class, time, or place. But for the householder, there definitely must be a classification of the vows, which are modified according to these four regulatory concepts. If one burns logs, oil, or coal for cooking or light, one destroys insects living within these natural products. One cannot insist that family go cold, live in the dark, or not eat cooked food because of the wish to refrain from killing bacteria living in these fuel products. However, the vow of non-violence implies great care to avoid the destruction of life. Another exception is the prince or ruler of a country who is forced to physically confine a murderer because he has taken the lives of a number of people.

We must always walk the law of Dharma according to our station in life and our spiritual understanding. The intent to refrain from violence, and carefulness in living, is what is important. We must continually weigh and balance the pros and cons of any given action. For instance, a person may be in a room with a rat with bubonic plague. To kill the rat is violent, but not to do so will endanger the lives of many other people. Which is more violent? We must take into consideration the harmony and disharmony of any action or inaction.

According to the Yoga Sutras, violence and untruth are obstacles to the practice of abstentions and observances, and are of four types:

1. To do violence or be untruthful to another person,
2. To do violence or be untruthful to one's self,
3. To allow others to do violence or be untruthful,
4. To encourage others to do violence or be untruthful.

Thoughts and actions of this nature give rise to pride, anger, greed, and thus delusion, moving us further away from the goal of cosmic consciousness. These stages can be considered as:

1. Mild,
2. Moderate,
3. Extreme.

Before performing any mental or physical action, you should reflect upon its consequences. As you move forward in the establishment of non-violence, your heart will be bathed in a stream of compassion and fearlessness, which will give birth to that blessed state called Bliss (ananda). The Yajur Veda states that when a yogi is fully established in non-violence, he cultivates the feeling of the Spirit toward all life-forms, and therefore does nothing that will bring him grief or attachment. Being non-attached he reaches closer to the goal of cosmic consciousness.

In the practice of yoga, the grosser manifestations of non-violence are controlled first.

1. Non-violence begins by first controlling physical violence of killing, striking, or hitting.
2. After this has been mastered, there is control of verbal violence by not speaking cutting or hurting words.
3. As physical and verbal non-violence are mastered, we begin to control thoughts, moods, and attitudes in the mind itself.

These stages are not a one-two-three process. They are interrelated and interact one with the other. We start with the gross and the obvious, working towards the subtle and less obvious.

To repeat, the purpose of the abstentions is to purify of phlegm the subtle mind channels and to gather the life-force that is now flowing through the purified channels. The ability to control these life-currents is initiated by the major first stage. It has three substages:

1. Purifying the astral channels to enable more life-force to flow through them.
2. Gathering these scattered life-forces so the mind and consciousness become more effectual and dynamic, bringing greater control over your body and mind.

3. Lifting these life-forces to balance the chakras and gain greater bliss, wisdom, and balanced being called cosmic consciousness.

II. TRUTHFULNESS
(Satya)

The second yama is truthfulness (satya). It has two levels:
1. Truthfulness means conducting our mind, speech, and action according to truth.
2. Truthfulness is the result of our mind, speech, and actions being unified and harmonious. In short, we are truthful to ourselves when the three common vehicles--mind, speech, and body--are harmonious, one with the other.

There should be a realization that words that harm are not truthful, and if in speaking certain words someone is hurt, those words should not be spoken! According to the science of yoga, you should examine all your words before speaking, and utter them only if they are useful and good. Complications arise when virtuous words lead to hurt. Many people find it difficult to distinguish between truth and untruth. Whatever the ultimate solution is for each individual, the guiding factor should be mindfulness so that there is:
1. No intention to harm.
2. A true understanding of truth in your own mind, speech, and actions as it relates to the whole of life.

As with each of the abstentions, truthfulness has three levels:
1. Intellectual truthfulness
2. Verbal truthfulness
3. Physical truthfulness

Intellectual Truthfulness
(Baudhika Satya)

Intellectual truthfulness can be practiced or lived if you have decided and accepted what truth is. Without intellectual truthfulness, it is impossible to speak or act truthfully. When the intellect is dominated by inertia and/or passion, the mind cannot discern between truth and untruth. The practice of truthfulness produces a steady mind and a steady intellect which produces a steadiness in truthfulness, upon which vocal and physical truthfulness depend.

What is truth? To those of you who would dive deeply into and perfect your own being, the answer is, You are Truth.

Verbal Truthfulness
(Vachika Satya)

It is only if you are established in intellectual truthfulness that you will be able to speak truth. Yogis are constantly reminding each other that what they speak should be spoken for the betterment of others. The Mahabharata states, it is good to speak truthfully, but better still to speak that which benefits others. The importance of this statement is emphasized in the fact that many people are compelled to speak what is truth, but do so with intentions to hurt. This statement helps us realize that there are many truths that can be spoken, but if we are truly practicing the vow of verbal truthfulness, we will speak that single truth that does the greatest good for the greatest number of people.

Another aspect of verbal truthfulness is keeping one's word. There are times when because of karma, circumstances, devastation, or other reasons, it is impossible to keep a promise you have made. For this reason it is said that if a person at least attempts to keep his word with the full intent of his mind, body, and being, he has in truth adhered to truthfulness. It is obvious that many difficult problems present themselves in attempting to adhere to verbal truthfulness. Here is an ancient story that represents and gives insight into this problem:

> Once upon a yogi time, a saint was meditating in a forest and a deer passed by. Shortly thereafter, a hunter came pursuing the deer and asked the saint, 'Did you see the deer?' The saint spoke saying, 'Yes, I have seen the deer.' Then the hunter asked, 'Which way did the deer go?'

> Now, if the saint tells the truth, the hunter will kill the deer. If, on the other hand, he does not tell the truth, he will violate the practice of verbal truthfulness. What should he do? It is late in the year, and if the saint does not speak truth, the hunter and family will starve. What should he do?

I leave you to solve this symbolic problem, adding two other thoughts. Some say truth should be spoken only with wisdom, while others say truth should be spoken without any consideration of loss or gain.

Physical Truthfulness
(Sharirik Satya)

Truth that has been understood intellectually and expressed in words proceeds outward into physical action. This is called physical truthfulness. . Truth must be unified in mind, speech, and action. Physical truthfulness which is akin to good actions uplifts the mind and tends to lift the pranic currents, extremely necessary for anyone traveling the mystical pathway.

The goal of abstentions-observances is to reach a state of renunciation. Non-violence and truthfulness are the keys by which this is done. However, the importance of wisdom in observing truthfulness, particularly in our modern age, is a key. The world will often use you, hurting others, if you are not wise in your truthfulness.

III. NON-STEALING
(Asteya)

For most people, non-stealing means non-theft. In yoga, however, it means not committing theft physically and/or not causing or approving of anyone else doing so--in mind, word, or action. To observe non-theft in deed, speech, and thought is called non-stealing (asteya).

Intellectual Non-Stealing
(Baudhika Asteya)

Observing intellectual non-stealing is the most difficult, for it implies that we should not even think about wanting to take what belongs to another. It does not mean, however, that we cannot see something another person has, admire it, and through our own efforts acquire the same thing that they have. For example, you may know a person who possesses a very special text. There is nothing wrong with thinking, 'I would like a copy of that text.' You must be willing to work for what you want if it is important for you to have it in your life. Intellectual non-stealing is best defined as not thinking of improperly taking anything that belongs to another. This honesty should occur even within the dream state.

According to many yogic texts, what you have not earned has not yet been presented to you. This is the great dictum. These texts teach, anything coming into your life you have earned. It belongs to you and will bring happiness. However, anything coming into your life that has not been earned, will bring struggle, difficulty, and perchance unhappiness.

Verbal Non-Stealing
(Vachika Asteya)

Most people overlook this important aspect of non-stealing. The practice of verbal non-stealing implies you should not steal what belongs to another on a verbal level, such as stealing one's dignity, pride, happiness, moment of glory, or mental values. Only high souls strive to overcome verbal non-stealing. It, also, means you should not verbally injure another's character, in any way, shape, or form.

Physical Non-Stealing
(Sharirik Asteya)

To take a physical object by deceit, force, skulduggery, or without permission is physical theft. Physical stealing is taking possession of something you have not earned, or something that does not belong to you. If a person wants something, he should realize it has to be earned. This produces a stability of the mind which is akin to pranic stability. From a spiritual level, pranic balance and self-sufficiency of the mind is what life is all about. Although all things flow from life, we should be more than willing to till and gather these gifts.

By the practice of the above abstentions, (non-violence, truthfulness, and non-stealing), you begin to gain the ability to cleanse, gather, and lift the life-force, and your goal of God-realization becomes even closer.

IV. CELIBACY
(Brahmacharya)

The fourth abstention is non-sensuality or celibacy. A great amount of literature has been written about this particular abstention. Vyasa, the great Hindu commentator, defines celibacy as the control of the genital organs. Manu, the Hindu lawgiver, states that a student residing under the guidance of his spiritual preceptor should observe abstentions and observances and keep his sense organs under control, striving for the upliftment of his soul. In this sense, celibacy tends to extend beyond the general meaning given. You will notice that Manu is not merely talking about control of the sexual desires, but control of all organs. Because of this, this abstention is referred to as non-sensuality.

According to Hindu tradition, the average human being's life is divided into four equal parts. The first quarter is referred to as studentship. It requires the practice of celibacy, and the study of the sacred scriptures and secular knowledge. After the completion of the first quarter, three pathways are then open to him:

1. He may immediately leave his studies and take up responsibilities conducting himself in a manner prescribed for householdership. This person is called a Vasu.
2. He may decide to acquire further knowledge for an additional twelve years. He thus delays entering the stage of householdership. During these additional twelve years, the practice of celibacy is still observed. A person entering this additional study is called a Rudra.
3. He may decide to spend the rest of his life in contemplation, study, and celibacy.

If he studies and practices celibacy until the age of 48, he is called an Aditya. If he practices celibacy for the rest of his life, he is referred to as a maishthika brahmacharya. And if he dedicates his entire life to the spiritual search as a monk, he is referred to as a Sannyasi.

The philosophy of yoga expressly states that the life of the householder is in no way inferior to the other pathways, for sannyasis are dependent upon the householder for food and clothing. The yoga philosophy states that the life of the householder is the best spiritual pathway for the average person. Hence the spiritual texts (Vedas) extol the life of the householder. One of the duties of the householder is to procreate a family and give to them wisdom.

Celibacy is observed only up until the stage of householdership. The holy texts emphasize repeatedly that procreation is a sacred sacrifice as well as a sacred ritual. It is an action that spiritual, liberation-seeking souls should feel comfortable with. There should be a realization that through this religious ritual, one is assisting souls to take birth that they might find release.

A great deal of controversy regarding brahmacharya springs from the idea that sexual indulgences cause weakness because they dissipate the seminal fluid. Overindulgence in anything is detrimental. When a person moves from total sexual abstinence into householdership, there should not be a period of unbridled sexual indulgences. All the sense organs are difficult to control. We first strive to discipline the gross aspects of our life and then move to the more subtle. Thus, the sex organs should be brought under realistic control, first.

As a person moves into the third quarter of his life, stricter regulations of sensuality are established. At this time, he regains greater control, moving toward reestablishing total brahmacharya. Finally, as he enters the last quarter, celibacy is completely re-established. In the first and fourth quarters, brahmacharya is observed in mind, speech, and body, whereas in the second quarter, the householdership phase, he participates in the joys of love, for the enrichment of his mind, body, and soul. The concept of sexuality linked with a healthy spiritual attitude, mentally, physically, and vocally, should be established at all times.

Let us look a little further at brahmacharya from its three levels:

Intellectual Celibacy
(Baudhika Brahmacharya)

The Gita points out that if and when a person broods over the objects of the senses, that soul develops attachment to those objects. From these attachments, massive cravings spring forth. It is from the springing forth of massive cravings that the mind-force is scattered. The main purpose of celibacy is to gather as well as preserve the pranic energy that manifests through this vital organ. Yogis have always indicated that discipline of one's sexual life is key to success in attaining and experiencing mystical communion with higher states of consciousness.

There are three important ideas concerning brahmacharya:
1. One should hold the opposite sex in a high, spiritual framework, rather than debasing thoughts.
2. One should consider sexuality to be noble and a means of bringing forth souls into this world in order to gain illumination, allowing them to taste the outer fringes of God's Bliss.
3. Nothing scatters the pranic life-force more than sexual craving.

Therefore, in order to gather the life-force and balance your life, you should meditate, when you meditate. When you are eating, you should eat. When you are sleeping, you should sleep. When you are studying, you should study. When you are praying, you should pray. When you are communing with God, you should commune, and when you are loving, you should love.

According to the law of abstentions: In all things, whatsoever you do, do it with gentleness and spiritual warmth. Remain forever unattached, so that your mind moves and unfolds unto life.

Verbal Celibacy
(Vachika Brahmacharya)

Vocal brahmacharya obviously implies control over a person's speech regarding sexual expressions and overtones. Obscene jokes and lewd songs should be avoided. It is my individual and personal philosophy, however, that one should never become fearful. With this in mind, we should understand that occasionally a joke may indeed be funny. It would be far more spiritual, and certainly more normal, to laugh at such a joke than to get uptight. It is wise to remember: seek and find balance in all things....

Physical Celibacy
(Sharirik Brahmacharya)

To those who have practiced celibacy in thought and speech, the observance of physical brahmacharya becomes easy. I wish to stress again, the householder should not be fearful of sexuality. There should be no fear of the opposite sex. There should be no fear of the ecstasy that Life has given us. Rather, these gifts should be considered the dewdrops of existence by which we come to fully understand the warmth and beauty that is of God. Each streamlet, each rivulet returns ultimately to the ocean of benefic existence. Fear not, but lift... lift... lift.

Regarding physical celibacy, there are a number of basic procedures that should be followed:

1. In the practice of physical celibacy, it is unwise to eat food cooked by a person who radiates strong sexuality or negativity.
2. A body that is not regularly cleansed produces energy secretions that cause physical, sexual excitation. Therefore, one should bathe daily, emphasizing in particular the underarms and pits of the body. These should be washed with warm, clean water, without irritating substances. If soap is utilized, the body should be thoroughly rinsed.
3. Undergarments should be exceptionally clean and changed daily.
4. Food that is eaten should be easily digestible and not of a stimulating nature such as spices.
5. Many writers, both eastern and western, tend to feel that self-realization is the highest goal in life and that the oppo-

site sex are demons who keep us from reaching this goal. This is obviously a falsehood. The only demons are inside ourselves.

There is a higher goal than self-realization, called God-realization. God-realization is self-realization directed back to all earthlings needing love, warmth, help, support, and understanding. People often become so concerned with their own realization that they become selfish and thus unspiritual. They become lost in a delusion of fear and apprehension, thinking the enemy is out there. The enemy is, has been, and always will be inside our own minds, moods, and attitudes.

This controversial subject is illustrated in the following true story of an ancient king. The king's wife fell in love with her coachman. When the king found out about this, he renounced his kingdom and wrote the well-known text Bhartrihari Shatakan. This true book begins:

> 'She who is constantly in my mind does not care
> for me and has fallen in love with her coachman,
> who himself is in love with another woman, while
> this other is yet still in love with me... Therefore,
> fie on my wife, on her lover, on cupid, on me, and
> on the woman who loves me.'

The king does not understand the true nature of human beings nor of spiritual realization. That which we love is often separated from us. As a matter of fact, all things that are not ours are always separated from us. All things are just borrowed by us, even though most of us do not know it. Thus, the ancient kriyic law teaches:

THAT WHICH IS OURS, NO PERSON, NO GURU, NO GOD CAN TAKE FROM US; THAT WHICH IS NOT OURS, NO PERSON, NO GURU, NO GOD CAN GIVE UNTO US.

To experience sex in a noble and spiritual manner is to taste of the outer fringes of God's bliss. For most human beings, sexuality is the closest experience they will ever have in which they are touching anything in this universe. If one is really touching, the mind will recognize that it is touching, and the soul is also touching. People who have loved understand. And what is love, other than touching that which we believe we are not.

Loving is a process by which we bring forth another soul toward illumination. The joy a soul feels as he is moving into the physical plane is Joy. It is likened to a soul returning to the ocean, or the river moving toward the mouth of the ocean, or the rivulet moving to the river. There should be a realization and understanding of what is really happening through the physical ecstasy of sexuality. You are opening a doorway for another soul. Whether the karma of that soul permits its own birth or not, you are opening the doorway enabling him to enter the world. Do you understand?

Loving is a way of directing large amounts of pranic energy out through your body. But only if you direct that pranic energy toward another individual with great physical and mental love, will you tap an equal amount within your universe. If you are wishy-washy, you will direct the energy out of your body, but you will not pull any higher forces into your body. Thus you might, therefore, become more dissipated.

V. NON-GREED
(Aparigraha)

Non-greed is the fifth and final abstention. It is the second most important yama to be practiced for it is the key to controlling the life-energy. Greed can be devastating in its scattering effect on the life-force. If greed were to be removed on intellectual, verbal, and physical levels, there would be no need to practice the other four abstentions. Non-violence is the countering force to balance greed.

The great sage Vyasa states that non-greed is the attainment of remaining detached from the enjoyment of sense objects, not detachment from the objects themselves. The craving for pleasures and gratifications of sense objects intensifies and activates beyond normalcy the organs of these senses, causing a person to commit violence, in one way or another, against others, and/or against his own self.

By the observance of non-greed there is a recognition of the nature of the mind, and a realization that we are not the mind. The goal of life is to harmoniously balance the greed-seeking tendencies of the mind by bringing them into balance. This does not mean, however, that we cannot enjoy life, beauty, love, or knowledge. It means we should not reach out beyond the bounds of spiritual propriety to physically take, to mentally want, or to verbally try to cajole that which is not ours.

Intellectual Non-Greed
(Baudhika Aparigraha)

Intellectual non-greed is established through meditation, deliberation, and discernment. Through these three intellectual processes you begin to understand that the senses in and of themselves have no judgmental, evaluative, or discriminatory faculties. It is the function of a sense organ to sense. It is the function of the intellect to establish what is beneficial to the entire vehicle and not merely for the titillation of the sense organs.

The kriya yogi understands that it is the function of the mind to mind, the heart to heart, the stomach to stomach, the feet to feet, the hands to hand, and the soul to soul. This is their nature. That which is pleasing to a given sense organ often can be destructive to other organs. Thus, it is the purpose of the mind to bring all the sense organs into balance. This usually means pulling the life-force away from the sense organs, not away from the objects themselves.

When our intellect is immersed in deep thought, our ears do not hear anything. It is only when the intellect impels the sense organs toward something that the sense organs grasp at that object. The intellect has the power to discern what is harmonious and what is inharmonious to our total being. Thus the intellect must discern what is proper for the sense organs to fix themselves upon. This action is called intellectual non-greed.

Why are the sense organs to be so guarded? Because as the organs reach out and attach themselves to things, the mind desires to possess these things. Once the mind possesses them, it becomes fearful of losing them; and not possessing them, the mind becomes distressed by the knowledge it does not possess them. In both cases, the mind becomes agitated. An agitated mind scatters the pranic life-force, not allowing the spiritual soul-power to gather these life-energies and direct them to the higher states of consciousness which allow us to balance and harmonize the lower states of consciousness. This is the truth underlying and behind the meaning, the purpose, and the necessity of the practice of abstentions. A Hindu poet states the only difference between poison (vish) and the sense objects (vishaya) is that poison kills when it is eaten, while the sense objects tend to kill when intellectually thought about.

The moth attracted by the flame loses its life. The elephant attached by the sense of touch is entrapped when man digs a ditch and places a real she-elephant near it. The deer is trapped when a net is spread across the forest area and a sweet tune played.

Attracted by the tune, it is caught in the net. The fish, seeking to taste the flesh on a hook, swallows the bait, is caught and killed. The black bee, loving the sweet smell of certain flowers, is drawn to the flower and does not leave. Evening approaches and the flower closes, killing the bee. Thus, the Garuda Purana points out that the moth, the elephant, the deer, the bee, and the fish, each attached to only one sense object, loses its life. How can man, attached to all five sense objects, not destroy himself?

One of the key concepts of intellectual non-greed is this: You should not feel high elation when good karma comes your way, nor should you become excessively depressed when negative karma comes your way. In so doing, you become detached and your mind becomes quieted. As your mind becomes quieted, more energy flows within your physical/mental vehicle. Collecting and gathering this energy allows an activation of the higher chakras. As the higher chakras are activated you can balance the lower chakras. Only as this energy is available and directed toward a chakra, which controls various states of consciousness, can you transcend to higher, subtler states of consciousness.

Many yogic texts speak about death. This should NOT always be interpreted as physical death. One of the key yogic meanings of the word death is, 'death of the power of the mind'. It is important that each soul seeking to unfold spiritually, gain control over his mind and sense organs, allowing the control over the prana in his mind and body. The sense organs are to be used in a wise, detached manner.

Verbal Non-Greed
(Vachika Aparigraha)

Verbal non-greed simply means that you should not use intriguing, enticing, or lurid words to activate the sense organs in yourself or in others. On a subtler level, it means you should not be too talkative or verbally superficial. The student is encouraged not to use words to indulge the sense organs. The practice of meditative silence (mouna) is very helpful in overcoming verbal greed.

Physical Non-Greed
(Sharirik Aparigraha)

Practicing bodily non-attachment means recognizing your realistic and necessary needs and striving for them. But you should not reach out beyond those essential needs. It is quite normal, not greedy, to need or want a pair of shoes, or clothing. Without this understanding, you can become uncertain and upset as to the distinction between your needs and your greeds. If it is not self-evident, the spiritual texts' advice is very clear. Become unemotional and meditate so that you can see more clearly. The individual's needs will vary as he moves through the four different stages of life (the ashramas).

For those souls who have good karma and tend without any excessive effort to acquire more things of the world than are needed, the Vedas indicate that these superfluous gifts given through one's own past efforts should be funneled into noble, humanitarian, and spiritual causes. The wealthy of both eastern and western cultures recognize this. It is called noblesse oblige.

Physical non-greed implies you should not be too attached to your family or other persons, for this may cause you to strive to possess more than you really need. It also implies that you should not become physically jealous or envious when you see prosperity occurring with other persons or in other families. There should be rejoicing in others' good fortune. Be aware that this good fortune will cause other obligations and complications to arise in their lives. Find satisfaction in the realization that you have:

1. Defined clearly your own needs at each stage of your life.
2. Acquired the necessary essentials of life through your own honest labors.

Finally, on a subtler level, the observance of physical non-greed means the repayment of all debts one has incurred. These favors and debts most often originate from friendships, social and business. There are also, however, deeper-level debts the spiritual soul must repay if he is to truly unfold spiritually. These debts are:

1. Indebtedness to one's parents,
2. Indebtedness to friends,
3. Indebtedness to one's culture,
4. Indebtedness to the sages and saints of the past,
5. Indebtedness to one's spiritual preceptor.

For a noble soul, it is easy to repay debts of a business or social nature. For the unevolved soul, however, it is difficult to even want to repay them. One repays indebtedness to his civilization by leaving the world better off than he found it. It takes a noble soul to understand how to repay indebtedness to the sages of the past and to the preceptor of the present. This is best paid by:

1. By growing spiritually,
2. By being radiant,
3. By teaching,
4. By fulfilling your spiritual obligations.

The soul who is firmly established in non-greed truly begins to understand what he is, what he has, and most likely what he is to become in the next incarnation. This is a rung closer to spiritual unfoldment and a step nearer to the eternal bliss in and of this world.

In taking any vow, whether it is to fulfill a debt to the sages of the past or a vow associated with abstention-observance, the following question often arises: With whom are these vows taken? The vows are between you and you. For example, the vow may be: Starting today, I will attempt to perfect this vow for the rest of my life. If someone likes and collects books, I don't think a wise vow would be: starting today, I'll never buy or touch another book. This is not a realistic approach. The approach should be: I am going to purchase only the most important books. In time I will find that what is holy and important is really within me. Through the practice of a vow there occurs a gradual inturning process which may take an entire lifetime. If at some point you do not fully live up to a vow you have made, do not become angry or upset with yourself. You will not accumulate any brownie points or demerits for practicing or not practicing the vow.

What is the vow all about? It is about gathering the life-force. Consequently, one of the key rules is that in practicing it, it must be with an undisturbed mind. In practicing the vow with an undisturbed mind, you will truly understand the essence of the abstentions. The purpose is to bring about peace of mind so the subconscious and conscious energies can be gathered. In taking any vow, if you do not have peace of mind, you are doing something wrong. You are not understanding the spirit of yoga, for any vow is ultimately taken to bring about peace of mind. If a person takes a vow to stop eating candy bars but keeps thinking about them all day and then feels guilty for breaking the intellectual vow, it would probably be far wiser for that person to buy a candy bar, happily enjoy perhaps only one-half of it, and then spend the rest of his day with a less scattered mind.

There are exceptions to this, however, for ultimately greater discipline of body and mind needs to take place, so sense objects can be entirely given up, bringing about a lessening of desire. You may struggle with a desire for one hour, but three years later, because of training and discipline, you may struggle with it for only five minutes. And later, you may struggle with the desire for ten seconds. When you say no to your mind, it is important that it understands that you mean no. Thus it will not react. But remember, the purpose of the abstentions is to bring peace, tranquility, and serenity to your mind. You must realize there are wise ways to discipline the mind. Seek out those wise ways.

Now, what if a person desires a candy bar and suppresses the thought? Has he practiced abstention? No, he has not. Here is the secret: Yoga deals with disciplining your subconscious mind, rather than your conscious mind. Through the practice of yoga, you are able to take your conscious mind into your subconscious mind and reorganize it to produce genuine gentleness and happiness. Some people appear to be nice and kind, at a conscious everyday level, but they are subconsciously violent. This is often revealed when they indulge. The purpose of yoga is to balance the scattered energies existing in the subconscious mind. We have to discipline our mind all the way down to the roots of our soul, in order to expand our consciousness and become more self-conscious. Yoga is all about cosmic consciousness. Cosmic consciousness can only come about after there is bliss. Only as we balance the subconscious energies, do we experience this bliss and awaken to more subtle, galactic states of spiritual consciousness.

***

Remember, it is always possible to be too petty, regarding the disciplines of abstentions. I learned very early in life that there is a difference between yoga and Hinduism. Yoga points out that following the letter of the law tends to cause emotional harm. Yoga states we should follow the spirit of the law. In following the spirit of the law you will come to recognize that a cookbook on life cannot be written, and that each and every situation is uniquely different. With this realization you see life more clearly. If you do become too picayune about the practice of the abstentions, it indicates there is something you do not understand. Perchance you do not understand the spirit of yoga... the spirit of freedom... the spirit of Truth.

Simply rebalance the currents and learn to accept your humanness. In the acceptance of your humanness, the spirit will be more at ease, and you will be one step closer to cosmic consciousness.

OM TAT SAT OM

Chapter 2

THE LAW OF OBSERVANCE
(NIYAMA)

Through the practice of the observances (niyama) you acquire:
1. The ability to pull pranic energy from the cosmic source into your body.
2. The ability to direct that energy into the lower chakras.
3. The ability to use that pranic energy to balance the chakras.
4. The ability to lift that pranic energy to a higher chakra.

According to the Yoga system of Patanjali, there are five observances. These are:
1. Purity (shaucha)
2. Contentment (santosha)
3. Austerity (tapas)
4. Study of the holy texts (svadhyaya)
5. Attunement to God (Ishvar-Pranidhana)

I. PURITY
(Shaucha)

Purity is the first observance. It has two levels, external and internal.

The sage Manu points out that:
1. The body is purified by water.
2. The mind is purified by truthfulness.
3. The soul is purified by knowledge and austerity.

Intellectual Purity
(Baudhika Shaucha)

Intellectual purity consists in observing the vow to lift your thoughts and emotions to a higher state of consciousness. Intellectual purity means drawing upon and activating the higher purity (sattvic guna). This spiritual greatness comes by drawing upon the energies flowing from the heart chakra. Most of mankind is still functioning at the mars chakra (solar plexus) level and it is only by reaching to the heart chakra that we can attain clearer spiritual states of consciousness. By performing the vows of observance, we attune to the higher chakras. As we attune to the higher chakras, the life-force begins to lift. In short, the function of this practice is to cause the life-current, that has been increased and gathered, to ascend to the higher chakras, producing higher states of consciousness.

Intellectual purity is achieved by continuously invoking noble thoughts. Intellectual purity can be achieved by repeating the sacred symbol OM, or some other mantra upon which you fix your mind. Mental purity is acquired by the practice of compassion, or intellectually practicing whatsoever brings you into a state of peacefulness, wherein you transcend thought, expanding consciousness into cosmic consciousness.

Verbal Purity
(Vachika Shaucha)

Vocal purity is the continuous purification of the mercury throat chakra by speaking what is consoling, harmonizing, gentle, uplifting, and straightforward. Purity of speech is attained by the practice of clear, strong chanting (pajan). It is also attained through various breathing techniques. In the manifestation of these techniques that produce vocal purity, the mercury throat chakra is activated and consciousness is centered therein. Thus, you lift the currents from the heart chakra to the mercury throat chakra, ever driving the spiritual river upward toward the ocean of existence.

Physical Purity
(Sharirik Shaucha)

Physical purity is observed externally and internally. External purity means cleansing your physical body with soap and water. In some parts of India, special medicines are used. (These are known as triphala and ubtan.) External physical purity implies gentle, harmonious sitting, and walking of the body, as well as abstinence from unusual gestures that may be suggestive. Physical purity means utilizing sacred gestures (mudras) that invoke and balance the higher life-forces. These will be dealt with in the chapter on postures (asans).

Growing food, collecting food, and eating food is an important part of physical shaucha. Fasting is also an important part of internal physical purity. When a yogi has achieved external and internal physical purity, he has the capacity to perceive the light within his temple. As this light becomes more intense, he becomes less attached to his physical sheath, becoming more aware that he is a soul functioning through the instruments of body and mind, rather than a body that has a mind and perchance a soul.

Internal body purity allows you to gather this light into a sphere or disc, at the sun center, and by so doing permits the sun current to descend, bringing forth a blessing to the mental and physical chakras below. It is through this process that God-Realization is attained.

1. External Physical Purity:

When man lived much closer to nature, he did not need to be reminded of the necessity of bathing. The body, being less covered, was washed by the rain and rubbed by the bushes and grass, which stimulated and kept the skin from gathering and holding onto surface waste matter. As man began to become more civilized, the use of clothing caused a heavy change in his environment. He began to bathe less frequently. The importance of external bathing was made clear when we talked about celibacy and the importance of a clean body.

The skin is the single largest organ of the body. It is continuously perspiring. Each square inch of our skin contains about 3,000 pores, called sweat glands. These are somewhere between 1/16 and 1/8-inch deep. This means that there are approximately 20 miles of sweat glands in the average person's body. If these pores become nonfunctional, a large amount of waste matter that is released daily remains in the blood system and organs. This then must be excreted by the kidneys, putting unnecessary stress on them. Most people do not realize is that this sweat (more accurately called perspiration) is really a fluid secreted directly from the blood system, laden with waste matter. If the pores are not kept clean, this waste matter tends to accumulate in the blood system and is very difficult to eliminate from the body.

Also, if the surface skin remains unclean, a number of things result:

a. The waste material on the skin becomes a key breeding place for bacteria.

b. Natural oily fluids will not be excreted and the skin becomes hard, dry, and tends to crack, opening the system to external infection. The skin is composed of three layers. The top layer is called the epidermis and is composed of cells that are short-lived and constantly being replaced by youthful new ones. These worn-out and discarded cells form a coating upon the skin which tends to accumulate if not washed off.

Many of these dead cells are rubbed off by clothing. However, a remarkable quantity of cells remains on the skin and needs to be washed off, thereby freeing the openings of the pores.

c. The body temperature and consequently one's health may be affected. The pores are vital in controlling body temperature, an important part of keeping the body functioning properly. There have actually been instances where people have sprayed their entire body with gold paint for carnivals and died within hours from heat stroke, caused by the paint clogging the pores of the body. Clogging of the pores will affect body temperature. It is important to keep the body temperature control functioning well.

In ancient days, early morning was the most auspicious time for bathing. Today, however, modern man finds the evening bath most auspicious, as he returns home from work and washes off the stress and strain of the day. Bathing and rubbing the body with a washcloth removes surface bacteria and increases the circulation. If soap is used, be sure to rinse the body well.

2. Internalized Physical Purity:

After external cleansing, the discipline of internal physical purity follows. See the outline of the purification techniques below. These six physical purification techniques are called shat kriyas or shat karmas. By practicing them, one gains greater mastery and purification of the physical and astral channels. It is through the practice of the abstentions and observances that the mental channels become clean enough to allow physical purification to take place.

These techniques are given in the interest of deeper understanding of the total process of purity (shaucha). They should be practiced only under the close supervision of a spiritual preceptor.

OUTLINE OF THE SIX PURIFICATIONS
-The Shat Kriyas-

1. Stomach Purification (Dhauti)
    i. Cloth stomach cleansing (vastra dhauti)
    ii. Water stomach cleansing (jala dhauti)
    iii. Fire stomach cleansing (agnisara dhauti)
    iv. Wind stomach cleansing (varisara dhauti)

2.Colon Cleansing (Basti)
    i. Water colon cleansing (jala basti)
    ii. Ground colon cleansing (sthala basti)

3.Nasal/Sinus Cleansing (Neti)
    i. Water nasal cleansing (jala neti)
    ii. String nasal cleansing (sutra neti)

4.Solar/Lunar Channel Cleansing--Eye Cleansing (Trataka)

5.Abdominal (Mars Chakra) Cleansing (Nauli)
    i. Preliminary to nauli: stomach lift (uddiyana)
    ii. Nauli

6.Skull Shining Cleansing (Kapalabhati)

A discussion of all the shat kriya techniques will be found in chapter 3.

II. CONTENTMENT
(Santosha)

Contentment is the second observance and is considered to be the most vital. It is best described as remaining content with what you have, and not desiring that which you have not earned. It means that you should not feel disappointed if less than what you expected comes into your life, nor should you feel over-elated if more than what you expected comes into your life.

Intellectual Contentment
(Baudhika Santosha)

Intellectual contentment means being psychologically prepared to part with anything that you do not need. On a deeper level, it means that you should not feel perturbed if that which you do not need is removed from your life. It also means that you should not complain against society, fate, or God if what you acquire is insufficient to meet your needs. Rather, you should meditate and reach an understanding of the laws of abundance as well as the laws of karma.

If you have a book and someone is trying to steal it, you should not feel perturbed or vexed. You have two choices:

1. You can give the book to the soul who is attempting to steal it and mentally move on; or
2. With realism and spiritual insight, you can protect the book. And with a peaceful mind spiritually move on.

The important factor in contentment is being content with whatever you have, yet at the same time, reaching out with a quiet, balanced consciousness. The sage Manu states that contentment consists of earning only what you daily need, in terms of the maintenance of your family, for hospitality and sacrifice. Contentment is the root of happiness; happiness is the root of a quiet mind; a quiet mind is the root of gathering energy; and gathering energy is the root of illumination.

Some people feel that loss and gain are predestined and therefore we should endeavor toward contentment independent of how karma flows. Others feel that loss and gain are not predetermined and we should therefore endeavor to attain contentment. In every stage of your life, in every action of your life, you should be contented. Without contentment, a troubled mind arises. A troubled mind arises, causing the life-forces to become scattered. The life forces scatter, and awareness of the higher chakras becomes unattainable. If awareness of the higher chakras becomes unattainable, the lower chakras cannot be balanced. Only if a person is content can he be peaceful, and only if he is peaceful can he understand life's beauty and meaning. A person not striving toward contentment, or not having attained contentment, will pathetically spend all his energies attempting to acquire objects for enjoyment. These individuals will be bound to the chains of expectation which produce a troubled mind.

Verbal Contentment
(Vachika Santosha)

Vocal contentment means giving up chattering and superficial talkativeness. Bitter words, shouts, and insults are vocal non-contentment. You will obtain contentment of speech by controlling and renouncing harsh and bitter words. A person striving to attain vocal contentment should speak little, avoid verbal controversies, and strive for periods of spiritual silence (mouna). Vocal contentment is an absolute necessity for attaining intellectual contentment.

Contentment can be obtained by understanding the kriya yoga philosophy and realizing the wisdom of life's way: That which is taken from you is not taken from you but rather converted or transmuted into that which you need more dearly. Understanding this wisdom of Life's way will bring contentment.

Physical Contentment
(Sharirik Santosha)

Bodily contentment means not being violent in any way, against anyone or anything. It implies that the body in no way, shape, or form should be dominated by destructive, gawky, or awkward movements. On a deeper level, bodily contentment means forgetting past injuries and insults on an emotional level to the degree that your body's mind strives not to hurt.

The sage Vyasa, commenting on contentment, states that in this world, gross sense objects are enjoyed by our external sense organs, and subtle objects are enjoyed by our subtle and astral bodies, however, these enjoyments are not even one-sixteenth the enjoyment derived from the extinction of craving. When bodily contentment is absent, greed increases in such a way that a man who possesses one thing desires to possess one hundred things; a man who possesses one hundred things desires to possess one thousand things; and a man who possesses one thousand things desires to possess a million. This is the nature of greed.

The movement toward contentment is one of the supreme goals of yoga. It is expressed in the following two ancient teachings:

1. If a man has God but not contentment, what does he really have? However, even if a man does not have God, if he has contentment, he has everything.

2. A mountain is great, the sea is greater, the sky is greater still, and Reality is the greatest of all. But greed surpasses everything, for it is greed that holds the four worlds in its grip. Therefore, the soul who renounces greed acquires contentment and has everything.

III. AUSTERITY
(Tapas)

The third observance is austerity which is defined as the power to withstand hunger, thirst, heat, and cold, as well as all other discomforts. It is through mental, verbal, and bodily austerity that a person releases within himself the yogic energy to attain the unattainable.

Intellectual Austerity
(Baudhika Tapas)

Within the mental consciousness of mankind flow two sets of contra-currents: one in the realm of thought and the other in the realm of emotion. For instance, in the realm of thought, one set of currents may say: I can do it. While the other set may say: I'm afraid to do it. In the realm of emotion the contra-currents may be: love versus hate. Mental austerity means balancing these contra-currents. Balancing them brings about a removal of attachment, ego, and conceit. When these are removed, the mind is no longer distracted. As the distracted mind becomes balanced and centered, the sense organs are held in check; and as the sense organs are checked, one is capable of withdrawing into the inner universe of the chakras. Having this awareness of a chakra is equivalent to having the spiritual power (siddhi) of that chakra.

The Gita states that mental austerity consists of:
1. Quietude of the mind.
2. Equanimity of the mind.
3. Silencing of the mind.
4. Control of imbalanced propensities.

Having attained these fourfold mental austerities, you purify the heart chakra. You therefore purify your attitude, which brings about a proper attitude. If quietude and equanimity of the mind are not attained, and angular propensities of the mind are not controlled, there will be massive scattering and dissipation of the life-currents that have been gathered through the process of abstention and observances. In essence, mental austerity means not allowing the sense organs to be attached to objects.

The Gita states there is a threefold gate of anguish which destroys self-awareness. These are:
1. Greed
2. Anger
3. Craving

It is important to note that if the intellect is enslaved by any one of these three, the mind will also be enslaved. It is the nature of the mind to run toward objects and thus outward and away from the chakras and balanced chakra awareness. In this way, the mind runs away from sagehood and cosmic consciousness. It is through mental austerity that the mind is withdrawn from its outward movement and brought back to inner awarenesses.

Verbal Austerity
(Vachika Tapas)

Austerity of speech means refraining from any commitment of vocal agitations. This usually includes the avoidance of bitter, harsh, or critical words, as well as harsh discourses or discussions, including those that may injure or hurt others. One should also refrain from speaking that which would give permission or approval for others to hurt. Austerity of speech means speaking only meaningful, beautiful, and necessary words. The vow of silence is often considered austerity of speech.

Physical Austerity
(Sharirik Tapas)

A person practicing physical austerity should be able to withstand thirst or hunger, heat or cold, loss or gain. The ability to undergo physical hardships is extremely important in the attainment of happiness. It is well-known that without undergoing physical hardships, self-discipline cannot be attained. Without self-discipline, contentment becomes impossible. It is said that Indra, the king of the gods, practiced austerity for 104 years and only then was able to acquire the knowledge of creation. Mystically, the practicing of physical austerity is extremely important.

It is by understanding that one learns to balance the great opposites: the left and right sides of the chakras (the ida and pingala), so that God-Realization (sushumanic awareness) can be attained. It is not enough to merely purify the body; the energies must be lifted and directed to and through all the chakras. If this energy can be brought into and lifted into the chakras, consciousness can move through the balanced channel to higher, subtler realms of super-consciousness.

The law-giver Manu states that the culmination of austerity comes through the service to one's parents and spiritual preceptor. The Gita points out that there are three types of austerity:
1. Dull (Tamasika)
2. Passionate (Rajasika)
3. Calm (Sattvika)

According to the Gita, austerities that are practiced with obstinacy are referred to as dull. Those practiced with the idea of acquiring something are called passionate, and those done without desire for any result other than contentment or balancing the inner mechanisms of the mind are called calm. That which is gained through dull and passionate austerities will not endure. The calm austerity purifies the mind, intellect, and the body. It is the only austerity to be practiced.

Yoga states you should always be moderate in all activities and conduct. You should regulate your work, your play, and your spiritual efforts so as not to unduly exhaust yourself physically, mentally, or spiritually. According to the ancient sages, the mind has been locked to clinging desires from the beginning of time. It is therefore important to cleanse the mind of these clinging desires. The yogi contends the mind cannot be cleansed without austerity.

IV. SELF-STUDY
(Svadhyaya)

The great sage Vyasa defines self-study as the recitation of the OM mantra, the Gayatri mantra, and the study of the scriptures, Puranas, and Upanishads. This self-study leads to illumination along with liberation. Self-study is the utilization of mystical techniques that lead to the realization of Spirit, as well as the fullness of life. These mystical techniques consist of the study of the sacred mystical scriptures of any and all religions which teach the means and modes to enlightenment.

Intellectual Self-Study
(Baudhika Svadhyaya)

Mental self-study consists of performing one or more of the following six techniques:

1. Meditation on the holy sound OM in the mental sheath, i.e., the mercury throat level chakra. This is best performed by mentally writing OM with your creative imagination. The best way to do this is to visualize a large, iridescent circle in the mercury chakra. After you visualize it, add an infinite number of small oms clustering around it until you have drawn what appears to be one of the flowers of God, with an infinite number of petals. Always stand back, attempting to see the total flower more fully. As you practice this meditation in the intellectual sheath, the flower should become larger and larger. With each new meditation, conceive that you are reactivating the flower, i.e., that it is alive and organic, not something drawn on a mental blackboard.

2. Mentally chanting one's own chosen mantra (Ishta mantra) in the intellectual sheath of the mercury chakra.

3. Mentally chanting Gayatri mantra by writing it creatively in the intellectual sheath of the mercury chakra. Gayatri

mantra is given only after a long period of discourse, spiritual self-discipline, and purification.

4. Reading and studying the sacred holy scriptures and philosophies, which leads to the realization of life's ideal.
5. Meditation upon the sacred, holy texts and philosophies.
6. Inward contemplation to internally find those things described in the holy intellectual texts.

Many teachers suggest writing the mantra, in the above techniques, with an imaginary pen-of-light on the inside of the forehead rather than in the throat chakra. If the technique is performed in this way, these words-of-light should again and again be visualized, gazed upon, and held in silent contemplation without any physical activity whatsoever. Mental self-study is one of the surest pathways leading to God-Realization.

Verbal Self-Study
(Vachika Svadhyaya)

Verbal self-study is practiced by reading aloud holy texts containing spiritual knowledge in whatever language they are written or translated within. Verbal self-study is also performed by teaching ancient knowledge for spiritual unfoldment, writing about spiritual wisdom, or writing commentaries on ancient texts. In Hinduism, these ancient texts consist of the Vedas, the Upanishads, the Gita, the Puranas, the Ramayana, and Mahabharata, along with writings of the six orthodox schools of Indic philosophy.

In the Yogic tradition, self-study consists in studying the Upanishads, Sankhya Yoga texts, the Yoga Sutras, the Gita, and all other texts--religious and philosophical--which the teacher or disciple feels may bear meaningful fruit. Verbal self-study also includes loud chanting of sacred mantras, sacred words, the names of God, as well as praying.

Physical Self-Study
(Sharirik Svadhyaya)

With any kind of study, cooperation of the physical body is indispensable. Whenever you think or read, your physical body sustains and assists you. For this reason, many people feel that intellectual self-study and verbal self-study are in truth, physical self-study.

Physical self-study means correct posture along with a physical way of life that reveals to each cell of your being what you have learned. Self-study (Svadhyaya) has a twofold meaning: 1) self-study of the holy texts, and 2) study of the self and its component parts. Physical self-study is the awareness of what your body can do, along with the awareness and discipline of the sense organs and sheaths.

Sri Vyasa points out that after any intellectual or verbal self-study, the student should concentrate on what he has been thinking about, reading, or vocalizing. During this period of concentration, he should consolidate what he has learned into a paragraph, then into a sentence, then into a phrase, and then, if possible, into a single word. Through this technique, whenever that single word is repeated, the entire phrase, sentence, and paragraph will be re-membered and total learning will take place. After the student has contemplated the intellectual and vocal data, he should then medi-tate on the self-study so it will move him from an intellectual level to a revelation of the Self.

In the yogic tradition, OM is the symbol of Reality. By recita-tion, concentration, contemplation, and meditation on OM, God-Realization is attained. It is within God-Realization that the seeker facilitates communication with God for the purpose of balancing his total life existence. This is an expansion outward toward cosmic consciousness which is not only an understanding of the meaning and nature of life itself, but an understanding of the meaning and nature of your own individualized life.

V. CENTERING ON GOD
(Ishvar-Pranidhana)

The fifth and last observance is called attunement to God (Ishvar-Pranidhana). It has been translated different ways by dif-ferent teachers. Some of the translations include: attunement to God, meditation on God, or devotion to God. Whatever transla-tion you give, the meaning should be quite clear. There must be an unreserved, unequivocal, absolute, and total dedication of all your actions intellectually, vocally, or physically, to your chosen Ideal in life (Ishvar).

Ishvar can best be translated as your individualized, personal deity. If you are a Christian, it will most likely be Christ; if you are Catholic, it may be Mary; if you are Hindu, it may be Krishna. For Buddhists it will be the Buddha, and for the Yogi, it is God beyond form. Centering on God is an absolute necessity that brings de-tachment into your spiritual life. It will overflow into all areas of your existence: consciously, subconsciously, and superconsciously.

Centering on God is beautifully expressed in the Gita: You have a right to work, but not to the fruits of that work.

Whatever action you perform, rather than for the purpose of obtaining something, it should be done because it is meaningful in and of itself. I once knew two men who were going to medical school. One wanted to be a doctor because he wanted fame and wealth. Every school day was ever so painful to him. The other young man wanted to be a doctor to help people. Every day was a new joy in his life. For the second young man, studying was complete in and of itself because he had given his soul, his life, over to his Ishvar: the God of healing. The other man was waiting for wealth and fame, and every day was painful.

This final observance is the apex of the preceding nine abstentions and observances. They all lead toward this one apex of primary, fundamental unfoldment. Without the attainment of this apex, the mind and the senses with their cravings, apprehensions, and expectations will scatter the pranic life-force in an ever-greater chaotic process, making mystical attainments and awarenesses very unlikely. With some degree of mastery of the attunement to God, the life-currents are intensely drawn inward. The senses are drawn inward, awareness is drawn inward, and you become aware of inward things. It is at this time that the boy becomes a man and the girl becomes a woman. Having reached adulthood, they reach upward toward Godhood. This is a movement from subjective meditation to objective meditation. It brings you to the ultimate: the indwelling-God. This indwelling Lord has been the teacher since the beginning of time, even unto the most ancient of times. It is by this means that all are to be taught. This is the wish of the guru.

It is by the dedication of all your actions and the fruits of your actions that purification, simplification, stabilization, and meditation of the mind become possible, bringing you to cosmic consciousness. It is through the practice of the ten abstentions and observances (yama-niyama) that the very foundation of the spiritual life is established, so that you might attain God-Realization even in this very lifetime, in this very body.

Remember this thought: Whatsoever you do, do it gently and with love... and only after forethought. Whatsoever you do, seek out your own illumination with greater diligence!

OM SHANTI, SHANTI, SHANTI

Chapter 3

THE CLASSICAL PURIFICATION TECHNIQUES

SECTION I:
THE SHAT KRIYAS

Classically, there are six major techniques for removing physical and/or mental impurities from all the channels (nadis), especially the solar and lunar channels. The removal of these impurities, called phlegm, is very important because it:

1. Allows the pranic energies to flow over the nerve(s), increasing resistance to disease.
2. Allows the pranic energies to flow through the astral channels increasing the horizon of awareness.
3. Inhibits accumulation of toxins in the body, thus improving health and mentality.
4. Extends your physical life.
5. Increases your perceptual awareness.
6. Increases your psychic attunement.
7. Leads toward enlightenment.

The shat kriyas are also referred to as shat karmas. Shat means six, six major processes. But, the actual processes and techniques number more than six. Two phases of the purification are important. First, there is fasting and diet control, which are extremely important. Second, these is the actual washing of various parts of the body.

You will realize by reading about these purification techniques that some of them are quite dangerous, unless practiced under the direct guidance of an expert. Not all of the purification techniques need to be practiced by one person. The danger of each technique is given as they are discussed.

A point of emphasis. While you are cleansing your body, you must understand that the body is a physical instrument which your consciousness uses, and that this cleansing should not produce any abhorrence or disdain. Rather, it should bring a realization that it is a fine, precision machine that must be well-oiled and kept in repair. This process is also part of self-study, or understanding your body and how it functions in relationship to consciousness.

There has been some confusion regarding kriya. This is so, because the word has three distinct meanings:

1. Kriya means action. Kriya yoga is the yoga of physical, mental, and spiritual action which leads toward the accumulation of positive karma in this lifetime. This positive karma is called kriya-mana karma. It includes the karma that is now being created and now manifesting to neutralize negative karmas of the past. It is, also, spiritual karma that is placed in the spiritual bank for a future lifetime.
2. Kriya specifically refers to purification techniques: mental, physical, and spiritual.
3. Kriya has a third meaning. It means a series of powerful, mystical techniques that lead directly to cosmic consciousness and/or God-Realization in a single lifetime.

One of the most important texts on yoga is the Gherand Samhita. (Samhita means collected texts and Gherand is the name of the ancient sage who compiled them.) This text points out that the shat kriyas are essential for the purification of individual states of consciousness (the chakras), as well as the various sheaths (koshas):

1. Stomach cleansing (dhauti)
2. Colon cleansing (basti)
3. Nasal/sinus cleansing (neti)
4. Solar/lunar eye cleansing (tratakam)
5. Abdominal cleansing (nauli)
6. Cleansing of the sun/moon chakra (kapalabhati)

I. STOMACH CLEANSING
(Dhauti)

There are four dhauti or stomach cleansing techniques which will be covered in this section. They include:

1. Cloth stomach cleansing (vastra)
2. Water stomach cleansing (jala)
3. Fire stomach cleansing (agnisara)
4. Wind stomach cleansing (varisara)

The two most commonly practiced stomach cleansing techniques are the cloth and water methods.

1. CLOTH STOMACH CLEANSING
(Vastra Dhauti)

The most common stomach cleansing technique is called cloth stomach cleansing, usually referred to as dhauti. This technique requires a soft cloth that is about 3 inches wide and approximately 5 feet long, although not all of the cloth is used. The cloth should be washed thoroughly and should have no loose threads. Sometimes the edges of the cloth are sewn.

The procedure is simple. You dip the clean cloth in warm water and then squeeze out most of the water. Taking the edge of the cloth with your fingers, place it as deeply back into the throat as possible and begin gently to swallow 1 foot of cloth. Allow the cloth to remain there for 1 or 2 minutes, and then slowly withdraw it. Remember, any rapid pulling of the cloth out of the throat might burn the sensitive membranes. Each day learn to swallow an extra 3 to 9 inches of cloth.

One of the chief benefits associated with dhauti is learning to control the regurgitative effect. It is natural for the throat to reject anything that is not food; therefore don't become discouraged if and when this happens. By learning to control the regurgitative process, you will gain greater control over your mercury chakra and your physical vehicle. It increases awareness that your body is just a physical vehicle which you use.

In the wintertime, the cloth may be soaked in warm water. In the learning stages of cloth stomach cleansing, some students put the cloth in milk and sugar. This is slightly defeating because pasteurized milk is phlegm-producing. Nonetheless, it makes the cloth more palatable. Later, water with a pinch of salt is utilized.

To perform dhauti, sit on your toes in front of a bowl in which the moist dhauti is contained. Open your mouth and place the cloth as far back as possible into the mouth, and push it down into the throat with the middle and index fingers. Try to swallow a little warm water while the cloth is in the throat. This, sometimes, will ease the regurgitative re-action. If there is vomiting or a strong regurgitative action and the cloth is expelled, you should quietly wait a few minutes. Then, regain composure, and attempt again to swallow it, after re-washing it. After a few days you will succeed in learning to swallow a little of the cloth. Do not get nervous if in the first few days your body rejects the cloth. All that is needed is the ability to swallow approximately 3 feet of it. Remember, the cloth will slide easily out of the throat/stomach because it will now be covered with phlegm.

There is a caution: Practice cloth dhauti only on an empty stomach.

Once you have accustomed yourself to swallowing the dhauti, it will not be necessary to wet the cloth; however, I recommend the cloth always be moist. When the dhauti has been swallowed, whether it be 3 or 6 feet, abdominal cleansing is performed. Remember that 1 to 2 feet of cloth should always remain outside the mouth so that you do not swallow the complete end. Some teachers suggest tying the end of the cloth to a wrist. This might sound ridiculous because in the beginning stages it's difficult to swallow a few inches. But mastery will happen. From the beginning, train right.

Occasionally, as you are pulling the dhauti out, your throat will constrict. Don't get nervous, and don't panic--you will be able to breathe although the cloth is in the throat. The use of any type of oil will help lubricate and relax the throat. Gentle rubbing of the throat can also be helpful. It is strongly suggested that other than the preparatory stages of learning to swallow only a few inches of dhauti at a time, this technique be practiced under the direct supervision of your guru or a qualified hatha yoga instructor. After your dhauti cloth has been used, wash it thoroughly in warm water to remove all phlegm. Dry it, fold it, and put it away in a clean place (such as a plastic bag) for the next time.

In the early stages of practicing dhauti, it should be practiced daily. After the technique has been mastered, it is usually practiced at the four seasonal changes to help maintain health. Stomach cleansing is normally done early in the morning on an empty stomach after an evening's fast.

This particular stomach cleansing technique assists in the removal of excessive phlegm and phlegmatic conditions. It is said to cure coughs and sneezes, disorders of the lungs, and bad bile. It also improves gastric disorders including gastritis and complications associated with the liver, stomach, gall bladder, and throat. Its major value is that it 'opens' the astral channels.

2. WATER STOMACH CLEANSING
   (Jala Dhauti)

Water dhauti is a process whereby the stomach is cleansed to remove excessive phlegm and bile, utilizing water instead of a cloth. Drink 5 or 6 full glasses of lukewarm water to which approximately 1/8 teaspoon of salt has been added for each glass of water. Three to five minutes after drinking this water, vigorously agitate the stomach by means of the stomach lift (uddiyana) or the abdominal cleansing (nauli). This induces regurgitation. As the water is expelled, it will wash out excessive phlegm and bile. If one has difficulty regurgitating, drink more water, or insert a finger into the throat to assist the regurgitation process. Be sure not to use too much salt. The amount of water drunk has a direct relation to the ease of regurgitation.

Needless to say, this technique should not be used for people on a low sodium diet, etc.

3. FIRE STOMACH CLEANSING
(Agnisara Dhauti)

Fire dhauti is performed by standing in a slightly squatting position with the legs 1 to 1-1/2 feet apart. Exhale forcefully and fully. Then hold the breath. Now, perform the stomach lift or the abdominal cleansing, vigorously and rapidly. Continue the rotational pumping action of the stomach as many times as you comfortably can. Slowly increase the number of rotations up to approximately 108. Gradually increase the number, always remaining comfortable. Stop the technique before becoming exhausted. At this point allow the breath to flow in and relax. This completes 1 round. The number of rounds that can be practiced is 1 to 5.

Fire dhauti is so named because it increases the gastric juices, the gastric fire, greatly improving digestion. Do not practice fire dhauti beyond your capacity. People with difficult abdominal problems or circulatory disturbances should avoid it. Fire dhauti increases the peristalsis action of the bowels and keeps them healthy. It cures constipation wherein many diseases begin. It is, also, very helpful in reducing fatty tissue around the belly.

4. WIND STOMACH CLEANSING
(Varisara Dhauti)

Wind dhauti, as well as fire dhauti, can be performed in a sitting posture but it is far more effective in a standing position. As you stretch your neck forward, relax the throat muscles and pull air into the mouth, swallowing it. Repeat this process, filling your stomach with as much air as possible. Pressing the chin strongly against the chest will help you to hold in the air. Having filled the stomach with as much air as possible, practice rolling the abdominal muscles (nauli) and lifting the stomach (uddiyana bandha). After this, belch out as much air as possible.

One difficult aspect of this technique is that if the air is not totally expelled through the throat shortly after swallowing the air, it will later pass out through the anus as gas. This may present some social problems. Wind dhauti is very helpful for clearing out trapped, foul gas and for bringing in more direct oxygen to the stomach and intestinal tract.

II. COLON CLEANSING
(Basti)

There are two types of colon cleansing. The first is water colon cleansing (jala basti), and the second type is ground colon cleansing (sthala basti).

1. WATER COLON CLEANSING
   (Jala Basti)

Our western culture is quite familiar with water colon cleansing. The procedure is simply to allow water to enter into the colon, thus removing excess waste material. Methods range from squatting in a river to using an enema bag. In India, a person squats in a river using a small tube to open the anus, and performs the stomach lift, which expels air from inside the large intestinal tract. Rolling and isolation of the abdominal muscles (nauli kriya) is then performed. This creates a vacuum in the abdominal area, forcing water to be suctioned up into the colon. The person then stands, rotates the stomach to wash the inside of the intestines, and expels the water and its contents.

There is a technique for opening the sphincter muscle by performing the horse seal (aswini mudra). In this technique you sit in the easy pose and repeatedly contract and expand the anus.

The benefits are that it washes out accumulations in the intestinal tract, making the wall linings cleaner. Thus, they function better. Water basti is far more effective than ground basti. Remember, all practices of the shat kriyas are always performed on an empty stomach. In modern times, an enema bag is the best method for performing water basti.

The benefits of basti are numerous. Ancient texts say that it cures diseases arising from the three humors, removes disorders of the blood, bones, and fat areas, and removes impurities of the sense organs, the mind, intellect, and heart. They also say that it makes a person happy, and most importantly, that it helps to overcome passionate activity and/or lethargy. This procedure awakens the digestive powers and cures flatulence. It obviously relieves constipation and purifies the intestines. It tends to overcome stomach difficulties and keeps them from arising.

Ancient tradition points out that basti should be practiced before any long meditation, lasting days. It should be performed only when necessary, such as during periods of fasting or periods of heavy contemplation. As always, remember that anything performed in excess can produce problems.

2. GROUND COLON CLEANSING
(Sthala Basti)

Sitting on the floor with your legs stretched out before you, take hold of your toes; the right toe with the right hand, and the left toe with the left hand. Bring your head toward your knees, as in the forward bend (paschimottanasan), however, do not bend forward very much. In this position, relax the abdominal muscles, and in that relaxed state, churn them back and forth with an upward and downward motion.

While performing ground basti, hold the anus lock contraction (mula bandha). It is very important that you do not exert yourself while practicing this basti. It should be practiced on an empty stomach; sometimes drinking a 1/4-glass of water beforehand is helpful. Ground basti helps relieve gas and assists the peristaltic motion of the bowels. In addition to improving digestion, basti makes the body feel light and less earth-bound.

III. NASAL CLEANSING
(Neti)

The third shat kriya is nasal cleansing (neti). There are two types: water nasal cleansing (jala neti), and string nasal cleansing (sutra neti).

1. WATER NASAL CLEANSING
(Jala Neti)

Water nasal cleansing is quite simple. You draw water in through the nose and expel it out through the mouth. The water should be neither hot nor cold. A very small amount of salt can be added. Water neti can be reversed. You can draw water in through the mouth and expel out through the nasal passages. Water neti prevents colds and thoroughly cleanses the nasal passages, which allows a greater assimilation of life-force to the nerves and astral channels.

2. STRING NASAL CLEANSING
(Sutra Neti)

String nasal cleansing is a procedure whereby a soft, untreated thread 12 to 18 inches long is carefully passed through one of the nasal passages and then expelled through the mouth. Before this technique is performed, the alternate breathing technique is practiced to establish which nasal passage is more open. The nostril that is more open is then utilized in this technique. The thread or soft string is wetted before it is inserted in the nasal passage. It is placed as far up into the nasal passage as possible. The opposite nasal passage is closed and air is exhaled through the open mouth. The mouth is then closed and one inhales deeply through the open nasal passage containing the string. This will draw the string into the throat. Normally, most people begin to sneeze immediately. You will find that the thread needs only be inserted an inch or two. Gradually, the thread will reach down into the throat. You can then grab the thread with the middle and fourth fingers, pulling it out of the mouth. Later, with one end of the string in the mouth and one end of the string in the nasal passage, the string is slowly and very cautiously moved back and forth. Any strong movement will burn the delicate nasal membranes. One relaxes for a few moments and begins the process over again. This technique is only for those who have gained a certain degree of mastery over their body. Caution: do not yank the string out because of any discomfort. If there is discomfort, carefully and slowly pull the thread out so as not to burn the membranes.

Another word of caution: This practice is not to be carried on hastily or it may cause irritation, bleeding, and damage to the nasal membranes. It is best to have mastered water neti completely, before moving on to string neti.

Neti destroys sinus diseases, and headaches caused by various factors, as well as neck problems. The sinus passages, nose, and throat are cleansed, improving vision and allowing added prana to enter the astral channels.

IV. SOLAR/LUNAR EYE CLEANSING
(Tratakam)

The fourth technique is the solar/lunar channel cleansing. This process is known in English as gazing. You will note that it is called gazing and not staring. Staring will produce undue stress and strain upon the eyes.

The procedure is quite simple. You simply fix your eyes upon an object. In ancient times a slightly shiny object was utilized, often a candle. In modern times a light bulb is often used.

A 7-watt bulb is best. Do not use anything above a 15-watt light bulb, as the intensity of the higher wattage bulb will tend to cause damage. Candles are not the best, unless you are in a draftless room. If in a drafty room, the flame of the candle will be unsteady and this will detract from the goal.

The best posture to utilize is the perfect pose. Sitting and facing a wall, write a small OM on the wall. The object to be gazed upon should be at approximately eye level, neither too far nor too close away. Sit back about 3 feet and gaze without moving the eyelids. The eyes will begin to water. This watering brings about a washing effect on the eyes, producing an eye cleansing. If the eyes begin to burn, you might close and gently rub them as though you were trying to rub sleep out of your eye. When the eyes have rested, repeat the process.

In certain Indic sects, the sun is used as the object for gazing. This is done only at sunrise, just as the sun is coming over the horizon. I do not recommend it! The retina of the eye can be damaged by the powerful rays of the sun, even at sunrise. I recommend gazing at an OM symbol. When your eyes are fixed without any blinking, your mind will be totally focused.

Slowly increase the length of the gaze, without exhausting the eyes. It is best to perform the eye-gazing technique in an area that is not cluttered with objects. Often a corner of the room is best. Those with eye difficulties should consult their health practitioner before beginning this practice. Properly performed, the benefits of the eye gaze are improvement of eyesight and the development of concentration.

ADVANCED TRATAKAM

There are three more advanced techniques which should be utilized only by advanced students under direct supervision. They are procedures in which mystical sections of the body are gazed upon. The three most common are:

1. Gazing at the sun center (the ajna chakra) with the eyes half open (Brumadhya drishti). This technique is the most superior.
2. Gazing at the tip of the nose (Nasagra drishti).
3. A process whereby the eyes are held open but no object is perceived because the attention is focused internally (Unmani and sambhavi mudra). This practice should not be performed by people who are mentally scattered to begin with. The visualization of 'no thing' confuses them. They believe no-thing to be nothing. Such effort tends to produce a state of unconsciousness, rather than consciousness upon 'no thing'.

The benefits from these techniques, according to ancient teachers, are the perfection of perception and the removal of diseases of the eye. They remove drowsiness and laziness, giving control over the amount of sleep needed. External attention and the power of concentration are eminently heightened.

V. ABDOMINAL CHAKRA CLEANSING
(Nauli)

The fifth shat kriya is abdominal or mars chakra cleansing. The preliminary to this technique, although not classical, is the stomach lift. The stomach lift is given as a recommended preliminary to the practice of nauli. It is usually mastered before nauli is attempted.

Stomach Lift
(Uddiyana)

THE STOMACH LIFT
(Uddiyana)

Uddiyana is sometimes referred to as the stomach lift, meaning the flying up. It is through this technique that the life-energies are made to fly up from the lower mars chakra region to the head. Place the feet approximately 1 to 1-1/2 feet apart. Bend the knees slightly. Inhale deeply and exhale quickly and completely, holding the breath out. Now contract the abdominal muscles, pushing them inward and upward. Now, relax them. Again, push the muscles forcefully inward and upward and relax them. It's important that the movement between the inward and upward contraction and the relaxation of those muscles is in rapid succession. Repeat this 3 to 4 times, then relax completely, allowing the air to flow into the lungs. Rest. Exhale the air. While the air is held outside the lungs, repeat the upward and inward contraction of the muscles, with alternate relaxation.

Uddiyana should always be practiced on an empty stomach. Uddiyana will help eliminate toxins from the digestive system as well as waste material from the alimentary tract.

NAULI KRIYA
(Abdominal Mars Chakra Cleansing)

Having mastered the stomach lift, stand with your feet about 1 to 1-1/2 feet apart. Bend the knees slightly, placing the hands upon the knees. Bend the trunk and chest forward, then exhale and hold the lungs completely empty. Now move the abdominal muscles upward and downward and with effort to the right and to the left. This will require will power, internal effort, and skill. Strong mind thoughts must be sent to these areas to bring them under control. Gain control over the sluggishness of these muscles. Remember, the lungs are empty, otherwise it is impossible to perform nauli.

This can be an extremely exhausting procedure and should therefore be practiced slowly. Thus, while the breath is out, one should rotate the stomach up and down, to the right and the left, only 3 times and come to a rest. Take a deep breath, exhale again, rotate the stomach 2 or 3 times, and rest again. One keeps repeating this, stopping long before the feeling of exhaustion sets in. If you are going to perform 6 or 12 rounds, it would be wise halfway through, to perform the total relaxation posture.

Nauli kriya is a way of splitting the recti-front abdominal muscles, causing them to move independently and alternately, rather than simultaneously as is their normal action. For some persons this can be accomplished in a few months. Those who have large bellies find this very difficult to practice. Fasting and weight loss are recommended. Persons with acute abdominal diseases should not practice this technique. Also, pregnant women should refrain from this practice. The ancient texts point out that the technique cures weak digestion and prevents disorders of the kidneys, stomach, and intestinal tract. It, also, purifies the mars chakra, and releases large sums of energy into the astral body.

VI. SUN/MOON CHAKRA CLEANSING
(Kapalabhati)

The last of the major techniques is known as sun/moon chakra cleansing. It can be performed either in a sitting yogic position or in a standing position. The standing position is exactly the same as that for uddiyana, with the feet being 1 to 1-1/2 feet apart. Pull and hold the upper lip over the upper teeth, tightly but gently. This opens the nasal passages. Then inhale and exhale forcefully but as quickly and as smoothly as possible, like the movement of a blacksmith's bellows. There is a split-second retention after each exhalation. The inhalation is slow and vigorous. The exhalation is faster and more vigorous. Remember, there is a split-second retention after the exhalation. Inhale and exhale as quickly as possible, without stopping. This obviously produces a somewhat shallow breath.

In this process the viscera are rapidly pushed up against the diaphragm, relaxed, and then brought back up again, producing some beneficial effects. The viscera massages itself, the viscera massages the diaphragm, and the diaphragm massages the lungs. This triple massage action, in conjunction with the rapidity of breath through the nasal passages, cleanses the lunar (ida) and the solar (pingala) channels. If practicing kapalabhati you feel dizzy or giddy, you should stop and perform the total relaxation posture.

Having performed kapalabhati, rest and then perform kapalabhati again. In the initial stages, kapalabhati is practiced once a day, either in the morning or evening. Later, it is performed twice a day, once in the morning and once in the evening. It may be increased to 6 times a day, 3 times in the morning and 3 times in the evening. There is a modification of kapalabhati called 'bellows breath' which is given in the chapter on pranayama.

Standard kapalabhati as given here cleanses the arteries, improves digestion, and removes excess fat and phlegm from the body. Ancient texts say it removes all diseases from the head and central nervous system. On a mystical level, kapalabhati (and bellows breath) awakens the kriya kundalini life-force, and drives it upwards to the higher spiritual chakras.

SECTION II:
THE PURIFICATION TECHNIQUES OF THE BODY

In yoga, cleanliness is next to godliness is a literal as well as a scientific truth. Cleanliness not only means external cleanliness but also internal cleanliness. To gain lasting benefits from the practical techniques of yoga, it is necessary to maintain a standard of body cleanliness far above that which is normally accepted in the everyday life. Along with bathing, lasting gains are to be sustained by the continual practice of a yogic diet and fasting.

The function of the purification techniques is based upon the concept that as long as the body has impurities, the pranic force cannot collect in the astral body. If the pranic energies are unable to accumulate, the mind will not generate or vibrate to its highest spiritual awareness. Consequently, there are four substances which, if they accumulate excessively in the body, are highly detrimental to spiritual attunement and/or spiritual unfoldment. These are:

- Lactic acid
- Carbon dioxide gas
- Bile
- Phlegm

1. The accumulation of lactic acid in the muscles makes a person exhausted and fatigued. Thus, the person lacks the mental acuity or energy to perform the spiritual tasks needed to attain cosmic consciousness.

2. Toxic gas, or carbon dioxide, when combined with water, produces an acid which is exceptionally irritating to the body and nervous system. This causes one to be edgy, restless, irritable, and heavily distracted. This makes it almost impossible to be serene and thus to concentrate. Without serenity and quietness of the body, placidity of the mind cannot be gained. Without placidity of the mind, meditation cannot occur. Without meditation, wisdom cannot be attained. Without wisdom, cosmic consciousness cannot be attained.

3. Without sufficient oxygen and prana, one becomes mentally sluggish, and accumulative waste matter will not be properly eliminated from the system. The body and mind will become apathetic and often pessimistic in attitude and thinking. This usually causes the liver to become sluggish and impaired, and the normal flow of bile is interrupted. When this happens, bile backs up into the body and gives rise to biliousness. Biliousness is a major physiological obstacle to the attainment of spiritual awareness, for it locks a person

more intensely into body awareness. As long as one holds to body consciousness it is impossible to experience cosmic consciousness. You must therefore be capable of increasing your oxygen and prana to the brain and mind.

4. An excessive amount of phlegm or mucus in the body is not only a medium for bacteria, it also inhibits the absorption of prana, making the body more susceptible to disease. This lack of absorption of prana to the astral body denies inner awarenesses. Without inner awareness, no cosmic consciousness is possible.

THE BODY'S ELIMINATION

If anything, the shat kriyas emphasize the need to improve the process of elimination. The shat kriyas should not be looked upon as going against our natural functions but rather as assisting them. Yoga places extreme demands upon the body and mind, therefore, the functions of the body and mind must be correspondingly heightened.

Through artificial living habits, modern man's natural power of elimination has been basically lost due to three major factors:

1. An overindulgence in foodstuffs lacking sufficient bulk. This distends the large intestine enough to deactivate the reflexes for elimination.
2. Lack of sufficient exercise due primarily to sedentary work.
3. Lack of sufficient exercise due to non-active play.

Because of these three factors, the abdominal muscles lose their tonus and the power of elimination. As the power of elimination becomes sluggish, waste matters accumulate and there is a rapid deterioration of the internal organs.

In kriya yoga, your being is symbolized by the astrological symbol of a circle with a dot in it:

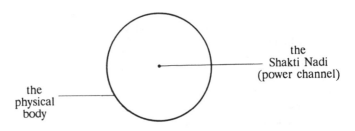

The circle symbolizes your total physical being, and the dot represents the alimentary tract, or the power channel (shakti nadi), extending from the mouth to the anus. The power channel is the power of the sun because your life is sustained by it, as this power channel manifests the three main functions necessary for earth life:

1. Digestion
2. Assimilation
3. Elimination

Physical and mental vitality and therefore, spiritual vitality, are dependent upon the high vibration of this power tract, especially at the abdominal plexus or mars chakra.

The single greatest handicap of the earth body is inadequate elimination. When elimination becomes extremely inadequate, the accumulation of fecal matter is drawn into the bloodstream, rendering the vitality of the red corpuscles somewhat inactive. Because of this, oxidation of the blood system is not as thorough. This produces a mental devitalization called lethargy, or moodiness. In normal everyday yogic language, it's called auto-intoxication. As this occurs, lack of spiritual vitality also ensues.

The blood that flows through and around the intestines is the self-same blood that flows through your brain. If the bowels become sluggish causing auto-intoxication, the blood becomes impure. When impure blood goes to the brain, it tends to dull the consciousness. When this happens, one's attitude becomes depressed, one's thinking becomes pessimistic, and spiritual self-awareness becomes impossible.

It is well-known that the cure for emotional depression, (the so-called blues), is to cleanse the alimentary tract. It is also well-known that in the European Middle Ages the so-called blue-bloods, the elite of Europe, suffered from blue blood because of their lack of physical activity, poor diet, and poor breathing habits. These blue-bloods were known for their emotional depression (the blues) and their emotional outrages. A word to the wise is sufficient.

Paying greater attention to elimination will greatly assist your spiritual unfoldment. The utilization of stomach cleansing and/or the ordinary enema is highly recommended. When utilizing these techniques, nothing should be in the water save the water itself. It is wise to use bottled spring water that does not have chlorine and/or fluorine in it.

Abdominal exercises should be practiced in connection with the enema. The best are the stomach lift (uddiyana) and abdominal chakra cleansing (nauli). Some critics of enemas claim that through their use, the colon might become flabby and weak. An excessive number of enemas should not be undertaken. Also, this will not occur if yoga asans are practiced. The abdominal exercises will also have a very important toning effect upon the solar plexus. The abdominal exercises along with enema cleansing will increase the peristaltic functions of the intestinal tract, in addition to increasing the digestive juices of the stomach, liver, pancreas, and gall bladder. Finally, these two working together will improve blood circulation throughout the entire body, especially in the brain.

Independent of the elimination of waste matter through the colon, there are three other major organs of elimination and purification. These are:

1. The kidneys
2. The lungs
3. The skin

Kidneys

The kidneys can be cleansed most easily by drinking larger quantities of pure water throughout the day, not at one time. The vast number of people today suffer from dehydration, due to lack of water intake. It is suggested that the water be taken between meals. Water taken with meals tends to dilute the digestive enzymes. Approximately 6 to 10 glasses of water should be taken each and every day. This water should be sipped, not gulped.

Lungs

The utilization of the lungs as an avenue of elimination will be extensively dealt with in the chapter on breath control. It is very important to breathe deeply a number of times each morning, afternoon, and evening, holding the breath long enough to allow the oxygen and prana to be absorbed into the physical and astral vehicles. With each inhalation, the oxygen is absorbed primarily into the physical bloodstream via the lungs. The prana, however, is absorbed directly into the membranes of the mouth and throat. Some of this prana goes directly to the physical brain, but the majority is absorbed into the astral vehicle.

Historically speaking, many yogis have recommended swallowing large quantities of air. This procedure arose from the observation that many flesh-eating birds are given to swallowing large quantities of air which helps purify their system and makes elimination easier. Snakes, after swallowing other animals, assist their digestion by also swallowing large quantities of air. I do not recommend this for the average person.

Skin

The fourth and final means of elimination is the skin. The skin is a valuable kinship organ to the bowels, lungs, kidneys, and liver, and is composed of two distinct layers:
1. Epidermis
2. Dermis

The epidermis is often referred to as scarf skin, or tissue. The epidermis lies over the outer surface of the body and consists entirely of flat cells devoid of nerves and blood vessels. This epidermis or upper skin is constantly shedding. New, live cells are constantly replacing the discarded cells. The epidermis lies on top of the dermis. The upper skin, or epidermis, is supplied by the dermis which continually forms new cells and pushes them upward toward the surface of the body. As these cells are created they become harder, drier, and flatter. Because the epidermis has no nerves or blood vessels, it does not bleed when pricked, nor does one feel pain. An unbelievable amount of epidermal dead tissue is being discarded each and every day of your life. This is most noticeable when the cells become gummed on the surface of the body because of body oils. It is well-known that persons who have had broken or fractured limbs and have had casts removed, found enough cast off epidermal cells to fill a small container.

The second layer of skin, the dermis, has blood vessels, lymphatic vessels, sweat glands, and nerves. It is through the dermal layer that we experience the sensations of hot and cold, smooth and rough, wet and dry, etc.

As indicated earlier, the organs of elimination are primarily the bowels, the kidneys, the lungs, and the skin. The bulk of impurities is eliminated by the bowels. Second in importance in elimination is the kidneys. After the lungs, the next important organ of elimination becomes the sweat glands in the skin, carrying away elimination by means of perspiration. When the kidneys are weak or partially inactive, the skin is called upon to do much of their work.

Most people think the skin is merely some sort of external covering or armor that protects the rest of the organs. Although this is true to an extent, there are several other important functions of the skin. These include:
1. Excretion of waste material,
2. An accessory organ of breathing,

3. Secretion of oily fluids,
4. Regulation of body temperature.

Excretion of Waste Material

One of the functions of the skin is to eliminate waste materials from the body through a process called perspiration. Intense perspiration can be induced by vigorous exercise or intense yoga postures. The inducing of excessive perspiration by performing asans helps in cleaning out clogged pores so they might normally regain their important function of removing large quantities of waste material from the body. The pores are one of the most important and most neglected organs of elimination. They are linked directly to the bloodstream. As the clogged pores are opened, they eliminate and relieve the burden on the kidneys.

It is interesting to note that perspiration contains fluids filtered out of the bloodstream itself by tiny sweat glands which then carry the waste materials to the surface of the skin. Consequently, you can see the importance of physical exercise and proper washing of the skin. When perspiration is analyzed, it is found to be made up of the same substances secreted in the urine. When the alimentary tract is obstructed or malfunctioning, again the skin is called upon to remove excess waste material which tends to produce heavy body odors. Heavy body odors indicate the need for drinking more pure water and internal cleansing, not just external cleansing. This is an important guideline.

An Accessory Organ of Breathing

The skin is also an accessory organ of breathing. Through the yoga asans and bathing, unclogged pores of the skin begin to breathe again, and to feed oxygen to important surface areas not easily covered by standard breathing. Modern physiology does not give much value to the concept of skin or pore-breathing. The yogis contend that the atmospheric pressure upon the body, when the pores are clean, produces a breathing effect which causes a surface oxidation of the skin. The word breathing also relates to the transference of pranic forces to and from the surface of the body. A clean skin surface increases the pranic flow.

Also, rays of the sun are of tremendous benefit to the skin, for they cause Vitamin D and prana to be absorbed through and into the pores. Consequently, regular sunbaths as well as air baths are highly recommended.

Secretion of Oily Fluids

The fourth important function of the skin is secretion of an oily fluid from the sweat glands, which lubricates and protects the skin from dry air. Due to many of our modern habits, there is a tendency for this oil to gum and clog the pores of our skin. Thus it is necessary to properly wash the skin. The use of bathing as a means of promoting healthy skin and cleansing the pores should be fairly obvious. However, there are a few points to be stressed.

1. One bathes without the use of excessive amounts of soap.
2. Be sure to rinse far more than you think is needed.
3. Utilize a soft soap rather than a harsher soap which tends to de-grease the skin.
4. Stay away from the detergents which are excessively drying and dangerous.
5. In any bathing, a cloth should be used and rubbed vigorously on the body to remove the excess epidermal skin and to assist in opening the pores and improving circulation.
6. There are two excellent times for bathing: early in the morning (before breakfast) and right upon returning home from work.
7. The temperature of the bath should be suited to your individual temperament and personality.
8. The major problem is people do not soak long enough. Soaking is very important. Soaking performs the same service for the skin as does flushing the colon for the large intestine.
9. The body should be dried with a thick, fluffy, clean towel. Rubbing the body with the towel will help stimulate the blood circulation as well as remove excessive dry skin loosened by the bath.

Regulation of Body Temperature

The skin also serves as a regulation of body temperature. You will note that if you take a cold bath, the flow of blood to the surface of the skin is quite notable. This immediately raises the body's temperature around the skin area to keep the body warm. We all know that in hotter weather we begin to sweat. As the sweat evaporates, it cools down the body by means of this evaporation. On an average day, the average person sweats or excretes approximately 1-1/2 pints of water. Persons engaged in heavy physical labor can sweat as much as two pints per hour. Here you can see how the body functions in trying to maintain a balance.

The performance of yoga asans assists in cleansing the body's pores for it increases body temperature. Warm liquids dissolve solids faster than cold liquids. When practicing the asans, the body temperature rises, enabling waste matter to dissolve faster and wash away more easily.

The Hot-Soak Bath

A hot-soak bath is highly recommended. The hot baths of Japan are well-known. The procedure is this: The water is drawn at a temperature of approximately 98 to 108 degrees. Some persons cannot stand this temperature; others find it extremely comfortable. You must acclimatize by finding a comfortable bath temperature and slowly increasing the water temperature while soaking. Over the months, you will raise the temperature of the hot-soak bath. In the hot-soak bath no soap is used. You just soak. The hot water opens the pores and raises the body temperature. This allows more waste matter to be dissolved away through the blood system, urine, sweat glands, etc. The soaking period lasts approximately 15 to 30 minutes, depending on your individual temperament. When the hot-soak bath is complete, take a cool shower. After cooling the body down, get back into the hot soak tub. The body is then rubbed dry in a standard procedure. Neither persons in a weakened physical condition nor those who are exhausted should use the hot-soak bath method. If you are in a negative mood, you should meditate prior to bathing. Then enter the bath to which hotter and hotter water is added.

CONCLUSION

This ends the discourse on the six purification techniques which cleanse and lighten the body, making it receptive to the absorption and storage of prana through the various prana-absorbing techniques of mantra, meditation, and breath control. It is through these prana-absorbing techniques that you absorb and accumulate enough life-energy to turn inward consciously to reach the later stages of yoga: sense withdrawal and samadhi.

The shat kriyas train the mind through disciplining the body. You will more fully realize that you are not a mind that has a body, not a body that has a mind, but that you are spirit which functions through body and mind. You realize that with a proper attitude, you must master them both. Only if you practice some of the suggested techniques will you feel their effects.

I wish to repeat the caution: Some of these techniques, if not most of them, should be practiced under the direct supervision of one who has mastered them. This cannot be stressed too strongly.

SECTION III:
NON-CLASSICAL PURIFICATION TECHNIQUES

Although we have completed the classical shat kriyas, there still remain 11 other purification procedures that you should know about. These techniques are also important.

THE STOMACH LIFT
(Uddiyana)

This has already been discussed under abdominal chakra cleansing as a preliminary to nauli. You should be aware that it is not one of the classical shat kriyas.

TONGUE CLEANSING (Chandra Dhauti)

There are two forms of tongue cleansing.

1. TONGUE CLEANSING
(Chandra Dhauti)

This cleansing technique is very important, and very powerful. It is highly recommended.

Obtain a silver spoon, sterling or silver-plated. Some people prefer using a silver butter knife. In either case, the procedure is the same. After you brush your teeth, put a little water in a glass, with a very small amount of salt. With the water, rinse the mouth and expel the water. Having washed the mouth, extend the tongue and take the silver spoon, or butter knife, and gently rub it across the tongue. The spoon is used upside down and the knife's dull side is used. Reach back as far as you can. Remember, it is very important to rub the tongue from the back forward. Do not scrape the tongue. It can be amazing, the amount of material that will come off the tongue, especially if you are not well.

Next rinse the mouth, expectorate, and repeat once or twice. When finished, wash, rinse, and wrap the spoon, putting it away to be used only for this purpose. You will find this procedure very invigorating. It allows a large amount of pranic energy flowing over the tongue to be absorbed into the tongue, moon chakra, and the astral body. You will find practicing this technique will make your eyes sparkle and your mind clearer. Practice this technique in the morning, and also in the evening, since kriya yoga is concerned with the dream state.

Any object could be used to clean the tongue. In Hawaii they sell plastic tongue cleaners. In China they were made of wood. However, silver as a symbol relates to the moon chakra. The spoon leaves small deposits of silver on the tongue which protect the tongue from infection. According to metallotherapy, certain metals fight infections. Silver, also, opens the moon center making one more psychic.

Here is an example to illustrate this: take a petri dish which has a culture on it, and drop in a silver dime (or any silver object). Bacteria will grow in the entire culture except in the area around the dime. The silver literally radiates ions and nothing will grow in that area. This is true of gold also. Utilizing silver and gold for money makes for a healthier society. People handling it will not communicate diseases.

2. TONGUE CLEANSING
(Hrid Dhauti)

There is another tongue cleansing that is referred to as hrid dhauti. Join together the index, middle, and ring fingers. Insert them into the throat and rub the tongue and root of the throat. Rinse the mouth with lightly salted water, gargle, and expectorate. Repeat this process 1 to 3 times. The hands, fingers, and fingernails should be cleansed ahead of time. Women utilizing this process need guard against scratching the delicate oral membranes with long fingernails.

SINUS CLEANSING

This technique also has great value. The thumb of the right hand is placed at the inside upper corner of the eye between the side of the nose and the eye itself. At this point in the eye socket there is a 1/4-inch notch where the optical nerve crosses. The thumb then massages this point.

When practiced, there is purification and balancing of what are often called the phlegmatic humors. These procedures not only purify and soothe the mind, but tend to induce clairvoyance and assist the perception through the third eye.

EAR CLEANSING
(Karna Dhauti)

It is important occasionally to remove excessive amounts of wax that are built up in the ears. People often complain of pains in the ear because there is a blockage in the tube leading from the nose to the ear. The best method of ear cleansing is to use an ear syringe filled with warm water. Cotton swabs can also be used for removing excessive wax. This procedure should not be done too frequently. Extensive cleansing or too frequent cleansing of the ears can be harmful. Do not use toothpicks, wire, or any object which may puncture the sensitive eardrum and cause deafness. Also, do not use tissues that may stick to the ear wax and be a source of infection.

TEETH CLEANSING

This is a normal technique used by most people. Most people use toothbrush bristles that are too hard and tend to scrape the enamel. Also, commercial toothpastes are exceptionally abrasive. Use only toothpastes that are low-abrasive, and/or a small amount of baking soda to brush your teeth. Finally, your teeth should be brushed in an up and down motion rather than in a back and forth motion.

VARIATIONS OF DHAUTI
1. STRING STOMACH CLEANSING
(Brahma Datuna Kriya)

String stomach cleansing is performed by taking about a dozen pieces of fine yarn, each approximately 7 feet long, folding them threefold and twisting them into a string. This will make a string approximately 2 feet long, the thickness of your little finger. At one end of the string a metal ring is firmly attached to assist in pulling the string from the stomach. Pure beeswax is then melted and the string soaked in it. About 1/2-inch of the string at the end opposite the metal ring should be free from wax so it will enter the throat without difficulty.

This string is known as brahma datuna. As the brahma datuna is made with yarn, it only needs to be made once, for it can be rinsed and reused. Historically, the brahma datuna was made of the pithy part of the leaf of the banana tree or the tender stems from the banyan tree. When the string was made from these trees, it could not be washed and had to be made fresh each time dhauti was to be used.

This method is very similar to dhauti, as studied in the preceding section. Having first emptied the colon and bladder, one stands (or sits) and pushes the soft end of the brahma datuna gradually down the throat. As with other dhautis, coughing and spitting may occur. The nose and eyes will begin to water and phlegm will be ejected from the throat. With patience, the process is repeated until 4 inches or so can be accepted into the stomach. After a week or two of consistent work, you will be able to insert a foot or two of string into the stomach. Then, taking hold of the ring with your finger, slowly pull out the yarn. The brahma datuna is then washed and hung up for the next use.

The effects and benefits of brahma datuna are very similar to the standard cloth dhauti. It promotes digestion and prevention of diseases caused by excessive phlegm. According to the ancient teachings, it improves and cures eye diseases. Brahma datuna is also known as danda dhauti. The basic distinction between these--brahma datuna and cloth dhauti--is the thickness of the brahma datuna and its porosity to absorb more phlegm and acid. Standard dhauti needs to be mastered before brahma datuna is practiced. This technique does not need to be utilized as cloth dhauti is complete in itself. Brahma datuna is given here for historical data more than anything else.

2. GAJI KARNI or KUNJAR KRIYA

Having emptied the colon and bladder, drink large quantities of water mixed with salt. Drink as much as you can, then a little more. Lean forward, place the palms on the knees and move the stomach vigorously back and forth causing regurgitation. In the wintertime, lukewarm water is used; in the summertime, cool water is used. Historically, the benefits of gaji karni include curing stomach and throat problems such as flatulence, gastritis, heartburn, belching, and indigestion. It increases the appetite and produces a mood of cheerfulness. Again, some people should beware of the use of salt.

3. VAMAN DHAUTI

This is a variation of gaji karni whereby excess water is drunk on a full stomach and the total contents of the stomach are emptied. This procedure is utilized when one feels that the food eaten is not of the purest nature, or that it is tainted.

VARIATIONS OF BASTI

1. AIR COLON CLEANSING
(Pavana Basti)

To perform air colon cleansing obtain a preferably silver tube or some other metal tube. The technique is similar to water basti, except that one fills the colon with air instead of water.

In a squatting position, insert the tube into the anus, drawing in a large quantity of air. When the air has been drawn, place the palms on the knees and perform uddiyana or nauli. Then press the intestines and pass the air out of the system. You may also wish to perform the cobra posture or the fish posture in order to assist the expelling of air. This procedure obviously is performed after jala basti. Historically, it removes disorders of the intestines, constipation, and flatulence.

2. GENITAL CLEANSING
(Uttara Basti)

In classical yoga, genital cleansing is used only by males. Historically, a flexible silver tube is placed into the urinary bladder by means of the urethra and water is forced through the tube to wash out the bladder. This procedure has been utilized to prevent or remove the formation of kidney stones. In the western world it is known as catheterization and is used for treating certain bladder infections. In females the entire vaginal pathway is washed with a syringe. This process is commonly called douching. In the practice of genital cleansing, one needs to be careful of irritations of the urethra walls as well as infections to the bladder.

This technique is given here for an historical understanding of the extent to which many persons practicing yoga have gone in attempting to cleanse the body. As indicated before, many of these techniques are to be utilized only as advanced procedures, under direct supervision, and only when needed.

Chapter 4

FUNDAMENTAL CONCEPTS
(ASANS)

We have already discussed the first two stages of yoga, namely the abstentions and the observances (yama-niyama), along with the purification techniques (the shat kriyas). The purpose of this chapter is to relate the next yoga stage: the yoga postures or asans. Each of the eight stages is a means by which you move from forgetfulness to illumination... from unhealth to health... from sadness to happiness... from constriction to expansion.

These eight stages to illumination are:
1. Abstentions (Yama) - Observances (Niyama)
3. Postures (Asan) - Energy-Control (Pranayama)
5. Sense-Withdrawal (Pratyahara) - Concentration (Dharana)
7. Meditation (Dhyana) - Contemplation (Samadhi)

Before discussing the postures, there are a few ideas and concepts that are important to understand.

THE PSYCHIC CENTERS (Chakras)
AND THEIR LIFE-ENERGY (Prana)

The first important concept is that of the chakras. Chakras are energy centers which activate and control your body and mind. Chakras can compare to a gasoline tank and crank case which must be filled with clean gasoline and good oil, in order to function properly. The postures properly utilized in yoga are a way of filling the chakras with the proper energy, at the proper levels. The chakras are located along the spinal axis of your being, from the base of the spine to the top of the head. Many western scientists and physiologists relate the astral chakras to the physiological plexuses which are located in the same areas, however, they are not the same. See the diagram on page 63 for a visual explanation of the chakras.

The second important concept is that of prana. It refers to the life-energies or the mystical forces which are often referred to as: kriya, laya, tantra, or kundalini energies. In the universe there is only one basic energy. It is called prana. Prana enters the human body, or any life-form that has a cerebral-spinal axis, through the moon center. This process occurs when we breathe. The moon center is the female center or the mouth of God, located at the back of the head near the medulla. In yoga it is called chandra chakra. See diagrams on pages 62-63. As we inhale, prana comes in at the moon center, descends through the five lower chakras, and then ascends back up through the same five lower chakras, but on the other side. It then radiates out through the sun center.

THE CHAKRAS

7. THE THOUSAND PETALLED LOTUS
    Transcending the six lower realms.

6. CANCER
    The feminine side of your consciousness
    LEO
    The masculine side of your consciousness

5. GEMINI
    The masculine side of the mercury chakra
    VIRGO
    The feminine side of the mercury chakra

4. TAURUS
    The feminine side of the venus chakra
    LIBRA
    The masculine side of the venus chakra

3. ARIES
    The masculine side of the mars chakra
    SCORPIO
    The feminine side of the mars chakra

2. PISCES
    The feminine side of the jupiter chakra
    SAGITTARIUS
    The masculine side of the jupiter chakra

1. AQUARIUS
    The masculine side of the saturn chakra
    CAPRICORN
    The feminine side of the saturn chakra

The sun and moon chakras do not play a part in modifying this life-energy. They are referred to as the luminaries, the HA and THA principles in hatha yoga, the solar and lunar forces. The hong and sau principles in kriya yoga. Prana, as it ascends and descends through the solar and lunar sides of each of the lower chakras, does become modified. At this time, energy is mystically modified or changed, just as magnetism produces electricity, or electricity produces light, or light produces heat. This modified energy is known as modified vital life-forces, or shakti.

In kriya yoga, the lower five chakras are named the mercury chakra, the venus chakra, the mars chakra, the jupiter chakra, and the saturn chakra. When the chakras were created in the infinities of yesteryear, they were divided into two segments: an inturning feminine state and an outgoing masculine state.

THE COSMIC WHEEL

Each chakra has a solar and lunar side.
Example:
    ARIES is the masculine side of the mars chakra, and
    SCORPIO is the feminine side of the mars chakra.

THE PATH OF THE PRANA

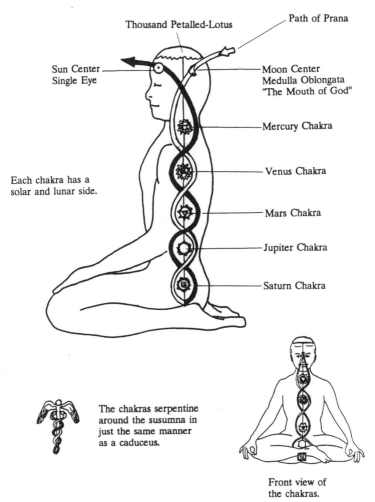

Thousand Petalled-Lotus

Path of Prana

Sun Center
Single Eye

Moon Center
Medulla Oblongata
"The Mouth of God"

Mercury Chakra

Each chakra has a
solar and lunar side.

Venus Chakra

Mars Chakra

Jupiter Chakra

Saturn Chakra

The chakras serpentine
around the susumna in
just the same manner
as a caduceus.

Front view of
the chakras.

THE FLOW OF THE LIFE-ENERGY

The Constriction and Expansion of the Chakras

In performing the postures, the prana flows into our vehicle, descending and ascending. We are trying to take this two-fold energy and balance it. There are two modifying forces in the practice of yoga: one is to constrict a chakra so that too much energy does not flow into it. The other is to expand the chakra so that more energy will flow into it. The postures are performed to either open or close a chakra, bringing that chakra into balance.

If a person has a very active mercury or throat chakra, he will usually eat a great deal of sugar, whether it is natural honey or candy bars. This usually implies that the chakra is too open. As the energy comes in and descends into that chakra, it pulls in or absorbs a tremendous amount of energy and complications can arise. Excessive energy tends to burn up the body. Any excess or shortage endangers bodily functions and thus the earth life. If he continues ingesting too much sugar, he might acquire sugar diabetes. In this instance, the aim of his performing the kriya yoga postures would be to close this mercury chakra, lessening the energy intake, and thus reducing the danger. As he closes off the mercury chakra, some energy will be pulled in, but most of it will by-pass the chakra. In effect, the massive craving for sugar will be removed and health will be maintained.

Here is another example: Despite the fact that our modern age is referred to as the enlightened age, a majority of people have a constriction in the mars chakra. Energy at the mars chakra tends to express itself as violence or merely as sex. At this stage we are trying to close down this chakra, so it will not pull in more energy, thus softening these two actions.

Here is a review of the chakric system as used in kriya yoga, as it relates to the postures. Conceive of the spinal column as a straw, running from the base of the spine all the way up to the throat area. There are five points along the straw, called the chakras, mercury to saturn. (See diagram on page 63.) These five chakras, however, are male and female, thus there are ten storage areas; each is sensitive to one of the ten pranic energies. When doing a posture, where you feel the pressure is where the energy is directed. If you are doing a posture that necessitates a headlock, the energy will be directed right to the mercury chakra. You affect the mercury chakra in one way or another with these energies. It is as simple as that.

On a deeper level, the ten pranic energies move through the five lower chakras and activate them. All of yoga, all of mysticism, ultimately comes back to the utilization and the control of these forces. We do not usually understand this in relationship to hatha yoga. Hatha yoga is usually regarded as bending and stretching and revitalizing and toning the body and organs by forcing fresh blood into them. Although this is important and very true, ultimately, there are deeper effects. It involves the theory of prana, and balancing those ten chakras.

Strengthening the Life-Currents

Anytime the prana current is strengthened in the body, two things occur:

1. Strengthening the current causes an increase in self-awareness. All yogic postures are ultimately directed toward increasing your self-awareness. As your self-awareness increases, you will become more aware of your body, taking better care of it. This will cause you to become more aware of your mind, and you will then also take better care of it.

2. Ultimately, this causes the energies to ascend to higher chakras. This ascendancy brings about a higher awareness, thus assisting in a more balanced self-awareness within your total being. Self-awareness assists in awakening greater balanced self-awareness.

The primary concern of most people is with body beautiful and a healthy body. For most people, the concept of self-awareness may not be meaningful for quite some time. It should be understood, however, that the idea of a healthy body is definitely important. The person who is not concerned with his physical body will never truly become concerned with his brain. If a person is not concerned with his brain, he will never become concerned with his thoughts. If he is not concerned with his thoughts, he will never become concerned with what lies beyond thoughts... thus, the importance of the initial stage.

These are the stages of evolution in which we attempt to influx the energy back in order to make our vehicle more aware. At the same time the energy fluxes back, it rises producing more self-awareness, and more balanced self-awareness. As we become more aware, we become more self-aware and we gain greater balanced self-awareness. We become more aware of how to live. We move from insanity to sanity. It is a movement from simple passion to compassion, from compassion to wisdom. Ultimately, this is the purpose of the yoga postures.

The Movement of the Ascending Current (Prana) and the Descending Current (Apana)

Let us discuss the concepts of the ascending current (prana) and the descending current (apana). Although there are ten currents, these two are most important. In most human beings the descending current is predominant. This imbalanced descending current tends to make a person irritable and/or restless. This body restlessness makes it difficult for one to inturn and meditate.

Although we are trying to transcend body awareness, for some people body awareness may be good. Those individuals who tend to be ungrounded need to bring the current back down into their body, and balance it, thus, becoming more aware of this world. When this area of their life is balanced, they will be able to move into the inner realms, transcending body awareness.

For the most part, however, we are trying to bring the current upward to reach higher awarenesses and to unify those forces. Any motion of the body tends to produce body awareness. And so, absolute stillness without tension is the answer. If you are tense, even though you are unaware of that tension, the current will still descend. For most of our lives, the current has been descending. Through the practice of kriya yoga, we begin to re-balance the current, bringing it upward.

Sooner or later, the descending current and the ascending current will meet. They will meet somewhere: at the sun center, the intellectual center, the heart center, the body center, the philosophical center, or the saturn center. We are trying to lift the currents so that when they do meet, they do so at as high a plane as possible. The higher centers are less emotional, less destructive, and the higher you reach within your vehicle, the greater will be your free will, and the greater will be your control over the free flow of your thoughts and ideas.

Centering as a Means to Attain
Balance (Illumination)

Explaining this a little more thoroughly, allow me to use the British airplane insignia as an illustration. It is represented by a circle within a circle, within a circle, and is similar to a target in archery: two rings around a bull's eye.

In like manner, the spinal axis (chakra system) or the center of our being has three similar rings. In most humanoids the outer ring is where the majority of the energies are flowing. This can symbolically be called the periphery of our everyday consciousness.

When the currents are flowing here, we become relatively mundane.

Yoga is a way of gently moving the currents from the outer periphery of your consciousness towards the center, the inner target. When this happens, you gain spiritual energy or power (yoga siddhi). This type of power, however, is not power over people, nor is it power over the world. It is power over yourself. It is the energy to control your mind and body, the energy to balance all your impulses. Even when an impulse seems to be good, if it is controlling you, that factor in itself becomes negative. If a person is forced to become a millionaire, though everyone may feel this to be a wonderful thing, it really is not, because that person has been forced to do something. In a mystical sense, rather than generate a million dollars by the force of the impulses of his mind, it would be far better for him to make less money of his own free will.

Ultimately, we are trying to take the energy from the outer circle, move it toward the inner circle, and then gently nudge it to the kriya center. Herein, the deeper forces of our being allow us to heal our own bodies and have the freedom to do what needs to be done: according to the wisdom of the moment and not according to heavy karmic compulsions of the past, whether they be from five years ago or five hundred lifetimes ago.

Mystically, yoga is all about centering. If pranic energy went down your spine, and then went straight up again, centered, unmodified by your ego, illumination would occur. You would have balance or freedom. This would produce knowledge infinite and bliss supreme. The problem is that our egos interfere. This is called karma. The energies become scattered because of this ego interference. The whole goal of yoga is to rebalance these energies, to bring these energies together into a mystical marriage called illumination. This is the highest goal.

Remember, there are an infinite number of phases in your life which need to be balanced. You must balance your diet life, your love life, your home life, your work life, your social life, your intellectual life. You must balance every aspect of your life. As the Gita points out so clearly: He who eats too much, he who eats not enough; he who sleeps too much, he who sleeps not enough; he who works too much, he who works not enough, will not attain balanced self-conscious awareness.

YOGA AND THE FEELING STATE

The kriya yoga postures were developed by the ancient sages of India after studying and observing various animals. As an example, most of us are familiar with a cat's stretch. If you have ever seen a cat get up, you know it just reaches its legs out and goes into its stretch. The cat stretch posture was derived as sages observed tigers and lions upon awakening. Likewise, all the other postures are related to animal instinctive behavior. The theory is that animals, in their natural jungle, know instinctively what ought to be done at any given moment. Man, however, living in his concrete jungle, has lost his attunement to the instinctual. Through the practice of yoga we regain that attunement to life.

Asan as a Way to Balance Your Being

The purpose of this chapter is to teach you the yogic asans. I have translated the word asan to mean pose. The word pose contains a subliminal inference of being in a state of balance. The goal is not just to be able to perform the poses rigidly in a calisthenic fashion. The goal is to balance the life-energies thus attaining happiness. The goal is simply to become happy. You cannot become happy, however, until you have balanced your life. Yoga is a way of balancing your life. There are mystical techniques whereby a teacher can look into a student's soul and see where his or her imbalances are. From this standpoint, suggestions are given regarding the use of certain poses.

The Feeling State Within the Asans

Another important point is that every yoga pose is linked to a feeling state. I am sure you have felt that certain days are different from others. For example, Hanukkah is different from today; today is different from Christmas; New Year's Eve is different from yesterday; Monday is different from Friday. In exactly the same way, each and every asan is really quite different. What makes it different is the feeling state linked within each pose's chakra.

Feeling vs. Emotion

To explain the difference between feeling and emotion is vital to understanding the use of yoga poses. In our present evolution and spiritual unfoldment toward a balanced life, most of the world is in a state of heavy emotionality. What we need to do, in our present stage of evolution, is take our emotions, and move them toward balance by emphasizing and energizing the positive emotions. We need to move from negativity to positive enthusiasm. We must move from negative emotions to positive emotions, giving verbalization only to the positive emotions. We must become enthused about life.

Life is a matter of enthusiasm, derived from the Greek words EN meaning in, and THEOS meaning God. Life is a matter of being in God; it is a matter of enthusiasm. With enthusiasm, we understand life's goodness, life's ecstasy, and then energize it. As you energize your life, your body's pores and glands begin to work more efficiently. Everything begins working better and everything begins a cleansing process on itself, physically, mentally, and spiritually. It's called regeneration.

There is still another step upward in our evolution, and it's moving from positive emotions that neutralize negative emotions to a feeling state. The word emotion comes from two Greek words, E and MOTION meaning to put into motion. An example will be helpful. You begin to meditate on something you consider beautiful, such as a hot fudge sundae. Now, you are emoting, your mind and body will be put into motion and you come out of your meditation, finding yourself making a hot fudge sundae. If, however, in your meditation you remain unemotional about the hot fudge sundae, merely meditating on it from a feeling state, you will come out of your meditation peacefully, without any compulsion to make a hot fudge sundae. The feeling state is a balanced state that tends to hold you within that awareness. The emotional state tends to throw you out into action. This is what we are mystically trying to stay away from.

The problem of the world is that everyone is emoting. The world at large is trying to hold onto things, and trying to acquire more and more. They are grasping and moving out toward objects with an attitude of: I've got to have this. I've got to have that. This is imbalance. Yoga rebalances our soul, rather than emoting and desiring. Thus, we establish a peacefulness, and become content within our soul. This is done by attuning to the feeling state within the yoga poses.

Balanced Feelings and Their
Relationship to Thought and Creativity

The first step in performing asans is establishing a quietude, bringing all the energies together, creating a feeling state. These energies balance your mind, your intellect, and your lifestyle. In the world of sports, you hear a player having a difficult day say, 'I

just couldn't get my head together. I just couldn't get it together.'
This concept is very yogic: the idea of getting it together, and then
reaching out to perform. This is really what makes a great athlete,
a great composer, or a great yogi. As you balance your thinking
and emotions, having removed all the extraneous energies, you can
then reach out in perfection.

One more thing should be said regarding the feeling state. It
relates to the philosophy of the great Indian sage, Gautama the
Buddha, who said, 'As you think, so you are... You are a result of
all you have thought....' The problem is that we have many
thoughts such as 'I need a house... I want a car... I want a spouse...
I want more money... I want to practice my yoga more.' There are
always a series of thoughts and usually one thought opposes
another. This brings no internal peace of mind or tranquility,
causing upset due to tension. To resolve this problem we must
come to the realization that although we are a result of all we have
thought, we must transcend thought. We must, through yoga, move
back to a feeling state.

For every set of thoughts such as 'I want... I need... I must
have,' there is one basic feeling. Although we are a result of all we
have thought, the control or the balancing of our lives comes from
generating a new feeling. 'Hatred does not cease by hatred; hatred
ceases not by force of arms; hatred ceases by compassion and
compassion alone...,' the Buddha said. From hatred we move to a
feeling of love or compassion. A balanced feeling state must be
established in the five lower chakric levels which will allow us to
balance negative thinking. If we replace a negative emotion with a
positive feeling, then we solve all the problems in that one area.

Another example would be when a person says, 'Oh, I should
stop smoking cigarettes... I should stop drinking wine... I should
stop doing this... I should stop doing that,' he is obviously struggling
within himself. If he gives up only one habit, he will still be
struggling with the others. Similarly, there are probably an infinite
number of patterns or habits in our own lives that we are trying to
bring into balance. It would take quite a few lifetimes to remove
all the negativities involved. But as you know, yoga is a way of
speeding up evolution by grouping things of this nature into one
feeling. If you take the imbalances of these symbolical negative
habits and replace them with one positive feeling, you will immediately have brought that whole, large section of your life into balance.

A more specific example of this is the person who eats a poor
diet. He or she may become interested in yoga for one reason or

another. Amazingly, within a relatively short period of time, and without any real effort, having attuned to a feeling state of yoga, that person will become very interested in changing his total diet; eating more vegetables, more fruit, etc. These types of food will automatically become more appealing to him. This illustrates the type of feeling I am talking about.

On the other hand, if he feels the pressure of 'I must eat this,' or 'I must do that,' he will not have the feeling I'm relating. The attitude behind the feeling of 'I must' is something very mechanical and artificial. But, when you have the feeling of health, then healthy foods will immediately come into your life; you will automatically want to eat them. These healthier inclinations just happen with ease. This is the feeling state you should be trying to attune to in the yoga asans and in all of yoga.

The essence of hatha yoga, the secret of the poses, is to hold a feeling state. I cannot emphasize this too often or too strongly.

Chapter 5

MYSTICAL HAND GESTURES AND HOLDS

MUDRA TO ASSIST DIRECTING THE
LIFE-CURRENTS

The next important phase in the mastery of the postures is the practice of mystical hand gestures called mudra. It is a symbolic language. Your five fingers on each hand represent the ten life currents. These relate to the five ascending and five descending life currents. As these energies flow through your vehicle, they flow from your fingers.

I am sure you have occasionally looked at your fingers and seen some small emanations coming from them. If you take the emanations coming from your thumb and index finger, closing them into a circuit, this brings the current back into the spine, energizing the chakras related to those fingers. This is called a regenerative system, as in electronics, whereby you take a small amount of energy and regenerate it back into the system. By performing mudras, you take a small amount of energy from the hands and regenerate it back into the spinal column's chakras whereby it can be more strongly emanated outwards. If you open your hands, keeping them separated, you disperse the energies. If you close the hands, by clasping them together, you bring the energies back together, recirculating and regenerating them.

Yoga is somewhat like zone therapy in which you work with certain nerves on the foot to affect other corresponding parts of the body. By performing the asans, by stretching bodily organs, you energize them, thus affecting other areas of the body and mind. By performing mudra, you regenerate the current back into the spinal column, allowing these energies to manifest with greater vitality and more harmoniously.

Mudra has a re-balancing effect as well as a regenerative factor. When you perform gnana mudra, the thumb and index fingers are used (see the gnana mudra diagram). The thumb radiates a particular energy force field, and the index finger radiates a different energy force field. When you bring these fingers together, this causes these energies to influx back into the spine producing a re-generative process, strengthening the sun and jupiter chakras.

Mudra has also another definite effect. A person can communicate directly by saying something. But there is another method of communicating without the use of words. It's communicating through symbols. Gestures are symbols. It's similar to the use of body language. The body's postures indicate certain moods. In the same way, mudras are a form of communication.

Yoga is concerned with communicating with ourselves. Mudras are a non-verbal communication of your conscious mind to your unconscious mind! In psychological terms, the body/mind complex is like an iceberg. Our conscious mind is similar to the hundred feet of ice above the water. Would you consider this to be a hundred-foot iceberg? No. It is a thousand-foot iceberg. One hundred feet of the iceberg, called the conscious mind, lies above the surface. However, nine-hundred feet of the iceberg is in the depths of the ocean, the subconscious mind. This portion remains unseen. To be successful in yoga, the conscious and subconscious minds must be brought into a harmonious union.

Mudras can be compared to the power of affirmation. It's like repeating a certain phrase, over and over again, to yourself. An excellent self-suggestion is, 'Every day in every way I am becoming happier and happier'. Another positive suggestion that can be repeated while performing a mudra is, 'Every day in every way I am becoming wiser and wiser'. This is applied psychology. If you repeat something, over and over again, you will create it in your life.

A mudra and the manner in which it is formed has a specific message. How does this apply to mudras? The gnana mudra (meaning knowledge), for instance, is a non-verbal communication, a symbolic gesture, a ritual in which the conscious mind is saying to the subconscious mind, (and the subconscious mind is saying to conscious mind), 'I will deliver knowledge up'. If you perform this mudra often enough, the effect of the symbol will begin to activate in your mind, bringing forth knowledge. You must, however, hold the symbol for some time in order to make it work. With suggestion you must repeat it over and over again, in order to gain the attention of the conscious and subconscious minds.

Another example of non-verbal communication will be helpful. A man and woman meet and nothing happens between them. They merely stand looking at one another. Something changes, however, when they meet and soft, melodious music is playing in the background. The music communicates something non-verbal to them. It helps to bring them together. You could say the music contains symbolic words. In the same way, the spiritual music of the mudra is a warmth communication, causing the conscious mind and unconscious minds to link together.

Performing the divinity mudra, in which the symbolic message is one of balance, is a way in which the minds communicate with each other, saying, 'Let there be balance'. In religious terms, the message is, 'Thy will, Lord'. A non-religious way of saying this is, 'Let me take direction from life'. The Taoists would say: 'Just flow... let life flow... follow life. The river knows where the river is going... follow the river... it knows for it has been following this stream of life for millions of years'. However, when things get tough, you have to do more than let life have its way. At this time, another mudra, with a more affirmative subconscious message may have to be utilized. Such a mudra is the wisdom gesture or the ego-transcending gesture. You might need to use a mudra that communicates a message that it is going to take more than just flowing with life. It's going to take some individual personality at this time. It's going to necessitate expressing another part of my soul in order to complete life's goal. You need to accept greater responsibility, not by manifesting the ego, but by putting part of yourself assertively into what needs to be done. Mudras energize certain chakras. A mudra is more than just a suggestion. It is a mystical way of activating parts of your mind and soul.

THE FIVE FINGERS AS THEY RELATE
TO THE LIFE CURRENTS

The mystical symbolism of the fingers themselves must be understood. This theory is based upon the concept that the psycho-mental energies coming up from the subconscious mind, and related to the chakras, differentiate themselves and emanate outward through the five fingers. Symbolically, these fingers, in relationship to the psycho-mental energies, reveal a process of complex cultural patterns whereby non-verbal suggestions and mind stimuli are utilized together.

In performing mudras, tactile suggestions are used to assist in controlling subtle semiconscious and/or unconscious energies. In yoga we are not just dealing with the physical body or the conscious surface mind. Yoga insists upon entering deeply into the semiconscious, preconscious, subconscious, unconscious, and super-conscious states of existence, in order to gain mastery over all the mind's energies holding us to everyday, limited, humanoid consciousness. Breaking this hold we enter into superconsciousness.

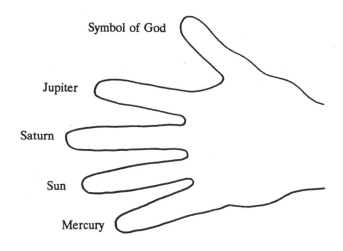

Symbol of God

Jupiter

Saturn

Sun

Mercury

Symbolism of the Fingers

Thumb: The thumb is the symbol of divine energy; energy that flows through our vehicle unconditioned by our subconscious patternings or karmic proclivities. The thumb is the symbol of will power. Power that can be drawn upon by our willing (not willfulness) consciousness.

Index: The index finger is known as the jupiter finger and is the symbol of our ego personality; it symbolizes energies controlled by subconscious mind patternings. Its energies produce expansion.

Middle: The middle finger, symbolizing the saturn force, is the most karmic or the most conditioned energies. This finger is utilized only in those mudras that require heavy, stabilizing forces.

Ring: The ring finger symbolizes the sun energies. These energies relate to the strength of the individual.

Little: The little finger is known as the mercury finger. It emanates energies that are important in the unfoldment of the intellect and of business.

ENLIGHTENMENT GESTURE
(Buddhi Mudra)

Buddhi Mudra

The enlightenment gesture is a meditative mudra in which the spiritual energies harmonize and mingle with the ego personality, allowing a manifestation of the spiritual individuality. The Buddhi mudra is performed by placing the tip of the thumb to the tip of the index finger, forming a circle. Both hands are placed together so that the knuckles of each hand come together. They are then placed in the lap at the mars chakra, the solar plexus area. This is an ancient Hindu mudra that is often associated with Lord Buddha, the great Hindu sage. The Buddhi mudra produces a quieting effect upon the mind and a regenerative effect upon the pranic energies of the neuro-hormonal system.

WISDOM GESTURE
(Gnana Mudra)

Gnana Mudra

This mudra is performed by taking the thumb, the symbol of Reality (Brahman), and your index (jupiter) finger, the symbol of the personality, and bringing them together, so that the tip of the forefinger comes down to the middle of the thumb. The three other fingers (the mercury, sun and saturn) are placed together and held outright. Traditionally, the hands are then placed in the lap upright. This is the gesture of knowledge or wisdom.

In this mudra a very important subconscious awareness takes place: Although God is within me and I am within God, I have the right to be me, as long as I do not interfere with life. This non-interfering with life is symbolized by the extending tip of the thumb. This slight extension symbolizes non-ego. Forming this gesture brings about a subliminal communication that allows you to harmoniously express yourself.

There needs be a realization that ultimate wisdom is not the annihilation of you nor of your ego. Although a teacher must teach what traditionally must be taught, he has the right to teach as his personality sees fit. In other words, he colors the teaching with his positive vibration and personality. He makes the teaching come alive. Enlightenment is not an annihilation of yourself. Yogananda expressed it this way: It may be wonderful to allow your concept of God to make a doormat of you; but if you are that doormat, it certainly isn't very meaningful nor pleasant.

If you are having some difficulty in your life and realize it is because of an ego problem, it may be good to practice this gnana mudra, in which the thumb of God extends beyond the index finger. By practicing this mudra in meditation, the ego begins to step aside and the natural harmony of life begins to manifest.

VARIATIONS

As well as placing the hands in the lap, gnana mudra can be performed in other ways:

1. With the right hand raised and held against the body, similar to the American Indian gesture of greeting.
2. Over the heart chakra with the hand upturned, close to the chest. This is performed while breathing certain kriya pranayamas.
3. With the hands placed palms upward across the knees, forming a stable back support and slightly forcing the spine to move forward. This is commonly seen in meditative postures.

CHALICE MUDRA
(Cup Mudra)

Cup Mudra

The chalice mudra is performed by cupping the hands and placing one of them on top of the other, placing them in the lap. The thumbs are touching, tip to tip. If you utilize the chalice mudra while performing any meditative pose, you place the right hand on top of the left hand, if the right leg is over the left. If the left leg is over the right, then place the left hand over the right hand, in a cup fashion. This pattern should be followed with all the postures.

These mudras are an important part of yoga. Unless you are performing them, you are not really practicing yoga. They are important because energy, and how it's controlled by gesture (mudra) and sound (mantra), produces deeper spiritual effects on consciousness.

Shanti Mudra

BLESSING GESTURE
(Shanti Mudra)

The blessing gesture is also called the shanti mudra. It is performed by taking the middle finger (saturn finger), and placing it on the fingernail of the index (jupiter) finger. Then simply touch whatever object it is that you wish to bless.

This mudra is known as the food blessing gesture, whereby you touch the edge of the plate before you eat, sending positive vibrations to the food. As you touch the edge of the plate, mentally chant, 'Om, shanti, shanti, shanti'. Shanti means peace. See the chapter on mantras.

If you look at this gesture, you notice there's a little bow between the two fingers. They are positioned together. This bow is called Govinda, and has the following meaning: If the personality is backed up by destiny (saturn finger), it is not an ego manifestation, but rather a manifestation of individuality.

OM Mudra

DIVINITY GESTURE
(Om Mudra)

The divinity gesture is performed by bringing the tips of the thumb and index fingers together. The thumb and forefinger merge and blend perfectly. There is no God, there is no me. There is just Life. There is a complete circle representing a balance between God's karma and your karma.

In the wisdom gesture, divinity is manifesting. In the ego-transcending gesture (ahamkara mudra), the individuality is manifesting. In the divinity gesture, they come together perfectly and only life manifests.

What would happen if you walked around, all the time, holding the divinity gesture? You would attain more peacefulness and less aggressiveness. This is why it is such an important mudra. Holding the divinity gesture indicates a peacefulness and solidarity deep within oneself.

When a person becomes threatened he often crosses his arms across his chest. Through this symbolism he is saying, 'You are not going to affect me'.

INTERLOCK GESTURE
(Gomukha Mudra)

The gomukha mudra is performed while reflecting or meditating. It is made by interlocking the fingers together in cup fashion. The interlock gesture is a symbol of the mind and the body harmoniously coming together. The two thumbs symbolize that

Gomukha Mudra

we as spirit manifest on two planes. The mind is symbolized by the left thumb. The body is symbolized by the right thumb. This mudra is also performed by bringing the tips of the thumbs together. The thumbs positioned in this way symbolize that we function through two vehicles which serve the one spirit. Holding this mudra produces a strong unifying effect on the mind and body.

EARTH GESTURE
(Prithvi Mudra)

The earth gesture or prithvi mudra is made by placing the hands in the wisdom gesture, and then turning the palms downward. The fingers are often separated and/or left open on the knees. In the earth gesture the energies are pouring downward to the earth itself, and then emanating back upward to the saturn chakra. The earth gesture gives stability.

Prithvi Mudra

Namaste Mudra

RESPECT GESTURE
(Namaste Mudra)

The namaste mudra is formed by placing the palms together with the fingers extended, the thumbs lying parallel to each other. The arms are bent and the hands brought to the chest at the heart level. This is a mudra of respect and humility. It symbolically means, 'My soul bows to your soul,' or 'My soul recognizes the divinity within you.'

EGO-TRANSCENDING GESTURE
(Ahamkara Mudra)

Ahamkara Mudra

Reversing the process of the wisdom gesture, produces the ego-transcending gesture. · The ahamkara mudra is performed by taking the thumb (the symbol of God) and placing it in the middle of the index finger so the index finger extends beyond the thumb. This mudra is the gesture of individuality or ego. This mudra is utilized by those persons having difficulty asserting themselves. It may be used when a person must teach or express himself and is lacking self-confidence. If one is fearful or introverted, this mudra is helpful as it brings out and expresses that which needs to be expressed.

In the gnana mudra, the ego is totally subsided and divinity is manifesting. With the God finger extending farthest, you are sitting back, allowing the more esoteric forces within the universe to manifest. In the gnana mudra, the thumb or God finger has the greater extension. In the ego-transcending gesture, the forefinger (jupiter) has the greater extension.

Some people have difficulty understanding the concept of ego and often become emotional about it, feeling the ego must be annihilated. This is not true. At times, however, we do need to put the ego aside. I want to stress that the ego-transcending gesture is often necessary and essential for the expression of our spiritual lives. There are times when we must very diligently work for that which needs to be done, not in an ego sense, but from the standpoint of our duty (dharma). The ego-transcending gesture assists in giving strength to put the ego aside at the appropriate time, place, and way. We must put the ego aside with the realization that we must now do that which needs to be done.

If a situation in your life arises, form the ego-transcending gesture, hold it in your thoughts, and the energies will regenerate. You are not trying to manifest your ego, but rather generate energy for your personality to do what has to be done. The ego often gets in your way and you have to learn to transcend it. When the boss says, 'You're doing it all wrong, wrong, wrong!' and your ego wants to react (which may be justified), this is the time to transcend the ego so that you can do your duty.

MUSCULAR CONTRACTIONS
(Bandhas)

During the practice of asans and breath control, holds or muscular contractions are often performed to hold the life-currents in the body. These contractions are called bandhas. There are three major bandhas.

ANAL CONTRACTION
(Mula Bandha)

Historically, this bandha is known as the root contraction. It is the most commonly used bandha and is achieved by contracting the anal sphincter muscle. It is usually combined with the stomach contraction (uddiyana bandha). The anal contraction is performed by drawing up and tensing the upper part of the anus. This prevents the life currents from just descending and becoming scattered. This contraction pushes the currents back upward to support the ascending vital breath. When the anal muscle is tightly lifted, the descending currents automatically ascend again. Performing the anal contraction forces the life currents back upward, lifting them to the heart chakra, producing greater love.

In most individuals, the descending currents drop down to the sphincter muscle, which has been pushed out because of overweight and other factors. When the sphincter muscle is pressed out, the currents just keep flowing down, accumulating in the saturn and jupiter chakras. This does not allow the currents to re-ascend with any force. Thus, the brain's capacity to think and memorize is lessened. This accumulation of current in the saturn-jupiter areas produces heavy emotionalities and thus cravings. When the sphincter muscle is contracted by means of this bandha, the energies re-ascend, balancing your system and producing a softening of the emotionalities and cravings.

The Hatha Yoga Pradipika states that the root contraction practiced continually brings perpetual youth. Almost all women automatically hold this contraction. It is not something a woman is taught. It is also performed through proper carriage of her body. When women perform this anal contraction along with the aswini mudra, great health and magnetism manifest.

THE STOMACH CONTRACTION
(Uddiyana Bandha)

The stomach contraction (uddiyana bandha) should not be confused with uddiyana, where there is a repetitive inward and upward movement of the stomach muscles. In the stomach contraction, one locks or holds the muscles. Uddiyana means flying up. By performing uddiyana bandha, pranic energy is forced to move upward from the lower abdomen area to the head. This bandha is performed by pushing the stomach muscles slightly in and up and holding them. Through the practice of the anal contraction, the current will flow into the mars chakra, activating martian energies. To get the energies beyond this chakra, we use ·this bandha. Pushing the stomach muscles slightly in and up opens the second gate of God (at the mars level), allowing the current to move beyond, flowing into either the heart chakra or mercury chakra. Energy at these higher centers produces spiritual awareness, philosophical attitudes, and a more dignified cultural life pattern.

Chin Lock Contraction

THE CHIN LOCK CONTRACTION
(Jalandhara Bandha)

Sometimes called the net-holding contraction, this bandha is performed by putting the head down into the crevice of the neck. With the hand, press forward slightly on the back of the head so that the chin rests firmly against the chest bone. The chin lock contraction is often used when one is holding a breathing technique with a meditative posture.

The chin lock contraction regulates the flow of ascending currents to the mercury chakra and to the brain. Caution, however, should be observed in the practice of the chin lock.

Chapter 6

RELAXATION TECHNIQUES AND STRETCHING EXERCISES

RELAXATION TECHNIQUES

It is not wise to come home from work or school and immediately perform yoga postures. There should be a psychological adjustment from one life activity to another. Your mind should orient itself to the symbolism, meaning, and purpose of the postures. You should attune to the feeling of yoga by beginning each practice session with a series of simple, yet meaningful relaxation techniques.

TOTAL RELAXATION (Sava or Savasana)

The total relaxation pose called sava is a classical yoga posture, and is also known as the sponge, or the corpse posture. The most appropriate name is the total relaxation pose, for this reveals

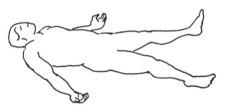

Total Relaxation
(Savasana)

the true nature of the technique. The process of yoga involves warming up the body, stretching the muscles, and squeezing out the old devitalized blood from the organs and muscles. This then forces in fresh blood and oxygen throughout the system, stimulating and purifying the muscles, subtle nerves, glands and organs. It is during the rest period following an asan that this process is finished.

The total relaxation pose is one of the most important postures. If you cannot do savasana, you cannot do yoga. Savasana is performed for a short period of time:

1. At the beginning of a hatha yoga practice session,
2. Between the different postures; and
3. At the end of the practice session, for a longer time.

Total relaxation is begun by lying on your back. The feet and legs are slightly outturned. The arms are at the sides with palms upturned. The limbs can be relaxed by individually lifting and dropping them gently to the floor as if they were dead weight. Your eyes should be closed, with your attention gently focused at the sun center, that point between the eyebrows at the root of the nose. There should be no furrowing of the brow caused by straining. The jaw is relaxed, letting the chin drop slightly. If the mouth is tense, the entire body is tense. At the sun center create a feeling of tranquility and send this feeling throughout your entire body.

Total relaxation, when practiced at the end of the yoga session, is usually called final relaxation or maha-savasana, meaning it is a longer rest period lasting from five to fifteen minutes. When performing asans, the key is to remain in this posture until the heart and pulse rates are quieted. To facilitate this, create a feeling of peace and relaxation. Mentally take this feeling to each of the 20 major parts of your body:

Left foot	Right foot
Left calf	Right calf
Left thigh	Right thigh
Left haunch	Right haunch

Abdomen
Stomach

Left forearm	Right forearm
Left upper arm	Right upper arm
Left side of chest	Right side of chest
Left side of neck	Right side of neck

Front of neck
Back of neck

Having relaxed the body, again bring your attention to the sun center and incorporate the most important feature of savasana, the affirmation. Affirmation achieves the goals you have set for yourself, mentally. Below are examples of appropriate affirmations:

Every day in every way I am becoming happier and
   happier.
Every day in every way my body is becoming
   healthier and healthier.
Every day in every way my mind is becoming
   steadier and steadier.
Every day in every way my mind is becoming more
   and more illumined.

Any of these affirmations or any combination can be used. The affirmation is neither said with great force nor anguish. It simply is a stimulation and a restimulation of the thought process. You are a result of your thinking, thus, yoga begins with your thinking and ends with your illumination. If you have ever been in a rowboat and thrown the anchor to shore, you pulled the boat to the shore, not the shore to the boat. Affirmation is the anchor. You throw the anchor out and pull yourself (the boat) to shore, which is a particular state of consciousness you are holding.

Some think the world is ugly, and they reaffirm this process by thought and action. They take their anchor, throw it out into their own world of ugliness, and pull themselves toward that ugliness. On the other hand, those who know the world is beautiful reaffirm it by thinking, how beautiful the world is! They throw their anchor to the shore of beauty. With affirmation you do not change the world, you simply change the direction of your boat, preconceived in your consciousness. If you think beauty, you will be drawn toward the harbor of beauty. If you think wealth, you will be drawn toward the harbor of wealth. If you think love, you will be drawn into the harbor of love.

In yoga, the emphasis is upon health, not unhealth; upon beauty, not ugliness; upon spiritual wealth, not poverty.

In savasana and maha-savasana, your mind should be flooded with strong, vibrant, positive thoughts. Having practiced the asans, you have stimulated and exercised your body. Now lie down and relax. All the freshly oxidized blood will go to the brain; all the new prana will go to the brain. At this moment your mind is like a battery, fully charged. What you think now will have a hundred times the force it normally does. Remember, you are not changing the world. You are changing your mind's direction.

Benefits: In total relaxation, spiritual, intellectual, and creative energies are released. If you do yoga, but do not have a rest period, you will not acquire the full benefits of the postures. In yoga you are not dealing just with the physical body, but with the mind and its pranic energy. Only when you relax does the pranic energy begin to give peace and awareness of higher states of consciousness. In savasana, with the help of affirmation, a peaceful relaxation and recharging of mind and body is attained.

PALATE MASSAGE

Women with long thumbnails may have to first trim one thumbnail to perform this technique. It needs only to be performed occasionally. Wash and rinse your hands thoroughly before beginning. Open your mouth and place the thumb on the hard palate located at the roof of the mouth. Proceed across the hard palate until you reach the soft palate. This is where the nerves relating to the stomach, chest, and brain lie. Massage the entire edge of the soft palate--from front to back and side to side.

Benefits: Massaging the palate will have strong psychological effects, helping to heal and regenerate the brain, body, and mind. It is based on the concept of reflexology, which states that nerves run from the surface of the skin to deep, internal organs. The largest organ of the body is the skin. To tone one part of the nerve is to tone that organ which is attached to that nerve.

EYE EXERCISES

Most of our learning occurs through the eyes, and most of our tension also occurs in the eyes. When there is tension in the body, there is tension in the eyes. Therefore, when the eyes are relaxed, the body becomes relaxed. When the eyes become relaxed, the mind also becomes relaxed.

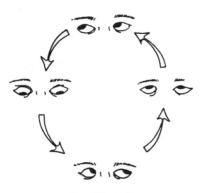

Eye Exercises

1. THE EYE MASSAGE

Double the fists, place the knuckles of each index finger into the inside sockets of the eyes, and rub gently. This slight pressure on the eyeball squeezes out old blood, allowing rejuvenated, fresh oxygenated blood to re-enter. The eye massage can be effective when your mind is extremely tired.

2. EYE MOVEMENTS

With the eyes closed, perform the following eye movements:

a. Move the eyes up and down in strong vertical sweeps.
b. Move the eyes back and forth in strong horizontal sweeps.
c. Make diagonal movements from upper-right to lower-left, and then from upper-left to lower-right.
d. Rotate the eyes in a circle, first in one direction, then in the other direction.

Do each series of movements 3 times. Upon completion of the eye exercises, rub the palms together vigorously and gently lay them upon the closed eyes. The heat generated by the palms passes into the ocular area, having a soothing effect.

Benefits: these exercises strengthen the eyes and relieve eye strain. They send blood, oxygen, and pranic energy to the brain resulting in clarity of thinking. The mind, also, becomes more relaxed and serene.

NECK ROLLS
(Grivachakrasan)

The neck rolls are a four-stage or four-directional technique: forward, left side, back, right side.

Neck Rolls

Understanding this will improve the proper rotation of the head.

1. Sit in any cross-legged or meditative posture that is comfortable. With the eyes closed, relax and slowly bring the head down, chin to your chest, allowing it to be completely relaxed.
2. Now, rotate to the head to the left. As you rotate to the left, bring your left ear over your left shoulder. Do not lift the shoulder to the ear.
3. Rotate your head back so it is touching the upper cervical region. Take the hand and press back on the chin to assure the head has been brought back as far as possible.

4. Now bring the right ear over the right shoulder, being sure that the right shoulder does not lift to meet the right ear. Now bring your chin back onto your chest.

Repeat this rotation 3 to 7 times in the same direction. Then, reverse direction and perform an equal number of rotations.

If the neck is stiff, the following exercises to precede the neck rolls are recommended:

1. Raise arms over the head, palms together, and reach for the ceiling. This will loosen stiffness in the neck.
2. Repeatedly bend your head from front to back.
3. Repeatedly bend your head from side to side.

Benefits: Rotating the neck releases tension in the neck and shoulders, producing a relaxation and positive stimulation of the nerves in the upper cervical area. The nerves become toned, and muscles of the neck become stronger and more elastic. The voice becomes more mellow. Prevents wrinkles of the neck.

SHOULDER MASSAGE

Place the left arm across the chest and bring your hand over the shoulder area. Cup the left hand over the neck muscles. Using the fingertips and the palm, gently knead from the base of the neck across to the outside of the shoulder blade and back to the neck again. Any sore spots should be gently pressed with the thumb in a circular motion. Now, repeat the process on the opposite shoulder.

Benefits: The shoulder massage alleviates muscle soreness and tension by pressing out deoxygenated blood and forcing fresh oxygenated blood into the muscles. This produces a state of deep relaxation.

FOOT MASSAGE

Using the thumb or knuckles, massage the large tendon under the arch of the right foot. Next, proceed to the area at the base of the toes, just above the ball of the foot. Massage any tight or stiff areas of the foot with the thumb and fingers. If a particularly sore area is encountered, massage more gently, but longer, until the soreness is relieved. Now, repeat the process on the left foot.

Benefits: Rids tensions in parts of the body corresponding to areas on the foot. Promotes overall relaxation of the body, while toning the inner organs of the viscera.

HAND MASSAGE

Use the thumb of one hand to massage the entire surface of the opposite palm, remembering to press gently but firmly. If soreness is encountered, use gentle circular motions until the soreness is alleviated. Next, clasp each finger (one after the other) with the fingers of the opposite hand, giving each finger a gentle twist in both directions, followed by a slight pull on the finger. Repeat with the opposite hand.

Benefits: Removes tension and soreness in the hands, fingers, and arms, while toning the inner organs by reflexology.

RAG DOLL

This stretch is actually very difficult to perform properly. It is difficult because the rag doll, as its name implies, requires limpness, and most individuals are extremely tense and stiff. Stand and stretch the arms toward the ceiling. Taking a deep breath and as you exhale, drop your body forward like a rag doll, letting the arms and neck hang loosely without any tension. Do not attempt to touch the floor. Do not be concerned about how far you have dropped down. The secret of the rag doll is relaxation.

If your body is stiff, or if you try to touch the toes, the muscles contract and little relaxation takes place.

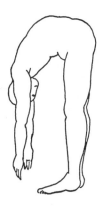

Rag Doll

Benefits: As the head is dropped down and totally relaxed, the blood vessels are opened and large quantities of blood run into the neck and chest. But most importantly the head and eyes are washed in healing blood. This flushes and cleanses the face and scalp. The rag doll stretch induces relaxation and control over the neck, chest, and arm muscles along with many of the facial muscles. It overcomes stiffness and tension in the legs and in the spine which improves blood and pranic energy flow. As the body drops down, it presses on the diaphragm and tones it. It presses on the viscera which is excellent for improving bowel movement. This stretch takes pressure off the heart, and is excellent for improving skin problems. It strengthens the blood vessels in the eyes, which usually means redness of the eyes disappears. The biggest single benefit is that more blood is carried to the brain, producing a mental vitalization and a greater alertness.

DYNAMIC TENSION
(Yogoda)

Mystically, the body is divided into many parts. These include the feet, calves, thighs, haunches, abdomen, stomach, arms, chest, and neck. The purpose of dynamic tension is to energize these parts of the body according to the following five stages:

1. Lie on the floor in a relaxed state. Gently close the eyes and mentally become aware that the separate parts of your body are combined to make one unified whole. Attune to the concept that the mind is also a part of the body and that you, the Spirit, control the mind and body. Come to realize that the Spirit within is the same Spirit within the universe. Realize that within the cosmic universe there are vast amounts of life energies which can be drawn upon.

2. Exhale forcefully, through the open mouth, all the air from the lungs.

3. Inhale as much air as possible through the nose. Then, simultaneously tense your whole body. During the inhalation and tensing, imagine energy flowing into your body through the medulla oblongata, the moon center. Will that this energy go to all the organs of your body. The tension should begin mildly, progressing to medium, and finishing with high tension. At the third level the body should be visibly shaking.

4. Exhale forcefully, all the air through the open mouth again, and then totally relax your whole body.

5. Hold the exhalation, without breathing for as long as possible, but without strain or effort. Now, relax and breathe, remaining in total relaxation until all body functions return to normal. During this relaxation, keep your attention gently focused at the sun center and affirm:

> I am the master of this body...
> I control this body-mind complex...
> I create this feeling of peace, tranquility, harmony, and equanimity from the cosmic energy that emanates within me and the universe...
> I am the creative principle...

Dynamic tension should be performed 3 times. It can also be utilized on any single part of the body.

Exhale, inhale, tense at a low level for a count of 3, and then relax. Repeat at a medium level of tension and relax. Now repeat at a high level of tension and relax. Each is done three times and there is a relaxation between each tensing.

Caution: Persons with high blood pressure, heart disease, or similar dysfunctions should proceed with extreme care, tensing only to the degree allowable by medical advice.

Benefits: The tensing of all the major muscles and organs in the body eliminates toxic substances. It stimulates the growth of red blood cells which carry a fresh supply of oxygen throughout the system. This results in increased vitality which can be felt almost immediately. Through the deep inhalation and exhalation, the breathing mechanism is toned and developed.

Mystical benefits: Dynamic tension causes a flow of pranic energy to various organs of the body; hence, the entire body/mind vehicle is rejuvenated. Since you are utilizing your free will to direct the energy, your will power and self-control are developed. The word will means the result of the interaction of the principle: I am aware that I am. It does not mean willfully.

STRETCHING EXERCISES

In yoga there are a number of stretching exercises which are not from the classical period. These stretches were introduced after the classical period and thus they are not mentioned in classical texts. The exercises are referred to as warming up, limbering up exercises. They are extremely important. They warm the body, making the muscles more flexible, and thus less likely to have accidents. The stretching exercises, also, prepare the body for deeper benefits from the asans themselves.

Physiologically there is a twofold basis for stretching prior to performing asans:

1. If you go into a posture with a tense and cool body, the muscle tissue and sinew attached to the bone may pull or tear. As you do the stretching exercises, there is an elevation in body temperature which assists in relaxing the muscles; therefore, there will not be the pulling and/or tearing that can be caused by exercising with cold, tense muscles.

2. Through stretching and breath-control, particularly the hold, along with mental suggestions, there is produced a stimulation of erythropoetin in the kidneys. This produces a gentle stimulation of the bone marrow which manufactures red

blood cells. These newly generated cells are then carried through the entire system. When these cells mature they will bring added oxygen to all parts of the body.

Most people's spinal muscles have very poor tonus, because the paraspinal muscles are very tense. Because of improper diet, lack of exercise, and incomplete waste removal, the body becomes extremely lethargic and tense. The body attempts to remove this accumulating waste material. It attempts to do so by dehydrating and storing it, often in the joints of the fingers, the knees, and in particular the spine. This accumulation is called calcification, and produces irritation, uncomfortableness, restlessness, and a general state of body awareness. Through proper stretching, asans, diet, and pranayama, these conditions can be overcome or reduced. These calcium deposits are called arthritis of the fingers or spine. Many people refer to this as the aging process. This is can become very dangerous when the pads or intervertebral discs of the vertebrae begin to become calcified, producing inflammation and complicating spinal movement. In extreme cases, this brings about calcification in which the fingers become like solid bones, or sections of spine become frozen. By performing the stretching exercises, along with proper diet, the spine can become more limber due to better paraspinal muscle tone.

STRETCH-LIFT

Before doing any asans, particularly before stretching the spine, begin with the stretch lift. Standing, lift the head as if you were attempting to touch the ceiling with the head. Raise the arms over the head, palms together, and reach toward the ceiling with your head. Then with the arms still raised over the head, palms together, reach toward the ceiling with your arms. Adjust your spine and lift higher. Gently lower the arms to the sides.

Benefits: The stretch lift aligns the spinal column prior to attempting any flexing or stretching. This exercise protects spinal muscles and nerves by adjusting the vertebrae and the intervertebral discs, thus assuring that the muscles and nerves of the spinal area will not be pinched.

Stretch-Lift

LIMB STRETCHING

Lie on your back and raise the arms over the head so they are lying on the floor. In this position perform the following stretches:

1. Inhale, stretching and extending the right arm as much as possible, until you feel a pull in the shoulder area. Relax and exhale. Repeat with the left arm.
2. Pointing the toes and arching the foot, inhale and stretch the right leg as far as possible. Keep a straight line from toe to hip, making sure the leg does not swing out to the side. Relax and exhale. Repeat with the left leg.
3. Now inhale and stretch the right arm and right leg. Feel a pull along the entire right side of the body from the fingers to the toes. Relax and exhale. Repeat on the left side.
4. It is also very helpful to stretch the left leg and right arm at the same time. Repeat, but stretch the right leg and left arm at the same time.
5. Finally inhale and stretch all four limbs simultaneously. Hold the inhalation and outstretched position as long as comfortable. Now totally relax for a few minutes.

SIDE SWINGS

Stand with the feet firmly planted 1 to 1-1/2 feet apart. The arms are stretched out to the sides, held level with the shoulders. Then rotate the body from the waist only, to the right and then to the left. When performed properly, there is a slight pull on the arm that is going behind the body, and the leg opposite the turn bends slightly, while the leg on the side you are turning toward remains straight. If you are turning to the right, there is a pull on the right arm; the left knee turns in slightly, and the right leg remains straight. The head is turned in the direction of the swing, as if you were looking over the shoulder at the arm behind you. As you build a momentum from side to side, you start throwing the weight of your body in the

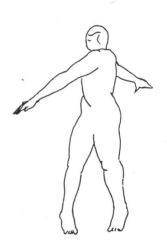

Side Swings

direction of the swing. Be sure to keep the shoulders down and
the arms level with the shoulders. Remember, twist only from the
waist. Keep the hips rigid. This stretch can also be performed by
gripping a cloth (a handkerchief or scarf) behind you, keeping the
arms stiff. The cloth is used when the arms are unusually weak or
stiff or if the shoulder muscles are undeveloped.

Benefits: The waist muscles are extremely important because
they support the most important muscle in the body, the diaphragm. This is a large, flat muscle, like a sheet of paper. As it
moves up and down, you breathe. If it becomes weak, less oxygen
is brought into the body and thus there begins an accumulation of
toxins in the body. The side swings break down fatty tissues in the
waist area, allowing the diaphragm to be freer, taking pressure off
the heart, lowering high blood pressure, and thus normalizing
blood flow and heartbeat. The side swing massages the internal
organs, particularly the lobes of the lungs and the upper intestinal
tract, promoting better elimination.

Half-Moon

HALF-MOON
(Ardha-chandrasan)

Of all the stretching techniques,
the half-moon is the most vital.
Stand erect with the feet anywhere
from 12 to 18 inches apart. If your
feet are too close together, there
will be lack of a firm base. Bring
your arms, palms together, over
your head, pressing against the ears.
You will immediately feel the stretch
in the entire chest region. Next,
with a simple sway, bend sideways
as far as you can, keeping the spine
in alignment. You must be careful
not to lean forward as you bend to
the side. If you bend beyond your
normal ability, your body can be
thrown out of alignment.   Now, repeat the technique on the
opposite side. The half-moon can be performed with a full chalice
(lungs filled with air) or an empty chalice (lungs emptied of air).

The full chalice directly affects the body; the empty chalice
directly affects the mind.

Caution: Persons who have slipped discs, or chronic backaches, etc., should begin very gently and gradually work up to performing the complete stretch. It is wise to get an OK from your health adviser.

Benefits: This stretch tones and stretches the thoracic cavity, thereby aiding the ability to take in more oxygen. It stretches the waist and abdomen and helps clean the body by acting as a stimulant to remove solid wastes. The half-moon tones the spinal column and realigns it. Most women find the half-moon helpful in strengthening the pectoral muscles which support the breasts.

Mystical benefits: The half-moon has a psychological effect that promotes balance. Although it is technically a stretching technique, it does activate the mercury chakra, the mars chakra, and the saturn chakra. Yet when done properly, it primarily affects the venus chakra.

ROCKING CHAIR
(Tadananas-karasan)

The rocking chair is a very important technique. Simply lie on your back and bend your knees and bring them to your chest. Clamp your arms under the knees or across the ankles and simply rock back and forth on your spine. It is not necessary to touch the back of the head to the floor. What is important is the gentle rock and building up a momentum. The speed and rhythm of the rock is dependent upon the individual.

Rocking Chair

Advanced technique: Sit on the floor in a cross-legged posture (sukhasan). Grab the toes of the left foot with the right hand, and the toes of the right foot with the left hand. Bend from the waist, touching the chin to the floor. Next, roll backwards on the spine, unbending the knees, yet keeping the legs crossed at the ankles, and touch the toes to the floor behind the head. Performing this advanced stage is almost like going into the plough posture. Then roll forward on the spine with the legs still crossed, bend the knees, and come again to a sitting position and repeat, building a momentum.

Benefits: The most important is the stretch massage and alignment of the spinal column. Secondly, it gives elasticity to the spine.
All of the muscles and nerves running lateral to the spinal column
are massaged. This obviously stimulates the sympathetic nervous
system. This stretch also massages the optic nerves that exist at the
back of the head. It massages the medulla oblongata, the part of
the brain that controls the relaxing of the stomach muscles, thus
relieving tensions within the digestive system. This stretch tends to
relax the eyes, which produces a quietude within the mind.
Because of the flexing of the moon center it produces relaxation
and greater control over the breathing mechanism.

Mystical benefits: Practicing the advanced technique stimulates
the memory track. This is one of the techniques practiced in the
advanced stages of yoga to stimulate recall of data experienced
earlier. By practicing this technique, you are able to remember
things which you have forgotten from previous existences. How far
back one can go depends on each individual soul. All asans affecting the moon center control the psychic element which allows
deeper, clearer dreaming. Thus, dreaming acquires more noetic
and less emotional relevancy, producing deeper insight regarding
the nature of reality.

THE CAT

The Cat

Stand and perform the
stretch lift to align the spine.
Kneel down on all fours.
Hands should line up in front
of the knees. Exhale and
hold the exhalation. Press
the chin against the chest and
arch the back toward the
ceiling, keeping your elbows
as straight as possible. Inhale
and hold. Bend the head as
far back as possible, slightly
bend the elbows, and curve your back into a U-shape. Exhale, repeating the above procedure several times in a row.

Benefits: Makes the spine extremely flexible, firms the stomach
muscles and removes fatty tissue from that area. Reduces tension
in the neck, and strengthens the thoracic cavity. It removes strain
in the shoulders which is marked in most Americans. Most importantly, the cat massages the kidneys, causing removal of uric wastes.

LEG BOUNCES

Often referred to as leg limbering. This stretch is an important preparation for many of the meditative postures and the butterfly pose as well. Sitting on the floor, extend your legs. Put either foot on the opposite thigh and gently bounce the knee toward the floor. Initially this is done without the hand on the knee. Keep your spine straight and be careful not to lean toward the leg you are bouncing. At first bounce gently, then more

Leg Bounces

vigorously. Next place the hand on the knee, pressing it to the floor with each bounce. Mentally take your consciousness into the muscles of the leg you are bouncing and think: stretch. Repeat using the opposite leg.

Benefits: It loosens the hip and knee joints. The meditative postures necessitate loose hip joints and flexible knees in order that you might sit quietly and thus meditate deeply.

Mystical benefits: This leg stretch makes the ankles flexible, which is important mystically. The ankles are symbolic stress points within your body/mind complex as they relate to the feet. The feet are neptunian and the thighs are jupiterian, both symbolic of philosophy and religion. Through this stretch you are symbolically stretching for a deeper meaning to life. Stretching the ankles has a deep psychologically quieting effect. In quietude, the meaning of life is found.

BUTTERFLY STRETCH

Sit on the floor. Bend the knees, bringing the soles of the feet together. Place the arms between the legs, using the hands to grasp the feet so as to keep the soles of the feet together. Draw the heels as close into the body as possible. Bounce the legs toward the floor repeatedly. The movement of the legs will look like the wings of a butterfly. Practicing over a period of months, the outsides of the legs eventually will touch the floor.

Butterfly Stretch

Benefits: The pelvic area is stretched; the joints in the knees and ankles are loosened. On a deeper level, the butterfly stimulates vitality and activates the entire body, making it alive, vibrant, and active.

Mystical benefits: Stimulates, releasing the kriya kundalini energies.

The Umbrella

THE UMBRELLA

Stand with the legs 8 to 18 inches apart with arms behind you, and interlock your hands. Now draw the shoulder blades together and keep the elbows as straight as possible. Keeping the arms and legs straight, bend forward at the waist and slowly bring the head toward the knees. At the same time, bring the arms up from behind and over the head. Hold for a few seconds and return slowly to an upright position. If you compare the rag doll and the umbrella, you will see the that difference is that rag doll is limp, whereas the umbrella is rigid.

Benefits: The umbrella tones and stretches the spine, flexes the shoulders, and stretches the thoracic cavity. It assists in stretching the legs, particularly those muscles behind the knees. There is a direct relationship between knee muscle relaxation and mind relaxation and quietude. This stretch draws large quantities of blood to the face, improving the complexion, the scalp, and the texture of the hair. As in any inverted or semi-inverted stretch where the head is lower than the heart, you nourish the brain.

Stomach Lift

STOMACH LIFT
(Uddiyana)

The stomach lift is not to be confused with uddiyana bandha described earlier. The stomach lift is used to facilitate the performance of uddiyana bandha along with providing the benefits listed herein.

Stand erect with the feet 12 to 18 inches apart. Inhale deeply and bend slightly at the knees. Lower the buttocks a few inches while keeping the spine straight and vertically aligned. Be careful not to lean forward. Placing the hands on the knees, exhale as much air as possible. Next, holding the breath, contract the stomach muscles in and up. Do this quickly, and then relax. Repeat this 1 to 5 times, then relax for a longer period. The stomach lift can also be done sitting. In order to achieve proper alignment before beginning uddiyana, the rocking chair is done before this stretch.

Benefits: The stomach lift tones the entire stomach-digestive area. It helps in overcoming constipation. It is excellent for toning the diaphragm muscles, driving the air out of the lungs and allowing fresh air in. Also, it lifts and closes the sphincter muscle.

Mystical benefits: It causes the life-current to ascend stronger than it descends. When this happens, sexual restlessness settles down, but is not annihilated. By constant practice, the stomach lift awakens the kriya kundalini in the higher chakras.

MOUNTAIN
(Parbatasan)

Usually this posture is performed in the lotus pose, but any of the cross-legged postures is acceptable. Simply lift the arms over the head close to the ears, keeping the elbows straight, palms joined together, trunk absolutely erect and straight. Stretch the torso upward as though you were trying to touch the ceiling with the fingertips. Be careful not to lift the buttocks off the floor.

Most yoga students do this posture by inhaling and holding to a count of 4 or 8.

The Mountain

This produces an added pressure on the lungs and forces a large amount of added oxygen into the bloodstream. This 8-count hold should be gradually built up to a higher number. Begin with a rapid 4-count, then slow down the count. Extend the count to 7 or 8 seconds.

Caution must be exercised so that the face does not turn red by holding too long. If you have high blood pressure, develop this stretch slowly.

Advanced variation: Sit in the lotus pose. Now slowly raise the body and rest on the knees and hands. Then raise both arms upward, close to the ears, keeping the elbows straight, trunk absolutely erect and straight. Stretch the torso upward and balance on both knees.

Benefits: The mountain is valuable in overall toning of the body. It increases vitality and stimulates the removal of body waste. It also strengthens the lungs. The mountain makes the whole thoracic cavity more elastic enabling one to take in more oxygen during inhalation. The average breathing cycle is less than two seconds. Independent of this very short breath-cycle, a minimal amount of oxygen enters the bloodstream because the air sacs of the lungs are sluggish. This stretch tones the air sacs enabling more oxygen to enter the bloodstream. All internal organs are vigorously and positively stimulated. This means the digestive organs improve their functioning because the gastric juices are improved. A sluggish elimination system is stimulated and more waste matter is removed from the body.

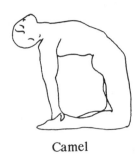

Camel

CAMEL
(Supta-vajrasan)

There are a number of variations to the camel. The simplest way to begin is by kneeling with the buttocks resting on the heels, bottoms of the toes on the floor, feet arched. Classically, the hands should grasp the base of the heels. Next, tighten the anal and stomach muscles and lift the buttocks off the heels, not by raising the legs but by pushing the pelvic region forward. As you are lifting, drop the head as far back as possible, arching the thoracic area. Once you are in the posture, begin to relax and let the weight of your body do the gentle stretching. It is easier to begin with the hands on the floor, and arch into the posture. Then place the hands on the base of the heels. However, this is not the traditional technique.

To come out of this posture without jerky movements, you first lower the buttocks slowly onto the heels, keeping your head all the way back. Once resting on the heels, bring the head forward into normal position and rest your hands on the thighs. Some persons lower the hands onto the floor before coming out of the posture, leaning on one hand and turning the body to the side for support while coming up. This is not proper but is suggested for people with weaker back muscles. After the body is strengthened, you can return to the standard process.

As a rule, take a deep breath and exhale two-thirds to three-quarters. Hold and then lift. Occasionally, when you lift and arch backward, you will feel a slight pressure in the chest area. When this happens, simply exhale more air. Some people take a deep breath, go into the posture with the throat open, and exhale while bending. In any heavy bend, the less air you have in the lungs, the greater will be your flexibility.

Variation: A simpler version of the camel can be performed by kneeling on the buttocks, resting on the heels, placing the hands on the floor behind the feet (rather than on the heels) and lifting into the posture.

Benefits: To improve digestion. The neck muscles become toned and fatty deposits that exist in the stomach/waist area are markedly reduced. The rib muscles which normally are very weak, are strengthened. The abdominal and rectal muscles are also strengthened. This allows the sphincter muscle to close. If the sphincter muscle is not closed, an enormous amount of bowel moisture is lost, causing heavy constipation. When the waste deposits in the colon are heavily dehydrated, stress and damage occurs, such as hemorrhoids. This is serious because the sphincter muscle is attuned to the saturn chakra's subtle nerves located at the base of the spine that allow the prana to ascend. The pain from hemorrhoids can be very extreme. It is not a mental state conducive to meditation. An instant remedy for hemorrhoids is to squat in a small amount of hot water. Gradually add hotter water. In 1 to 3 minutes the hemorrhoids will shrink and the pain will go away. Relief lasts for many hours or even days. Repeat as needed.

By practicing the camel, the neck becomes strong and stomach and waist areas are markedly reduced. Digestion is improved and any stomach problems are corrected. The ribs are strengthened. The camel assists in improving sciatica, an injury to the nerve of the inner thigh.

THE LION
(Simha Mudra)

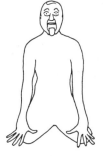

This lion posture is also referred to as the kali mudra. It is performed by sitting in the lightning bolt posture with your hands resting on the knees, palms downward. Take a deep breath, stretch the fingers, and feel a emanation of energy pouring into the earth. Next, the tongue is

The Lion

extended as far out and downward as possible. The eyes and mouth are opened widely.

All these movements should be performed simultaneously. Hold for a few seconds, release, and swallow lightly.

Benefits: A tremendous amount of blood is rushed into the face and neck area, thereby feeding and strengthening the organs in the head. It relieves sore throats and protects one from sore throats and stiff necks. The lion strengthens the neck and tongue muscles and tends to alleviate postnasal drip. It tones and relaxes facial muscles. The movements bring blood to the fingers, allowing better circulation, making the hands warmer and preventing calcium deposits. It produces improvements in the digestive process. The body slims down, and sluggishness is removed.

Mystical benefits: The lion is most significant because it affects the tongue, a key mystical organ, linked to the moon center. Stretching the tongue gives greater control over the moon center and produces the following:

1. It brings about greater dream perception. Those who do not dream begin to remember their dreams after practicing the lion for a number of weeks. Those who normally dream very little dream longer and more perceptively.

2. Control over the door to the other world, the astral world. This is the greatest mystical effect. For most people, the door is absolutely closed. The lion pose assists in opening this door. You thus become more receptive to higher vibrations. Control of the moon center allows you to close the door to lower vibrations, if you wish.

3. It causes deeper normalization of the breathing mechanism. This occurs because the moon center controls breathing. Breathing tensions are removed and there is a greater balancing of the ascending and descending currents.

When the lion is practiced along with other yoga techniques, it helps produce clarity of thinking, serenity of the mind, and the visional state.

In advanced yoga, one practices tongue milking. This is a procedure in which the tongue is massaged. A small silk cloth (rayon or nylon is acceptable) is moistened and placed over the extended tongue. The wet silk adheres to the tongue making the milking process easier. The tongue is encapsulated in the hand, is then pulled down and from side to side. This technique stretches and exercises the tongue. The mystical benefits of the lion, therefore, are heightened.

There is another technique practiced with the tongue that should be mentioned at this point. In India, many students begin the practice of yoga at a very early age, planning to spend their entire lives practicing it. Some teachers, therefore, cut the muscle below the tongue by 1/12-inch, rubbing salt and butter into the cut. Obviously, this is extremely painful. After many cuttings over a period of from 12 to 36 months, one is able to extend the tongue down past the chin. The tongue is then trained to be flipped back and put into the soft palate cavity. This helps in producing the visional state. If done improperly, death due to suffocation will occur. I do not recommend that anyone go through this process. It is mentioned only for historical reasons. If ever considered, it should be done only under the direct supervision of a teacher who himself has had the operation and learned the secrets of tongue rolling.

Chapter 7

THE CLASSICAL POSTURES
(ASANS)

KRIYA YOGA--THE ART OF BALANCED BEING

Kriya yoga is unique in that it conceives the mind and body to be one organ. What happens in the body likewise occurs in the mind, and what happens in the mind likewise occurs in the body. In kriya yoga, the physical muscles are stretched, thereby squeezing out the old blood. Then, the freshly oxygenated blood is circulated through all the muscles and organs. When the body is stretched and relaxed, tension is relieved, and fresh blood revitalizes the inner organs, including the brain. When tension of the body is relieved, the mind is calmed. When tension of the organs is relieved, the mind becomes still. This process can be reversed. Relaxing the mind by controlling your thinking causes relaxation of the body. However, this method is more difficult. Thus, yoga places the emphasis on moving from the physical to the mental.

Of all the various yogas, kriya yoga is the most important for it moves beyond control of just the body and the everyday mind, to the control of your total being and consciousness, which exist on many planes. Most individuals begin the practice of yoga concerned only with bodily states such as a more healthy body, the ability to relax, and a longer life. Although the goal of yoga extends far beyond this, these are valid and worthwhile goals. Kriya yoga, however, is a system of learning and perfecting eight stages of self control in order to completely attain spiritual health: cosmic consciousness.

THE FIVE STAGES OF EVERY POSTURE

Every posture has five stages in it. Practicing the yoga postures is similar to playing a musical instrument. To a very large degree, it necessitates timing and attunement to a feeling. If you ask a musician how long a full note is, he cannot give you an exact, definitive answer. Every musician knows the length of a note is a matter of its relationship to other notes. In short, timing is proportional and relative. It is a feeling state, close, but different in each master's mind.

In the same way, the feeling state within a particular posture is subjective, but very closely linked to that posture. From that feeling follow five stages which make up the completed posture.

1. The first step is mentally attuning to the posture. Here the mind establishes a feeling state appropriate to the posture. For example, when a tennis player is about to serve, he must attune his mind to a particular attentiveness. He mentally goes through the delivery of the ball before actually tossing it up. This collectiveness, this attentiveness, is the feeling which was spoken about. The feeling will be different with different postures. The closer the postures are to each other, the closer will be the feeling.

   This feeling state before going into a posture is important. If you hold a positive feeling, it will cause the mind states relating to the posture to become balanced. This feeling state draws the energies into balance. It produces a quietness and brings energies to the specific energy center (chakra) according to the pose performed.

2. The second step is the flowing into the posture. Move into the posture as gently, as smoothly, and harmoniously as possible. If you have ever watched how a cat stretches, you will perceive the ease and grace with which you should go into any posture. The flow or sweep into a posture is one motion. There should be no jerkiness.

3. The third step is holding the posture motionless. This is most important. People who move awkwardly have an extremely difficult time holding the mind still... concentration is almost impossible. People who are always fidgeting and/or always making extraneous movements, have their energies scattered. There is a relationship between bodily stillness and mental equilibrium.

   The secret of the posture is the hold. It is in the hold that the bodily energies are brought into balance. It is within the hold that the life energies are lifted and sent to the chakras, healing karma imbalances. The mind always follows the feelings. If you feel anger, holding to that feeling causes the energies to become more out of balance. Eventually they become so far out of balance you will be compelled to think, to speak, or to act in a negative way. But reversing the process, and holding to a balanced quietude, will cause the anger to soften or lift. When this feeling is held in the hold of the posture, it affects your subconscious mind. Thus, it has far stronger and longer lasting positive effects. It is also at this stage that the kriya kundalini ascends into the various chakras.

4. The fourth step is sweeping out of the posture. This should be done with one motion. Struggling to get in or out of a posture produces jerkiness and consequently an imbalancing of the energies. This defeats the purpose of the poses. In short, you should flow as smoothly out of the posture as you flowed into it.

5. The fifth and final step is total relaxation. This rest period is the second most important stage, for it is here that all the energies are balanced, reducing the emotions and producing positive feelings.

Although five stages are indicated, they are actually one total harmonious whole. There should be no ruptures or awkward movements between any of the stages.

Finally, there is a great difference between doing calisthenics and the yoga postures. Calisthenics is aimed at rapid contractions in order to enlarge and strengthen the muscles. Yoga stretches the muscles, toning and then relaxing them. It is, therefore, essential to learn to differentiate between stretching and straining. When the stretch becomes a strain, it is no longer yoga.

GUIDES TO PERFORMING THE POSTURES

Choosing the Postures

Every posture is not for everyone. In the practice of yoga, everyone practices the observances (yama) and abstinences (niyama), but not everyone should perform all the postures. Know your body, and know the postures. With the assistance of a qualified instructor, map out a personal program of yoga that meets your individual requirements, physically and mentally. Always inform an instructor when a posture is uncomfortable or exceedingly difficult for you. Never feel you are a failure if you cannot master a certain position, even after a few years. Remember, in performing the asans, you are competing only with yourself, not with another person.

Yoga is more than exercise. It affects the total psycho-mental-physical functioning of your entire being on many levels. When you are attempting to improve your life, self-discipline is needed. Self-improvement begins by doing the best you can with what you have. Start from whatever point you are at, and watch your attitude.

Right Side or Left Side?

Some yoga postures can be performed in two ways. The masculine position utilizes the right side of the body, thereby energizing the life-current (prana) into the physical. The feminine position utilizes the left side of the body, thereby energizing the life-current into the mental. You should become equally adept at performing a posture in both ways.

It is highly recommended the postures be practiced in the way you find more difficult. The feeling of discomfort is an indicator of which side of your vehicle is lacking. It is here that the energy needs to be directed to strengthen your being. In general, place less emphasis on the postures that are easy for you to do. When there is no feeling of discomfort on either side, women should first perform the posture in the masculine position; men should first perform the posture in the feminine position.

Bending Forward and Backward

Bending the body affects the prana current in one of two ways. The basic rule when performing bending postures is to do a backward bend after each forward bend. Those postures which cause the spine to bend forward open the energy centers (chakras) and allow the current to flow in. Those postures which cause the spine to arch backwards, allow the energy to ascend upwards to the higher centers. Therefore, to attain true balance with kriya yoga postures, you must determine if it is desirable to pour energy into a given center or to take the energy out of a given center. A final goal is to balance all the energy centers.

If you do not know which energy center is to be balanced, it is best to work with the center at the base of the spine, and then move upwards. When a particular chakra is balanced, the prana flowing in and out of the chakra is balanced. There is neither too much energy pouring into the chakra, nor will the chakra stop the proper amount of energy from flowing into it.

Holding Contractions (Bandhas)

Some postures utilize the anal contraction (mula bandha), the stomach contraction (uddiyana bandha), and/or the chin lock (jalandhara bandha). Where applicable, they are indicated in the text. These contractions assist in directing the flow of the current upward. Their importance should not be underestimated.

Breathing

Breathing techniques are extensively dealt with in the chapter on pranayama. In the early stages of yoga, the concern is with learning to slow down the breathing. If the lungs are full of air and held while doing the poses, the body is mainly influenced. If the lungs are empty and held while doing a pose, the mind is influenced. This stage of yoga should be practiced only after studying the chapter on pranayama.

Duration of the Hold

In the beginning, the postures should not be held longer than a few seconds. Gradually, the length may be increased by a few seconds at a time until a hold of a minute or so is achieved. In the advanced stages of yoga, certain postures may be held for longer periods, but only when indicated by and under the supervision of a qualified instructor.

Eye Position

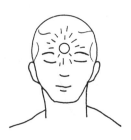

Eyes gently focused
at the sun center

While performing the postures, the eyes can be either totally closed or half closed. The latter position is known as unmani mudra. It is preferred by some as it allows light to enter and stimulate certain centers of the brain. At first, it is far better to close the eyes completely. This assists in drawing in one's consciousness, closing out the external physical world. The average person concentrates better with the eyes totally closed. Whether your eyes are closed or half closed, the attention of your awareness should always be focused at the sun center (ajna chakra), at the root of the nose between the eyebrows.

There should be no stress or strain when focusing at the sun center.

Series of Three

Each pose should be performed 3 times. Here is the pattern:
1. Go into the pose, come out, rest;
2. Return to the pose, come out, rest;
3. Return to the pose, come out, and perform the total relaxation pose (savasana).

Beginning a Practice Session

Begin each practice session with a period of total relaxation (savasana), drawing your mind deeply inward. Let go of your awareness of the everyday world. Consciously tell your mind to release its problems, worries, and apprehensions. Create a feeling of peace within yourself and affirm the goal(s) you hope to achieve through your practice of yoga. Proceed with any of the relaxation techniques and stretching exercises you find particularly meaningful and beneficial.

Final Relaxation

End each yoga practice with the total relaxation pose, lasting from 5 to 15 minutes. When in the total relaxation pose, peacefully bask in the joy, warmth, and in-turnedness of your be-

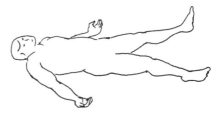

Total Relaxation
(Savasana)

ing. Be sure you use your affirmations to gain the greatest positive effect from yoga. These affirmations will be found in each section of the classical poses, in the next section. They will assist you in developing a positive dynamo of creative thinking and a positive attitude toward life and self.

Regularity of Practice

When you practice is not as important as regularity in practice. Make a commitment to study and practice daily. Say to yourself, 'I will study 15 minutes and practice 20 minutes each and every day'. By adhering to this commitment, you establish self-discipline. If the body obeys your mind when it is told to do the postures, the body will also obey when your mind tells it to relax.   From this follows greater happiness, contentment, and wisdom. You can extend the work-out period according to your needs, after you have established the basic daily pattern.

Illness

Traditionally, if a person is ill, the yoga postures should not be practiced. Some teachers believe, however, if a person is ill, doing the postures very gently will help recuperation. It is recommended that one perform only the simplest postures with extreme gentleness if one is ill.

In cases where one suffers from chronic disease or functional disorders, additional care needs to be taken. Ailments such as high blood pressure, diabetes, emphysema, gastritis, colitis, organic impairment, and so forth, are not to be considered lightly nor should they be ignored. In cases such as these, yoga should be practiced only after first consulting with an expert teacher and/or health practitioner. Only then should the individual proceed.

Pregnancy

During pregnancy one must be extremely cautious in performing any postures which highly activate the pelvic region and might inadvertently induce labor. An additional danger in performing inverted postures such as the headstand, shoulderstand, plough, and so forth, is the possibility of the umbilical cord becoming wrapped around the fetus, thereby causing problems. In the first three months it is permissible only to practice those postures which utilize the upper part of the body and the limbs. In the last six months of pregnancy it is best to practice only relaxation techniques, breathing techniques, and the milder stretching exercises. If you are pregnant, find a woman expert who teaches yoga and pregnancy. Talk to her about your personal yoga program.

For the expectant mother, the most valuable technique is total relaxation which should be practiced extensively. In this position, you should place your hands on the stomach and breathe slowly and regularly. With each inhalation, mentally draw into your consciousness all the love and compassion of the universe. With each exhalation, mentally send that energy through your arms and hands to your child. With this technique, a feeling of peace and harmony is transmitted to the unborn child and penetrates into its consciousness on the physical and mental planes. This feeling makes the child's mind more balanced, making its life more positive. This positive feeling will remain in the consciousness of the child its entire life.

Beginning Students

Beginning students, especially older persons, should limit their practice to the relaxation techniques and stretching exercises for a number of weeks. The degree of speed to which one can proceed should be determined by the wisdom of a qualified yoga instructor.

Clothing

Wear comfortable, loose-fitting clothing which in no way inhibits movement, especially at the waist, neck, thigh, and shoulder joints. A leotard or gym suit is excellent. Shoes are never worn during hatha yoga practice, nor should stretch socks be worn. When practicing the postures in the privacy of your home, it is beneficial to perform them in as little clothing as possible. Women who are well-developed may find that some support is helpful, in some postures. Men might find it wise to wear at least a jockstrap.

Practice Area

The area in which you practice yoga postures should be clean, dry, and well-aired. The room should be quiet, and there should be no drafts. The postures should be performed on a mat, blanket, large towel, or rug, used solely for this purpose.

North, South, East or West?

In general, it does not matter which direction you face while performing hatha yoga postures. The exceptions are the meditative poses. The directions to face while forming the meditative poses are covered in the chapter on performing the meditative poses.

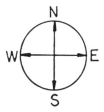

Eating Before Practice

The stomach should be at least half empty before you practice the postures. Allow 3 to 4 hours after eating a solid meal. On a half-empty stomach, you will have greater agility and a feeling of lightness. Also, there will be no overtly active digestive processes occurring when you are forming the postures. As many of the postures relate directly to the organs of digestion, this might interfere with their benefits.

Daily Liquid Consumption

Water is one of the greatest body-purifiers. Most people do not drink enough water. It is recommended that the yoga student consume at least four 8-ounce glasses of water daily.   The water should be cool and drunk slowly.   Water flushes your system and stimulates the processes of elimination whereby waste and toxins are expelled from the body.

To assist this cleansing, the yogi cleansing vitality drink may be used in the beginning stages.   This drink is made by adding the juice of 1/2 lemon and 1 to 3 teaspoons of blackstrap molasses to 8 ounces of hot water.   A little honey can be added.   The lemon juice helps in cleansing the body of phlegm and waste, whereas the molasses increases the body's iron and mineral supply which increases your strength and energy.   Almost everyone has a low iron count.   The blackstrap molasses will correct this.   It is recommended that this yogi drink be taken every third or fifth night, before sleep, for a number of weeks.   The yogi drink is used only when one first starts the practice of yoga.   After that, it is used only when needed.

Purification Techniques (Shat Kriyas)

In order to further cleanse the body, it is recommended the student study the chapter on purification techniques, before beginning serious practice of the asans.   Those not listed below are best performed only under the direct supervision of an experienced teacher.

1. Water colon cleansing (jala basti).
2. Water nasal cleansing (jala neti).
3. Solar/lunar eye cleansing (tratakam).
4. Sun center gazing (brumadhya drishti).
5. Stomach lift (uddiyana).
6. Solar/lunar chakra cleansing (kapalabhati).
7. Tongue cleansing (chandra and hrid dhautis).

The descriptions of the classical yoga postures follow.   They are given according to the key chakras upon which they have their greatest effect.

ASANS AFFECTING THE SATURN CHAKRA

WARM-UPS

One-Leg Lift
  (Eka-uttana-padasan)
Leg Lifts
  (Uttanatavasan)
Gas-Relieving Pose
  (Pavana-maktasan)
Palm Tree Pose
  (Tadasan)
Flying Bird Pose
  (Yanoddiyanasan)

FORWARD BENDING POSES

Creeper Pose
  (Lapasan)
Posterior Stretch
  (Paschimottanasan)
Squat Pose
  (Utkatasan)
Tortoise Pose
  (Pada-prasaran
  -kachchapasan)
Bat Pose
  (Chamagadarasan)
Right-Sway
  (Pingala Bharad-vajasan)
Balancing V-Leg Stretch
  (Vistrita-padasan)

BACKWARD ARCHING POSES

Half-Cobra Pose
  (Ardya-bhujangasan)
Hero Pose
  (Virasan)
Cobra Pose
  (Bhujanasan)
Left-Sway
  (Ida Bharad-vajasan)

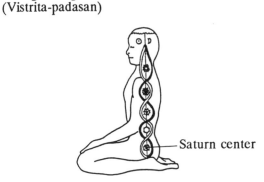

Saturn center

Special Note for Practicing the Asans

In the practice of the forward bending and backward arching postures, the forward bending pose should always be done first, followed by a backward bend.

Remember: the forward bending postures open the chakra channels, whereas the backward arching postures cause the energy to surge up that open channel to the higher chakras.

AFFIRMATIONS FOR THE SATURN CHAKRA

The following affirmations are to be utilized in the hold position of the saturn chakra poses. These affirmations are not to be confused with mantras, covered in a later chapter.

1. Be invincible, be of steady courage, and have a goal.

2. God-Realization is mankind's highest duty.

3. I will do that which will not have to be undone.

4. I will do what I can, having full confidence in natural law.

5. I realize that a soul who has never been against the wall is not likely to climb over.

6. If a system causes suffering, re-systematize.

7. Brotherhood is given us; friendship must be acquired.

8. You cannot hear the earth move; great powers make very little noise.

9. In the end we will all return to mother earth for the solution.

POSTURE DESCRIPTIONS

ONE-LEG LIFT
(Eka-uttana-padasan)

One-Leg Lift

Lying on your back, slowly lift one leg straight up at a right angle to the body, hold, then lower the leg. Now lift the opposite leg, repeating the process. Lift the legs singly as indicated, 3 or 4 times, then lift both legs together 3 or 4 times. Gradually increase the number and duration of the lift as abdominal strength is gained. After resting and deep breathing, sit up, draw the soles of the feet together close to the body, and butterfly the knees up and down. The legs may also be lifted together for short periods of time in preparation for the leg lifts.

Benefits: Leg lifts ease constriction of the muscles and cartilage in the legs and knees, toning and flexing the hamstring muscle. They assist in toning the abdomen, strengthening weak abdominal muscles--a common cause of lower back pain. The butterfly movement stretches leg and knee tendons in another direction, and the combination of the two gently prepares the legs and thighs for the lotus posture.

LEG LIFTS
(Uttanatavasan)

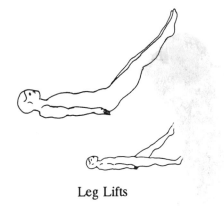

Leg Lifts

Lying flat on the back, keep your legs straight and joined together. Place the hands at the sides of the body, palms facing down. Raise both legs, keeping them straight and lifting them approximately 2 feet off the ground. Keep your gaze affixed to the toes. Slowly lower legs to the floor. Repeat a number of times, resting between each lift.

Benefits: Tones and strengthens the stomach muscles; also tones and strengthens weak abdominal muscles, a common cause of lower back pain. Eases constriction of the muscles and cartilage in the legs and knees. Helps in the improvement of bowel elimination.

GAS-RELIEVING POSE
(Pavana-maktasan)

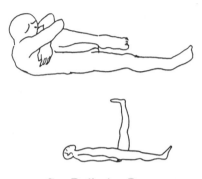

Gas Relieving Pose

Lying on your back, slowly bend the left knee and lift it toward the chest. Place the hands around the knee and press firmly into the chest, keeping your other leg straight. Hold for 3 seconds. Raise the left leg and stretch it upward at a right angle to the body, pressing your foot outward toward the ceiling. Slowly lower to the floor. Repeat with the right leg and then both legs. This technique can also include bringing the forehead to the knee as you bring the knee to the chest. Gas-relieving can also be practiced after drinking a glass of water.

Benefits: Tones stomach muscles, relieves flatulence, improves the complexion.

PALM TREE POSE
(Tadasan)

Palm Tree Pose

Stand straight with your feet together. Inhale, filling the lungs and stomach with air.

Raise the hands straight up, spreading the palms. Balance the entire body on the toes while gazing forward. The body should be kept absolutely erect and still. The anal contraction should be utilized.

Variation: This posture may also be used walking backward and forward in one of the rare motion asans.

Benefits: This pose is utilized by young people to increase height as well as to give room for the internal organs to develop.

FLYING BIRD POSE
(Yanoddiyanasan)

Kneel erect with the toes touching the ground, heels up and buttocks aligned with your knees (off the heels). Firmly affix the right knee on the left heel and raise the right heel up. Stretch the arms to both sides and retain this balanced position for as long as possible. Repeat, using your other leg.

Flying Bird Pose

The heel comes off the floor.

Benefits: Relieves rheumatic pain in the knees. The waist is strengthened and one attains inner balance and tranquility.

CREEPER POSE
(Lapasan)

Go into the plough pose. Outstretch both legs and arms as wide as possible. In this outstretched position both arms and legs should remain straight and firmly on the ground. Legs should be kept outstretched as wide as the arms.

Creeper Pose

Benefits: The arteries and intestines are cleansed and strengthened. Skin diseases are corrected. Disorders of the nose, ear, mouth, and eyes are corrected. The back and waist become flexible. Appetite is increased.

POSTERIOR STRETCH
(Paschimottanasan)

Sit on the floor, legs straight in front of you. Lean forward slightly and wiggle so you feel that you are sitting on the

Posterior Stretch

buttocks as you would on a chair. Sit erect and stretch arms over the head. Exhale and drop your body forward, the head coming down toward the knees. Hold for 1 to 4 seconds. Return to the sitting position with arms stretched upward over the head, inhale, and drop the arms to the lap. Relax.

Benefits: Restores elasticity to the muscles, particularly the hamstring muscles. Makes the spine flexible, tones abdomen and inner organs, and prevents sciatica. A good pose for diabetics. Relaxes and makes the mind more flexible.

SQUAT POSE
(Utkatasan)

Stand erect, feet 12 inches apart. Lower the body by balancing on the toes. The arms are then wrapped around the knees or clasped in the lap. Anal contraction should be utilized in this pose.

Squat Pose

Variation: Stand erect, feet 12 inches apart. Keeping the feet flat on the floor, bend the knees and drop to the floor. Clasp arms around knees. Hold 5 seconds.

Benefits: The squat assists in elimination of constipation. It strengthens calf muscles; loosens hip joints; exercises feet.

TORTOISE POSE
(Pada-prasaran-kachchapasan)

Sit on the floor with your legs forming a V-leg stretch position with the soles of the feet together. Bend forward and place the arms under the knees. Bend the body forward, moving your feet outward, until the legs are as straight as possible and the forehead touches the floor.

Tortoise Pose

Benefits: This is an advanced exercise for the thoracic and lumbar regions and strengthens the back. Sends blood to the head. The hands and feet gain strength and the stomach also becomes strong.

BAT POSE
(Chamagadarasan)

Sit on the floor with your legs extended in front of you, forming a V-leg. Lean the chest forward, placing the arms under each knee. Then press the arms

Bat Pose

straight out to the sides, pushing the elbows with the knees. This will force the legs and head to raise. Retain this balanced position for a short time.

Benefits: This is a very useful pose for improving digestion; strengthening the joints, hands, and feet; pushing out accumulated gas, making the chest strong and the body healthy in general.

SWAY POSE
(Bharad-vajasan)

Sit on the floor with the legs swung to the left, bent at the knees. Interlock the fingers and place them behind the head. Pull shoulders back and, holding the spine erect, sway to the left toward your feet. Relax the arms and sit quietly. Now sit with the feet to the right; resume the position of the arms upward, hands behind the head, and sway to the right. Hold each sway 3 seconds.

Sway Pose

This posture, like many of the poses, can be performed by stretching either to the left or to the right. When you sway to the left, it is called the left-sided sway (ida bharad-vajasan), when you sway to the right, it is called the right-sided sway (pingala bharad-vajasan).

Benefits: Stretches the thoracic cavity, spine, and shoulders. Reduces the waistline.

BALANCING V-LEG STRETCH
(Vistrita-padasan)

Assume the plough position. Spread the legs in a V-position and hold onto the feet with your hands. Bend the knees and bring your legs forward, swinging the body into a balanced sitting position with the arms and legs straight. Hold 3 seconds and return to the V-plough position. Release legs as in the plough and assume the total relaxation pose.

Variation: This pose can also be

Balancing
V-Leg Stretch

assumed while in a sitting position by bending the knees, taking hold of the outsides of both feet, balancing on the buttocks, and then extending the legs into the balancing V-leg position.

Benefits: Brings flexibility to the legs and back and concentration to the mind. Relieves constipation.

Cobra Pose

COBRA POSE
(Bhujangasan)

Lie flat on your stomach, forehead on the floor, fingers at shoulder level, heels together, feet flat on the floor. Slowly raise your head up and back. Continue lifting the shoulders and spine in one smooth motion, keeping the stomach and pelvic area on the floor. Lift using the back muscles with the hands to guide you. Elbows should not be straight but should remain slightly bent. Hold 3 seconds. Lower in reverse order, spine, and back, then shoulders. When shoulders are on the floor, roll head forward, forehead to the floor.

Variation: While in the full cobra pose slowly turn the head and look over your right and left shoulder toward the heels. Center the head and release the posture.

Benefits: Energizes the sympathetic nervous system, strengthens the back muscles, prevents spinal displacement and many orthopedic difficulties. Assists in curing dysmenorrhea and delays menopause. Massages all internal organs.

HALF-COBRA POSE
(Ardha-bhujangasan)

Stretch your left leg back as far as possible. The right knee is bent with the foot flat on the floor. Place the right hand on the right knee, left hand and spine bent slowly backward until left hand, spine, and left leg look like a semicircle. Hold 3 seconds. Repeat with the left knee forward.

Benefits: This is an excellent

Half-Cobra Pose

stretch for all the muscles, ligaments, nerves of the legs, stomach, spine, and arms. An excellent stretch for the entire body.

HERO POSE
(Virasan)

Kneel on the floor and sit on your heels. Gently spread the feet so the buttocks come to the floor between the feet. Sit for 3 seconds. Place the hands on the floor and lift your body back to its original kneeling position. Stretch out the legs and relax in total relaxation (savasana).

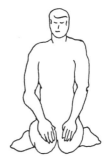

Hero

Variation: Sitting on the floor, place your left heel on the outside of the right hip on the floor. Then bring your right leg over and on top of the left knee so the knees are aligned and your left knee remains below the right knee. Then bring the right foot alongside the outside of the left hip. With fingers interlocked, place them on the knees. Hold this position for as long as you comfortably can and relax. (Also see the gomukha pose described in the chapter on the meditative poses.)

Benefits: Excellent for menstrual disorders. Stretches the knees and feet; tones the thighs.

Hero
(Variation)

ASANS AFFECTING THE JUPITER CHAKRA

WARM-UPS

Twist-Around-Waist-Pose
  (Utthita-kumdhakasan)
Triangle
  (Trikonasan)
Pigeon
  (Kapotasan)
Eagle
  (Garudasan)

FORWARD BENDING POSES

Elephant Pose
  (Gajasan)
Symbol of Yoga
  (Yoga Mudra)
One-Leg Posterior Stretch
  (Eka-pada-paschi-
  mottanasan)
Lizard Pose
  (Chatush-padasan)
Shooting Bow Pose
  (Akarna-dhanurasan)
Head-on-Knee Pose
  (Utthita-jamushira-
  samyuktasan)

BACKWARD ARCHING POSES

Hanuman Pose
  (Hanuman-asan)
Bow
  (Dhanurasan)
Navel Pose
  (Nadhi-asan)
Rocking Navel Pose
  (Rocking Nadhi-asan)
Half-Locust
  (Ardha-salabhasan)
Full-Locust
  (Salabhasan)
Soles-on-Head Pose
  (Ditarita-pada-
  mastakastarshasan)
Arch
  (Setu-bandhasan)
Supine Hero
  (Supta-vijrasan)

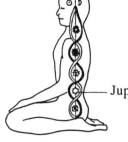

Jupiter center

AFFIRMATIONS FOR THE JUPITER CHAKRA

The following affirmations are to be utilized in the hold position of the jupiter chakra poses. These affirmations are not to be confused with mantras, covered in a later chapter.

1. I can afford to wait if I am ahead of time.

2. Moving through life fighting for a principle, I will be careful not to violate a greater one.

3. The secret of success is not asking for more, but using what I already have.

4. Deciding what I would do if I had a chance to live my life over again, now, I will start living it.

5. It is a worthy ambition to aspire to rule if I start by ruling my own world.

6. I will look to a philosophy that increases the do's and decreases the don'ts.

7. I will increase my peace of mind with a workable philosophy.

8. The most successful success is successful thinking.

9. Habits habitually help or hinder.

10. Even the slowest soul may increase his speed.

POSTURE DESCRIPTIONS

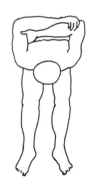

Twist-Around-Waist

TWIST-AROUND-WAIST POSE
(Utthita-kumdhakasan)

Stand erect, placing the feet 2 to 3 feet apart. Place the arms behind the back with elbows bent and grasp the left elbow with the right hand and the right elbow with the left hand. Clasp the elbows with the hand of the opposite arm. Inhale as fully as you can and hold. Bending forward, twist your body from the waist only, in a circular motion, slowly and carefully so there is no trace of dizziness. This rotation is a four-stage movement, similar to the neck roll: forward, sideways, backward, sideways, forward again. Move the body in a full circle in one direction with one inhalation held. Exhale. Inhale and hold, reversing the circular motion in the opposite direction. This pose should be done whereby you make the circular motion in both directions; however, the left direction should be done first. This pose can also be exercised making the circular rotation with an empty chalice.

Benefits: This is one of the most powerful and useful postures for correcting disorders of the stomach as well as reducing the abdomen. Strengthens the chest and improves appetite and digestion.

Triangle

TRIANGLE
(Trikonasan)

Stand tall. The feet should be 3 feet apart. Slowly bend to the left until the left hand is on the floor or on the ankle. Right arm is straight over the head close to the ear. Breathe normally. This pose should be done on both sides; the left side should be done first.

Benefits: Tones the spinal nerves, makes the waist muscles supple, keeps the body youthful, stimulates the peristaltic action of the bowels and intestines, and strengthens the legs. Circulation of the blood is markedly improved. The spine, neck, shoulders, and arms become fairly strong.

PIGEON
(Kapotasan)

Kneeling down, bring the heels and toes of the feet together and assume the lightning bolt pose with knees slightly apart forming a V-position. Insert the arms between the thighs and taking the hands one over

Pigeon Pose

the other, cover the soles of the feet with the palms. Retain the breath and raise the head. Lower the head while exhaling.

Benefits: Strengthens the nerves of the chest, neck, hands, and feet. Tones, massages, and strengthens muscles of the chest and neck. Helps awaken the tiny air sacs in the lungs, improving the respiratory system. Also relieves tension in the cervical area.

EAGLE
(Garudasan)

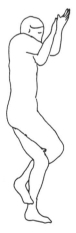

Raise the right leg and wind it fully around the left. Similarly wind the arms around each other and join the palms or perform the interlock gesture (gomukha mudra). Standing like this on one leg, place the wrists on the tip of the nose in such a way that the formation looks like the beak of a bird. Repeat the posture on the opposite leg.

Benefits: Strengthens the nerve tissues, muscles, and bones of the arms, legs, and hands. Firms the legs, thighs, and hips. Enlargement of the kidneys is often reduced. Also helps in

Eagle Pose

developing poise, concentration, and balance as do the other balancing poses.

ELEPHANT POSE
(Gajasan)

Elephant Pose

Stand erect and bend from the waist, placing the extended arms outward so the palms are flat on the floor facing forward. Keep the legs and the arms absolutely stretched. Walk forward and backward in this posture. This is another moving asan. (Also see the palm tree pose.)

Benefits: Assists the circulation; tones the muscles of the extremities. Because of the inverted position of the body while in this pose it aids in increasing the blood flow to the chest, neck, and head, nourishing the muscles and nerves in these areas.

SYMBOL OF YOGA
(Yoga Mudra)

Symbol of Yoga

Assume the lotus posture. Clasp hands behind the waist. Inhale and exhale, slowly lowering the head toward the floor. Hold 1 to 3 seconds. Lift to a sitting position.

Benefits: Stretches lower back muscles; relieves constipation.

ONE-LEG POSTERIOR STRETCH
(Eka-pada-paschi-mottanasan)

One-Leg Posterior Stretch

One-leg posterior stretch is performed exactly the same as the full posterior stretch, except you bend one of the legs and place the heel either against the inner thigh or on top of the thigh of the opposite leg. For example, you would place the right foot on or against the left thigh, with the opposite leg extended (in this case the left leg). Now, pull the head to the extended knee, bending forward, holding the big toe of the outstretched leg with both hands. The ankle may also be held. Return to a sitting position and repeat with the opposite leg extended.

Benefits: Restores elasticity to the muscles, particularly the hamstring muscles. Makes the spine flexible, tones the abdomen and inner organs, and prevents sciatica. Relaxes and makes the mind more flexible. This is a good pose for diabetics.

LIZARD POSE
(Chatush-padasan)

Lie on your stomach. Spread the hands and feet apart at approximately a 45-degree angle from the center line of your spine. Inhale fully. Balance the body on the toes and the palms by

Lizard Pose

bringing the hands slightly back. The arms might have to be bent slightly to begin with. Hold, exhale, and rest. Repeat 2 to 6 times. This is an extremely difficult pose and should be mastered slowly over a long period of time.

Benefits: Makes the body strong, and increases the prana energy intake, purifying the blood and astral vehicle.

SHOOTING BOW
(Akarna-dhanurasan)

Sit on the floor with both legs extended. Grasp the right foot with the right hand, the left foot with the left hand. Pull the right foot up to the right ear, still holding the extended left foot with the left hand as it is positioned on the floor. Hold 1 to 3 seconds. Repeat with the left leg to the ear.

Benefits: Renders the hip joints supple; improves posture; tones legs.

Shooting Bow

HEAD-ON-KNEE POSE
(Utthita-jamushira-samyuktasan)

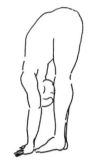

Head-On-Knee
Pose

This is a standing posterior stretch. Stand erect and bend forward from the waist. Place the palms on the floor so they are at a distance of approximately 1 foot from the toes. Exhale and touch the knees to the head as long as you comfortably can. Repeat 2 or 3 times.

Benefits: Improves digestion, reduces the abdomen, and makes the spine flexible.

HANUMAN POSE
(Hanuman-asan)

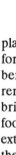

Hanuman
Pose

Stand straight with the feet placed together. Place the left leg forward about 3 feet. Inhale, bending the left leg as the left foot remains flat on the floor, and bring the chest forward. The right foot remains straight as it is extended behind you. Retaining the breath, raise the arms, bending them at the elbow, forming a trident position with the arms and head. Stand in this pose as long as you can retain the breath. Exhale, lowering the hands to the sides, bringing the left leg back, and resume a normal standing posture.

This posture is not repeated with the right foot forward. Only the left foot is brought forward, based on its symbolical relationship to the ida (feminine) astral currents predominating in the physical vehicle.

Benefits: The lungs and chest are developed. The body becomes healthy and the prana intake and storage is strongly increased.

BOW
(Dhanurasan)

Lying on the stomach, forehead on the floor, bend both of the knees and grasp the feet or ankles with the hands. Lift the thighs, head, and shoulders by pushing the feet away from the head at the same time you are pulling the hands toward the head, like a lever. It is easier if you lift the thighs first. Hold 1 to 3 seconds. Stretch 1 to 3 times.

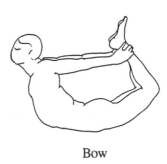

Bow

Benefits: Tones spinal nerves; helps remove or prevent constipation; strengthens lumbar and thoracic sections of the spine; improves posture. This is a general toner for the total body. It exerts great pressure on the spine and stomach, strengthening the vertebrae. The spine becomes more elastic. Releases trapped gases in the stomach, and relieves constipation and dyspepsia. The muscles and nerves of the shoulders, arms, hands, and thighs are benefited.

Warning: Those who suffer from heart disease or high blood pressure are warned not to attempt this posture without proper guidance from a qualified medical person.

NAVEL POSE
(Nadhi-asan)

Lie on your stomach. Stretch the hands out in front of you. Inhale, filling the lungs to capacity, and hold. Raise

Navel Pose

the legs, keeping the knees straight. Lift the arms and head, balancing at the navel. Keep this boat-like posture as long as you comfortably can. Exhale and resume a resting position.

Benefits: Cures indigestion and disorders of the stomach. Increases the efficiency of the spleen and liver.

ROCKING NAVEL POSE
(Rocking Nadhi-asan)

Rocking Navel Pose

Perform the navel pose described above, but rock in a seesaw rhythm as long as you comfortably can, holding the breath. Be sure the elbows and knees do not bend.

Benefits: Same as the navel pose but increases the benefits more quickly.

HALF-LOCUST POSE
(Ardha-salabhasan)

Half-Locust Pose

Lying on your stomach, chin to the floor, make fists with the hands and place them under the thighs. Spread the legs into a V-position and slowly raise the left leg as high as possible without bending the knee. Hold for a few seconds. Lower the left leg. Repeat the procedure using the right leg.

Benefits: Tones the stomach and back muscles. Fills the air sacs of the lungs, making them more elastic. Strengthens the thigh muscles; removes excess fat. Tones sympathetic nervous system.

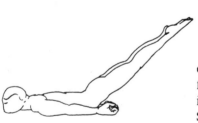

FULL-LOCUST POSE
(Salabhasan)

Full Locust Pose

Lying on the stomach, chin to the floor, make fists with the hands, placing them under the thighs. Spread legs in a V-position, slowly raising the legs as high as possible without bending the knees and hold for 2 seconds. To assist the lift, it might help to clasp the hands under the pelvic area and push down against the floor.

Benefits: Tones the stomach and back muscles; fills the air sacs of the lungs, making them more elastic; strengthens the thigh muscles; and removes excess fat. Tones sympathetic nervous system.

SOLES-ON-HEAD POSE
(Ditarita-pada-mastakastarshasan)

Lie face down, placing the palms next to the shoulders with elbows close to the body. Lift the head back and raise the upper part of the body, keeping the lower pelvis on the floor. , Bend the legs at the knees, lifting them off the floor and bringing the toes to touch the back of the head. This is an extremely difficult pose and should be developed slowly over a long period of time. It must not be rushed.

Soles-On-Head Pose

Benefits: Makes the body supple and buoyant and the spine elastic. Markedly activates the kriya kundalini by bringing the holy feet to the most holy part of the body: the thousand-petalled lotus, the head.

ARCH
(Setu-bandhasan)

Lie on your back, bend the knees, heels should be close to the hips, arms relaxed at the sides. Inhale, gently arch the back, making the body a slant board.

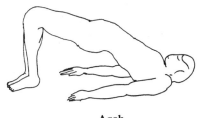

Arch

Now, contract the anal sphincter muscle. Be sure your shoulders are on the floor. As you maintain the position, hold the breath (without strain) and gently hold the anal contraction. Now exhale and lower the body slowly.

Benefits: Sends blood to the brain and reverses gravity's pull on the organs. The anal contraction stimulates gonadal strength and disperses the hormonal fluids throughout the body. Strengthens the spine and back muscles. Helps firm legs and thighs and tones abdominal organs.

SUPINE HERO
(Supta-vijrasan)

Supine Hero

Kneel on the floor and sit on your heels. Gently spread the feet so the buttocks come to the floor between the feet/heels. Supporting yourself with your elbows, gradually slide down so that your entire back rests on the floor. Hold 3 seconds. Lift to a sitting position. You may use your elbows again for support and then place hands on the floor and lift yourself back to the original kneeling position.

Variation: While the back rests on the floor in this pose you may also form the namaste mudra, placing the palms together, arms bent and hands brought to the chest at the heart level, fingers pointing to the ceiling.

Benefits: Excellent for menstrual disorders. Stretches the knees and feet; tones the thighs. It has all the advantages of the cow pose (gomukhasan). Also feet, palms, knees, thighs, stomach, waist, and neck become strong and healthy.

ASANS FOR AFFECTING THE MARS CHAKRA

WARM-UPS

Cock (or Balance Pose)
(Kukkutasan)
Fists-Balanced Pose
(Tolanglasan)
Parrot
(Shukasan)

FORWARD BENDING POSES

Reverse Pose
(Viparitakaranasan)

Peahen
(Mauri-asan)
Boat Pose
(Naukasan)

BACKWARD ARCHING POSES

Half-Wheel Pose
(Utthitardha-
chakrasan)
Wheel Pose
(Chakrasan)

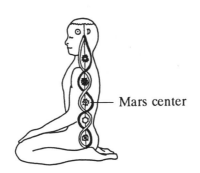

Mars center

AFFIRMATIONS FOR THE MARS CHAKRA

The following affirmations are to be utilized in the hold position of the mars chakra poses. These affirmations are not to be confused with mantras, covered in a later chapter.

1. I will keep depression from making me oppressive.

2. I will be spiritually worth more each day.

3. Steady persistent improvement is the basic law of nature.

4. I understand that trials temper temper.

5. If I am to rise higher, I must help others to unfold.

6. If I wish my consciousness to unfold, I must feed it, rest it, exercise it.

7. A diamond is beautiful. May I be a living diamond.

8. Water is easily eliminated, but most difficult to compress.

9. I will aspire to do useful work.

10. I will take inventory of this day for it will give me accurate understanding of what my work will be tomorrow.

POSTURE DESCRIPTIONS

COCK (BALANCE) POSE
(Kukkutasan)

Form the lotus posture. Take both hands and squeeze them between the back leg and the calf of each leg, as far in as possible, the right hand between the right calf and leg and left hand between the left calf and leg. By leaning backward, push and pull the arms so the legs are ultimately wrapped around them near the elbows. Then lean forward and lift. Now place the palms on the ground and balance your whole body with the two hands. Look forward and maintain this posture as long as you comfortably can.

Cock (Balance) Pose

Benefits: Strengthens the arms and chest. Improves the digestion as well as the function of the liver, removing excess fat in the hands and feet.

FISTS-BALANCED POSE
(Tolanglasan)

Sit in the lotus posture, making fists of the hands, and place them firmly under the back of the hips. Lean back and now balance the body on the fists you have just made. Stretch the knees forward and the head backward. Knees and the head must be at the same level so the body is a straight line parallel to the floor. Hold the breath in.

Fists-Balanced Pose

Benefits: Relieves constipation, keeps the stomach healthy, and strengthens the fingers.

PARROT
(Shukasan)

Sit on your heels and toes as in the lightning bolt pose, forcing the heels together. Place the palms firmly on the ground with the arms touching the outsides of the legs. Inhale, retaining the breath, and balance the body on the fingers in such a way that the pose looks like the form of a parrot.

Parrot Pose

Remain in this position for a few seconds. Repeat 2 different times.

Benefits: Muscles of the fingers and arms become strong.

REVERSE POSE
(Viparitakaranasan)

Lying on the back, slowly lift both legs up toward the ceiling. Tuck the chin into the chest. Continue to swing the legs up, supporting the back just under the hips with the hands, elbows on the floor. Hold for 1 second. Roll down

Reverse Pose

out of the pose, keeping the head and shoulders on the floor. Repeat 1 to 3 times.

Benefits: Tones the reproductive organs, clears the complexion, massages all the internal organs, and helps concentration.

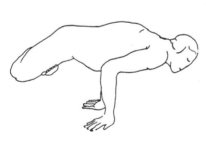

PEAHEN
(Mauri-asan)

This in effect is a lotus pose (padmasan) in the peacock position. It is sometimes called padmasan peacock. While extending and stretching the legs outward in the back, in the peacock position, a lotus posture is performed.

Benefits: Same as the pea-

Peahen Pose

cock, however, the benefits are developed more slowly.

The peacock pose: Kneel. Join your two arms together, resting hands on the floor, palms down, fingers pointing toward the toes. Bring the abdomen down against the elbows, which are supporting the body. Stretch the legs out in back of you. Inhale and raise both legs as you balance on the hands. The body is parallel to the floor.

BOAT POSE
(Naukasan)

Lie on your back. Inhale and raise the arms and head off the floor, keeping the palms close to each other with the thumbs intertwined. Now raise the legs above the ground, the same

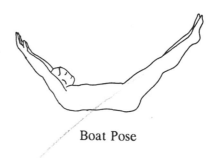

Boat Pose

distance as the arms have been raised so the body is a straight line parallel to the floor. Keep the knees and arms stiff and held together. This pose is held as long as the breath can be retained comfortably. Exhale as you return to a resting pose.

Benefits: This pose tones the large and small intestines; tones stomach and abdomen and strengthens lower back muscles.

HALF-WHEEL POSE
(Utthitardha-chakrasan)

Stand erect. Raise the arms above the head with the palms facing the ceiling, fingers pointing back. Exhale. Bend forward, inhaling. Then take the head and arms and swing them comfortably as far back as possible without bending the knees.

Benefits: Tones the liver, spleen, and intestines.

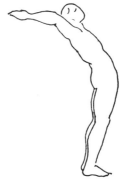

Half-Wheel Pose

WHEEL POSE
(Chakrasan)

Wheel Pose

Lying on your back, bend the knees, feet resting flat on the floor close to the hips. Hands should be brought up and placed at shoulder level, elbows up, palms flat on the floor, fingers pointing toward the feet (like a back-bend). Use the hands and feet to slowly push up. Hold 3 seconds. Slowly walk the feet and hands toward each other to perform the full wheel posture. Lower slowly. Do this posture only once.

Benefits: Tones the back and legs completely. Strengthens the stomach. Brings blood to the head. Strengthens and makes flexible the chest, back, stomach, and waist, as well as the neck, arms, hands, legs, knees, and feet. Gives excellent control over the body, making it agile and flexible. Prevents bad posture in old age. It tones the extremities.

ASANS AFFECTING THE VENUS CHAKRA

WARM-UPS

Child's Pose
  (Moodha-asan)
Mountain (or Hill)
  (Parbatasan)
Thigh Pose
  (Janu-asan)

FORWARD BENDING POSES

Right Prone Spinal Twist
  (Pingala Jathara
  -parivartanasan)
Crow Pose
  (Kakasan)

Heron Pose
  (Vakasan)
Swan Pose
  (Hansa-asan)
Crane Pose
  (Krounchasan)
Sri Mahavira Pose
  (Mahavira-asan)
Head-to-Knee Side Stretch
  (Parshvottanasan)
Black Bee Pose
  (Bhringasan)

BACKWARD ARCHING POSES

Bird Pose
  (Khagasan)

Left Prone Spinal Twist
  (Ida Jathara-
  parivartanasan)

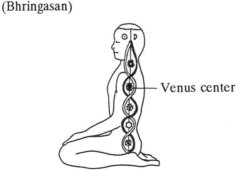

Venus center

AFFIRMATIONS FOR THE VENUS CHAKRA

The following affirmations are to be utilized in the hold position of the venus chakra poses. These affirmations are not to be confused with mantras, covered in a later chapter.

1. The ancients are reputed to be wise only because their contemporaries were so ignorant.

2. Poise is the power to keep the balance.

3. Adversity is often necessary to develop balance.

4. The difference between what we ought eat and what we eat is an education in and of itself.

5. I must back up my ideas or I will be a back number.

6. Anything that is truly mine can never be taken from me.

7. I will build and preserve that which is meaningful in life.

8. I will dig until I strike rock--then I will build.

9. When I think of self, I will prefix it with the word, higher.

POSTURE DESCRIPTIONS

CHILD'S POSE
(Moodha-asan)

Child's Pose

The child's pose is often considered a relaxation pose though it actively affects the organs and glands of the body. Sit in a kneeling position as in the lightning bolt pose with the feet flat on the floor, sitting on the buttocks. Allow the hands to relax alongside of your body keeping your head, neck, and trunk straight. Slowly bend forward from the hips so the stomach and chest rest on the thighs and the forehead is brought to the floor in front of the knees. As the forehead touches the floor, slide your arms, palms upward, so they rest comfortably alongside of you. Completely relax in this position.

This posture provides a resting position after postures that flex the spine backward and those that stimulate the thigh muscles. It is suggested as a resting pose after invigorating postures, particularly inverted poses such as the headstand, for it helps the body and blood flow to swiftly regain balance.

Benefits: Relieves lower back pain in the muscles and ligaments; relaxes the back muscles; massages the internal organs including the diaphragm and chest, bringing a fresh blood flow to them. Places pressure to the chest and lung area, assisting and stimulating the respiratory process; improves the complexion.

MOUNTAIN (OR HILL)
(Parbatasan)

Mountain
(Hill)

Variations of this posture are also described in the chapter on the stretching asans. This particular version is performed by sitting in the lotus posture. Holding the hands, palms together, raise arms over the head and lift the body so you are balanced on your knees--making sure the buttocks are lifted.

Benefits: Makes the spine flexible; stretches the rib cage, assisting in deeper and better breath control.

THIGH POSE
(Janu-asan)

Stand straight with the feet placed together. Place the left foot on the right thigh near the groin. The right arm goes over the right shoulder, the left arm goes behind the back, and the hands are joined by gripping the fingers. You now assume a half-sitting posture. Place your left knee either on the ankle of the right foot or on the ground. Repeat this posture by reversing the leg position.

Benefits: Removes the weakness of the calves and joints of the feet; tones thigh muscles; relieves tension in the shoulder and back area; promotes balance.

Thigh Pose

PRONE SPINAL TWIST
(Jathara-parivartanasan)

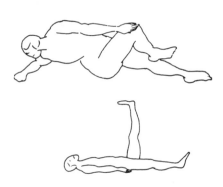

Lie on your back and lift the right knee to the forehead with both hands. Now, lift the head up to meet the knee. Return the head to the floor. Next, bring the right knee across the body to the floor on the left side with the left hand. Extend the right arm outward to the side, even with the shoulders, trying to keep the right shoulder and elbow down on the floor while you press the right knee to the floor on the opposite side with the left hand. Turn the head to look at the right hand. Release by again bringing your forehead to the right knee with both hands. Lower the head and lift the leg to a 90-degree angle. Then lower the leg to the floor as in the leg lift. Relax on your back. Repeat with the opposite side.

Prone Spinal Twist

This posture, like many of the postures, can be performed by bending or stretching to the left or right. When you are bending to the left, it is called the left prone spinal twist (ida jathara-pari-vartanasan). When this posture is performed by bending to the right, it is known as the right prone spinal twist (pingala jathara-parivartanasan).

Benefits: Assists the lumbar and pelvic areas, relaxes the neck, and helps prevent bursitis in the shoulders. Gives a gentle twisting motion to the torso, massaging the organs, especially the liver, stomach, and kidneys. Allows the life-force to flow without obstruction to the spine.

CROW POSE
(Kakasan)

Squat on the toes, keeping the knees apart. Rest hands firmly on the floor in front of you, elbows bent. Place one knee on the corresponding arm; ease the other knee up on the other corresponding arm, i.e., right knee to right arm, and left knee to left arm. The knees are placed on the upper arms. Hold as long as you can balance. (See related note under the swan pose.)

Crow Pose

Benefits: Improves concentration; strengthens wrists.

HERON POSE
(Vakasan)

Stand straight and bend from the waist, placing both palms on the ground (pointing ahead), bending the elbows slightly. As you bend the knees, place them on the upper part of each corresponding arm, as close into the armpits as possible. The feet should be in line with the elbows and below the hips. Balance the entire body on the arms. This posture

Heron Pose

should be held only for a few seconds, gradually increasing the duration. (See related note under swan pose.)

Benefits: Nerves and muscles of the arms are strengthened and the chest becomes quite strong.

SWAN POSE
(Hansa-asan)

Swan Pose

The swan pose is performed the same as the heron pose except the knees are placed outside the arms very close to the bent elbows. Stand straight and bend from the waist, placing both palms on the floor (pointing ahead), bending the elbows slightly. As you bend the knees, place them on the outsides of the arms very close to the bent elbows. Balance the entire body on the arms. This posture should be held only for a few seconds, gradually increasing the duration.

Benefits: The same as the heron. Enlarged tonsils are improved. Digestion is improved. The desire to eat is heavily softened.

Note: The three preceding postures (crow, heron, swan) all look the same. But close examination will reveal that the placement of the knees on the arms differs. In the crow, the legs/knees rest on the upper arms; in the heron, the legs/knees are in the armpits; in the swan the legs/knees are by the elbows on the outsides of the legs.

CRANE POSE
(Krounchasan)

Crane Pose

This posture is somewhat related to the crow, heron, and swan except while balancing in the pose the toes are brought to the wrists. Stand erect. Bend from the waist, placing both palms squarely on the floor. Place both knees on the elbows in such a way that the body is balanced on the hands. Bring the toes of both feet to rest near the wrists. Hold as long as you comfortably can.

Benefits: Strengthens the arms; broadens the chest. Improves the pranic energy ingestion and storage.

SRI MAHAVIRA POSE
(Mahavira-asan)

Stand erect and extend the right foot, bending the knee forward about 3 feet. The left leg is extended backward. Inhale and retain the breath. Clench the fists and bring them a little above the chest. Expand and stretch the chest. Remain in this pose as long as you comfortably can hold the breath. Repeat this pose with the left foot forward.

Sri Mahavira Pose

Benefits: Develops the chest; strengthens and improve the prana intake and its circulation. Invigorates lungs and arms. Prevents disorders caused by phlegm in the chest. The name of this asan suggests deep, mystical benefits.

HEAD-TO-KNEE SIDE STRETCH
(Parshvottanasan)

Stand erect, feet 12 inches apart, hands clasped behind the back. Inhale. Exhale and bend forward, bringing the head toward the left knee. Hold 1 to 3 seconds. Return to a standing position. Inhale and relax. Repeat to the right.

Benefits: Stretches and tones the entire leg; massages the liver and stomach; strengthens the back; improves complexion, hair, eyes, and mind.

Head-To-Knee
Side Stretch

BLACK BEE POSE
(Bhringasan)

Sit in the lightning bolt posture, knees wide apart, in a V-position. Inhale, holding the breath. Bend forward and place the chest on the knees and the elbows in front of you between the knees. Raise the head upward a little

Black Bee Pose

and inhale a maximum amount of air through the mouth. Retain the breath in a motionless pose as long as comfortable.

Benefits: Keeps the intestines healthy; prevents stomach disorders. It purifies the apana current, which is one of the key prana forces associated with the elimination organs of the body.

BIRD POSE
(Khagasan)

Bird Pose

Form the lotus posture and lie on the stomach. Fill the lungs fully, taking hold of the rib cage on both sides with your hands. Press the elbows as near together as possible above the back. Raise the head, neck, and chest from the ground without wobbling and sustain a hold as long as you are reasonably comfortable. When you can no longer hold the breath without strain, exhale and return to a normal position, lowering the head, neck, chest, and elbows, bringing the arms to the sides.

Benefits: The kidneys and intestines are massaged and cleansed. Urinary disorders are corrected.

ASANS AFFECTING THE MERCURY CHAKRA

WARM-UPS

Three-Lock Pose
(Tri-bandha-asan)
Shoulderstand Pose
(Sarvangasan)
Balanced Pose
(Tulasan)

FORWARD BENDING POSES

Back-Leaning Pose
(Poorvottanasan)
Knee-Pressing Ear Pose
(Karnapidasan)

Right Half-Spinal Twist
(Pingala Ardha-
matsya-indrasan)

BACKWARD ARCHING POSES

Bridge Pose
(Setu-bandhasan)
Left Half-Spinal Twist
(Ida Ardha-matsya-
indrasan)

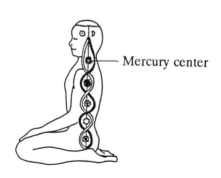

Mercury center

AFFIRMATIONS FOR THE MERCURY CHAKRA

The following affirmations are to be utilized in the hold position of the mercury chakra poses. These affirmations are not to be confused with mantras, covered in a later chapter.

1. Recreation means re-creation.

2. The mind, like a ship's nest, gives a long vision ahead--anticipate!

3. Similar causes produce similar results in the hands of similar people.

4. When in doubt, I must seek added information.

5. Self-expression makes for self-preservation.

6. I am a slave until I command my own time.

7. The secret of failure: the pestiest pest of all pesty pests is a pessimist.

8. What I am given by the world depends on what I give to the world.

9. What makes the world a better place to live in, begins within myself.

10. I receive the qualities that I give to another at the same time I give them.

POSTURE DESCRIPTIONS

THREE-LOCK-POSE
(Tri-bandha-asan)

Stand erect, keeping both feet together. Exhale, raising both arms over the head, grabbing hold of each elbow with the opposite hand. Simultaneously perform all three contractions (bandhas): the anal bandha, stomach bandha, and chin lock. Then stand on the toes and stretch the entire body upward while the arms remain on the head. The contractions are held as long as comfortable. Relax out of the pose. Repeat twice.

Benefits: Independent of increasing the height, it causes an intense regeneration and activation of stored prana. It reverses the degenerating forces of the body, producing renewed vitality and youthfulness.

Three-Lock Pose

SHOULDERSTAND POSE
(Sarvangasan)

This is an extension of the reverse posture. Lying on the back, slowly swing the legs to the ceiling. Tuck chin into the chest and continue to roll up the spine, supporting yourself high on the back with the hands, elbows on the floor. By placing the hands higher up the back toward the shoulders, you will achieve a straighter shoulderstand. The chin should be placed in the crevice of the neck to achieve a chin lock. Hold 1 second. To come out of the pose, first lower the legs somewhat behind the head (before bringing them forward out of the shoulderstand). Relax the hands and arms in front of you on the floor. Now slowly roll out on each vertebra, bringing

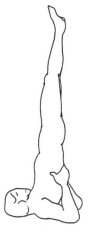

Shoulderstand Pose

the legs down, keeping them straight and close to the body. Keep the head and shoulders on the floor by slightly raising the chin upward. Repeat 1 to 3 times.

Benefits: The chin lock stimulates the thyroid gland to produce thyroxin. It reverses the pull of gravity on all the internal organs and removes congestion of the liver and spleen. Assists in curing constipation and piles; restores gonadal health and vitality; prevents varicose veins, and acts as a powerful blood purifier. It is the best posture for nourishing the brain, lungs, and heart. It strengthens eyesight and cures indigestion as well as chronic headaches and gastritis.

BALANCED POSE
(Tulasan)

Balanced Pose

Sit in the lotus posture (padmasan). Place the palms forward on the ground to the left and right of the thighs. Place the weight on your fingers and palms and gently lift the body. This posture is maintained only a few seconds to begin with, gradually increasing the duration of the hold.

Benefits: Strengthens the arms, palms, chest, and shoulders. Helps the cleansing of the stomach and intestinal tract.

HALF-SPINAL TWIST
(Ardha-matsya-indrasan)

Half-Spinal Twist

Sit on the floor with both legs extended. Bending the right knee, place the right foot across the left knee so it is resting on the floor on the outside of the left knee. Support yourself with the right hand on the floor behind you, arm straight. Place the left arm on the outside of the right knee and grasp the right ankle with the left hand. Inhale, and as you exhale, push the left elbow against the outside right knee to help twist your body to the right.

Keep the hips straight, turning the torso and head.   Hold 3 seconds, return to the center and relax. Reverse and stretch to the opposite side.

This posture, like many of the postures, can be performed by bending or stretching to the left or to the right. When you bend to the left, it is called the left half-spinal twist (ida ardha-matsya-indra). When you bend to the right, it is called the right half-spinal twist (pingala ardha-matsya-indra).

Benefits: Keeps the spine elastic, tones the spinal nerves, prevents lumbago and muscular rheumatism of the back. Good for constipation and dyspepsia.

BACK-LEANING POSE
(Poorvottanasan)

Lie on your back, keeping the knees, heels, and toes of both legs together. Place the hands at the sides, palms down, raising the legs back over the head--exactly as in the plough position. Touch

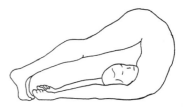

Back-Leaning Pose

the floor with the toes while the legs remain straight with the knees locked.   Stretch the arms back over the head and hold the toes with the corresponding hand, that is, right hand to right toe, left hand to left toe. Push the legs back over and away from the head far enough so the chin touches the chest.

Benefits: Considerable pressure is exerted on the upper part of the body, particularly the neck, chest, and shoulders.   These therefore become extremely elastic. The blood is purified.   The lungs and heart are properly cleansed. This produces a steadying of the mind, and senility is delayed or defeated.

KNEE-PRESSING-EAR POSE
(Karnapidasan)

Go into the plough position. Bend the knees, pressing them against the ears, keeping the hands straight and either extend-ed flat on the ground behind you or extended out to their sides even with the shoulders.

Knee-Pressing Ear Pose

Benefits: The ears, neck, waist, and back are strengthened. Hearing is improved. Disorders of the spleen, liver, and digestion are cured. The spinal cord is strengthened and becomes more flexible. This is a technique for overcoming obesity.

BRIDGE POSE
(Setu-bandhasan)

Bridge Pose

Perform the shoulder-stand pose and hold your weight firmly with both hands supporting the back. With hands on the back, keep the back arched. The back does not touch the floor in this pose. Now, slowly lower the legs and place the feet on the floor. The waist must be kept arched off the floor to look like a bridge. The chin should be placed in the crevice of the neck. Do this posture only when ready.

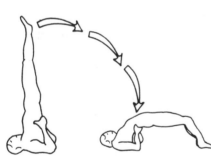

Movement from the shoulderstand to the bridge pose.

Variation: A modified and simpler version of the bridge is performed by going into the pose from a lying position rather than from the shoulderstand. Lie on the back. Bending knees, lift the lower part of the body and arch the back upward, placing the hands above the waist, assuming the bridge position. The chin should be in the crevice of the neck as in the shoulderstand posture.

Benefits: Regular practice makes the spine more flexible and strong, improving digestion and curing intestinal disorders. Reduces abdomen and prevents backaches. Regulates the thyroid and parathyroid glands.

ASANS FOR AFFECTING
THE SUN AND MOON CHAKRAS

THE POSTURES

The Meditative Poses

Prosperous Pose
   (Swastikasan)
Easy·Pose
   (Sukhasan)
Celibate Pose
   (Guptasan)
Zen Pose
   (Vajrasan)
Lotus Pose
   (Padmasan)

Locked Lotus
   (Baddha-padmasan)

Frog Pose
   (Mandukasan)
Sage Goraksha Pose
   (Gorakshasan)
Adept Pose
   (Siddhasan)
Union Pose
   (Yogasan)
Cow pose
   (Cow-faced Pose)
   (Gomukhasan)

The Other Poses

Headstand
   (Shirshasan)
Sage Dhruva Pose
   (Dhruva-asan)
Tripod Headstand
   (Vrikshasan)
Palm-Stand Pose
   (Hasta-shirshasan)
Lotus Head Pose
   (Padma-shirshasan)
Spiritual Prostration Pose
   (Sash-tan-gadan-dawatasan)

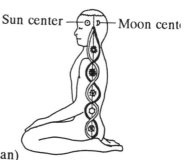

Sun center — Moon cent‹

For a complete description of the meditative poses, see the chapter on meditative postures.

You will note that with this series there are no forward and backward bending poses. Each is in a state of equilibrium or balance. This is what the sun chakra (ajna chakra) and the moon chakra (chandra chakra) symbolize.

AFFIRMATIONS FOR THE SUN AND MOON CHAKRAS

The following affirmations are to be utilized during the sun chakra and moon chakra poses. These affirmations are not to be confused with mantras, covered in a later chapter.

THE SUN

1. The sun is the keystone of my existence.

2. An optimistic atmosphere helps take the place of sunshine in the winter months.

3. Be as wise as the sunflower: face the light!

4. The best place to develop leadership is right where I am.

5. A plant absorbs the sunshine by day and builds it into its life by night.

6. If you don't like your heredity, do better by your posterity.

7. Fear is ignorant; caution is intelligent; therefore, daily, I transmute my fears into cautions!

8. I will not tax myself with trifles.

9. The greater my sorrows, the more valuable my smiles.

10. Ability, reliability, and ambition form a grand trine.

THE MOON

1. The moon is the keystone to my subjective, inward existence.

2. The moon shines by the light of the sun.

3. A plant absorbs the sunshine by day and builds it into its body by night.

4. The greater my sorrows, the more valuable my smiles.

POSTURE DESCRIPTIONS

HEADSTAND
(Shirshasan)

Use a corner of the room where no objects are.   A pad for the head is suggested. Kneel.   Interlock the fingers, placing the hands on the floor.   Form a triangular base with the forearms. Bring the head into the cupped hands by leaning forward and placing them at the back of the head. Be sure that both elbows are flat on the floor. Now begin by lifting the hips, bringing the feet to the floor and walking forward, feet toward the head. Because the head is cupped in the hands on the floor, walking will bring the body into a vertical position. Be sure that the neck is not bent. When the trunk of the body is vertical, lift the legs. Here use the back muscles to help lift the legs upward. Don't kick. Absorb pressure on the arms and elbows so that little weight is on the head. Hold 3 to 4 seconds. Return to the floor. Relax in the pose of the child and then in the total relaxation pose (sava). Be sure to exercise the neck before and after.

Headstand

In the initial stages of the headstand you may practice near a wall until you gain security in holding the pose; then continue to practice the pose without the wall. It is important not to become too dependent on the wall.

Do not do the headstand if you have high or low blood pressure, weak eye capillaries, are overweight, or have constrictions in your neck and shoulders.

Benefits: Increases circulation to the brain, improving concentration.   Reverses the pull of gravity on all the internal organs. Prevents varicose veins.   Helps in curing neurasthenia by stimulating the brain and nerves; assists the removal of asthma, hernia, lymphatic disorders; reverses the aging effects; nourishes the hair follicles.

SAGE DHRUVA POSE
(Dhruva-asan)

Sage Dhruva
Pose

Stand erect.   Bend the right knee, placing the right foot on the left thigh near the groin with the sole upturned.   Bring palms together to the chest near the heart chakra forming the namaste mudra.   This is also called spiritual gesture (pronam mudra). This posture has been used for thousands of years by yogis as they stand on the banks of the Ganges River chanting the OM-kar, Gayatri, or ishta mantra.   (See the chapter on mantra.)

Benefits: This   posture   vitalizes   one's body and mind.   It keeps one from becoming lazy.

TRIPOD HEADSTAND
(Vrikshasan)

Tripod
Headstand

Differing from the standard headstand, the tripod headstand is performed by supporting yourself while resting on the palms instead of the forearms. Kneel with the tops of the toes against the floor and buttocks on the heels in the lightning bolt pose.   Place the palms on the floor in front of you, approximately 6-12 inches apart, in line with the knees.   Lower the head to the floor, placing it somewhat above the hands so the head and hands form a triangle.   Then pushing with bent toes, raise the feet and entire body upward with help from the back muscles.   Stretch the length of the body upward like a staff.   Balance equally on the palms and head, but press with the arms so the majority of the weight of the body is on the palms, not the head.   Maintain this posture motionless for as long as comfortably possible.

This posture can also be done by forming the tripod stance with the head and palms as described above and then pushing with the toes, raising the feet and bringing the knees smoothly to the elbows. Then with the help of the back muscles, lift the knees off the elbows, extending the body into the headstand.

Benefits: Beneficial to the head, neck, chest, eyes, and heart. Blood circulation to the head and lung area is markedly improved. Improves digestion and helps control the sexual drive. Prohibits the hair from turning prematurely grey.

PALM-STAND POSE
(Hasta-shirshasan)

Stand erect, bend forward, placing the palms in front of you approximately 1-1/2 feet apart. Place the legs over the head with the feet firmly held together, toes pointing toward the sky. In our western tradition this is known as a handstand.

Benefits: Yogis believe this posture has more benefits than even the headstand because the circulation of the blood increases, and it is the blood that purifies the body. The face and eyes acquire a spiritual luster. Prevents colds and coughing; relieves indigestion and headache. It nourishes the brain and enhances the strength of the arms as well as the mind's sense of psychological balance.

Palm-Stand
Pose

LOTUS HEAD POSE
(Padma-shirshasan)

Perform the lotus posture (padmasan) and enter into either a standard headstand (resting on the head and forearms) or the tripod headstand (resting on the head and palms) by placing the head and forearms (standard headstand) or head and palms (tripod headstand) on the ground and raising the body. This pose should not be held for more than approximately 2 minutes. It can also be done in the reverse way, i.e., going into either type of headstand and then forming the lotus pose while in the inverted position.

Lotus
Head Stand

Benefits: Head, eyes, and chest become strong.   Digestion is markedly improved.   Constipation is relieved.   Colds are cured and/or prevented.

SPIRITUAL PROSTRATION POSE
(Sash-tan-gadan-dawatasan)

Spiritual
Prostration Pose

Lie on your stomach and stretch your arms fully over the head, crossing one wrist over the other so that you touch the guru's left foot with your left hand and his right foot with your right hand.   The spiritual prostration pose is also utilized in showing spiritual respect.

Benefits: This pose is used in paying respect to spiritual preceptors and holy people.   It engenders humility, softening arrogance, and enhances respect and devotion.

ASANS FOR AFFECTING
ALL THE CHAKRAS AT THE SAME TIME

WARM-UPS

Yoga Push-Up (Crocodile)
(Makasan)

FORWARD BENDING
POSES

Moving Crocodile
    (Moving Makasan)
Plough
    (Halasan)
Right Spinal Twist
    (Pingala Matsy-indrasan)
Peacock
    (Mayurasan)

BACKWARD ARCHING
POSES

Fish
    (Matsyasan)
Left Spinal Twist
    (Ida Matsy-indrasan)
Scorpion
    (Vrishchikasan)

AFFIRMATIONS FOR ALL THE CHAKRAS

The following affirmations are to be utilized in the hold position of each of the following poses. These affirmations are not to be confused with mantras, covered in a later chapter.

1. I am health, vim, vigor, and vitality.

2. Every day, in every way, I am becoming more and more vigorous.

3. My body and my mind are strengthened daily.

4. Each day I realize the difference between dynamic force and tension.

5. My body is a totality; so is my spiritual life and my earth life.

POSTURE DESCRIPTIONS

YOGA PUSH-UP
(CROCODILE)
(Makasan)

This posture is some-
times referred to as the
crocodile pose. Lie on your
stomach with legs stretched
backward and support them
on bent toes, heels upward.

Yoga Push-up

Then place the hands alongside and in line with the shoulders,
palms resting on the floor, elbows bent and close to the body,
forehead on the floor. Inhale and lift the body a few inches off the
floor, resting your entire weight on the palms (pressure on the
wrists) and toes. The length of the body from head to heels should
be lifted equidistant and parallel to the floor. In lifting, be careful
not to thrust the buttocks higher than the rest of the body. In this
raised position the body should be stiff and rigid as a steel bar or
tree trunk. The anal contraction (mula bandha) and stomach
contraction (uddiyana bandha) are also performed as you go into
and hold this posture.

Benefits: The entire body is exercised. Causes extensive perspiration which should be rubbed back into the body. Circulation
is quickened and the body and bloodstream are highly purified. It
also strengthens the arms, fingers, legs, stomach, and feet.

MOVING CROCODILE
(Moving Makasan)

Perform the yoga pushup
or crocodile. (See full description above.) Keeping
the body stiff, walk or jump
about. This is a very ad-
vanced moving asan.

Moving Crocodile

Benefits: In general this
is an excellent asan for invigorating the entire body. It increases
the blood circulation, purifying it. The benefits are the same as the
crocodile, however it also tones and strengthens the calves, arms,
chest, and pectoral region.

PLOUGH
(Halasan)

Lying on your back, slowly lift the legs to the ceiling and continue to swing them over and behind the head, toes resting on the floor. The chin is tucked into the chest. Hands and arms are flat on the floor,

Plough

palms down, pointing away from the body. Hold 1 second. Roll out of the pose the same as in the shoulderstand, keeping the shoulders and arms on the floor, lowering the spine, vertebra by vertebra, keeping the legs close to the body as you lower them to the floor. Repeat 1 to 3 times.

Benefits: Most effective of all postures in bringing elasticity to the spine, especially in the neck and upper back, which in turn maintains youthfulness, develops abdominal muscle tone, and assists in curing dyspepsia. Relieves constipation. The spinal nerves and muscles of the back are toned. Improves circulation, increases the appetite, and improves the digestive power. Reduces obesity and relieves backaches, improving or curing any intestinal weaknesses.

SPINAL TWIST
(Matsy-indrasan)

Sit on the floor, legs extended. Bending the right knee, put right heel under the perineum, left foot on the floor across the right knee, right arm on the outside of the left knee, right hand grasping the left foot or ankle. Left hand and arm are wrapped around and behind the waist, hand toward the opposite thigh. Now turn and

Spinal Twist

look over the left shoulder. Exhale and turn further. Feel the twist in the entire torso, especially in the waist and neck. Push right elbow against the outside of the left knee as you hold the pose to help you turn further. Hold 3 seconds. Repeat with the opposite side.

This posture, like many of the postures, can be performed by bending or stretching to the left or right. When you are bending to the left, it is called the left spinal twist (ida matsy-indrasan); when this posture is performed by bending to the right, it is called the right spinal twist (pingala matsy-indrasan).

Benefits: Helps cure congestion of the liver and spleen. Assists the kidneys, massages the internal organs, helps cure rheumatism of the back, prevents constipation. Assures flow of insulin from the pancreas; strengthens the lower back, allaying lower back pain.

PEACOCK
(Mayurasan)

Kneel. Join the two arms together, resting hands on the floor, palms down, fingers pointing toward the toes. Curving the fingers up helps in balancing. Keep the hands firm. Bring the abdomen down

Peacock Pose

against the elbows, which are supporting the body. Stretch the legs out in back of you. Inhale and raise both of the legs from the floor as you balance on the hands. Either hold the legs parallel to the floor or lower the forehead and lift the legs upward.

Benefits: Excellent for strengthening stomach muscles, wrists, and shoulders. As the elbows press within the abdomen, circulation to the internal organs is increased, improving digestive abilities. The abdominal viscera are toned and the chest and thoracic cavity are strengthened. This is a good pose for persons with diabetes as it gently massages the spleen. Aids in eliminating toxins from the body. In general this is an excellent pose for invigorating the entire body.

FISH POSE
(Matsyasan)

Sit cross-ankled, grasp toes, push down on the elbows as you lie back and slide the top of the head to the floor. A mat is suggested. Arch the body, the chest in particular. Let the knees drop as close to the floor as pos-

Fish Pose

sible (usually only one knee can touch the floor at first). Feel relaxed. Breathe deeply.

Easier variation: Keep legs outstretched placing the palms on the floor under the small of the back at the hip area as the back and neck are arched into the fish position. Use the elbows to lift the body en-

Fish Pose
(Variation)

abling the top of the head to slide to the floor.

Benefits: Stretches the thoracic cavity; stimulates the trachea and larynx and improves speaking and singing voice. Sends rich blood supply to the brain, improving mental acuity. Prevents constipation. Tones and relieves mental tensions. Renders knee and ankle joints flexible. Cures disorders of the stomach. Strengthens trunk and legs.

SCORPION POSE
(Vrishchikasan)

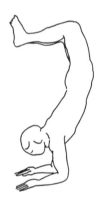

Kneel. Bend forward and place the forearms on the floor, palms down. Press on the floor with the forearms and swing the legs up and straighten them somewhat. As you perfect this pose, the legs will be straighter. Keep the head above the floor and balance yourself.

Benefits: Tones all the muscles in the spine. Increases circulation. Increases the strength of the arms. Makes the spinal cord elastic. Helps overcome laziness. Prevents disorders of the kidneys, liver, spleen, and stomach.

Scorpion Pose

Chapter 8

SALUTATION TO THE SUN
(SURYA-NAMASKAR)

The salutation to the sun is a sequence of twelve poses that are practiced in a flowing movement. Here are the steps:

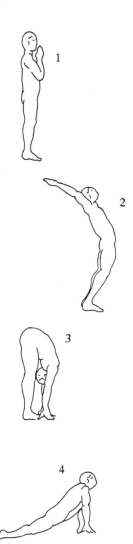

1. Stand erect facing east. Join the palms together forming the namaste gesture. Place the feet and heels together and inhale.
2. Release the hands, raising the arms upwards, and at the same moment bend backward from the waist. The legs should remain straight.
3. Now bend forward placing the palms on the floor at the outsides of the feet. The thumbs should be in a straight line with the toes. The legs should remain straight and the head should touch the knees. Heels must remain close together and on the ground. In the initial stages, the knees can be slightly bent if you are unable to keep them straight, but as soon as possible the legs should be kept straight, making a standing posterior stretch. (Note: when the hands are lowered to the floor in step 3, they are to remain in that same position until step 11).
4. Next, place your right foot back as far as possible, bottom of the toes touching the ground. The palms remain in position as above while doing the next step (5). Keep the chest erect and the head slightly tilted back. Gaze upward toward the sky.

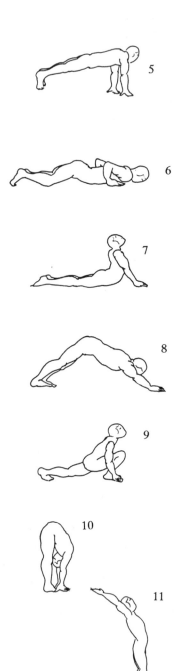

5. Take the left foot and bring it back, placing it close to the right foot. The toes of both feet are bent, and the knees are off the floor. Keep toes, heels, and knees together. The neck and head should remain in alignment, somewhat like the crocodile pose, except the body is raised higher, and the arms are straight. The weight of the body is on the toes and arms, rather than on the toes and wrists. Continue gazing upward.

6. Bend your knees and touch the floor with the knees first, then the chest, then the forehead in a sweeping motion. The pelvic and stomach areas do not touch the floor. The toes and hands remain on the floor.

7. Lower the abdomen and then the pelvis to the floor, moving into the cobra pose. The head is arched back and the feet have changed position so the insteps (tops of the feet) are now on the floor.

8. Keeping the hands/palms on the floor, raise your body from the waist and place the heels on the floor, stretching the waist backward and up so that the body forms a V-shape.

9. Bring the right foot forward and place it between the palms, keeping the left leg straight. The neck and head are raised, gazing upward. Arch the back at the waist.

10. Bring the left foot next to the right in such a way that the palms are in line with the feet. Keeping the legs straight, bend forward from the waist, placing the head to the knees.

11. Raise the hands off the floor, swinging them up alongside of the head and arch backward from the waist, as the legs remain straight. This is the same position as in step 2.

12. Straighten the body, bringing the head to an erect position. Now lower the arms to the sides and assume a normal standing position and assume the namaste mudra. (In step 12, the feet should occupy the same place on the floor as in step 1. Keeping this in mind will help you ease from one position into the other position. Glide from one position to another without extraneous movements or shifting).

To derive maximum benefit from the salutation to the sun, perform all 12 positions with the breath, or use the following alternating breathing pattern:

Position 1: exhale
Position 2: inhale
Position 3: exhale
Position 4: inhale
Position 5: exhale
Position 6: inhale
Position 7: HOLD
Position 8: exhale
Position 9: inhale
Position 10: exhale
Position 11: inhale
Position 12: exhale

Also, repeat this salutation 5 to 15 times to derive maximum benefit.

Benefits: The body becomes strong and vibrant. The twelve poses exercise the entire body, including all the organs. The arms and legs become flexible and symmetrical.

Mystical benefits: Awakens the kriya kundalini producing visional states of meditation.

At the hold points in this salutation, the mantra: OM SRI SAVITUR VA-NAMAH is to be mentally recited with reverence. (See chapter on mantra for further clarification.)

You will find the salutation to the sun illustrated, which will make understanding easy.

SALUTATION TO THE SUN

Chapter 9

SALUTATION TO THE MOON
(CHANDRA-NAMASKAR)

The salutation to the moon is a sequence of twelve poses that are practiced in a continuous flowing movement. These are the steps:

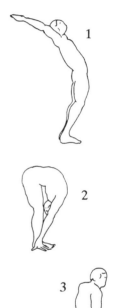

1. Standing upright with feet approximately 12 inches apart, bring the arms and hands over the head and bend backwards from the waist into forming a standing half-wheel. (This position is the same as position 2 in the salutation to the sun).

2. Keeping the legs straight, swing the arms down, creating a half-circle motion and place the hands, palms down, at the sides of the feet. The head rests on the knees, forming the standing posterior stretch. (This position is the same as position 3 in the salutation to the sun).

3. Bring your left leg back as far as possible, the side of the ankle touching the ground. Simultaneously bring the right leg forward, bending the right knee forward so the entire weight of the body is resting on the toes of the right foot. Now, lift the right heel off the floor, lowering the body so the buttocks rest on the heel. The hands, palms down, are kept on the sides of the right foot.

4. Stand up, and in a flowing movement switch the position of the legs. Bringing the right leg backward, touch the base of the toes to the floor, toes bent. You should now be supporting yourself on the left foot and right knee, in a half-kneeling position. Bend the

left foot forward slightly. Then lift the upper part of the body, raising the arms along the sides of the head, stretching them upward. Stretch the chest forward into a curve, as in the Hanuman pose.

5. Place both hands in front of you on the floor and with the toes bent, bring your left foot backwards alongside the right foot and perform danda. That is, sit on the heels with the toes bent and then lean forward with the palms resting on the floor. Then lift the chest and upper part of your body forward as in the cobra pose. The toes remain bent and the hips are lifted up off the heels while the heels remain on the floor.

6. Now, bend the left foot forward so the weight of the body is on the toes of the left foot, bringing your right foot backward. Keep your hands on the floor alongside the left foot. (This is the same idea but opposite leg as in step 3).

7. Now, stand up and again in a flowing movement, switch the position of the legs; the same idea but opposite leg as in step 4. Bring the left leg backward, touching the base of the toes to the floor with toes bent. You should be supporting yourself at this point on the right foot and the left knee which is in a half-kneeling position. Now lift the upper part of the body, raising the head and stretching the chest forward, making fists of both hands, and raise the arms along the sides of the head, the thumbs pointing toward each other. Bend the head slightly back.

8. Place the hands alongside of the right foot. Extend the body forward and bring the right foot back to meet the left foot with the toes bent to the floor. Stretch the upper part of the body forward to assume a pose similar to the full cobra pose. However, the arms are straight and the weight of the weight of the body should be on the toes and palms.

9. Place both knees on the ground. Bend the legs back, bringing the body back until your hips are resting on your heels, in a sitting position. The toes are bent and supporting the body. Bend forward to touch the ground with the head. The arms are outstretched and the hands and palms are on the floor over the head.

10. Again, place the buttocks on the heels with toes bent and raise the arms alongside the head, bending them back as far as possible.

11. Place the palms on the ground and jump to bring the feet between the hands. Sit erect, putting the weight on the toes.

12. Stand erect with the hands in namaste mudra.

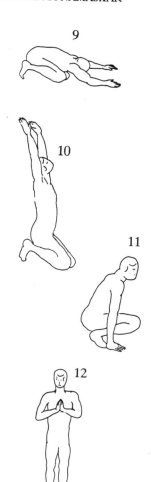

The salutation to the moon should be performed 5 to 15 times.

Benefits: The entire body is exercised, making it healthy, symmetrical, and vibrant. Digestion is improved.

Mystical benefits: Awakens the kriya kundalini and produces visional states in meditation.

At the hold points of the salutation to the moon, the mantra: OM SRI MAHA-CHANDRA VA-NAMAH should be recited mentally with reverence. (See chapter on mantra for further clarification).

On the following page you will find the moon salutation illustrated which will make its understanding easy.

SALUTATION TO THE MOON
(Chandra-Namaskar)

Chapter 10

MEDITATIVE POSES

ATTENTION WITHOUT TENSION

In practicing the meditative poses, you seek a feeling of stillness, quietude, essential firmness, and foundation. In all the yoga asans, but particularly in the meditative poses, you must establish motionlessness. Reaching that stillness of the meditative pose, the mind penetrates into your superconscious.

The feeling of stillness attained in a meditative posture will penetrate to the depths of your being. When this occurs, there is a mystical click, and you then become aware you have moved deeply within yourself. You now know that you are in a meditative state, and not just day-dreaming.

The meditative postures begin with rendering the body motionless. To establish this same motionlessness internally, there can be no stress or strain of any kind. There is a need to practice the yoga asans, otherwise you will be thinking, 'My knees hurt... My spine needs to be stretched a little more... My back hurts... ' If there is any body awareness in a meditative pose, then the stillness of the posture has not penetrated into the center of your being. Body awareness indicates you have not relaxed into the posture, and thus it has not yet become a meditative pose. In the meditative pose there must be absolute attention, without any tension! When you attain absolute attention without physical or mental tension, there is loss of body awareness. This loss does not produce a state of unconsciousness, but rather a total concentration on the mind state. As long as you are in body awareness, there is an outgoing tendency of the mind. This generates a need to move the body, to feed it, or to do something with it. When you transcend body awareness, you move into pure awareness of the mind state. This is the land of milk and honey wherein spiritual things happen and karma is softened.

This centering is called attaining the shanti principle. In western tradition it's achieving internal peace and quietude. This is achieved when you are peaceful to the core of your being. Here, there is a unification of the physical and mental into consciousness, creating a state of balanced, centered awareness, wherein exists tranquility, harmony, and equanimity. It is from this principle that the ancient science of kriya yoga was developed.

We must be unified in thought, word, and action, with what we are truly feeling, whether it is living our lives as students, teachers, parents, or lovers. The unification of the external and internal is somewhat similar to playing a musical composition, as the composer felt it when he wrote it. It is not playing the music letter perfect, as it was written. Notes are only a map to the higher consciousness of the composer's mind. Music is playing the music from the core of your being, feeling the composer's feelings. So likewise, life must be played out, feeling the Composer's Feelings. Understand?

This unification means moving beyond the externals, and moving beyond actions, words, emotions, thoughts, and moving to the feeling state. The feeling state is the precursor of all else. Therefore, when you move into a meditative posture, you are to move beyond the body and mind stillness and find the harmonious balance of your entire being. Enter into meditation.

One of the major problems in life is the Gemini complex which symbolizes the duality of our life. In psychology, it is called ambivalence. This duality is expressed as not knowing who or what we are, nor what we truly want. The problem is not this duality, but the continual bouncing back and forth between the extremes. One minute we want this, the next minute we want that. Few of us ever truly make up our minds. This duality manifests because of the nature of your mind and your body. Each is trying to gain its own wish.

Until this unified state of awareness is realized you will just scatter your energies and not make much progress. Wherever you may be, or however you see yourself, success and attainment begin with this unified meditative state. This also brings about an expansion beyond what and where you are, beyond something greater than you conceive yourself to be.

The common problem is that we think in the same breath, 'I would like a college education... I would like to teach... Wouldn't it be great to get married?... I'll go to Europe next year... I want cosmic consciousness... I want a new car...' All these desires are scattered, Gemini-fashion, throughout your lower being. Each desire is going in a different direction. Soon, you are so bound up in these scattered energies that you are going nowhere. Even when you begin moving in one direction, you are not truly happy because your heart is emotionally linked to many other things and directions. From this perspective, the secret of beginning yoga is to ask yourself, 'Who and what am I?' Finding this answer, you must become one person so that you can move on to truly find the higher Self.

The meditative poses are a way of settling down all these energies. These energies are called desires or karmas. When they are quieted, you become aware of who and what you are. The meditative poses make this attainment very easy. This is accomplished in two stages:

1. You become aware of all your needs, desires, or karmas. Your strongest or most intense piece of karma is revealed to you. You become aware of which direction your desires are taking you.
2. However, there is a realization that you do not have to follow the direction of those strong desires. You do not have to be controlled by your desires or karmas; rather, you can and should control them.

This concept can be illustrated. There are doctors, who knew from the age of seven that they must become doctors. These persons find very little joy in doctoring, because they are driven by something. That something is a subconscious craving. It is karma. On the other hand, there are those who throughout medical school are never sure they want to become doctors. They do not feel they must become doctors. Rather, they consciously choose the direction of their career. In this choosing, they find great satisfaction. It is important to distinguish between these two, for they represent the two types of people. Those who find joy in what they are doing, and those who are compelled. By knowing and understanding the feelings within yourself, you can be free of your desires, not being forced to go in their direction. Life is about choosing, rather than being forced.

When the myriad energies of your desires settle down, then you can choose without compulsion, for you have brought about a resolution of the duality within your being. This is what meditation is all about. The meditative poses are essential for reaching this state of balance, for it is the final state of unification of the body-mind complex. In this state lies the shanti principle, the peace and harmony principle. The final process of yoga is found in the utilization of the meditative postures.

GUIDE TO PERFORMING THE MEDITATIVE POSES

1. It is vital that a special area in your home be set aside for the practice of the meditative poses. The area should be free from drafts. The use of lightly-scented incense, flower fragrances such as rose, jasmine, or sandalwood, will greatly help create a tranquil mood. Music should not be played during your meditation time. A special rug or blanket (traditionally made of wool) is used. It should be used exclusively for this purpose. This establishes your own vibration into the meditation mat. Other suggestions will be given in the chapter on meditation.

2. Wear comfortable, loose-fitting clothing which does not bind or cut off your circulation, especially to the limbs, waist, and neck. If you wear trousers, care should be taken to avoid an over-accumulation of cloth in the underside of the thigh and knee area, as it will produce an undesirable tourniquet effect. It's best to wear little or no clothing.

3. Begin with some relaxation techniques and stretching exercises, like total relaxation, neck rolls, rocking chair, leg bounces, and so forth. The stretch-lift is utilized prior to going into any pose, to align the spine.

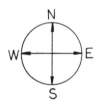

4. Historically, the meditational poses are performed facing east during the daylight hours. After sunset, you face north toward the polar star. This allows you to orient yourself to the center of your universe.

These two symbols, the horizon of light and the north pole, are symbolic of the sun center (ajna chakra), which is the point of balance within your being. In Biblical symbolism, this point is referred to as the single eye.

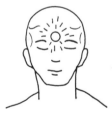

Eyes gently focussed at the sun center

5. The eyes are either completely closed or half-closed, called unmani mudra. The attention is gently focused upward, at the sun center, between the eyebrows at the root of the nose. This will cause your awareness to be centered within your consciousness. Be sure there is no furrowing of the brow caused by stress or strain. At first, the eyes can be completely closed, removing external distractions.

6. All meditative poses are formed in one of two ways. The masculine position (surya) is formed when the right leg is on top thereby activating the solar force. The feminine position (chandra) is formed when the left leg on top, activating the lunar force. All meditative poses should be practiced in both positions in order to balance both sides of your being. Start with the feminine position first. If one position is more uncomfortable, this indicates which side is lacking in energy (prana). This pose needs to be practiced more often, so as to strengthen it. The uncomfortable position should be practiced more extensively. When the flow of energy is equal, there is no discernible difference of tension. Women should begin with the sun position; men should begin with the moon position.

7. While performing a meditative pose, the anal contraction (mula bandha) and the stomach contraction (uddiyana bandha) should be utilized. These bandhas assist the release and the lifting of the kriya kundalini life-force. Also, when doing pranayama, use the chin lock, when holding the breath.

8. If your knees or ankles become stiff while in one of the meditative poses, gently come out of the pose, extending the legs in front of you. Place the hands on the knees, and alternately bounce the legs gently against the floor. This relieves tension in the joints and prevents cramping of the calf and thigh muscles. You now resume the meditative pose.

   If there is a tightening or stiffness felt at the small of the back, perform total relaxation (savasana) for relief. Usually one does not go into total relaxation when moving from one meditative pose to another.

9. At first, meditative poses are held for only a short time. Gradually, increase the period from 1 to 9 minutes. Later you can work up to 48 minutes. Historically, students do not practice meditative poses for longer than 3 hours.

10. Meditative poses are practiced 3 hours after eating. This allows you to achieve maximum benefits from the poses.

    The following are the key meditative poses.

    1. Prosperous Pose (Swastikasan)
    2. Easy Pose (Sukhasan)
    3. Celibate Pose (Guptasan)
    4. Lightning Bolt (Vajrasan)
    5. Lotus Pose (Padmasan)
    6. Locked Lotus (Baddha-padmasan)

7. Frog Pose (Mandukasan)
8. Sage Goraksha Pose (Gorakshasan)
9. Adept's Pose (Siddhasan)
10. Union Pose (Yogasan)
11. Cow Pose (Gomukhasan)

THE PROSPEROUS POSE
(Swastikasan)

Prosperous Pose

The prosperous pose is also known as the auspicious pose, the tailor pose, and the happy pose.

This Sanskrit word means cross and refers to the equilateral Eastern cross. This cross is similar to the Greek cross where each segment is of equal length, but is unlike the western cross which has a long vertical segment and a shorter horizontal one. The cross has arms on it symbolizing the spinning of creation and evolution. The Eastern cross has a resemblance to the German cross. However, the German cross spins in a counter-clockwise motion, symbolizing non-evolution.

To perform the prosperous pose, sit erect and raise the arms over the head alongside the ears, stretching upward to align the spine. Now place the sole of the right foot between your left thigh and calf and place the sole of the left foot between your right thigh and calf. In the prosperous pose, the hands may be in any comfortable mudra. Gnana mudra is suggested.

It makes little difference which leg is on top when performing the prosperous pose. You should, however, practice first with one leg on top and then with the opposite leg on top. Whichever position is more uncomfortable, practice that position a little more.

There are two theories regarding the symbolism as to which leg is should be on top. The first theory is that the leg on top symbolizes the side of your being which is stronger: either the solar, physical, right side or the lunar, mental, left side. The other theory declares the bottom leg symbolizes that side of your vehicle which forms the foundation of your life.

EASY POSE
(Sukhasan)

The easy pose is known also as the comfort pose. It is a comfortable meditative pose most often used by beginners or elderly persons.

To perform the easy pose, sit erect and raise the arms over the head alongside the ears, stretching upward to align the spine. Then simply place the legs in a simple cross-legged

Easy Pose

position. Either leg can be on top when performing the easy pose. Decide which position is more uncomfortable and practice that position to balance out your body. In the easy pose the hands are often placed in the OM mudra.

Benefits: The easy pose is an excellent beginning meditative pose. The neophyte can easily cross his legs and immediately begin to attain stillness. One can begin practicing breathing techniques right away without working to perfect a more advanced meditative pose. Persons with heavier thighs find the easy pose the most comfortable. The easy pose does not produce as great a stability as does the adept's pose. Do try the adept's pose.

CELIBATE POSE
(Guptasan)

The celibate pose is also known as the hidden pose. To perform it, sit erect and raise the hands over the head close against the ears, stretching to align the spine. Place the left foot under the body with toes pointing backward so the ankle rests on the floor. The sole is upturned. Place the right foot on the ankle of the left foot. Be sure to keep the heel

Celibate Pose

between the anus and genitals, pressing upward on the perineum. Place the hands on the respective knees in the wisdom gesture. This posture should be practiced by alternating the position of the feet, in order to balance the flow of the life force.

Mystical benefits: This posture subdues the sexual drive.

LIGHTNING BOLT POSE
(Vajrasan)

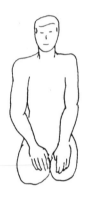

Lightning Bolt
Pose

This pose is also called the Zen pose, after the Zen monks who rarely utilize any other posture. It is also known as the kneeling pose and the firm pose. Vajra means lightning bolt. The pose is so named because it releases suddenly the life-current from the base of the spine, sending it to the top of the head.

Before forming the lightning bolt posture, sit erect. Place the buttocks on the heels and raise the arms over the head close to the ears, stretching upward to align the spine. The pose is performed in a kneeling position with the tops of the feet flat on the floor, the heels and knees together. The buttocks rest on the heels, exerting pressure on the nerves existing in the lower coccyx region. They do not rest on the floor.

The hands are placed in either of these two gestures:

1. Earth gesture (prithvi mudra) or
2. Enlightenment gesture (buddhi mudra)

Many people find this pose produces a strain on the knees and insteps of the feet. Consequently, it is one of the meditative poses which is not practiced much. This pose should be practiced more frequently.

Benefits: The weight of the body on the feet drives out old blood and pumps fresh blood in. Secondly, there are more bones in the feet than in any other part of the body, and they are constantly being pushed downward because of the body's weight. This pose exerts pressure in the opposite direction, relieving strain and fatigue in the muscles and bones of the feet. This has strong positive effects on the whole body.

According to zone therapy, or foot massage therapy, all the organs of the body are rooted in reciprocity to the feet. A nerve in the foot, when stimulated, sends a current to the corresponding organ, stimulating it and then relaxing it. Accordingly, this pose produces a tremendous invigoration of many internal organs. In addition, it lifts the spinal column and gives greater support to the back than when sitting normally. It also relieves pressure on the diaphragm making breathing easier.

Mystical benefits: Unlike the lotus pose or adept's pose, in which the buttocks are on the floor producing a feeling of stability or firmness, the lightning bolt pose lifts the body. This produces a feeling of elevation, loftiness within the mind. When the tops of the feet are pressed against the floor, a tremendous mind-body quietness is produced. The feet are important spiritual symbols. Pushing new blood into them symbolizes a regeneration of the spiritual life.

LOTUS POSE
(Padmasan)

Lotus Pose

The lotus pose is the most significant of all the meditative poses, and is referred to as the symbol of yoga. It is fundamental to doing many other yoga postures. It is inaccurately referred to as the yoga pose.

Padma means lotus, which has a twofold mystical significance. First, the lotus grows in muddy water, but due to its inherent nature, the blossom is forever untainted. Thus, this pose symbolizes an adamantine state of consciousness whereby you are unaffected by the negative or gross conditions of life. Secondly the lotus flower guided by the wind moves freely over the water, yet is deeply rooted at the base of the pond. Thus the lotus pose symbolizes the stability of the spiritual search.

To perform the lotus pose, sit erect and raise the arms over the head close to the ears, stretching upwards to align the spine. Bend either leg and, using the hands, turn the ankle so the top of the foot rests on the thigh of the opposite leg. The heel should be up-turned and as close to the groin as possible. Place the other foot on the thigh of the opposite leg in the same manner. The knees should press against the floor, and the toes should be as far to the outsides of the body as possible. Either leg may be locked over the other. The hands may perform one of the following mudras:
1. Wisdom gesture (gnana mudra)
2. Earth gesture (prithvi mudra)
3. Enlightenment gesture (buddhi mudra)

Most people cannot sustain the lotus pose for more than a few minutes. It is permissible to come out of posture, extend the legs and gently bounce them in an alternating rhythm. Having relieved the tension in the legs, return back into the lotus pose. For more advanced students, the historical texts advise the lotus pose not be held more than 3 hours.

The lotus pose should be developed and perfected over a number of years. Few people take the time to correctly develop this posture. They seem embarrassed if they have not mastered it within a few months. Consequently, many have injured the sciatic nerve and/or developed a trick knee because they stretched the legs too extensively, too soon. A word to the wise...

Caution: All yoga asans are not for everyone. The lotus pose, in particular, cannot be mastered by everyone. It would not be wise for persons with blood circulation problems to attempt the lotus pose, as this posture closes down the blood supply to the legs.

Benefits: The lotus pose tones and stimulates the nerves in the lower coccyx region, increases the spine's flexibility. It stimulates the organs of elimination. Thus the bowels are cleansed. The lotus pose also softens and regulates the breath cycle.

Mystical benefits: The lotus pose assists deep inturning. It is used to increase awareness in the inner planes, which is most beneficial for spiritual unfoldment. Secondly, the lotus pose closes off the saturn, jupiter, and part of the mars chakra, allowing the life-currents (prana) to enter into the higher spiritual chakras. This produces detachment. In this state of detachment, thoughts and desires can be experienced clearly. Thirdly, the pressure of the interlocked thighs stimulates certain nerves in the coccyx region of the spine. This mystically opens the balanced channel (sushumanic) located between the mental (ida) and the physical (pingala) channels as well as unlocking the Gate of God. It is here that the life-currents are balanced releasing kriya kundalini energy.

LOCKED LOTUS POSE
(Baddha-padmasan)

The locked lotus is unique among the meditative poses in that it actively involves the upper part of the body.

To perform the locked lotus, sit erect and raise the arms over the head close against the ears, stretching upward to align the spine. Form the lotus pose, drawing the feet close to the groin and as far to the outsides of the body as possible so that the feet are over the

Locked Lotus Pose

edges of the thighs. Place the right arm behind the back and grab the toes of the right foot. Cross the left arm over the right and grab the toes of the left foot. Realign the spine, relax, and hold as long as comfortable. When coming out of locked lotus pose, release the hands and slowly bring them forward. Because this is a difficult position to attain and maintain, there are two alternative methods to move from the lotus to the locked lotus. First, while in the lotus pose, tie the end of a handkerchief to one of the big toes. Tie another handkerchief to the other big toe. Cross your arms behind your back and take hold of each end of cloth. The left hand grasps the left toe's handkerchief. The right hand grasps the other handkerchief. Gradually pull on the cloth until you are able to grab your toes. Continual practice over a period of time will perfect your locked lotus pose without using the cloth.

The second method is different, yet you can receive most of the benefits of locked lotus while performing this modification. In the lotus pose, take a piece of cloth at either end and hold it in front of you. Straighten your arms and raise them over the head in such a way that while still holding the cloth you bring it behind your back a little above waist level. The insides of the arms should be facing each other. The wrists are turned inward, and the hands are facing outward. Gradually move the hands from the ends of the cloth to the center, at which point the insides of the wrists should be touching. This movement brings together the shoulder muscles, pressing the upper cervicals. Practicing over a period of time will strengthen the upper back muscles and facilitate doing the locked lotus.

Benefits: The entire rib cage is stretched, improving the breathing mechanism. It prevents nasal allergies. It reduces the hip area and strengthens the pectoral muscles. The locked lotus also corrects most digestive problems, cures constipation, and shrinks hemorrhoids. It produces steadiness of the mind, thereby improving the intellectual capacities. It helps overcome laziness and drowsiness. If you practice the locked lotus daily, the yogis say you will live to be 125. This may be an overstatement. However, the pose is known to assist longevity, because it regenerates the entire vehicle.

Mystical benefits: This pose opens the heart chakra. Gross emotions are dropped and subtler feelings are transmuted into compassion, love, insight, and inspiration. Locked lotus produces greater dream awareness.

Frog Pose

FROG POSE
(Mandukasan)

The frog pose is so named because a frog has the capacity to take in and retain large amounts of air. Accordingly, this pose is performed with full chalice. This means the breath is held while the lungs are filled with air.

To perform the frog pose, sit erect and raise the arms over the head close to the ears, stretching upward to align the spine. Kneel, spreading the knees apart into a wide V-shape. Separate the heels slightly, pointing the toes toward each other, and press the buttocks down onto the heels. The frog pose is simply the lightning bolt pose with the knees spread. The hands are placed downward on the knees in the earth gesture. While in the posture, inhale fully and retain the breath as long as comfortable. Exhale slowly and repeat the breath cycle, extending the length of the hold with each progressive inhalation.

Benefits: The pressure of the heels into the buttocks stimulates the nerves leading to the organs in the pelvic cavity. This promotes the removal of waste material. Large accumulation of fluids in the body (commonly referred to as water retention), are removed by the practice of the frog pose. In short, the frog pose has a diuretic effect, as well as bringing relief from constipation. This promotes overall improved health.

Mystical benefits: The frog pose awakens the kriya kundalini currents in the center channel. Holding the breath in this pose causes the ascending currents (prana) to become stronger than normal, increasing the activity of the higher chakras.

Sage Goraksha Pose

SAGE GORAKSHA POSE
(Gorakshasan)

This pose is also known as the butterfly pose, bearing a marked similarity to the butterfly stretching exercise. This pose is also called the ankle-knee pose, and is named after the sage Goraksha. It is one of the more difficult meditative poses to perform.

To perform the ankle-knee pose, sit erect and raise the arms over the head close to the ears, stretching upward to align the spine. Place the soles of the feet together, drawing them up to press against the perineum. The knees should be pressed totally flat against the floor. The hands are placed on the knees in the wisdom gesture.

Caution: In the beginning, the ankle-knee pose must be practiced with care. If performed with a wrong mental attitude, it can produce an over-stimulation of the sexual organs.

Benefits: There is a strengthening and an activation of the hormonal processes, producing a slimming of the physical body and making it supple. It, also, strengthens the muscles of the thighs and pelvic region. It removes restlessness and/or irritability, improving nervous disorders. For the male householder, it is therapeutic for treating impotency.

Mystical benefits: Whether male or female, exerting pressure on the perineum produces a sublimation of the sexual energies which are transmuted and lifted to the higher chakras.

ADEPT'S POSE
(Siddhasan)

One who is an adept is a sage, an individual who has attained profound knowledge. This wisdom comes from the quietude of an undistracted mind. An adept is one who has the capacity to think or reflect without emotionality. A sage is one who has attained proficiency in awakening the

Adept's Pose

higher centers of consciousness to reveal the great secrets of life.

The adept's pose is the most commonly used of all the meditative poses. It is also known as the perfect pose or the sage pose. The adept's pose is one of the easier meditative poses and is considered perfect for meditation because there is no locking of the legs, which cannot be sustained very long, by most people.

The adept's pose can be performed in one of two ways. The masculine position of the adept's pose is performed with the right foot on top. The feminine position of the adept's pose is performed with the left foot on top. The position you utilize is determined by whether you wish to balance the physical principle of your being, or the mental principle. The masculine position of the adept's pose will be described.

Sit erect and raise the arms over the head alongside the ears, stretching upward to align the spine. Place the left heel at the base of the spine, under the perineum. Then place the right heel against the pubic bone or just above the genitals. The perineum is the soft underpart of the pubis, between the anus and scrotum. Under the perineum runs a nerve that leads directly to the urogenital organs.

The hands are to be placed in any of the following mudras:
1. Wisdom gesture (gnana mudra)
2. Interlock gesture (gomukha mudra)
3. Chalice gesture (cup mudra)
4. Enlightenment gesture (buddhi mudra)

In the wisdom gesture, with the hands placed on the knees, the body is forced to lean slightly forward. This puts a gentle pressure on the jupiter chakra at the small of the back. This relieves stiffness or discomfort resulting from trying to sit too straight. Bringing the spine forward brings about a sense of ease in the adept's pose.

Caution: The adept's pose is basically used by celibates who have taken a vow of chastity. If one is married, it is not advisable to practice the adept's pose for long periods of time. However, a small amount of practice is recommended even for the householder, as this pose tends to bring temperance.

There is no such thing as a modified version of the adept's pose. If the bottom left heel is to the side of the perineum and placed against the opposite thigh, this is a different posture entirely. If a householder practices this pose for extended periods of time, it should be practiced with the bottom of the left heel to the side of the perineum, resting it against the opposite thigh.

Benefits: The adept's pose has three distinct advantages over the lotus pose. First, it does not block off as much blood flow to the legs. However, the blood pressure is lowered and circulation throughout the body improved. Secondly, it does not irritate the sciatic nerve, which runs from the pubic region down the thigh to the leg. Next, the pressure on the perineum produces a quietude within the mind.

Over and above this, the pose forms a solid base with the legs, giving a marked sense of physical and mental stability. This pose, also, produces a detached, philosophical attitude, improving creativity and intellectual capacity. Stress is relieved and sleep is improved.

Mystical benefits: It produces inner visional states in the form of heightened dream awareness and spiritual visions. Intense practice of the adept's pose will cause the dream state to become exceptionally clear, a desirable goal.

UNION POSE
(Yogasan)

Union Pose

The union pose is not one of the more commonly known meditative poses, yet it is extremely helpful in achieving the goals of yoga. It is often referred to as the yoga pose.

To perform the union pose, sit erect and raise the arms over the head close against the ears, stretching upward to align the spine. Perform the lotus pose. Place the hands through the thighs, near the knees. Twist the hands so that the wrists are facing forward and touching the floor under the body. Now, while pressing with the hands, simultaneously lift the entire upper part of the body approximately 2 to 3 inches off the floor. This will cause the shoulders to lift slightly.

The union pose is basically the lotus pose with the wrists in a forward position near the knees.

Benefits: The downward pressure of the hands lifts and stretches the entire spinal column, relieving pressure on the pads between the vertebrae. It stimulates circulation, removing drowsiness when one is studying or working for extended periods of time.

Mystical benefits: The reversed position of the hands has mystical significance in that it symbolizes the individual mind turning inward and tapping knowledge from the universal mind. Lifting the spine awakens the kriya kundalini life-currents.

COW POSE
(Gomukhasan)

Cow Pose

The cow pose is sometimes referred to as the cow-faced pose. It is not commonly known, yet it is very important. It derives its name from the word meaning cow, the most sacred of all Indian animals. In yoga, the cow's milk is a lunar symbol indicating fruitfulness and expansion. The jyothi light used in religious ceremonies to symbolize the flame of existence, or the eternal light, is often made from the butter of a cow.

The cow pose can be performed in either of two positions. The masculine position cow pose is formed with the right leg on top, benefiting the physical side of your being. The feminine position cow pose is formed with the left leg on top, benefiting the mental side of your being. Symbolically, the masculine position produces a fruitfulness of the body, whereas the feminine position produces a fruitfulness of the mind. The feminine position will be illustrated.

Begin in a sitting position and raise the arms above the head close to the ears, stretching upward to align the spine. Kneel on all fours, bringing the left leg across and over the right leg. Keep the legs spread and lower the buttocks to the floor between the legs, drawing the calves in toward the sides of the body. The feet are not under the body but are lying to the side of the hips. The coccyx region is pressed against the floor. Next, raise the right arm over your shoulder, palm at shoulder blade level. Lower the left arm and bring it behind the back, bending it at the elbow, with the palm facing outward. Then clasp the fingers of both hands together. Right palm faces the body; left palm faces away from the body. Both are clasped behind the back. The right elbow points upward toward the ceiling and the left elbow points downward toward the floor.

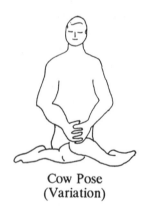

Cow Pose
(Variation)

Variation: The following is a variation of the hand placement while forming the cow pose. After attaining the position of lowering the buttocks to the floor between the legs and drawing the calves in toward the sides of the body, place the right hand on top of the left knee and the left hand on top of the right hand. The knees and hands are aligned atop one another in the following ascending order from the floor: right knee, left knee, right hand, left hand. The thumbs are extended and pointing outward with the fingers held close together. Straightening the arms, press the knees together toward the floor until you feel a pressure at the small of the back. It is essential that the knees and hands are aligned with the coccyx pressed against the floor. (In the masculine position cow pose, the order would be reversed: left knee, right knee, left hand, right hand.)

The cow posture, more than any other meditative pose, necessitates the anal contraction since the V-shape of the outturned legs causes the anal sphincter muscle to be pushed out. The cow pose is an extremely strenuous pose and in the early stages should not be practiced for more than 5 or 10 seconds. Gradually the pose can be extended, a few seconds at a time, up to a period of 5 minutes.

Benefits: The cow pose regenerates the entire vehicle by stimulating the nerves at the base of the spine. Regular practice tends to retard the aging process by keeping the vertebrae in the lower region of the spine from calcifying. This pose places a counter pressure on the feet, thereby relieving the strain of the normal arched position. The cow pose stimulates nerves in the feet leading to various internal organs, thus relaxing and revitalizing them. Also, the cow pose relieves the chronically stiff-kneed by relaxing the two lateral muscles at the back of the knee. As the walk is relaxed, the mind becomes more relaxed, producing a mental stability and tranquility.

Mystical benefits: The strong pull at the base of the spine and the small of the back activates the saturn and the jupiter chakras. Once these centers are opened, the kriya kundalini rises to the higher centers. This activates the heart chakra and the mercury chakra. The contraction of the anal sphincter muscle causes the ascending kriya current to continue its movement upward, with greater force. Finally, the jupiterian symbolism of the cow pose is extremely auspicious for spiritual endeavors such as chanting or reading the holy scriptures. According to ancient tradition, the rewards of such endeavors are most fruitful.

Chapter 11

BREATH-CONTROL
(PRANAYAMA)

SECTION I:
AN INTRODUCTION

Yoga differs from western medical philosophy. This is not to say that doctors are wrong and yogis are right but that they have different theories. The medical field has been very conservative in acknowledging many concepts and theories that yoga has adhered to since the beginning of time. When it was first discovered that blood circulates, medical science denied this. When a number of other scientific physiological concepts were first developed, medical science denied them. The point is, the scientific community has constantly had to give ground, somewhat begrudgingly, to new concepts. This conservatism is not negative, for it has kept much superstition out of the medical field and is utilized as a safeguard, but it has also caused many medical discoveries to develop at a very slow pace. Allow me to elaborate on two very basic concepts in which yoga and the medical field differ.

One of the fundamental distinctions between yoga philosophy and western medical science lies in the concept of prana, Life-energy. Yoganandaji called these energies life-trons. They are also called the vital airs. In this chapter we will explore this concept. Many teachers have tried to superficially equate prana with oxygen, but they are distinctly different. When you inhale oxygen, it chiefly enters the capillaries in the lungs, and is transferred into the blood-stream. Although prana also enters the bloodstream it is primarily absorbed by the mucous membranes and moves toward the nerves, energizing and vitalizing them. This contributes to increasing the physiological functions of the organs, plexuses, and brain centers.

It is difficult to prove the existence of something like prana; however, there is one significant indicator that can demonstrate how oxygen and prana are two different things. We know that breath is life, and we are also quite familiar with the oxygen/carbon dioxide cycle known in internal respiration. Now, if oxygen is life, rather than breath is life, why is it that a dying man cannot be kept alive by a supply of pure oxygen? The answer: It is not simply oxygen which keeps a person alive, there is something else. In yoga is it called prana, the life-breath.

Secondly, although medical science tends to look upon the body as a single vehicle with many physiological organs including a brain, the yogi looks upon the body as a triune being having three very distinct vehicles, as well as consciousness.

1. The physical body
2. The astral body
3. The causal body

These three bodies are capable of functioning separately, yet at the same time, have interrelationships which modern psychologists have recently begun to recognize as significant in developing a deeper understanding of consciousness. These interrelationships are also important to the yogi, who moves to higher states of consciousness. This movement is referred to as transcending everyday consciousness.

This triune body is the temple of Spirit (atma) and is composed of five sheaths:

The Triune Body		The Five Sheaths
Physical Body (Sharira)	➤	Food Sheath (Anna-maya-kosha) Prana Sheath (Prana-maya-kosha)
Astral Body (Sukshma Sharira)	➤	Mind Sheath (Mano-maya-kosha) Intellect Sheath (Vijnana-maya-kosha)
Causal Body (Karana Sharira)	➤	Bliss Sheath (Ananda-maya-kosha)

Maya means temporal; kosha means sheath. Joining these two words together, maya-kosha can be defined as a temporary sub-vehicle or sheath used by the bodies. These five sheaths and three bodies are modes and means for the expression of consciousness.

The utilization of the two concepts, prana and the triune vehicle, is important in a scientific-cultural attempt to establish a dynamic healthy vehicle. If an athlete is going to be successful in the Olympics, he not only needs a strong body but also a steady mind. However, everyone today knows that it takes more than body and mind to win. Winners have access to something more. It is his mind that disciplines his body to bring in that gold medal by defeating the competition, sometimes by as little as 5/100ths of a second. Such victory is not achieved by sheer physical prowess, but by strong direction given to the mental and physical vehicle, from a deeper level of that soul's being.

When your breath is irregular, your mind will be unsteady, incapable of giving you this type of direction. Consequently, pranayama is practiced to give:

1. Greater discipline to the physical body;
2. Increased ability to concentrate or study;
3. A realization of higher states of consciousness.
4. Ability to draw upon that extra special something, when needed.

The attainment of all three of these require control of the breath, or the practice of pranayama.

Finally, the triune body has more than just muscles and nerves running throughout. There are also astral channels called nadis through which pranic energy flows. The channels exist in the astral and/or in the mental bodies rather than in the physical body. Many people are unaware there are life-currents in the earth, flowing in regulated patterns which can be charted. They exist in the ocean, and even in the sky there are predominant, varying air currents. Just as most people are unaware of these life-currents flowing through the earth, they are also unaware that there are astral currents. These life-currents run throughout our physical vehicle. They flow through our muscular/skeletal structure, the blood and lymph system, the spinal fluids, as well as through the more subtle organ of the brain, known as mind.

According to yoga, these channels are clogged with phlegm. The function of yoga is to remove the gross and subtle phlegms. When the nadis are cleansed, prana can flow through, thereby increasing physical strength, concentration, and meditation. When the nadis are purified through proper yogic techniques, prana stimulates and vitalizes the gross, subtle, and super-subtle levels of your being, giving the underlying consciousness control over the grosser vehicles.

PRANAYAMA: CONTROL OF THE LIFE-FORCE

Yama means control; prana means life-force. Pranayama therefore means control of the life-force. Breathing is an external manifestation of prana. Prana is your very life, the ultimate force that causes you to move, think, and create. By regular practice of pranayama you gain the ability to direct and control the life-force within you. This is done through your thinking process, thoughts being the agents which direct the life-force. Prana can be stored in various organs of your body and in your chakras. It can mentally be transmitted to various organs to improve vitality, overcome disease, and bring serenity and enlightenment.

The average human being breathes approximately 15 to 18 times per minute. In a normal breath cycle, you exchange one pint of air. By learning the habit of breathing more deeply through the practice of pranayama, you begin to automatically breathe in an additional three pints of air! Through the development and habitual practice of pranayama, you learn to exhale more forcefully. These allow a greater supply of oxygen and prana to be absorbed into your system. According to yoga, bodily health is not only determined by nutritional factors contained in the bloodstream but also by its content of oxygen and prana. Pranayama super-oxidizes the blood. It supercharges it with oxygen and prana. This not only brings an extended life, but a more vital life. Higher states of consciousness also become more attainable.

The student should be reminded that pranayama is a powerful tool and best practiced under the guidance of a competent teacher.

PRANA

Life is infinite and all-pervading. Life manifests itself through the duality of a primordial energy called prana, and a primordial nature called matter. There is no single object or substance that does not contain this energy/matter complex, whether it be classified as matter or mind. Just as subtle vapors upon cooling become gross matter and take the form of a cloud, or of water, or of ice, so in exactly the same manner, prana evolves as mind in its various forms. It is prana which vibrates and appears as the life-force, even in the atoms.

There is an unbelievably close correspondence between the microcosm and the macrocosm. In creation and evolution, prana first evolves itself as cosmic mind, and then becomes grosser and grosser. It then evolves itself as the astral elements of ether, then air, then fire, then water, and finally earth. (These elements should not be confused with the gross physical elements in chemistry.) Prana does not change; however, the energies formed do change.

In the creation of your body, prana becomes more and more gross, first evolving as:

1. Mind, and then as the brain center;
2. Then as the mercury chakra in the realm of the astral throat;
3. Then as the venus chakra in the region of the astral heart;
4. Then as the mars chakra in the region of the astral navel;
5. Then as the jupiter chakra in the region of the astral gonads; and
6. Finally, as the saturn chakra in the astral region at the base of the spine.

In this way a physical body is born within the womb of its mother. After evolving a body, prana abides in its dynamic form in the saturn chakra. In the average person this prana remains in a static state throughout the entire womb life and earth life. Through yoga practice, this energy is released and activates latent gray-matter. This improves the functioning of your everyday states of consciousness which include wakefulness, sleep, and the dream state.

Although medical science admits the existence of the nerve currents and their importance to life, they have not as yet located the exact position of the dynamo where the nerve energies are generated and/or stored. Although it is very difficult to detect these through external instruments because of their subtlety, they can be known. They can be known through the instrument of your own mind.

Nerve energy is one of the most important energies required for bodily and mental functions. We continually use up this nerve energy in our everyday activities of wakefulness and dreaming. It is only in meditation that this energy is regenerated. Sleep, very similar to meditation, is also an inturning process whereby nerve energy is regenerated. During sleep, however, we function at a subconscious level and therefore there is no conscious direction or conscious release of this energy, and there is no conscious control of the life-energy. In short, there is no pranayama. How is prana to be controlled? It is controlled by practicing various breathing techniques and/or mantras.

When prana stops flowing, all bodily functions stop. It is interesting to note that most westerners tend to think that life stops when breathing stops; yet doctors and yogis know that prior to, and more basic to the bodily functions of breathing and heartbeat, life is dependent upon something more: brain function. If this were not true, the body would not die when receiving pure oxygen, adrenalin, or intravenous sugar, and so forth. Doctors admit that this is a mystery, but the yogi states that it is a mystery that is explainable: the flow of prana.

Pranayama is very necessary for physical life, for physical improvement, and for maintaining vigorous health. Pranayama and its mastery are also absolutely essential for attaining mental unfoldment and spiritual progress. The ancient sages, through intuition and by experience, discovered this. They understood the importance of the control of prana in maintaining health and increasing one's mental capacity.

The breath-prana is the central factor in sustaining our lives. The breath-prana is the central factor in sustaining our consciousness. We can live an extended period of time without food, a long period without water and/or sleep, and without air it is impossible to sustain life for more than a few minutes. But without prana, life stops immediately.

The average person breathes by inhaling-retaining-exhaling, in a very personal pattern. Each person's breathing pattern is more unique than his fingerprint. The science of pranayama is the most intense yogic technique that can be utilized for expanding your life, improving your intellect, creativity, and retentive memory. It is the key to spiritual progress.

Ancient texts point out that pranayama properly performed cures diseases and improves one's life, but improperly practiced can cause complications of the mind and body. Most westerners seem to ignore this, thinking there could not possibly be anything unbalancing about breathing. Breathing control, however, is like a sharp axe. If flayed about, it can cause damage. Discipline and caution are needed in both.

The science of pranayama as it relates to your individual being can be divided into the following sections:

1. Your individual bodily idiosyncrasies,
2. Your individual mental idiosyncrasies,
3. Your individual karma,
4. Your individual locality sector,
5. Your individual time track.

More will be said about these later.

The purification of the body, mind, and astral vehicle can only be attained through the control of the life-force. It will increase your youthfulness, concentration, and power of meditation. It will also improve your power of creativity and recall, until ultimately it removes the darkness of ignorance and reveals to your individual self, the Spirit within.

The effects of pranayama are more constructive when practiced in conjunction with the other yoga stages.

CHAKRIC ENERGY
IN YOUR UNIVERSE

The physical body, according to yoga, is a miniature universe; a microcosm. Let me explain this further. The secret of the study of kriya yoga is locked within the word kri-ya, composed of two root words:

KRI = meaning lunar energy; the active principle (maha-shakti).

YA = meaning solar energy; the passive principle (Lord Shiva).

Your body and mind contain solar and lunar energy. Solar energy flows through the right nostril, whereas lunar energy flows through the left nostril. The right nostril is called pingala nadi; the left nostril is called ida nadi. These two main channels run from the nostrils all the way down to the base of the spine where they join. The word nadi is best defined as an astral channel. Being an astral channel, it is located in the astral or subtle body, not in the physical, gross body. The nadis cannot be seen, yet they do affect the physical body. Suspended and centered between these two channels, from the base of the spine to the top of the head, is the third and most important channel called sushumna.

PINGALA is the channel of the sun (right side),
IDA is the channel of the moon (left side),
SUSHUMNA is the channel of divine fire (centered).

The yogi, through his disciplining and yoga practice, is ultimately trying to bring the prana into the balanced channel of divine fire (sushumna), so that it flows upward from the lower centers of consciousness, to the higher centers. The reason that yoga is so concerned with stretching and loosening the spine is to make this sushumanic pathway clear. Thus, the life-energy can flow upward unimpeded, affecting the higher center and producing cosmic consciousness.

The normal flow of the life-force is through the lunar and/or solar channels, the sushumna remaining fairly inactive.

From the base of the spine to the top of the head, however, these three channels intersect a number of times. These intersections or conjunctions are called mass-energy-converters or "chakras."   These mass-energy-converters regulate the physical body's mechanism and the mental/astral body's mechanism as well. They regulate them in exactly the same manner that a flywheel regulates an engine.   If you can conceive your total vehicle as a complex series of engines necessitating seven flywheels, you will understand more clearly the reason the yogi strives to regulate the chakras through control of the life-force and pranayama techniques. It is important to recognize that these chakras, according to the yoga philosophy, are not physical like the nerves, but are astral centers of energy that regulate and control the neuro-hormonal system which in turn controls the body/mind functions.

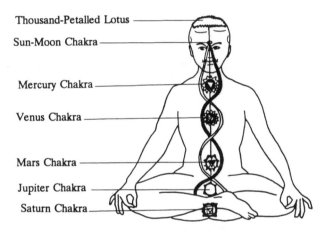

Thousand-Petalled Lotus
Sun-Moon Chakra
Mercury Chakra
Venus Chakra
Mars Chakra
Jupiter Chakra
Saturn Chakra

The Chakras

1. Saturn center (muladhara chakra): This center is located in the pelvic area, just above the anus, at the base of the spine. Mula means root and dhara means vital part. Joining these root words together, muladhara can be defined as the root support or the foundation upon which all the other centers are built.

2. Jupiter center (svadhisthana chakra): This center is located at the small of the back, just above the organs of procreation. Sva means vital-force and has an equivalent meaning to the English word soul (not to be confused with Spirit). Dhisthana means abode.   Thus the jupiter center can be translated as seat of the soul, or the seat of the memory track. (Spirit is immortal; soul is the memory of the Spirit).

3. Mars center (manipuraka chakra): The mars center lies in the realm of the navel region. Its meaning is the island of

jewels. In English it is referred to as the solar plexus. In a mystical sense, this is the level that mankind has evolved to. In short, this is where the individual consciousness dwells. Proof is that when one experiences great ecstasy or great anguish, one does not feel it in the head but in the pit of one's stomach.

4. Venus center (anahata chakra): This chakra lies within the cardiac or heart region. Anahata means heart.
5. Mercury center (vishuddha chakra): This center is located in the throat region of the body. Vishuddha means pure.
6. The moon center (chandra chakra): Chandra means moon. The moon center exists at the back of the head at the region of the medulla oblongata.
7. The sun center (ajna chakra): The ajna chakra is located between the eyebrows. Ajna means to command. This center is also known as the third eye and the eye of Shiva.
8. The thousand-petalled lotus (sahasrara chakra): This center is located at the top of the cerebral cavity. It extends beyond the physical body.

These are the major chakras that are referred to in yoga. There are, however, others. For instance, there are also two small chakras between the mars chakra and the heart chakra. They are called:

1. Manas chakra, and
2. Surya chakra.

The manas chakra means mind center. That is, mind in relation to the sense organs.

The surya chakra means solar chakra. This chakra should not be confused with the mars chakra, which in western physiology is often called the solar plexus; nor should it be confused with the sun center (ajna chakra). It is the surya chakra that releases the kriya kundalini fire.

These two chakras, manas and surya, relate to the seeds of the genitals and are often referred to as kama-rupa, meaning the form of passion. Some western mystics have referred to these two chakras as the Christ center, for the passion of anguish and the passion of ecstasy are to be found here.

The yogis clearly indicate that these two chakras are not to be entered into, for mankind tends to attune only to the passion of anguish. Consequently, in yoga we move directly from the mars chakra to the heart chakra which relates more to love than to passion.

In the palms of the hands and the feet there are four separate chakras, one in each appendage. These are often seen in the hands of great saints or avatars such as the Buddha. They are represented by lotuses or crosses. These chakras, like all chakras, open and release a vibrant red pranic energy which tries to balance one's astral being. In mystic Christianity this red fluid is often referred to as blood and the opening of the chakras is referred to as bleeding.

There is another chakra, known as lata chakra. It is located at the front of the forehead and is often seen on statues or photographs of Avatars like the Buddha. You see three centers:

First, a jewel at the root of the nose known as the ajna chakra. We talked about this center before.

Second, a large outcropping at the top of the head which is the thousand-petalled lotus. This chakra corresponds to the pineal gland. We talked about this center before.

Third, in between these two chakras on the forehead is the third jewel known as lata chakra. This forehead chakra relates to the pituitary gland and its psychic functions.

As indicated earlier, the chakras are subtle mental vortices of energy. Nonetheless many modern Hindus have attempted to relate rather than correlate them with the plexuses of the body and the neuro-hormonal flow. One such suggested system is as follows:

The saturn and jupiter centers correspond to the gonads.

The mars center corresponds to the abdominal organs, i.e., the stomach, spleen, liver, and pancreas.

The venus center corresponds to the heart and the main blood vessels surrounding the heart.

The mercury center corresponds to the thyroid, parathyroid, and thymus glands.

The sun center, forehead center, and the thousand-petalled lotus correspond to the brain, pituitary, and pineal glands, respectively.

In the system of yoga, only seven major chakras are considered:
1. Saturn chakra
2. Jupiter chakra
3. Mars chakra
4. Venus chakra
5. Mercury chakra
6. Sun and moon chakras
7. Thousand-petalled lotus

As you see, there are seven rather than eight, for the sun and moon chakras are considered to be one chakra (in esoteric yoga). Each chakra has a ruler or lord. And each lord of the chakra has a wife or mistress. This symbolizes that within each chakra is a male and female principle. The whole process of kri-ya yoga is to bring about a reunification of these two forces, producing a total harmony within our being. The solar principle is referred to as the passive observer, whereas the lunar principle is referred to as the active doer.

When these solar and lunar principles are balanced by bringing the energies up the center channel, rather than through the male and female channels, you attain to the seventh major realm wherein you transcend the limitation of your solar system. This is called thousand-petalled lotus consciousness, or cosmic consciousness. It is a transcendency over your unconscious, subconscious, preconscious, and post-conscious states of being.

The purpose of the asans, pranayamas, and meditation is to awaken and lift the kriya kundalini energy innate within your body-mind complex. The kriya kundalini energy is symbolized as a thrice-coiled sleeping cobra (naga) lying in the saturn chakra. According to yoga, this dormant energy has to be:

1. First, awakened,
2. Then aroused,
3. Then sent upward through the spinal column, piercing all seven chakras, and finally entering into the thousand-petalled lotus where it reunites with the All-Consciousness of existence.

Many physiologists and psychologists claim that the average person is only utilizing about 3% of the gray matter within his nervous system. The gray matter is what you think with. The yogi contends, however, that it is more like one-third of 1%. This means that only a very small percentage of the massive gray matter within your vehicle is being stimulated and used by your everyday consciousness. Through the practice of pranayama, inhaled oxygen is absorbed more rapidly on the surface of the muscles than on the surface of the nerves, producing a static electrical charge. The heavy focusing at the cerebral regions while doing the techniques drives more blood in that direction. Consequently, as the static electricity follows the normal flow of blood, it acts as a catalyst or stimulus in awakening a greater quantity of brain cells. With this awakening comes greater perception, greater retention, greater recall, greater creativity, and that which yoga stresses: greater positivity, buoyancy, and happiness.

Another reason the average person uses only a small portion of his gray matter is because his breathing patterns, unhealthy diet, and overweight are not conducive to a proper feeding of the brain. Consequently, in order to protect itself, the brain mechanism renders the vast majority of its gray cells dormant. Because of this, the body's brain requires only a minimal amount of blood, oxygen, sugar, and so forth to sustain its life. By removing the phlegm and impurities, and by super-charging the bloodstream with oxygen and 'prana-izing' the nerves over a sustained period of time, the conscious mechanism begins to recognize that the brain cells can now safely reawaken, producing an expansion of consciousness, referred to as cosmic consciousness.

The gray matter is not only concentrated in the cranium; it is found within the entire length of your spinal column, and also exists in some peripheral ganglia (collections of nerve tissue outside the brain and spinal cord) which are formed at specific points along the spinal column and branch into larger networks of nerves called plexuses. If the gray matter of the brain can think, feel, and so forth, why not the gray matter of the spinal column? Have you ever experienced great excitement or anger? Where did you feel it? In your head or in your solar plexus?

It is through the technique of pranayama that you extend the frontier of consciousness beyond your everyday athletic life and scholastic studying, and enter the true and final frontier. This final frontier, consciousness itself, is to be explored and conquered. The yogi, through his concentration and meditation, becomes aware of states of consciousness that are not necessarily meaningful to everyday life, but surely are meaningful in the exploration and attempted understanding of the vital fundamental factor of consciousness itself.

The yogi contends that he remembers through recall events extending back into the fetal stage, along with experiences of preexistence. Based upon the experiences and feelings of preexistence, the theory of reincarnation has been espoused. I suggest that a more acceptable solution to these frequently occurring past-life recalls is cellular memory. Within our consciousness there lies, as it were, our mother and father who represent guiding elements in our choosing, selecting, conditioning, and evaluation of life conditions. Independent of this sociological factor, there is also an actual cellular memory from the memory bank of the seed of our father and the egg of our mother, locked into the lower levels of our consciousness which can be activated. Your human physiology or your microcosm is one of the greatest computer storage banks of earth life experience. And who knows what other consciousness lies in other levels of that storage bank. To a philosopher, these are exciting concepts, but they are to be utilized in guiding and directing your life here and now on this earth, into a more meaningful, fruitful, satisfying existence.

Regulating unconscious habits is an extremely valid area of research. As university researchers move into this area with greater interest, they shall find more effective ways to balance abnormalities, as well as expand the good life.

Allow me to give an example of how these unconscious habits manifest. As an individual learns to type, he must concentrate on the location of the keys and which finger must touch which key. Once learned, however, the human consciousness no longer needs to think about it. The habit becomes unconscious and is stored within the brain and spinal column. As a matter of fact, thinking about how to type the word onomatopoeia, interferes and may even cause one to mistype it. Yoga suggests that you can regulate these and other types of unconscious habits which are stored within specific areas of the spinal column, by the proper energizing of prana through the use of yoga. These techniques will assist to either neutralize and/or increase the effectiveness of these deep unconscious conditionings.

Whether a person is striving toward the perfection of winning a gold medal in the Olympics, or developing his fullest mental and/or spiritual physical capacities, it is well-known that a disciplined mind, along with a relaxed state of consciousness, is needed.

As we face ever greater stresses and challenges, we need to call on our retentive memory and our past experiences to help solve life's problems. We need our ability of free association, our perception of present experiences, our creative imagination, and an optimistic viewpoint to win. Through the practice of pranayama these all become possible and we reach more fully to our potential.

If individually or collectively we are to move from the lethargic indifference of watchers of the world and become participants, whereby we become leaders, discoverers, and lovers, we must revitalize our physical and mental being for that wondrous adventure and challenge which life holds.

In truth, we are mankind adrift within a boat. Some of us have come to the realization that we can no longer be satisfied with just holding our own. We must press forward to assist the world as never before, to solve and resolve the problems of living, as well as to expand the joys of being. We need new data, we need new viewpoints, we need new creativity, to meet our tomorrow. Where do the answers exist? They exist deep within you.

Finally, what is it that makes life meaningful? Whatever it is, does it not have its basis in the matrix of consciousness? It is this very matrix of consciousness that the yogi seeks to understand and to master through pranayama and other yoga techniques. In this self-mastery we ascend the high road to the ultimate evolutionary meaning of life itself. Not life as some abstract concept, but life whereby our individual life is found, sustained, and lived.

PRANAYAMA AND THE ASTRAL CURRENTS

According to the Gautamiya Tantra, there is no principle, no austerity, knowledge, state, treasure, or other thing superior to pranayama. It states that whatever spiritual disciplines are performed without pranayama, become fruitless.

Prana, the universal life-energy, enters the human body through the moon center, descending down through the cerebral spinal axis, reaches the bottom, and then ascends again. As it ascends and descends, it is modified by the nature of the chakras. As this prana is modified by the chakras, the prana is differentiated into what are called vital airs (vayus). The word chakra-current relates a more meaningful translation. Here is a brief summary of the chakra-currents.

1. prana:
   The first principle of the vital airs is known as prana. It has the same name as the ascending solar energy itself. The life-energy known as Prana should not be confused with this type of prana. English authors attempt to differentiate between the two by capitalizing the P in major Prana and using a lower case p in this type of prana. This prana manifests itself as hong-sau, and assists in sustaining the respiratory processes within the physical body, which sustain physical life. The activity of this prana is centered in the venus center. Prana is ingested into the body, just as, and when, oxygen is ingested into it.

2. apana:
   The second principle of the vital airs is known as the downward current and is the energy which relates to and circulates through the saturn chakra. It controls secretion and related excretory functions of the gross body. Some texts

point out that apana is expelled from the physical body in much the same way as carbon dioxide is expelled from the lungs.

3. samana:

The third principle of the vital airs is the energy which functions through the mars center and regulates the gastric fires. In short, it controls the process of digestion.

4. udana:

The fourth principle of the vital airs is the energy that manifests through the mercury center in the throat. It regulates the diaphragm and thus the depth and rhythm of respiration. Udana is very important, for at the time of death its function is to release the astral body from its hold onto the physical body. A familiar manifestation of the astral body separating from the physical body is the death-rattle, a particular sound in the throat sometimes heard at the time of a person's death.

5. vyana:

The fifth principle of the vital airs is the energy prevailing the entire body, but which centers in the jupiter chakra. It is extremely important in vitalizing the tissue cells and controlling circulation.

These vital airs or specialized functions of the chakric energies are involuntary. It is the task of the yogi to intensify and gain voluntary control over these energies and consequently their functions.

The average human being breathes about 22,000 times a day. With each breath cycle, the apana strikes the static latent spiritual energy known as kundalini in the saturn center of the cerebral-spinal axis. It is the function of the yogi to take what is usually a rapid and extremely shallow breath cycle and intensify it so that the striking force of the respiratory cycle will awaken the kriya kundalini. The average lung in normal breathing is filled to only 1/6th of its capacity. In the practice of pranayama the lungs become filled to a much greater capacity. This releases more apana which consequently more strongly strikes the sleeping kriya kundalini.

When pranayama is successful, the kriya kundalini is awakened and two sensations are felt in the spinal area:

1. A bubbly sensation, ascending along the spinal axis; most often at the heart center area.
2. Heat, descending over the spine. This is referred to as kriya fire, tapas, or dumo fire.

As the kriya kundalini is awakened and ascends up the sushumna channel, it revitalizes and re-energizes each chakra, purifying the astral channels related to each. Ultimately, it reaches the highest center of the astral body, the thousand-petalled lotus, where it unites with the higher kriya kundalini, or super kriya-kundalini, called maha-kriya kundalini. When this happens, the intermixing of the two kriya kundalinis polarizes every cell of the physical body and every petal of the astral body. In essence, the key function of pranayama is to force the upward current to flow downward and strike the latent kundalini, causing the downward current to rise. By reversing their directions in this way, they are intermingled and great psychic heat is generated. It is usually most noticeable at the mars center or solar plexus.

This is the great fire ritual of old.

There are three kriya kundalinis:

1. Brahma-kriya kundalini:
   These are redissolving kriya currents. They are located at the saturn center. They produce a bubbling sensation and are gross.

2. Vishnu-kriya kundalini:
   These are recreating kriya currents. They are located at the mars center. They produce a sensation of heat within the spine and are subtle.

3. Shiva-kriya kundalini:
   These are sustaining kriya currents. They are located at the thousand-petalled lotus center. They produce a sensation of bliss and are super-subtle.

The advanced student might note the inversed relationship of the three forces: Brahma, Vishnu, and Shiva.

There are three knots located along the spinal column. Discomforts such as pain, lightheadedness, dizziness, nausea, and disorientation may arise because the kriya kundalini is not success-fully passing through these three knots in its upward ascent. These knots (granthis), are located at the saturn center, the venus center, and the sun center. The knot at the saturn chakra is known as the knot of Brahma; the second knot at the venus center is known as the knot of Vishnu; and the third knot at the sun center is known as the knot of Shiva.

Prana, like the ocean tides, ebbs and flows in and out of the physical and astral bodies. At sunrise, prana enters the sushumanic channel; at noon it is equalized both in the astral channel and the bloodstream; at sunset prana rushes through the physical arteries; and at midnight it rests in the hollow of the heart and in the blood vessels as well.

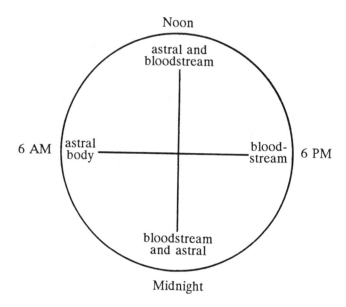

From noon until midnight, prana circulates when the blood and the physical energies are at their peak. From midnight until noon it is polarized in the nadis. Intellectual activity is much sharper and at its peak at this time. This explains the mystery of why so many creative artists, in all ages and countries, have been night-owls, preferring post-midnight and wee early morning hours for their creativity.

We shall now turn our attention to the guides to pranayama. These guides should be read and fully understood before beginning the practice of pranayama. They will assist you to more effectively utilize the techniques. Please read them carefully.

GUIDES TO PRANAYAMA

1. The breathing techniques should not be performed on a full stomach. Do not practice pranayama on a full stomach, nor should you practice it in a state of hunger. This means you should wait a reasonable amount of time after a small repast and a few hours after a full meal. Usually 2 to 4 hours after a full meal is the proper amount of time before beginning extensive pranayama.

2. Pregnant women and persons who have scarlet fever should not undergo the practice of extensive pranayama.

3. Although pranayama produces many physiological and psychological states that are desirable, its major aim is the release of the pranic energies, gathering them, and then bringing them to the higher chakras so that a meditative state can be attained.

4. While practicing these pranayamas the neck, spinal column, chest, and waist should be kept in a straight line, at full attention without tension.   The following asans are recommended and can successfully be used in the practice of pranayama:

   The Meditative Poses:
      a. The easy pose
      b. The adept's pose
      c. The lightning bolt pose
      d. The hero pose
      e. The lotus pose

5. Extensive practice of pranayama should be begun for the first time, either when the sun is at zero degrees of the zodiacal sign Aries, or zero degrees of Libra. These configurations occur in the springtime on March 21st and at the fall equinox on September 23rd, respectively.

6. Persons who are physically weak should not practice the following pranayamas until they have improved their physical vitality through diet and asans:
      a. Bhastrika (bellows breath)
      b. Prachhardana (forceful exhalation and hold breath)
   The following pranayamas should not be practiced in the winter:
      a. Sitkari (the cold maker)
      b. Sitali (cooling breath)
      c. Chandara-bhedana (moon-piercing breath)

7. The following pranayamas should not be practiced during the summer:
      a. Bhastrika (bellows breath)
      b. Surya-bhedana (sun-piercing breath)
   Those persons who find their minds to be extremely scattered will find the following pranayamas useful in rapidly acquiring the power of concentration:
      a. Bhamari (the bee breath)

   b. Sarva-dwara-baddha (solar-bound breath)
   c. Sukshma-shwasa-prashwasa (gentle and soft
         exhalation breath)
Those persons wishing to develop brute physical strength
should practice the following pranayamas:
   a. Bhastrika (bellows breath)
   b. Vaya-viya-kumbhaka (balancing both chalices
         breath)
During the practice of these particular pranayamas, one's
diet should consist of easily digestible and nourishing foods.
Light-oil foods are also highly recommended.

8. Kriya yogis state that a long life is an extremely important
   factor in the unfoldment of wisdom and spiritual insight;
   consequently they have developed the following pranayamas
   for prolonging physical life:
      a. Dergha-shwasa-prashwasa (deep abdominal
            breathing)
      b. Bahya-abhyantara kumbhaka (full chalice/empty
            chalice hold breath)

9. Remember, behind the physical food sheath (called the
   anna-maya-kosha, which is the essence of food energy) is the
   vital sheath (called the prana-maya-kosha, which is the
   essence of prana), which is composed of prana. Prana is the
   very link between physical body consciousness and the desirable astral consciousness. A vigorous vital sheath gives powerful consciousness in the astral world.

10. According to the kriya yoga philosophy, earth life is com-
    posed of a given number of breaths. The average number
    of breaths for the average human being is fifteen per
    minute. If one reduces the number of breaths per minute,
    one extends the life-span. When the breath is suspended it
    increases the inner spiritual vigor.

11. If you can control your Prana, you can control all the forces
    of your inner universe. The control of the inner cosmos is
    the beginning of life control. Learn the secret of controlling
    the little wavelets of prana in your mental cosmos, and the
    secret of control of the Prana in the external cosmos be-
    comes clear. The yogi who becomes an expert in the secret
    of pranayama becomes a soul radiating joy, light, and spiri-
    tual energies.

12. It is important from a psychological perspective that prana-
    yama not be practiced in a damp or foul-smelling place.

Also, to procure the mental and spiritual benefits from pranayama, it is important that you,

    a. Control your diet,

    b. Control your work/rest cycle,

    c. Control your sleep.

13. The sage Patanjali gives the following classifications for pranayama. They are:

    a. External (bahya)

    b. Internal (abyantara)

    c. Retention (kumbhaka)

14. Determining how and when to do pranayama depends on:

    a. Your individual nature,

    b. The length of time you have,

    d. The number of repetitions you are able to do.

15. Empty chalice: Empty chalice refers to the practice of pranayama wherein the lungs are devoid of air, and held empty. This causes the pranic energy to drive toward the mental vehicle, affecting the mind.

Full chalice: Full chalice refers to the practice of pranayama wherein the lungs are filled with air, and held. This tends to drive the current toward the physical vehicle, markedly affecting the gross body.

All the asans can be performed with either ida or pingala pranayama. That is to say, they can be performed with either empty chalice or full chalice, according to whether you want to direct the energies to the body or mind.

As an example, the shoulderstand activates the mercury center which controls the thought processes of the mind and the organs which enable you to verbally communicate those thoughts. The shoulderstand performed with ida pranayama (empty chalice) will markedly affect the functioning of the mind. When it is performed with pingalic pranayama (full chalice) it drives the energies more toward the physical, vocal organs. If you have difficulty concentrating, with due caution, you should practice the shoulderstand with empty chalice, driving the energies toward the mental processes. This will produce greater powers of concentration. On the other hand, if you have difficulty speaking, whether it is stuttering or not being able to speak at all, practicing the shoulderstand with full chalice will tend to improve the vocal organs. If the vocal organs have been inactive for an extended period of time, producing actual decay, it is dubious whether this technique would be of any help.

16. In order to determine the intensity, length, and duration that pranayama should be practiced, the physical and mental fitness of the student should be gauged, either by the student himself or by an experienced instructor.

17. The best time for practicing pranayama is early in the morning, just preceding sunrise. This time is best for those pranayamas used to gain spiritual development. Just after sunset is also a good time. This period of time is best for utilizing techniques to produce quietude and restfulness.

18. The ancient texts point out that pranayama should be practiced four times a day. This is most difficult for a working person and thus it is important to understand that fifteen minutes in the morning and fifteen minutes in the evening will produce excellent benefits and also spiritual unfoldment.

19. Pranayama should be practiced in a clean, comfortable place.

20. One of the most important guidelines in the utilization of pranayama is that it should be practiced with regularity: in the same posture, in the same place, and at approximately the same time each day.

21. At no time during the practice of pranayama should there be tension caused by the yoga posture, or by any mental apprehension you may be experiencing. An accumulation of saliva in the mouth usually indicates a state of tension. If saliva does accumulate, more completely relax your body and mind before beginning pranayama. Also, if saliva accumulates in the mouth, do not swallow it while holding the breath, but do so just before exhalation. In short, you cannot swallow and continue to hold the breath. If you must swallow, immediately exhale.

22. In pranayama, all breathing is done through the nasal passages, with the exception of a few esoteric methods: kriya, sitali, sitkari, etc. You should inhale and exhale through the nose, unless otherwise indicated.

23. Some people often experience slight quivers of the body which may produce heavy perspiration. If this occurs, the perspiration should be rubbed back into the body after finishing the pranayama. Both conditions will disappear after a little practice.

24. Pranayama is best practiced in a meditative posture while sitting on a folded wool blanket. Although any simple cross-legged posture is acceptable, the adept's posture, the hero posture, and the lotus posture are the most beneficial.

Sitting on the floor is very important for it lowers your blood pressure, etc.   However, If you do not have the capacity to sit on the floor, a chair is acceptable.   What is most important is that your body is relaxed and as motionless as possible.   The eyes should remain closed during the entire process.   There are two reasons for this:

    a. If the eyes are kept open, a burning irritation may result.

    b. If the eyes are kept open, the mind will more than likely wander, scattering the pranic energies.   This defeats the purpose of concentration.

25. In all pranayamas the anal contraction (mula bandha) and stomach contraction (uddiyana bandha) are held; and in many pranayamas, after the inhalation and hold, the chin lock contraction is practiced and then released just before exhalation.

26. If heavy ringing is heard in the ears, or pressure is felt within the ears, either lessen the intensity and/or duration, or stop the pranayama entirely for a while.

27. It is important not to immediately follow pranayama with the practice of asans.   Usually 1/2 hour should elapse before beginning asans.   Simply do the asans first, rest in savasana, followed by mantra, then pranayama.

28. Whenever you are exhausted, do not practice pranayama.

29. The key thing to achieve is an even duration of inhalation and exhalation.   (Although there are some pranayamas that do differ in their ratio of inhalation and exhalation).   If you inhale for 10 seconds, you should exhale for 10 seconds, with approximately the same intensity.   Remember this equation:

$$(D)(I) = F \quad \text{Duration x Intensity = Force.}$$

If the breath becomes disrupted when attempting to master an equal duration of inhalation and exhalation, the best approach is to markedly lessen the duration of the hold, or to shorten the inhalation.

30. When an even duration of inhalation/exhalation has been mastered you can then begin to practice with a more extended suspension following inhalation.   This is called full chalice control (antara-kumbhaka).

31. Only after full chalice control has been mastered should you attempt to practice extended suspension following exhalation. This is called empty chalice control (bahya-kumbhaka).

32. I think it is important to point out that some students develop constipation in the initial stages of practicing the chalice. This is temporary and usually disappears. Therefore, be sure to drink added water. Eat food with more fiber in it.

33. One of the greatest benefits gained by the practice of pranayama is a marked change in mental attitude and mental outlook. These attitudinal changes include:

   a. A reduction of fears,
   b. A reduction of cravings,
   c. A more creative imagination,
   d. A more optimistic, buoyant outlook,
   e. A greater ability to concentrate.

34. While performing pranayama, be cautious as you increase the intake of air so you do not bloat the abdomen in the inhalation process. This is a key factor in all pranayamas.

35. Students should know that after extensive practice of pranayama, the hold will become instinctive in their breathing patterns. This is known as kaivalya-kumbhaka, the illumination hold.

36. Persons suffering from high blood pressure or heavy cardiac difficulties should never attempt to hold their breath. Those with low blood pressure should retain their breath after inhalation only.

37. Fainting: In full chalice, if the air travels above the mercury chakra to the brain, fainting may result. A tightly held chin lock can remedy this because it prevents 'air' from rapidly moving upward to the brain. The chin lock should only be practiced in the presence of a mature individual who understands the deeper mental aspects of pranayama. If fainting occurs, the ears can be rubbed and/or cold water splashed on the face.

38. It cannot be stressed too strongly that these techniques must be practiced without strain to the body or mind. Do go slowly, but do practice every day.

39. In many of the pranayamas the following technique is utilized. It is a valuable procedure to know. It is called Shiva mudra. (See diagram in this section.)

a. Bring the right hand to the nose.

b. The index and middle fingers are tightly folded and closed into the palm.

c. Now place the right thumb at the right nasal passage. The thumb is appropriately used to close off the right nasal passage.

Shiva Mudra

d. Then place the ring and little fingers at the left nasal passage. They are appropriately used to close off the left nasal passage.

e. This closing off is done by making a pinching motion with the thumb, and the ring and little fingers. It is done alternately, i.e., closing off the right nasal passage with the right thumb while inhaling through the left nasal passage, and then closing off the left nasal passage with the ring and little fingers while exhaling through the right nostril.

40. A little unsalted butter or light oil (olive oil) in the mouth and throat, prior to an extensive practice of pranayama, may be very helpful, as it will lubricate the mucous membranes preventing them from drying out and cracking.

41. If discomforts occur either during or because of pranayama, the practice should be stopped for a few days or weeks.

42. The great sage Manu points out that just as the impurities of metal are burnt out when placed in a furnace, likewise the impurities of the organs of the body and mind can be burnt out by the furnace of the breath in the practice of pranayama.

43. Patanjali points out that pranayama purifies the blood and promotes good digestion. It also gives agility, strengthens flexibility of the mind and personality, and ultimately rends asunder the veil of darkness concealing the realities of our individual existence. It, also, rends asunder the veil of darkness concealing the truths of existence. All that is needed is the daily practice of pranayama without stressing the body/mind complex. Slowly but surely destiny will unfold.

With these thoughts in mind, let us turn to the preliminary techniques of pranayama.

SECTION II

PRELIMINARY PRANAYAMAS
-The Breath Cycle-

Symbolically, the cycle of the breath: the inhalation, hold, exhalation, hold, is a microcosm of a more galactic cycle of the universe. This cycle is called the breath of God. In the external, gross world this cycle is called summer, winter, and the two solstice points, spring and fall. It is at the solstice points of spring and fall that the hold of the macrocosmic breath occurs. This is an esoteric statement. It is given for those who wish to meditate on a deeper realization: Man is a part of, not apart from, nature.

Applying this deeper truth to the microcosm of our individual universe, the sustainment of bodily life by prana is automatically regulated, by our individual breathing patterns.

Below are the three Sanskrit words which define the stages in the breath cycle.

1. Puraka is breath inhalation.
2. Rechaka is breath exhalation.
3. Kumbhaka is breath suspension.

Breath suspension can occur between inhalation and exhalation, or between exhalation and inhalation. This suspension is often referred to as the hold.

There are six preliminary practices to assist you in the successful attainment of the goals of pranayama. These are:

1. Deep abdominal breathing (3-part breath),
2. Increasing the inhalation time,
3. Increasing the exhalation time,
4. Increasing the combined inhalation/exhalation time,
5. Increasing the full chalice breath suspension time,
6. The vitalizing breath.

Generally, the average person completes approximately 16 to 18 breath cycles per minute. Increasing the length of the inhalation, exhalation, and suspension substantially reduces the number of breath cycles per minute, thereby calming and rejuvenating the mind and body, as well as giving added longevity. These preliminary pranayamas purify the nadis, allowing successful completion of the higher goals of pranayama.

In many of the preliminary and classical pranayamas you are instructed to close the throat. This is a very important part of the technique. It refers to closing the glottis which allows for a slower and deeper inhalation and exhalation. If the air rushes into the throat too rapidly, it is an indicator that the throat is too open. The air is inhaled and/or exhaled through the nostrils, but because the throat is closed, the air passes through the nostrils more slowly and more gently. Closing the glottis puts pressure on the air entering the lungs and gives a time delay, assisting in a far greater absorption of oxygen and prana. This is important.

THE TECHNIQUES

1. DEEP ABDOMINAL BREATHING
(Dergha-shwasa-prashwasa)

This deep breathing technique is called deep abdominal breathing or sometimes the 3-part breath, or diaphragmatic breathing. While in a meditative pose, exhale slowly through the nasal passages, and without holding begin to inhale slowly. While you are inhaling, progressively:

a. Extend the stomach walls,
b. Expand the chest, and
c. Lift the collarbone.

When the lungs are full, without holding the breath, begin exhaling slowly through the nasal passages as you:

a. Lower the collarbone,
b. Contract the chest, and
c. Contract the stomach muscles.

Remember, each inhalation begins at the stomach and each exhalation begins from the top of the lungs.

This order is extremely important to gain maximum inhalation and exhalation. When performed properly, the breathing is one steady, continuous flow. Beginning students usually concentrate so heavily upon the abdominal wall, the chest cavity, and the rib cage, that they combine these 3 movements into one breath. It should not be done this way. Although the breath should be inhaled in a flowing movement, be sure to follow the order of lifting the stomach, then expanding the chest, then collarbone, and so forth.

Benefits: The benefits include heavy oxidation of the bloodstream which has a toning effect on the entire body; purifies the nose, chest, and lungs. It strengthens the liver and stomach, producing increased digestive powers. The body becomes very agile. The life span is markedly increased.

2. INHALATION EXTENSION

Sit in a meditative pose. Slightly close the throat and inhale as slowly and as long as possible. (Closing the throat causes the air to flow in more slowly. If the air rushes in too rapidly this means the throat is too open. If it takes 10 to 20 seconds to flow in, it is an indicator that the throat is closed. (See ujjaya pranayama in the section on the classical pranayamas.) Time yourself. Without strain, extend the inhalation time. Remember, the incoming breath should not be so slow that the in breath breaks. Practice each day for a few weeks.

3. EXHALATION EXTENSION

Sit in a meditative pose. Inhale quickly through the mouth. Slightly close the throat, and as slowly as possible exhale with air passing through the nose. Time yourself. Extend the time, but without strain. Practice daily for a few weeks.

4. INHALATION/EXHALATION EXTENSION

Sit in a meditative pose. Close the throat almost completely. Inhale as slowly as possible and without any hold, exhale. Exhale as long and as softly as possible. Without holding, inhale. Repeat 3 times. Time yourself. Practice daily for a few months.

5. EASY BREATH
(Sukha-purvaka)

The easy breath is also known as the comfortable breath. It is simple to perform if you are acquainted with nerve purification or alternate breathing. The distinction between alternate breathing and the easy breath is that in the easy breath the ratio of the breath-retention time is increased while the inhalation and exhalation time remain the same.

Sit in a comfortable meditative pose and form the wisdom gesture with the left hand, placing it on the left knee. With the right hand, form the Shiva mudra: Place the right thumb over the right nostril and ring and little fingers over the left nostril; the index and middle fingers are cupped in the palm of the right hand. Closing the left nostril, inhale through the right nostril for 5 seconds. Hold for 5 seconds and close the right nostril with the thumb. Release the left nostril and exhale for 10 seconds. Inhale through the left nostril for 5 seconds, hold for 5 seconds, and exhale through the right nostril for 10 seconds. This completes one round.

While performing easy breath you should feel the spiritual qualities of peace, joy, love, and happiness entering into your system and circulating along with the breath. As the breath is exhaled, feel these divine qualities radiating out into the world to be shared with all sentient life forms. Breathe 7 rounds per day for some time. Add from 3 to 5 rounds each week, until you are breathing approximately 32 to 40 rounds per day. This may be done in 2 or 3 sittings during the course of the day. When you are able to breathe 40 rounds per day at a ratio of 5-5-10, the ratio can then be increased in this manner:

$$5 - 5 - 10$$
$$5 - 7\text{-}1/2 - 10$$
$$5 - 10 - 10$$
$$5 - 12\text{-}1/2 - 10$$
$$5 - 15 - 10$$
$$5 - 17\text{-}1/2 - 10$$
$$5 - 20 - 10$$

Each time the ratio is increased, begin by breathing 7 rounds per day, adding 3 to 5 rounds per week until a total of approximately 40 rounds per day is practiced at the increased ratio. Then you may go on to increasing the time of the hold, taking from 6 to 12 months to reach the final ratio. When the 5-20-10 is reached, it need not be increased further; merely increase the number of rounds per day.

Benefits: The easy breath causes the mind to become steady and clear; you gain great powers of concentration.

6. VITALIZING BREATH

Stand erect and place the hands on the hips. Turn the head to the left, open the mouth wide, and exhale forcefully. Bring the head forward and inhale as deeply and as fully as possible through the nose. After you have filled the lungs, tense all muscles in the body in such a way as to produce a slight quivering of the muscles. Totally relax and still facing forward, exhale through the mouth in two short exhalations. The vitalizing breath is reverse psychology, forcing the muscles to tense more than they are already tensed; in so doing they can relax more as you release the tension. Through this technique you gain mastery over tensions in the body.

Benefits: The vitalizing breath energizes the body by forcing new prana and oxygen throughout the entire vehicle. This exercise is most beneficial when you are very tired and need a lift.

Chapter 12

BREATHING TECHNIQUES
(PRANAYAMA)

SECTION I:
THE CLASSICAL TECHNIQUES

Having thoroughly gone over the guidelines to pranayama as well as some important preliminary techniques, we now turn to the classical breathing techniques for gaining control of the life-force (prana).

1. THE DRAWING BREATH
(Ujjaya)

This pranayama is also known as the HA-SA breath and the hissing breath. The root word jaya means success in the spiritual venture. It is often used in yoga affirmations to promote spiritual success. The prefix uj means superior. Thus, the name indicates a method of eminence among the classical techniques.

The drawing breath is performed in a meditative pose. Then do the stomach contraction. Close the mouth and exhale completely through the nasal passages. Inhale slowly and evenly while partially closing off the glottis. The glottis is the opening between the vocal chords, at the upper part of the windpipe. This causes the air to rush past the partly closed glottis, producing a soft humming sound within the throat. The passage of the incoming air is felt on the roof of the palate and makes a 's-a-a-a-a' sound. This sound should definitely be heard. Be cautious not to bloat the abdomen in the inhalation process, as the entire abdominal wall is pulled inward and upward by the stomach contraction.

It is important that the incoming breath reaches from the throat to the heart only. Make sure as you are inhaling, to feel that the breath is traveling to the heart only. As you inhale, feel and imagine they are traveling from the nose to the throat and then to the heart. On the exhalation it should travel only from the heart to the throat and then to the nose. In short, you are only using the air from the upper portion of the lungs, not the lower portion.

When the lungs are full, form the chin lock contraction and hold as long as comfortable. Release the chin lock and exhale slowly and steadily until the lungs are empty. The glottis is half closed. The brushing of the air against the palate should make a 'h-a-a-a' sound. The exhalation can be either through both nostrils, or through one nostril, while the other is closed with a thumb. Passage of the outgoing air should be felt on the roof of the mouth.

This pranayama is repeated 3 times. The number of repetitions is slowly increased, so as not to strain yourself. There are no restrictions to the drawing breath. It can be practiced at any time, and in any place. It's usual limit is 3 to 9 minutes.

Benefits: Ujjaya relieves excessive heat from the head and improves digestion. It is helpful in curing consumption, asthma, and other pulmonary diseases. It soothes the nerves and tones the entire body. It is excellent for alleviating high blood pressure. Some texts indicate it's an expectorant. Ujjaya can be done in a reclining position without the hold.

Mystical benefits: Through the constant practice and mastery of HA-SA pranayama, unconsciousness can be obliterated. Decay of the physical body can also be retarded, even after the death state. It gives remembrance of past lives, of bardo plane experiences, and is well utilized for controlling dreams.

2. SKULL-SHINING
(Kapalabhati)

The skull-shining technique is similar to the bellows breath with two exceptions:

    a. In skull-shining, the inhalation is slow and the exhalation is vigorous.

    b. In skull-shining there is a split-second retention after each exhalation.

Skull-shining can be performed in a sitting position or in a standing position. The standing position is exactly the same as in uddiyana, with the feet being 1 to 1-1/2 feet part. Pull the upper lip over the upper teeth, firmly but gently, to open the nasal passages. Then inhale and exhale forcefully but quickly and smoothly, like the movement of a blacksmith's bellows. There is a split-second retention after each exhalation. The inhalation is slower; the exhalation is faster and more vigorous. Inhale and exhale as quickly as possible, without stopping. This produces a somewhat shallow breath.

Skull-shining is sometimes treated as a preliminary to bellows breath. The restrictions are the same as for the bellows breath. Read them carefully. For more extensive data, see the chapter on the shat kriyas.

Benefits: Brings heat to the body when it is cold. Improves digestion, and helps cure asthma and consumption. It also decreases fat, particularly around the stomach area. The benefits are the same as for bellows breath.

Mystical benefits: It opens the door to the center (sushumna) channel. It's an excellent pranayama for awakening the kriya kundalini. It is very helpful in opening the three knots in the sushumna channel. These three knots are called Brahma granthi, Vishnu granthi, and Rudra granthi in the sushumna, located at various levels of the spine. These knots inhibit the kriya kundalini energy from ascending all the way up the center channel and reaching the sun center.

3. BELLOWS BREATH
(Bhastrika)

In this pranayama, as the name implies, the air is rapidly forced in and out of the nasal passages with no hold. Make a fast, vigorous exhalation. Inhale just as forcefully and as rapidly. This continuous repetitive action will imitate the sound made by air rushing out of a bellows. In bellows breath, the inhalation and exhalation must be forceful, yet long. Often, the middle and forefinger of the right hand are held together in a straight manner and placed under the nasal passages. The exhaling air should strike against these fingers with full force. After 10 cycles, take a slow deep inhalation and hold for 2 seconds. Then slowly exhale through the left nostril only. After resting for a short time the bellows breath should be repeated with as many cycles as are comfortable. Then take a slow, deep inhalation, hold, and exhale slowly. If you find that the sound of the air lessens or that the vigor is not as intense, reduce the number of cycles within a round.

Restrictions: This pranayama must be done in moderation. You should be very cautious in its practice. When practicing, some people experience a throbbing in the ears, or their nose will begin to bleed. These are indications to stop. Other pranayamas should be used to strengthen your vehicle before this technique is resumed. If dizziness results, stop the practice immediately.

Persons with weak lungs and bodies, as well as those with problems such as glaucoma, pus in the ear, or high or low blood pressure, should not practice it. If practicing this pranayama for weeks, I recommend the ingestion of milk, cheese, and ghee (clarified butter).

Benefits: Brings heat to the body when cold. It improves digestion and helps cure asthma and consumption. It is also an expectorant. This pranayama decreases fat, particularly around the stomach area. It's excellent for losing weight.

Mystical benefits: Rapidly awakens the kriya kundalini. It opens the door to the center channel. It is helpful in opening the three knots in the center channel. These knots in the spine inhibit the flow of kriya kundalini energy from reaching the sun center.

4. SUN-PIERCING
(Surya-bhedi or Surya-bhedana)

The sun-piercing pranayama is a process for passing energy or consciousness through the sun center (ajna chakra). It is a powerful mystical technique given by the guru to his closer disciples.

In this technique, the breath is inhaled only through the right solar nostril and exhaled only through the left lunar nostril. Sit in a meditative posture, and perform the anal contraction along with the chin lock contraction. Form the wisdom gesture with the left hand. Bring the right hand up into the Shiva mudra. Press the ring and little fingers of the right hand, blocking the left nasal passage completely. Inhale slowly and completely through the right nostril. When the lungs become full, close the right nostril with the thumb of the right hand. Hold the breath for 5 seconds. Increase the tension of the anal contraction. Still keeping the right nasal passage closed, relieve the pressure on the left nasal passage by releasing the pressure of the ring and little fingers of the right hand. Exhale slowly and thoroughly through the left nostril. When the air is completely exhaled, close the left nasal passage. Now open the right nasal passage by releasing the pressure of the thumb. Inhale slowly through the right passage. Throughout this pranayama, pressure is applied to the nasal passages in such a way that the air coming into and going out of the nasal passages makes a sound similar to a leak in a tire. The eyes are to be closed and the mind is totally absorbed on the sound of the air entering and leaving the body. Remember: all inhalations are through the right nostril; all exhalations are through the left nostril.

Each inhalation and exhalation should be approximately the same length and intensity. The force of each inhalation should equal the force of each exhalation. The mathematical formula is:

$$Force = Intensity \times Duration.$$

Great heat is generated by the practice of this pranayama. You should rub any sweat produced back into the body, either with the hands or a small towel. This is important, as it keeps the body from becoming weak.

Sun-piercing should be repeated 3 times in the early stages with 1 to 3 pranayamas added each day until somewhere between 21 and 32 can be performed without strain. This can usually be done within 5 to 10 minutes, and should be followed by total relaxation.

Restrictions: Practice this only in the winter months. However, those who are of the wind or phlegm humors can practice in the summer months. Persons with high blood pressure or coronary difficulties should not hold their breath after the inhalation!

Benefits: The pressure on the nostrils allows the lungs to absorb more oxygen and prana than in most other pranayamas. This soothes and invigorates the nerves, increases the digestive power, and cleanses the sinuses. As it causes heavy perspiration, it removes most of the impurities from the body.

Mystical benefits: This is one of the greatest pranayamas for awakening the kriya kundalini energies. The proper use and mastery of this technique allows the disengagement of consciousness from the gross body allowing traveling into the astral planes. It is an excellent mystical technique for softening certain types of karma.

5. COOLING BREATH
(Sitali)

Sit in the easy pose. Roll the tongue lengthwise into a tube while projecting the tip of the tongue a little ways outside the mouth. Draw the air through the curled tongue with a 's-s-s-s-sa' sound. The air is drawn in as through a drinking straw. Fill the lungs completely. When full, withdraw the tongue and close the mouth, and perform the chin lock contraction for about 5 seconds. Exhale thoroughly with a "hu-u-u-u-m" sound through the left nasal passage after releasing the chin lock. Repeat this process from 5 to 10 minutes. Usually 3 rounds are sufficient.

Restrictions: This should be practiced in the summer. Those who suffer from high blood pressure or coronary problems should not practice this technique.

Benefits: It heals the body, and removes excessive heat from the head, clearing the eyes and ears. It is an excellent technique for cooling the body. It relieves hunger and thirst. The cooling breath activates the liver and reduces phlegm and bile, thus improving digestion. This technique is excellent for preventing high blood pressure (but not for curing it).

6. THE COLD MAKER
(Sitkari)

The cold maker is a variation of the cooling breath and is sometimes called the wheezing breath. Sit in the adept's pose and curl the tongue backwards so that the tip of the tongue touches the upper palate. Keep the lips slightly parted, clench the teeth and inhale while producing a 'See-e-e-e-e' like sound. Fill the lungs to capacity, but do not retain the breath. Exhale immediately through both nostrils. You are inhaling through the mouth and exhaling through the nostrils. Repeat the process from 5-10 minutes. Usually 3 rounds is sufficient.

Restrictions: Persons suffering from high blood pressure may find this a painful process.

Benefits: It heals the body, and removes excessive heat from the head, clearing the eyes and ears. Cools the body. Relieves hunger and thirst. It activates the liver, reducing phlegm and bile, thus improving digestion. This technique is excellent for preventing high blood pressure (but not for curing it). The benefits are the same as those for the cooling breath.

7. THE BEE BREATH
(Bhamari)

In this pranayama you produce a soft humming-like sound of a bee. Sit in the hero pose and close the right nostril with the right thumb. Inhale through the left nostril. When the lungs reach full capacity, retain the breath for 3 seconds. Then slowly exhale through the same nostril, and at the same time, with the throat, produce a humming sound for the entire length of the exhalation. The exhalation should be as long as possible. Allow this 'e-e-e-e' sound to totally pervade your mind. Gradually increase the duration of the exhalation and the intensity of the humming, but without stress.   Repeat approximately 10 times in earlier stages, and gradually move to an ultimate count of 108.

Benefits: The bee breath produces a most harmonious voice. It cures insomnia. It is an excellent technique for learning concentration.

Mystical benefits: It enables you to hear the mystical OM sound on the psychic level. It is one of the key pranayamas for awakening the kriya kundalini energy. It quiets the mind and increases concentration allowing you, in time, to enter the outer fringes of samadhi.

8. MIND-QUIETING BREATH
(Murccha)

Sit in lotus pose. Close the right nostril with the thumb. Inhale through the left nostril as fully as possible, retaining the breath. Form the chin lock contraction. Fix your gaze at the sun center, at the root of the nose between the eyebrows. Make a strong mental effort to extinguish the noise activities of the mind. The mind should become so extremely quiet that it enters into the deep stillness of contemplation. Exhale through the left nostril and repeat the process using the right nostril. Gradually increase the duration of the hold as you practice this technique over a period of weeks.

Benefits: This pranayama gives you the ability to bring extreme quietude to the mind by removing the noise factor from the mind. It stops all the thought processes, without producing unconsciousness.

9. THE FLOATING BREATH
(Plavani)

Form a comfortable and steady meditative posture. Then inhale through both nostrils in such a way that the stomach becomes extended like a balloon. Be sure that the air has settled or accumulated in the stomach area. Retain the air as long as comfortable. Then exhale fully. Repeat 6 to 12 times.

Benefits: It increases the digestive fires, removing constipation, thus giving general health and strength to the body.

Mystical benefits: It purifies the astral channels and also the pranic currents. Historically, this is the technique yogis use to levitate upon water, like a lotus leaf. The levitation does not refer to the water of a lake. It refers to the water element of the jupiter chakra.

SECTION II:
THE NON-CLASSICAL PRANAYAMAS

There are many important traditional techniques that could best be called non-traditional because they are not given in the classical texts. They have been passed down for many generations because they have been found very useful. These techniques should also be practiced with great mindfulness as they are helpful in attaining the goals of yoga, including mastery of the senses and higher insights into the nature of the Self. All the cautions indicated in the Guides to Pranayama should be held in mind while performing these techniques.

1. IDENTICAL MOTION BREATH
(Sama-vritti)

This pranayama exercises the yogi's capacity to achieve uniformity in the duration and intensity of all three stages of a pranayama: inhalation, hold, exhalation.

This pranayama is best practiced by first inhaling and exhaling only, with no hold. Having attained a degree of uniformity in the duration and intensity, you should then attempt to practice full chalice. Inhale for 10 seconds, hold the breath 10 seconds, exhale for 10 seconds, and immediately begin to re-inhale. After mastering the 10-10-10 ratio, you should then attempt to master this technique using the empty chalice: Inhale for 10 seconds, immediately exhale for 10 seconds, and hold with no air in the lungs for 10 seconds. In the beginning practice stages of full and empty chalice, you may inhale and exhale with no hold for 2 or 3 cycles, and then hold on the third cycle. Repeat 3 cycles without a hold.

Restrictions: Use extreme caution in any pranayama where the breath is held if you are not in good health.

2. IRREGULAR MOTION BREATH
(Visama-vritti)

Irregular motion consists of 3 irregular breathing cycles. In this technique, the length of the inhalation, hold, and exhalation are not equal and thus an interruption of the breathing cycle is attained.

In the first cycle of irregular motion breathing the ratio is 1:4:2. The inhalation is for 1 unit of time, the full chalice is for 4 units, and the exhalation is for 2 units. For example, you would inhale for 5 seconds, hold for 20 seconds, and exhale for 10 seconds. The length of the inhalation is arbitrary. It depends on the lung capacity of the individual. The important factor is the time ratio.

In the second cycle, the ratio is 2:1:4. For example, the inhalation could be 10 seconds, the hold 5 seconds, and the exhalation 20 seconds.

In the third cycle, the ratio is 4:2:1. For example, the inhalation could be 20 seconds, the hold is 10 seconds, and the exhalation 5 seconds.

Performing these 3 cycles consists of 1 round. You should complete 3 rounds and rest in total relaxation. Again, the duration of the inhalation, exhalation, and hold is determined by the individual's strength and lung capacity. Under no conditions should you produce any type of stress.

Restrictions: This difference in ratio can easily create breathing difficulties and dangers for the student if practiced for any length of time. As with all more advanced pranayamas, expert guidance should be obtained before you extensively practice.

3. HELD MOTION BREATH
(Stambha-vritti)

This is a kumbhaka breathing technique. It's a technique whereby emphasis is on the suspension of the breath. There are two modes to this breathing technique: Empty chalice and full chalice.

  a. The breath is exhaled forcefully through the open mouth. The mouth is closed, and the breath is suspended for as long as comfortable. This is called empty chalice (Ida stambha-vritti).

  b. Inhale fully and quickly through the open mouth. Then the full breath is suspended and held as long as comfortable. This is full chalice (Pingala stambha-vritti). When releasing the air, the mouth is opened and the breath is released suddenly, but not forcefully.

4. EXTENDED FOUR-PHASES MOTION BREATH
(Abhyantara-bahya-stambha-vritti)

The fourth traditional pranayama is a combination of the previous three. Inhale as slowly and quietly as possible, holding as long as comfortable. Next, exhale as slowly and quietly as possible, holding as long as comfortable. These four stages complete 1 round. Repeat anywhere from 3 to 12 rounds, depending on the strength of your lungs.

5. NADI PURIFICATION; ALTERNATE BREATHING
(Nadi-sodhana or Nadi-suddhi)

The nadis are the channels in the astral body which carry the pranic energy. Nadi purification is also widely known as alternate breathing. Nadi purification is performed by sitting in any comfortable meditative pose. With the left hand, perform the wisdom gesture, over the left knee. Perform Shiva mudra. The right arm is bent at the elbow with the middle and index fingers tightly closed against the palm. The right thumb is pressed against the right nostril; the ring and little fingers are against the left nostril. Empty the lungs completely through the right nostril. Then inhale slowly but steadily through the right nasal passage and totally fill the lungs. During the process of inhalation the left nasal passage is totally blocked by the ring and little fingers. Without any retention of the air, press the right nasal passage with the thumb. Release the left nasal passage and exhale slowly yet steadily through the left nasal passage. Inhale slowly through the left passage and, without retaining the air, close the left nasal passage with the ring and little fingers. Release the thumb and exhale through the right nasal passage.

In short, you inhale through one nasal passage and exhale through the other, with the exception of the initial exhalation which is made through the right nasal passage followed by an inhalation through the same passage. Remember, as you shift from one nasal passage to another, there should be no jerkiness. The inhalation and exhalation should be one continuous flow of air. It is important that the inhalation and exhalation are approximately of the same duration and intensity. Breathe 7 rounds.

Advanced retention: The process above is technically complete for the average person. However, there are two other steps that may be added while under the guidance of an experienced teacher. These include:

a. Having mastered equality of the inhalation and exhalation, you can then proceed to practice retention after inhalation.

b. Having mastered retention after inhalation, you can then proceed to practice retention after exhalation.

Restrictions: In the early stages of nerve purification, many people perspire extensively and begin to shake. This can be overcome by mentally and physically relaxing to remove tension from the muscles. This should be done before beginning the technique. Practice of the two retentions should be attempted only with permission and guidance of an experienced teacher. The texts point out that serious dangers may arise from extensive practice of alternate breathing retention, without proper guidance. Remember, persons suffering from cardiac difficulties or high blood pressure should never attempt to hold the breath. Persons with lower blood pressure may retain the breath after the inhalation only.

Benefits: The blood system is oxidized and prana is brought to the nerves. This pranayama invigorates the entire body, giving alertness to the mind as well. A lightness of the body is produced, appetite is balanced, and sound sleep results.

Mystical benefits: The mystical benefits include the activation of the solar and lunar channels producing a deep peace, astral awareness, and the releasing of the kriya kundalini.

6. FOUR PHASE LIBERATION BREATH
(Chatur-mukhi)

Sit in lotus pose. Turn the head toward the left shoulder and immediately inhale through both nasal passages. Do not retain the air. Immediately exhale only through the left nasal passage without closing the right. Now turn the face toward the right shoulder and inhale immediately through both nostrils, then immediately exhale through the right nostril without closing the left. While inhaling and exhaling there should be a loud sound, indicating that the inhalation and exhalation is being done forcefully. Bring the head forward and place the chin against the chest. Inhale quickly and forcefully through both nostrils and then exhale immediately through both. Next, looking upward, gaze at some distant point above the head. The eyes are then closed, the head is turned to the left, and the entire process begun again. Repeat 6 to 12 times. As you gain efficiency, the number can increase.

Benefits: Strengthens the nerves in the throat, neck, and nose. It also produces a quieting of the mind.

Mystical benefits: Because you are breathing through the ida and pingala, there is purification of the astral channels.

7. EXTENDED FORCEFUL BREATH
(Dirgha-sukshma)

In this technique the breath is used to move a tuft of cotton, gradually increasing the distance between the cotton and the nasal passages. The emphasis is upon developing drawn out and extended inhalations and exhalations.

Sit in the easy pose and place a chair about two feet in front of you. Place a small tuft of cotton on the chair. Exhale and if the cotton moves, place it further from you. Continue to increase the distance of the cotton and the length of the exhalation. As the external distance increases, the inhalation will be felt in the heart, navel, at the base of the spinal cord, and finally in the soles of the feet.

Benefits: Through practice of this pranayama the breath becomes deeper and stronger, yet remaining gentle. A steadiness of the mind is produced, which is helpful in developing powerful meditations.

8. GENTLE AND SOFT EXHALATION BREATH
(Suksama-shwasa-prashwasa)

In this technique the breath is used to move a tuft of cotton, gradually decreasing the distance between the cotton and the nasal passages. The emphasis is upon developing a smooth, soft, gentle inhalation and exhalation.

Sit in the easy pose and place a chair a distance of about 1 foot in front of you. Put a small tuft of cotton on the chair. Exhale and see how far the cotton is moved by your exhalation. Maintain this distance for about a week, trying not to move the cotton with the exhalation. After practicing for 1 week, move the cotton 2 inches closer, exhale and see if the cotton moves. Continue practicing until you reach a stage of development where the cotton does not move at all, even though it may be quite close to your nasal passages. In other words, you are developing a smooth, soft, and gentle exhalation. During this practice, concentrate on the subtleness and lightness of your inhalation and exhalation. While extensively practicing this technique your food should be light.

Mystical benefits: This pranayama helps make the breath extremely subtle. It produces a steadiness of the mind which is helpful in developing powerful meditations. It is an excellent pranayama for raising the kriya kundalini.

9. THE FIRE BREATH
(Agni-prasana)

Sit in the adept's pose. Place the palms on the knees and exhale the air out of the stomach through both nostrils. Inhale, lift the stomach inward, and exhale rapidly. The fire breath is done using both nasal passages for inhalation and exhalation. This inhaling and exhaling must be done repeatedly and rapidly, drawing the stomach in and out. This process is performed 15 to 30 times.

Benefits: Improves digestion, reduces fat on the body. It is one of the best exercises for reducing the abdomen.

Mystical benefits: This pranayama is excellent for raising the kriya kundalini.

10. OM WITH EXHALATION BREATH
(OM Sahita Rechaka)

Sit in the lotus pose. Inhale, taking the breath down to the base of the spinal column. Feel that the breath is going down to the base of the spinal column. Open the lips and produce a harmonious, humming OM sound while exhaling slowly and continuously. Immerse yourself into this sound with the eyes closed. Pronouncing the OM mantra should take at least 40 seconds: devote 30 seconds to the 'O' and 10 seconds to the 'M'. Inhale and repeat the process. This technique can be performed as many times as you find comfortable.

Benefits: This technique enables easy inturning, being absorbed in the mantra sound. It extends the breath, making it subtle, and thus quieting the mind and steadying the intellect. The mind is pulled away from sense objects, thus concentration becomes fixed. The life span is definitely increased.

Mystical benefits: With a good amount of energy poured into this pranayama, the astral OM becomes audible, as are the sound of bells, conches, thunder, and flutes. By inturning and meditating on these pleasant sounds, you will rapidly enter into samadhi.

11. MANTRA WITH RETAINED BREATH
(Sargarbha-sahita-kumbhaka)

In this technique, the breath is inhaled, held, and exhaled while a sacred sound is mentally chanted. In this particular technique the sound utilized is OM, because it is the cosmic sound of the universe.

Sit calmly in a meditative pose, making sure the neck and the waist are in alignment. The left hand forms the wisdom gesture and is placed on the left knee. The right hand forms Shiva mudra. Close the right nostril with the thumb and mentally chant OM. Inhale through the left nostril and mentally chant OM, 8 times.

Close the left nostril with the ring and little fingers, mentally chanting OM, 32 times while retaining the breath. Release the thumb and exhale through the right nostril, mentally chanting OM, 16 times. Reverse the process, by inhaling through the right nostril to a count of 8, retaining the breath with both nostrils closed to a count of 32, and exhaling through the left nostril to a count of 16.

While mentally chanting, the OM may be counted on mala beads or by using the fingers of the left hand. The counting may be done by mentally keeping track. Each mental OM should approximate 1 second of time. Therefore the inhalation = 8 seconds; hold = 32 seconds; exhalation = 16 seconds. If the 8-32-16 count is too intense or causes stress, use a 4-16-8, or 2-8-4 or 1-4-1 count. As the nadis become cleansed and the pranayama mastered--over a period of months, you should attempt to extend the count to 16-64-32. The highest count is 32-128-64.

Restrictions: Persons with high blood pressure should never attempt to hold the breath and consequently this pranayama is not recommended in such cases. As with all pranayamas, the ability to hold the breath comes gradually. You should extend the count without stress.

Benefits: This pranayama gives special mental strength and flexibility. It quiets the sense organs and the mind. It enables you to control hunger and thirst. Consequently your meditation is very deep. Some texts point out this technique practiced over an extended period of time causes the mantra OM to become visible to your mind.

12. THE THREE LOCK BREATH
(Tri-bandha-kumbhaka)

Sit in the lightning bolt or Zen pose and stop the breath wherever it is. Perform the three bandhas: anal contraction, the stomach contraction, and chin lock contraction. Then, hold the breath as long as you can. Release the three contractions and inhale slowly. Repeat this pranayama approximately 6 times while fixing the mind on the breath.

Benefits: This pranayama increases the power of concentration and steadies the mind.

Mystical benefits: Controls and steadies the pranic flow, enabling you to more rapidly attain samadhi. You become aware of the metaphysical secrets related to the retention of the breath.

13. SOLAR-BOUND BREATH
(Sarva-dwara-baddha)

Sit in the lotus pose. Inhale through both nostrils, filling the space from the base of the spine to the throat. Retain the air while closing the senses with the fingers: Close the ears with the thumbs, the eyes with the index fingers, the nostrils with the middle fingers, and the lips with the fourth and fifth fingers on the upper and lower lips, respectively. See the diagram of yoni mudra. Gaze at the sun center which is at the root of the nose between the eyebrows. Retain the breath as long as you can comfortably. Then remove the fingers from the nasal passages and exhale. Repeat a number of times. Increase the number and duration of the hold each and every day.

Mystical benefits: During the retention, the light of the third eye will appear. Some people first see checkered flame patterns arising in the sun center. This divine light or flame leads the yogi to knowledge of the astral and subtle bodies. The appearance of this light also enlivens and steadies the face of the neophyte. The mind ceases to wander and the Gate of God (Brahma-randhra) is thrown wide open.

14. BALANCING ASCENDING-DESCENDING BREATH
(Prana-apana-samykta)

Sit in the adept's pose. Inhale through both nostrils taking the air down to the navel. Take the air in with the feeling that it is going down to the navel. Form the chin lock contraction and hold. Raise the vital descending breath (apana) from the base of the spine to the navel. Mix this descending current with the inhaled air (the ascending current). Form the anal contraction and the stomach contraction. Try to balance the movement of these two vital breaths retaining the full chalice as long as possible. Then exhale. Increase this practice daily.

This technique may seem vague to the non-initiated student and should be followed under the guidance of an experienced teacher. It necessitates a mindful state of consciousness, allowing the student to be aware of these currents and thus the ability to control and mix them. This is true pranayama: The control of the life-force.

Benefits: This pranayama gives physical brilliance and luster to the body.

Mystical benefits: This technique awakens and lifts the kriya kundalini.

15. FORCEFUL EXHALATION AND HOLD BREATH
(Prachhardana)

Practice of this technique consists of throwing the breath outside the body and holding it there.

Sit in the lotus pose. Through both nostrils, exhale the air contained in the stomach. This must be done forcefully as though you were regurgitating. Then hold the empty chalice. Relax, breathe normally for a few moments, and then repeat the process.

Benefits: Cultivates the power of concentration and the ability to develop sense withdrawal.

16. BALANCING BOTH CHALICES BREATH
(Vaya-viya-kumbhaka)

Sit in the lotus pose and gaze at the sun center which is at the root of the nose between the eyebrows. Exhale and inhale quickly through both nostrils 12 to 24 times. Then exhale completely and perform the three contractions. Hold the empty chalice as long as you can comfortably. Inhale when needed, through both nasal passages. Hold the full chalice. Exhale, through both nostrils, when you feel uncomfortable, as though regurgitating. This entire process constitutes 1 round. Practice 2 or 3 rounds daily, increasing the number according to your individual capacity.

Benefits: Produces weight reduction. The body becomes slim and vibrant. Chronic colds are cured. Phlegm in the nose, throat, and lung areas is removed.

Mystical benefits: Through this pranayama the neophyte attains the power to move the breath from the base of the spine all the way up into the head (Brahma-randhra) which awakens the kriya kundalini.

17. FULL CHALICE/EMPTY CHALICE HOLD BREATH
(Bahya-abhyantara-kumbhaka or sahita-kumbhaka)

Sit in the easy pose. Close the right nostril and inhale slowly through the left nostril, taking the air down to the base of the spine. Feel that the air is going down to the base of the spine. Hold the full chalice and then perform the 3 contractions as long as possible. Exhale through the right nostril. Hold the empty chalice as long as possible. Alternate by inhaling through the right nostril, hold, then exhale through the left nostril and hold.

Benefits: Produces a long life and the other general benefits associated with pranayama. The power of inhaling, exhaling, and retention is increased.

18. MANTRA REGULATED BREATHING
(Sapta-vyahrita)

Sit in the hero pose. Inhale through both nostrils and mentally chant the following mantra:

OM Bhuh...	OM Bhuwah...	OM Swaha...
OM Manah...	OM Janah...	OM Tapah...
OM Satyam....		

This mantra should last the length of the inhalation. Hold the full chalice and mentally chant the mantra 3 more times. Exhale while mentally chanting the mantra 2 times. Hold the empty chalice and mentally chant the mantra 7 times.

Benefits: The mind stops wandering and merges itself in deep concentration. Consequently, meditation and samadhi are induced. Useful for developing your intellectual powers.

Mystical benefits: When this pranayama is performed along with this spiritually forceful mantra, it gives the ardent student the visional state.

19. COUNTER-CURRENT NADI BREATH
(Vi-loma)

Vi-loma can be defined as going against the grain, or going against the natural pattern. The inhalation and exhalation, rather than being a continuous stream, is a process of several interruptions, which extends the normal time of inhalation and exhalation.

Stage 1: The inhalation.

Sit in a meditative pose. Inhale for 2 seconds and pause for 2 seconds; again inhale for 2 seconds; pause for 2 seconds; and continue until the lungs are full. Form the chin lock contraction and hold the breath 5 to 10 seconds. Exhale deeply but slowly with the throat somewhat closed, producing a 'h-a-a-a' sound as in the drawing breath (ujjaya). Relax the chin lock contraction before exhaling. Repeat the cycle 5 to 10 times and then rest in the total relaxation pose.

Stage 2: The exhalation.

Having rested for some time, return to a meditative pose. Inhale with the throat somewhat closed, making the sound 's-s-s-s-a,' while filling the lungs to capacity. Form the chin lock contraction and hold the breath 5 to 10 seconds. Exhale for 2 seconds, pause for 2 seconds; again exhale for 2 seconds, pause for 2 seconds. Continue until the lungs are empty. This completes 1 cycle of stage two. Repeat the cycle 5 to 10 times. Rest in savasana.

Variation: Vi-loma is one of the few pranayamas that can be performed while lying down.

Restrictions: Vi-loma is an advanced pranayama. It is recommended that you master the drawing breath and the nadi purification procedures before attempting to master this technique.

Benefits: This pranayama has strong and positive effects on the blood pressure. Stage one improves low blood pressure; stage two improves high blood pressure.

20. REGULATED NADI BREATH
(Anu-loma)

The name suggests a technique that flows in the natural pattern. The inhalation is done through both nostrils and the exhalation is done through alternate nostrils.

Inhale through both nostrils fully and completely. Hold the breath for 5 seconds. Closing off the left nostril, exhale slowly through the right nostril. Completely empty the lungs. Inhale completely through both nostrils and hold for 5 seconds. Close off the right nostril and exhale through the left nostril (using Shiva mudra). This completes 1 cycle of anu-loma. You can perform 3 to 7 rounds at one sitting.

Restrictions: This is definitely an advanced pranayama. Less advanced pranayamas should be mastered first before going on to this one. Try to master the following techniques first: sun-piercing, nerve purification, the drawing breath, and vi-loma. Persons with heart ailments or blood pressure complications should refrain from this technique.

Benefits: Soothes and invigorates the nerves, increases the digestive power, cleanses the sinuses, gives a feeling of lightness to the body, and promotes sound sleep.

Mystical benefits: It awakens the kriya kundalini. Mastery of this technique will enable you to disengage your consciousness from your physical vehicle and move into the astral planes.

21. OPPOSITE NADI BREATH
(Prati-loma)

This particular pranayama is concerned with inhalation through alternate nostrils and exhalation through both nostrils, exactly the opposite of regulated nadi breath, the technique just given.

Sit in a meditative pose. Close the left nasal passage and inhale through the right nasal passage until the lungs are filled. Close off both nasal passages and hold the breath for approximately 5 seconds. Release both nasal passages and exhale slowly, yet deeply and completely, through both nostrils. Close the right nostril and inhale through the left until the lungs are filled. Close both nasal passages and hold 5 seconds. Release both nostrils and exhale slowly and completely. This completes 1 round. Practice 3 to 7 rounds per sitting.

Restrictions: This is an advanced pranayama. Other less advanced pranayamas should be mastered first. Prati-loma should not be practiced by persons who have nervous disorders or by those who are suffering from blood pressure complications.

Benefits: Improves digestion; soothes the nerves; tones and invigorates the entire body. Acts as an expectorant, and cures consumption, asthma, and other pulmonary diseases. Calms the mind and promotes sound sleep.

Mystical benefits: Practicing this pranayama produces re-membrances of previous incarnations. It heightens your conscious awareness, even through the death state.

22. REGULATED COUNTER-CURRENT NADI BREATH
(Anu-loma/vi-loma)

Sit in a meditative pose. Close the right nasal passage and rapidly inhale through the left nostril in one continuous stream. Hold with full chalice. Exhale through the right nostril and then inhale with the same. Continue rapidly, alternating left and right nostrils from 12 to 18 times.

Benefits: Removes impurities of the nose and lungs. The mind becomes clearer, the body healthier, and the brain exceptionally buoyant.

23. MOON-PIERCING BREATH
(Chandra-bhedana)

This technique is a powerful mystical process of piercing the moon. It has deep metaphysical significance and historically is only revealed to advanced disciples. This technique must be practiced only in relationship to a specific time, place, diet, and fasting.

Sitting in a comfortable meditative pose, close off the right nostril and inhale through the left nostril while mentally making a mantric sound, such as OM. Retain the breath in the throat, lungs and stomach. After you can no longer comfortably hold, exhale through the right nostril slowly.   Repeat this as many times as comfortable.

Note: If the left nostril is closed off for whatever reason, patiently lie on your right side for a minute or two, and the left passage will naturally open.   You can then proceed with the technique.   The same is true of the right nostril.   If it is closed off, lie on your left side. Proceed with the technique.

Yoga points out that approximately every two hours, a nasal passage closes off while the other opens.   The opening and closing of the nasal passages refers to the shifting of energies in the ida and pingala nadis.   According to yoga, this two-hour breathing cycle is controlled, for most of us, by the movement of the rising sign which occurs every two hours.   In a male, if a masculine ascending sign rises, the right nasal passage should open; if a female sign ascends the left nasal passage should open.   The reverse is true in women.   There are, also, other factors that affect these conditions.

Restrictions: Historically, the teaching of this technique and its practice are done so in strict relationship to a specific time, place, and diet.

Benefits: Removes excessive heat from the body. Reduction of bile.

Mystical benefits: The moon-piercing breath helps release you from body consciousness whereby you become aware of the inner astral states of consciousness, including the visional state.

Chapter 13

SENSE-WITHDRAWAL
(PRATYAHARA)

Having studied and practiced the outer steps of yoga: yama-niyama, and asan-pranayama, we now move to the inner steps: sense withdrawal-concentration, and meditation-samadhi.

HOW YOUR PSYCHIC MECHANISM FUNCTIONS

In eastern psychology, the totality of your awareness: consciously, unconsciously, subconsciously, preconsciously, and superconsciously is called chitta. Literally translated it means mind-stuff and is composed of three separate functions:

1. Mind or sense organs (manas)
2. Intellect (buddhi)
3. Ego (ahamkara)

According to yoga psychology, the brain is a system consisting of gross and subtle organs. The gross organs are linked to the external sense organs: the ears, skin, eyes, tongue, and nose, which convey experience of external objects to the mind (manas) and the intellect (buddhi). The external sense organs experience external objects. The subtle organs likewise experience these objects, conveying this experience to the mind, which transfers it to the intellect where the experience is converted into data and knowledge. It is then evaluated by the ego, and if found acceptable, is brought up into consciousness. The subtle organs are called chakras, and classify everything into ten catagories. For example the venus chakra classifies love feelings and emotions; the saturn chakra classifies duty and confinement. The ego lives in the mercury chakra. Though these seem as if they are separate processes, they are actually only one, comprising the totality of mind-stuff (chitta). Here are two examples to illustrate this process:

1. Two men are in a room and a dog enters. One man fearfully runs and hides in the closet. The other man befriends and plays with it. Why are their actions so different? Because the mind-stuff of each man differs.

Both men saw the dog. This sense data was transmitted to the minds (manas) of both men. In the intellect (buddhi) of the first man, his data was transformed into a perception of danger, because in his memory was the strong subconscious thought: 'There is a dog. A dog once bit me. All dogs bite. That dog is going to bite me. I must protect myself.' In the intellect of the second man, the perception of the data was transmitted, because of memories, into the following thoughts: 'There is a dog. Dogs are man's best friend. Dogs are amiable and enjoyable to play with.' Here, you can see the subtle interplay of mind, memory, intellect, and ego in each man. Thus, you see why yogis spend so much time balancing out their memory tracks.

2. The sense organs perceive a piece of cake which has the odor and the flavor of chocolate. It is brown, moist, and rich. The senses of sight and smell transmit their data to the mind (manas). In the intellect (buddhi) the data is transformed into a perception, giving rise to the following thought: 'It is chocolate cake.' The ego then says, 'It is for me. It will make me happy, and it will give me energy.' And the individual eats the piece of cake.

MIND-STUFF
(Chitta)

The concepts of consciousness (chitta), mind (manas), intellect (buddhi), and ego (ahamkara) are further expanded to give a better understanding of how they function. Chitta is the totality of consciousness. It includes the sense organs, intellect, and ego sense. The mind-stuff has no direct relationship to the sense organs. It functions through three qualities called lethargy, passionate activity, and compassionate activity. In Sanskrit, these are called tamas, rajas, and sattva, respectively. Here is a further explanation of the functioning of chitta.

1. Sense organs (manas):

This is the faculty that perceives the sense objects. It receives impressions (sense experiences) and carries them to the intellect (buddhi) for distinguishing and classification. The five sense organs relate to the five lower energy centers (chakras) which store data, even from past lives.

2. Intellect (buddhi):

This is the faculty that discerns, and discriminates making judgmental values, having the potential to make distinctions or interpretations accurately or inaccurately. The intellect is the consciousness behind the sense organs that classifies sensory data. It is the evaluating factor; it interprets data.

3. Ego-maker (ahamkara):

The ego-maker exists in the lower mercury center. The ego-maker is the faculty that says, 'I am me. I am what I experience and what I interpret through these experiences.' The ego is also a storage bank that interprets particular experiences according to how 'I' conceive 'me'.

The ego is the false self in relationship to Spirit (atma), which is the true Self. The spirit is that which is real; all else is unreal. The ego is unreal from the standpoint that perceptions are transitory, ever changing. When you close off the senses, sensory data disappear; only memory remains (and it changes with time). The Spirit, on the other hand, is unchanging. The ego is artificial or transitory, for how you see yourself is based upon your sense experiences and judgment of your intellect. The ego is simply a combination of sense data and the evaluations of that sense data.

An important factor regarding the ego is that it is not negative and is not to be destroyed or punished. It is a necessary evolutionary stage in our total unfoldment. The problem with ego consciousness is this: believing that it is the final reality, the ego process stops and does not continue in its evolution. The technical term for this process is called ignorance. Ignorance is the cause of all suffering.

HOW YOGA RELATES TO THE
THREE FACTORS OF MIND-STUFF

The sun and moon centers are the manifestations of the individual soul and its full potential. The spinal column can be considered a mini-universe. The ascending and descending energies (prana and apana), flowing on the outer surface of the chakras relate to various states of consciousness. Through the practice of yoga you purify these two energy channels (nadis), opening up the constrictions within the center of the spinal column. This will enable you to lift the currents to the thousand-petalled lotus. The thousand-petalled lotus is the symbol of full and total realization of

the true Self (atma).   Here within this state of consciousness lies
true joy, love, bliss, and wisdom.

However, in the pursuit of this evolutionary goal, mankind en-
counters two major obstacles.   These are karma, and his own nature (memory track).

1. The first problem is the manifestation of karma from the
   past.   It makes no difference whether this karma is from
   three days ago or from three lifetimes ago.   Through the
   eight processes of yoga, you can break free of this storage of
   karma contained within and around the energy centers of
   your spinal column.   As this karma is balanced out you move
   away from these areas and move through the center channel,
   freeing the mind-stuff, momentarily, of past karmic emotionalities, and delusions.   You see life as it is, not as you have
   lived it.   Once seen, it becomes a new, powerful, positive
   memory to further spiritual unfoldment.

   Where is an individual's karma?   Karma exists as seed-
   karmas (vasanas) in the pericarp of the heart of the causal
   body.   Vasanas (the v is pronounced like a w) are not actual
   karmas, but are seeds of karma awaiting an appropriate
   moment to sprout.   At the proper moment, the causal body
   releases from its heart, these seed-karmas that now flow
   down from the mercury center to the saturn center, and
   back up to the sun center.   After leaving the causal body,
   the seeds circulate in the astral body becoming caught in the
   nets of various astral chakras.   Here they mix with the forces
   of your spiritual nature as well as the desire of that chakra,
   becoming a force to be dealt with here in this life, at this
   time.   The breath, with its inhalation and exhalation, creates
   moisture and heat which cause the seeds to sprout and grow
   in the astral vehicle.   They then circulate and drop down to
   the physical body producing physical karmic conditions.

   Through the practice of sense-withdrawal, the yogi with-
   draws the chitta from the senses.   In so doing, he masters his
   destiny by withdrawing energy from the karma!   By breathing
   through the center channel of sushumna rather than the sun
   and moon channels (pingala and ida), heat is generated
   whereby the karmic seeds are roasted or burnt up.   Thus,
   they cannot sprout.   Although the karmic seeds are still released into the astral body through the pores in the membranes of the pericarp of the heart of the causal body, and
   although the seeds are still caught in the nets of the astral

chakras and released into the physical vehicle, because they have been roasted, they will never sprout.

You may wonder if the heat from the solar channel can roast the karmic seeds. It cannot, for this heat is on the outer surface or periphery of your mind/body complex and therefore does not have direct contact with the karmic seeds. Also, the heat of the solar channel is not intense enough to roast them.

2. The second obstacle to man's attainment of the higher goal of self-realization is his nature, best known as his total memory. The memory of the past hinders us from going anywhere but back to the past. The average human being, by his very nature, is totally engrossed in the lower segment of the spinal column, specifically the saturn, jupiter, mars levels of consciousness. He becomes lost in his search for the ultimate reality as perceived through the sense organs. This he does with such intensity that he feels he is what he perceives. As an example, if a man feels misery over a long period of time, he begins to believe he is misery. If a person experiences joy, he says, 'I am happy,' and believes he is happiness.

Furthermore, when you feel pleasure, why is it that it does not continue? The answer lies in the fact that pleasure and pain are a two-sided coin. They are inseparable. Inevitably, pleasure follows pain, and pain follows pleasure. The yogi attempts to escape from this pleasure-pain principle by pulling away from sensory data, withdrawing the mind-stuff from the sense organs. This enables him to lift the life-current away from the lower chakras, and to ascend to the higher chakras.

The concepts of pleasure and pain are directly related to the concepts of aversion and attraction. The emotions of extreme aversion and extreme attraction are inimical to a quiescent mind which is necessary to acquire the ability to in-turn, and gain an awareness of the higher Self in order to obtain depth of wisdom. Therefore, in your daily life and yogic practices, attempt to detach yourself from all heavy emotionality which impairs your intellect and consequently the discerning powers. This detachment allows you to attain a way of life that is wiser than would be when judgments are made through emotionality. Many extreme aversions and attractions are not always conscious. A person does not always have an awareness of the tremendous proclivities of the mind that drive it and interfere with logical patterns.

You must begin by becoming detached from the gross and more obvious objects, and then move to detachment from inward and more subtle objects. In this way, you can turn inward and upward, attaining the goal of life. As you move toward detachment, you should not be unduly upset when experiencing the undesirable. It is, also, important that you not become unduly elated when pleasant, desirable experiences manifest.

The Bhagavad Gita points out: 'Everyone acts according to his own nature, against which no effort is ever successful.' It is the nature of the tongue to appreciate taste. It doesn't matter whether a person is a householder or a monk, that which is sweet, tastes sweet. The tongue cannot behave against its own nature. The goal of yoga, therefore, is not to change the sense organs, but to transcend them.

Why should one make such an effort to control the sense organs? Because deep in the sense organs lies the force of attractions and aversions. It is ever awaiting to jump forth and manifest. Desirable objects attract us and undesirable objects repel us. The repulsion gives us pain. Although the attraction gives us momentary pleasure, it brings apprehension and fear that we shall lose it. Thus, again we have pain. When the mind dwells on a physical object, the feeling of attraction arises. These basic feelings are rooted in the feeling of possession. Attraction causes possession. Possessiveness is the cause of human suffering, as it destroys the intellect's power of discernment. The more you are in control of the sense organs, the less likely you will lose this power of discernment.

The experience of taste belongs to the sense organs. This sense of taste is responsible, as are other sense organs, for the creation of attraction and aversion. Although it is the nature of the senses to function, they should not be allowed to manifest uncontrolled. The senses need to be guarded and disciplined. We should ever remain completely detached. Always remember, detachment does not mean indifference.

Summary. The theory of yoga points out that when the five gross sense organs, as well as the mind and intellect, become passive, a state of sense-withdrawal is attained. It is important to understand that passive or inactive sense organs should not be construed to mean that the sense organs are malfunctioning. The mind has merely pulled away from their force and they have become inactive.

Sense-withdrawal is a state of consciousness that differs from the normal three states of consciousness which every human being experiences. These are:

1. The wakeful state,
2. The dreaming state,
3. The dreamless sleep state.

The goal of sense withdrawal is valuable, because it leads to a fourth state beyond these everyday three, by enabling you to reach into your inner soul.

DEFINITION OF SENSE-WITHDRAWAL

Sense-withdrawal is the yogic technique by which you take the naturally extroverted and outgoing forces of the sense organs and cause them to become introverted, and inturned. This is done by drawing the senses away from their respective objects.

The Vishnu Purana points out that sense withdrawal is the action whereby you control the sense organs which naturally feel drawn outward toward their gross objects, by turning inward away from the gross objects themselves.

According to Patanjali's Yoga Sutras, sense withdrawal occurs when a person disciplines his sense organs to follow his intellect. In this way, the sense organs can easily withdraw from their objects, rather than be forced to follow them. The sense organs are controlled, by not allowing them to come into contact with their respective objects, and disciplining them to follow the intellect.

Another clear meaning of sense-withdrawal is, 'mastery of the senses'. When external objects are present, the sense organs cannot recognize them without the command of the mind. In a state of sense-withdrawal, the mind detaches itself from the external objects and becomes internalized. Consequently, the sense organs which normally run after these external objects cease their running and become stilled. In yoga, this idea is expressed through the symbolism of the bee. Just as the drones follow the queen bee, so the sense organs follow the mind. When the mind is internalized, the sense organs become stilled and renounce their craving for objects. Conversely, when the mind renounces the craving for objects, the sense organs become stilled.

The Bhagavad Gita states that the sense organs are extremely powerful, for once a person is drawn toward external objects, the objects attach themselves to the mind, agitating it. It teaches us that the wise soul keeps the sense organs constantly under control and thus his intellect becomes steady.

Katha Upanishad points out the mind follows the senses and the sense organs follow the external objects. Thus, the mind becomes lost as a ship in a storm. A wise soul disciplines his mind and gives direction to the sense organs, like a trained horse in the hands of a trainer. If he is unwise, his mind will not be controlled and his gross sense organs will wildly run, as do restless steeds.

Most humans find life quite painful. Why? Because they are locked to the possessiveness of things and cannot adjust to ever-changing life conditions. They seem unable to break this bondage because they attempt to release themselves from objects, without first having control over their sense organs. Through control of the sense organs they become truly detached. As they become truly detached, they no longer experience the negativity of the mind.

The key word is detachment: not detachment from objects, but detachment from our reactions to these objects, and our sensory perceptions of the objects. When the yogi talks about detachment, he is talking about detachment toward all things. This means detachment toward pleasure as well as pain; it means detachment toward external as well as internal objects. The average person finds it impossible to release himself from the shackles of worldly objects. This is called bondage. The cause of this bondage results from sense organs constantly running after objects, which produces heavier cravings. Cravings just grow, they cannot be satisfied.

The third chapter of the Bhagavad Gita beautifully expresses this concept of craving and attachment:

'Cravings cause addiction.
When that addiction is thwarted your mind becomes confused.
Confuse your mind and you lose the power of discernment.
Lose the power of discernment and you forget life's meaning.
Lose life's meaning and you miss the purpose of life.
Miss the purpose of life and you become unhappy... and what is
    life without happiness?'

Until the mind is completely controlled, sense-withdrawal cannot be perfected. Without the perfection of sense-withdrawal you cannot attain samadhi. Without samadhi there is no permanent happiness. When sense-withdrawal has been mastered, concentration, meditation, and samadhi are very easily attained.

The major obstacle to the attainment of the goal of yoga is sense attachment. The first rule of yoga is the ability to control the sense organs. Control the sense organs, and you dissolve away the dark desires deep within. These deep, dark desires need to be dissolved away, for they destroy discernment and consequently Wisdom. The foe is to be subdued. The foe, the enemy, is craving.

THE PROCESS OF SENSE-WITHDRAWAL

Unless the student has acquired mastery over the first four gross steps of yoga, sense-withdrawal is impossible.

The two most valuable supports in establishing sense-withdrawal and gaining control over the life-force are pranayama and mantra. It has been found that mantra, being more subtle than pranayama, is often difficult to sustain, especially when the mind is drawn toward objects. Breathing techniques are more helpful, as they are less subtle than mantra. Pranayama enables the mind to let go of what it is attracted to. Once the mind has let go of the object through pranayama, you may use mantra to go deeper. Pranayama purifies the external, gross sense organs, and brings them under control. Pranayama has an affection to the five gross organs and thus has a powerful and positive effect on them. This will enable you to drive beyond gross sense objects into higher states. It is through the practice of pranayama and mantra that sense-withdrawal is attained and made deeper.

Until some degree of mastery over the five gross sense organs is attained, it will be impossible to understand the five subtle organs. Without knowledge or understanding of the subtle sense organs, it is impossible to understand subtle astral objects such as the astral body. Here again is the importance of mastery over the gross levels of consciousness so that there can be attainment in the subtler realms.

When the intellect is attached to gross objects, it is then that the intellect ceases to function in the subtle realm. The sense organs function only in the initiation of the intellect. Thus control of the intellect is essential for the attainment of sense-withdrawal. The sage Goraksha says, 'As the tortoise is able to draw its limbs, so should the yogi draw in his sense organs'.

During meditation, the external sense organs remain inactive. When a person is in deep meditation, his eyes see nothing, his ears hear nothing. In short, his senses do not sense anything. During the process of meditation the gross sense organs cease to function and do not acquire any data regarding gross objects. This is so because the mind is inactive. As soon as the mind is truly quieted, the gross sense organs cease to have contact with external objects. This total process is called sense-withdrawal or pratyahara.

TWO TYPES OF SENSE-WITHDRAWAL

During sense-withdrawal, the intellect continues to be active, for it distinguishes and discerns. It is the sense organs that become inactive. Throughout this process the sense organs remain calm. Over and above sense-withdrawal of external gross objects there is still another subtler level that needs mastery. During meditation or extremely deep contemplation, the mind and intellect come into contact with subtle objects through the subtle sense organs. The yogi must also be capable of subtle sense-withdrawal from these subtle objects.

There is sense-withdrawal from gross sense organs and sense-withdrawal from subtle sense organs. This means that there are two sets of objects: gross objects, usually referred to as physical objects, and subtle objects usually referred to as astral objects.

The gross objects are those enjoyed by the gross sense organs. The subtle objects are those read about in the scriptures or often heard about from those on the spiritual pathway. These subtle objects can only be perceived and thus enjoyed through and by the astral body. These subtle astral perceptions are known more commonly as clairvoyance, clairaudience, and psychometry.

If a person is desirous of realizing the Self and obtaining release from limitation, it is absolutely necessary that there be both levels of sense-withdrawal. Only when both levels are mastered does the yogi enter into awareness of the super-subtler realm and its super-subtle objects. Herein lies samadhi. Not until the intellect is completely divested of all its attachments to the gross and subtle objects, can sense-withdrawal be completely attained, allowing yoga concentration to begin.

THE STAGES OF SENSE-WITHDRAWAL

There are four stages of sense-withdrawal:
1. Progressive detachment
2. Exclusive detachment
3. One-organ detachment
4. Controlled detachment.

Let us briefly look at each of these.

Stage 1. PROGRESSIVE DETACHMENT
       (Yatamana)

This first stage of detachment deals primarily with love and hate. These two extremely powerful emotions are deeply ingrained in human consciousness, and drive us toward given objects. We usually think of love as being the only emotion that draws us toward an object. Yoga points out that hate drives the mind to that object and ironically holds us to that object of hate.

Feelings of love and hate are the main cause of grief. In the majority of cases, people experience grief because they love possessively. With the help of the intellect and the utilization of sense-withdrawal, these two emotions are controlled and craving is softened by withdrawing the sense organs from these two sets of mental objects. It must be understood that the word love (kama or bhakti) is not to be confused with unselfish love (prem).

Stage 2. EXCLUSIVE DETACHMENT
       (Vyatireka)

Exclusive detachment implies that with the assistance of the intellect, you are able to observe life in general, along with your own life, clearly recognizing the seeming negativity that exists in various objects. You are able to perceive which objects in the world cause the greatest amount of pain, because of mankind's attachment to them, and not because of an innate negativity within the object itself. When you are able to perceive the dangers within certain objects you will be able to determine which objects are detrimental to your own lifestyle. This is done by determining and establishing:

      a. Which of these negatives have been properly renounced. Effort must be regenerated toward those objects that have been renounced, insuring they remain renounced, and that those objects which

need to be renounced, and have not been renounced, be renounced.

b. Which of these negatives are being renounced, and
checking to be sure that they are being properly
renounced. Note what added effort is needed to
successfully complete this task.

c. Which of these negatives are to be renounced,
placing them in order of importance and in a
chronological order. A plan should be established
for proper, harmonious renunciation.

Through this threefold process, you attain detachment
from objects.

Stage 3. ONE-ORGAN DETACHMENT
(Eka-indriya)

By persistent indulgence in emotionalities, these emotional forces enter as impressions into the depths of your
memory banks in the chakras. This produces a very
deep, unconscious interference with the functions of the
intellect. The deeper the emotional impression, and the
more frequent its impression upon the mind-stuff, the
more will a given sense organ activate. For example,
most of us would not be upset if a newspaper were burnt,
but most of us would certainly be upset if we saw someone burning a textbook.

The symbol, textbook, has made a much deeper emotional impression in our subconscious mind than did the
newspaper.

Through one-organ detachment, the yogi assures that
these interferences do not take place. One-organ detachment is a technique. However, it is a technique that
you do all day long, each day of your life. If even one
single sense organ remains uncontrolled, sense-withdrawal
or the other higher stages of yoga cannot be attained.
You must determine which sense organ produces the
greatest emotionality and refrain from activating or stimulating it.

Stage 1 tends to be more concerned with people and
personalities. It implies you should not allow the egotistical personality of a professor to interfere with your wish
to learn a given subject. Nor should you allow your
boss's aggressive nature to cause you to lose interest in
your job.

Stage 2 is more concerned with objects surrounding you. Thoughts such as, 'I do not have a car. Therefore, I am not very important'. Your happiness should not be determined by objects.

Stage 3 relates more to your inner dreams and spiritual unfoldment plans. These are not dependent on gross objects, but must be renounced so that you find happiness, joy, and wisdom along your pathway of life.

Remember, the cause of unhappiness is your attitude and your attachment to objects, not the innate quality of objects.

Stage 4. CONTROLLED DETACHMENT
(Vashikara)

With extensive practice of the above three stages of sense-withdrawal, you ultimately reach a stage in which the deep, buried impressions do not arise and disturb the intellect. When the intellect is not disturbed, even in the presence of gross or subtle objects, controlled detachment is acquired. In this way, detachment becomes an everyday part of your life.

DETACHMENT EXERCISES

1. EXERCISE A

Sit in a meditative posture with eyes closed, and visualize two people, one whom you like very much and one whom you dislike. Examine your thoughts, emotions, and feelings, and see if in some small way you can balance out or understand your personality. Determine why there is such a strong difference in the feelings regarding these two people. It is best to think of two people of the same sex. Thus, if you think of a man whom you like, also think of a man whom you dislike. If you decide to think of a woman you like, also think of a woman you dislike. By inturning, withdrawing, and examining your mental reactions as you visualize these two people, you gain insights helping you to become more detached.

2. EXERCISE B

Sit in a meditative pose with eyes closed and think of an object that you want. Or, think back a few years to that time when you really wanted something. Now, mentally revert to your early childhood and remember how happy you were before you ever knew that such objects existed. By examining these two aspects, you will gain insights into your life and personality. For example, today, many people are totally addicted to television and cannot live without it. But they lived very comfortably and happily before television was invented. What happened to their minds? Do you understand?

3. EXERCISE C
Visualize a person that you have strong negative feelings toward. Now mentally say something to that person: 'Hi, there... I like you... Help me to understand you...' Say it with feeling, and watch your mental reactions. Reaffirm positive mental statements toward that person until you can create within yourself great positivity regarding him. Do not allow the image to produce more negativity than positivity. An insightful thought to remember: The image within your mind is not that person, external to you. In this inward mental state, withdraw your senses and become more detached, recognizing that your thoughts and attitudes have absolutely nothing to do with that person. Understand?

4. EXERCISE D
Visualize someone you really like. Imagine them asking you to do something that you would prefer not to do. Mentally say to them: 'I'm sorry, I don't wish to do that'. It is very difficult to refuse to do something for someone you like. Watch your mental reactions to this process. It will give you insights and help in producing detachment... and more freedom.

In the practice of all these techniques, a few minutes a day is not enough. They are exercises that should be performed quite frequently, until you gain insight and freedom and become detached. Become detached but not indifferent.

SENSE-WITHDRAWAL TECHNIQUES

1. THE NETI TECHNIQUE
The neti technique is an important technique whereby you attain sense-withdrawal from gross and subtle objects. It's an important technique for assisting detachment from all objects. This technique breaks the illusion that you are the body, and the illusion that you are that which your mind thinks (you are).

Sit comfortably in a meditative pose. Close your eyes and turn inward. The room should be quiet, the time very late or very early. The temperature in the room should be comfortable. It should be pleasant with no distractions, physically or emotionally. The time of your practice, each day, should always be the same. Sit on a folded blanket with your body at full attention without tension. Become mentally and physically as comfortable as possible. Keep the spine straight. Wear warm, comfortable, loose-fitting clothes. The body must now remain perfectly motionless.

Now begin. Take a deep breath and relax. Be at full attention without tension. You are beginning to meet your mind. Though sometimes difficult, it is worth it. Let your thoughts flow. Watch them, without judgment... just watch them. Be yourself. Watch your thoughts, unconcernedly. Be mindful of what is happening in your inward universe... meet your mind. As you are mindful of the thoughts and as you see a thought, mentally think and mentally feel: Neti, neti, neti. This means, 'I'm not this thought; I'm not that thought; I'm not thought'. In essence, you will experience an important realization: I am not this thought that I see, nor am I this thought watching that thought... I am not thought at all.

Insofar as you do not identify yourself with the stream of thoughts, you begin to realize the real Self. This process is so simple to describe, yet so, so difficult to perform. It is important to master. You will realize through this procedure, that thoughts are not really you. This technique should be practiced for 3 to 7 minutes a day. It would be helpful to practice it for the rest of your life. You will, however, find major benefits within weeks, if not days.

2. YONI MUDRA TECHNIQUE

The yoni mudra technique is another procedure for attaining sense-withdrawal. It is extremely important for it astralizes your consciousness, allowing you to move into the subtler realms. (See the diagram of the yoni mudra.) Sit erect, resting the elbows on a table or some other small support. This support should be high enough that you can easily place your thumbs on your ears without slumping forward or straining upward. Place the thumbs comfortably but tightly on each of the tragus so that they close the openings of the ears. The eyes are closed and focused at the root of the nose at the eyebrows. The jupiter fingers (index) are placed below the eyes to hold them firmly. They are pressed lightly so as to prevent movement of the eyeballs, assisting the eye hold at the ajna chakra. Each middle finger rests gently on the nasal passages;

the ring fingers are placed on the upper lip and little fingers on the lower lip. Now take a deep breath, hold, and press the fingers so that all the sense organs are stopped. This is known as yoni mudra.

While holding your breath comfortably, mentally turn inward, with such intensity that you forget the whole external universe. This is sense-withdrawal. Full attention is focused at and on the ajna chakra, looking for and perceiving the light that is literally there. At first, most people perceive only darkness. Later, it appears to be a

Yoni Mudra

circular darkness at the sun center. Without straining, continue to look. Later, a hazy will-o'-the-wisp, then a circular egg-shaped light will appear. Still later, a circle of light can be seen. This circle of light then takes on various colorations: gold, then blue.

When the breath can no longer be comfortably held, release all the fingers. Exhale slowly. Inhale slowly, hold again, turning yet deeper inward.

3. THE WIND-UP WATCH TECHNIQUES

Sit in the adept's pose. Place a windup watch approximately 1 foot from your body. Close the eyes and concentrate on the ticking sound. Now turn inward and silently chant OM, until you no longer hear the ticking. Then listen again for the ticking for a few seconds. Turn inward again silently chanting until you no longer hear the ticking.

Repeat this technique a number of times.

Chapter 14

CONCENTRATION
(DHARANA)

The four earlier stages of yoga are called the outer limbs. The four later stages of yoga are called the inner limbs. They are: sense-withdrawal, concentration, meditation, and contemplation. There are also many higher states of contemplation (samadhi) called the innermost limbs. The four inner limbs cannot be separated from the four outer limbs, as they form one continuous movement, moving you toward your goal. Through the practice of motionlessness, pranayama, and chanting (mantra), along with the use of mental imagery, the yogi produces a mind-energy that enables him to move into a state of concentration-meditation-samadhi.

It is important to realize that sense-withdrawal, concentration, meditation, and contemplation (samadhi) form an active sequence, making a coherent, consistent whole. The practice of sense-withdrawal leads to concentration yet continues beyond and through meditation into contemplation. As sense-withdrawal is slowly mastered, concentration begins. As concentration is finally mastered, then and only then does meditation commence. Following this, contemplation or samadhi slowly manifests. One cannot truly say, however, where sense-withdrawal ends and concentration begins; or where concentration ends and meditation begins; or where meditation ends and contemplation begins. These separate movements occur simultaneously with eminent speed when the sage sits and practices the inward art. It is for purpose of explanation that we break down yoga into parts.

For example, the ancient texts state when you hold your mind on any given gross object for 12 seconds with no distraction whatsoever, you have technically attained concentration. This is not an easy state to attain, for during those 12 seconds, the mind may not be interrupted by any internal or external secondary thought whatsoever. Also, the ancient texts indicate if 144 seconds of concentration are attained, this will manifest as a state of meditation, of one second. If you can hold a concentrated thought for 144 seconds without any secondary thoughts or interruptions, a movement of meditation will arise. This is an effortless holding of the object in the mind. If 1,728 seconds of meditation (or 29 minutes) are sustained, a state of contemplation (samadhi) is reached. If contemplation can be held for 48 minutes (a muhurta) liberation (kaivalya) is attained.

This data, though accurate insofar as time is concerned, does not indicate the subtle inward distinctions between the states of concentration, meditation, and contemplation. It does, however, give an interesting guideline. This mathematical calculation is based upon information in the Kurma Purana.

Concentration, meditation, and contemplation together perform a deep, yogic function. This continuum in Sanskrit is called samyama. It has a number of root meanings. Samyama means holding consciousness together. The expression 'holding together' clearly points out that in samyama there is a combined action of concentration, meditation, and contemplation, with a dynamic thrust. The thrust is inward and upward so that the matrix of consciousness may be explored, understood, and ultimately transcended.

Concentration, meditation, samadhi are something the yogi does, not something the yogi is. These operations are not of the body but of the mind. They are described as the inner limbs of yoga, and definitely entail subtle astral action: internal mind action which is called kriya yoga, the yoga of mind action, the yoga of spiritual action. The action of concentration can only be performed when the mind is free from distraction. You learn to do something by doing, therefore, you learn to free the mind from distractions by trying to concentrate. You learn to ride a bicycle by trying to ride a bicycle, not by sitting on the porch steps thinking about it. In this case, thinking merely becomes a distraction to learning. Likewise, a distracted mind cannot learn to concentrate. Without being able to concentrate, you can never truly free the mind. You learn to free the mind from distraction by trying to free it.

Concentration, like meditation, is a function of the mind, rather than a condition of the mind. It is a function that you perform. It may be helpful to compare concentration with walking. Walking is not a condition within which you find yourself but a function you perform in order to travel somewhere. This concept applies to meditation and contemplation as well.

The ancient texts point out that just as gold ore is purified by heating it in a crucible, so too the mind is purified by placing it in the crucible of concentration. Concentration is the crucible of controlled, determined thinking.

CONTROLLING THE MIND

In yoga, the mind-stuff is normally divided into three stages of evolution, each characterized by a specific quality:
1. The dull or the lethargic state, called tamas.
2. The overactive or the emotional passionate activity called rajas.
3. The calm, equanimity state, referred to as the illuminative state of compassion, called sattva.

These three qualities are called gunas, and they have an evolutionary process. The mind is first dull, and then, breaking away from its lethargy, becomes passionate. In passionate activity it runs wild, yet this is higher than no action at all. Then, the mind must rebalance its passion and become compassionate. This is the highest state. (See diagram of the gunas.)

The Unfoldment of the Gunas

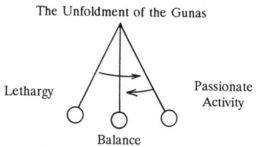

Lethargy

Passionate
Activity

Balance

Most human beings, physically and mentally, are an interaction of these three qualities, called gunas. This interaction causes the average person at one moment to become dull and lazy, at the next moment to be hyperactive, and in the next moment, compassionate and wise. The cycle repeats itself again and again. Independent of these interactions, there is a basic continual state of consciousness that prevails. Thus, we say one is lethargic, passionate, or serene.

When the mind is overcome by dullness (tamas), it lacks the power to differentiate between wisdom and foolishness. When the mind is overcome by passionate activity (rajas) it is drawn toward ambition and discontentment. In this state, the mind is consumed by feverish unrest and irresistible and insatiable cravings. The result is the person becomes more and more entangled in the externals and the superficiality of life. In this state, no matter how much the mind achieves, it is forever unsatisfied until it is ultimately consumed by its own craving. When the mind is ruled by equanimity (sattva) it unfolds, is collected, serene, and wise. This is the state needed for the attainment of spiritual insight. Through concentration, this is attained.

In India, the mind is known as the great bird, because it flies from one object to another just as a bird flies from one tree to another. In some literature, the mind is also likened unto a monkey because it continually jumps from one object to another. But the mind, despite its jumping, flying, and flitting, is attached, either directly or indirectly, to some basic karmic idea. I refer to this as the stickiness of the mind. It is a ticky-tacky quality that inhibits the mind from exploring and discovering newer, greater ideas. Just as the scientist concentrates his mind and invents new things, just as the mathematician concentrates and conceives a new formula, so the yogi concentrates his mind and opens it to new wisdom: knowledge of himself and of his universe. The power of concentration unglues the staid, jaded mind. It frees the mind from notions that inhibit its unfoldment.

Concentration is a technique for centering and rebalancing the equilibrium of the mind-stuff. Most human beings are out of balance with life. This disharmony causes one to be scattered and dull.

In the Bhagavad Gita, Sri Krishna points out the necessity for equilibrium, saying: 'Arjuna, the practice of yoga is not for him who eats too much or eats too little; nor is it for him who sleeps too much or keeps awake excessively. He who moderates his eating, his work, his recreation, his sleep, he alone is capable of mastering yoga'.

The practice of concentration begins with a concerted effort to remove the physical and mental imbalances of your lifestyle. This effort is reciprocal, for as you learn to concentrate and gain success in yoga, your life will become more balanced and meaningful. However, it is necessary to remove the impediments to concentration.

IMPEDIMENTS TO CONCENTRATION

There are a series of impediments to the practice of concentration. The student should be watchful so as to overcome them.

1. The major obstacle to learning concentration is unbridled emotionality. You must move forward to bridle your emotions, as you move through life.

2. Those engaged in heavy daily work schedules may find it difficult to find the energy and time needed for concentration practice. The energy and time must be carved to allow for this important practice.
3. Extreme physical or mental weakness will impair your ability to learn concentration. Mental and physical shortcomings will not prohibit your learning, but will definitely retard the process. Proper practice of postures and breath-control will correct these conditions.
4. Lack of an intuitional understanding of the importance of concentration will keep you from its goal. Concentration is not only important in a spiritual sense, but also in the psycho-bio-mental functioning of your individual being.
5. Concern over gain or loss in the mastery of concentration will seriously inhibit your unfoldment. Simply perform the exercises quietly and consistently, without thought of how well you are doing. You will be surprised at your rapid progress.
6. Lack of proper attitude toward your own mind will keep you from progressing. On all levels of your being realize this important psychological concept: I am not my mind. I have a mind and a body, but they are merely instruments for my expression. I am the self-existent one.

YOGA THEORY OF MIND CONTROL

Mankind does possess the ability to concentrate. For the vast majority of people, however, concentration is involuntary and un-controlled. Concentration is a result of the forces and power of the sense organs over the mind. It is essential that you are able to concentrate consciously, with volition, upon whatsoever the mind wills. Concentration means you are able to hold to the state of concentration as long as the related task is to be performed.

In like manner, concentration also means being able to let go of the state of concentration when it is no longer necessary to hold to a related task. For example, when solving a given problem the mind must focus on the problem for a period of time. When the problem is solved, you and your mind must let go of the problem. In our everyday lives, we often spend too much time concentrating on a problem, thinking we will solve it simply by focusing our atten-tion to it. This is not always true. It is wisdom to realize that thinking or decision-making is not problem-solving. Sometimes, letting go and returning to the problem when your mind is fresher, is wisdom. As in all of yoga, the key is disciplining the mind to let go when necessary.

In short, concentration from the yogic viewpoint is practicing techniques whereby you gain conscious control over your mental faculties. When concentration is mastered, the scattered energies of the mind are gathered together like a brilliant searchlight, removing darkness, enabling you to perceive into the distance. Only if you can use your mind and intellect, undisturbed by distracting emotionalities and cravings, can you truly be free and achieve the goals you have set for yourself in this lifetime.

There is a story in the Mahabharata about an archery tournament in which a wooden fish was set on a high pole at a distance. The eye of the fish was used as the target. Many kings and princes came forth, trying to hit the eye, but they all missed the target. Before each one released his arrow, the teacher asked him what he saw. All replied that they saw a fish on a pole. Finally, when Arjuna was asked this question he replied, 'All I see is an eye'. He alone hit the mark with his great power of concentration. You must of necessity close out all disruptive and irrelevant awarenesses so you might hit your mark.

The word concentration comes from a Latin word meaning one-pointedness. Concentration begins with the ability to direct the mind and maintain a full and exclusive attention on the object of concentration. As concentration is mastered, a second step occurs. The ability to stop the mind and look back at the machinery of thinking itself.

The function of concentration is to bring the mind to a focus, which like a searchlight, gives it the power to:
1. First, pay attention to the object of concentration.
2. Then shift from the object of concentration to an interest in the mind itself, as a state which has various functions.
3. At a later time, take great interest in the mind, not as a state of consciousness, but as an entirety.
4. Later still, acquire an interest in pure consciousness.

In the process of concentration, there is a self-restriction due to the mind being held to one object only. This self-restriction is accepted, for it is a limitation which is necessary in order to finally transcend not the object, but thought itself. This heavy self-restricting limitation is called the descent to hell. All avataras in world history, always descended to hell before they ascend into heaven. Perchance, this is food for thought.

A major distinction between concentration and meditation is that concentration is a self-constriction of the mind in which the state of restraint is held with great effort. Meditation, on the other hand, is an effortless holding of the mind to its object with an expansiveness. Western psychologists sometimes refer to this process as unrestrictive free association. In yogic literature, it is called the stream of consciousness.

In concentration there is an effortful movement of the mind, but it is neither a tensing nor a forcing. The activity of the mind in concentration is best described as an intense, calm directing of the mind. You are to achieve attention without tension in the yoga asans, so also in concentration and meditation there should be attention of the mind without tension. Neither intensity of thought nor daydreaming should be confused with concentration. Fanciful thinking or building castles in the air are quite different mental pursuits. Mental activities are not to be confused with concentration.

HOLDING THE MIND TO AN OBJECT

Concentration is holding the mind to a single object, even if the object be simple or complex, large or small, concrete or abstract. The practice of concentration begins with an object that is simple, small and concrete--for example, a diamond.   One then slowly moves to large, complex, abstract concepts. In the beginning practice of concentration, you may need to create a particular image in your mind, or repeat a particular sound in order to keep the mind on the object of concentration. When the power of concentration is firmly established, there will be no need for the props of mental imagery or sound. Through gentle control of the mind, after many practice sessions of concentration, you will learn to induce a mood. When you have truly learned concentration, inducing the mood of the object becomes automatic and you need not visualize it. The object of concentration is held by the mind itself. When this transpires the mind becomes active and a fountain of thoughts will burst forth.

Before this level of concentration is achieved, the student is advised to practice with a simple, concrete object of his own choosing. Yogis in India often use the symbol of the sacred cow because of its connotation of non-violence and its ability to give so much: butter, milk, ghee, oil for the temple lamps, and so forth. Let us assume you are concentrating upon the cow. The following general procedure for concentration may be used:

CONCENTRATION PROCEDURE

Form a meditative pose. Gently try to visualize the cow. Try to draw your mind to its simple, physical anatomy--the horns, hoofs, tail. You may then move to its subtler qualities, such as its milk; and further into yet subtler qualities, such as its placidity. You may look into some of the cow's more abstract qualities. With control but without tension, you draw from the concentration all that you can relate to the cow.

Here, you may find it helpful to utilize the seven rays of discernment in order to reach an understanding of the object. The seven rays correlate with the seven interrogative pronouns: who? what? where? how? which? why? and when? In this procedure you might ask:

> Who is this?
> What is a cow? Is it an animal? Is it a symbol?
> Is it a source of food ...?
> Where does this animal live?
> > In India? On a farm in Wisconsin?
> > In Lincoln Park Zoo ...?
> How does this animal survive?
> > By eating grass? By chewing its cud?
> > By sleeping long hours ...?
> Which cow is this?
> > A sacred cow? A pet cow? A milking cow?
> Why is this cow an animal?
> When is this cow not a cow?
> When it is a sacred symbol?

The seven rays of discernment technique for concentrating is a way of extracting data as well as helping in concentrating the mind. This can be done by asking some other questions, again using the seven rays of discernment.

When you are learning to concentrate, you may find it necessary to continually return again and again to your object of concentration for an extended period of time before you have totally grasped the meaning of the object.

There are three secrets for controlled thinking or yogic concentration.

The first is: It does not matter how many times your mind wanders in concentration, what matters is how gently you bring your mind back to the object. As the mind focuses upon an object of concentration, it is the nature of the mind to wander. In the example we talked about, the mind might wander from the cow to the thought of hunger. The nature of the mind is to wander. The secret, which cannot be over-stressed is, when the mind wanders you should not jerk it back with anger. This only releases forces in the mind that destroy the concentration. Rather, gently, ever so gently, without reproach, draw the mind back and re-unite it on the object of concentration. Continue drawing the mind back to the object until the mind realizes it is easier to hold to the object of concentration than to wander elsewhere. Concentration begins when the mind, of its own volition, holds to what you are concentrating on without any heavy aberration.

Learning to concentrate is similar to learning to ride a horse. If the horse becomes restless, you cannot spur the horse. A student learning to ride who spurs the horse in this manner will only cause it to gallop or bolt rather than quiet down. Likewise, the mind must learn to obey its master. In the earlier practice of concentration, you may find the mind wanders as many as 70 times. With daily practice, within six months, you may find the mind wandering only 50 times. This is great progress! After a year's practice, it may only wander 10 or 15 times. In three years, it may not wander at all, but remain completely fixed on whatever object (gross or abstract) you are concentrating upon.

The second secret of concentration is that you must be careful not to engage in tangential thinking which takes you away from the object of concentration. For example, if you are thinking of a cow, do not hold too long to the concept of milk, which may lead the mind to thoughts of cats, which may lead it to thoughts of dogs, which may lead to other thoughts. Be careful not to engage in tangential thinking.

If you concentrate on a cow, hold your mind's eye and your attention solely on the cow, realizing fully that you are attempting in one sense to isolate the cow from the rest of its universe. Although in reality this cannot actually be done, the effort to do so is a yogic technique whereby you learn to separate your own consciousness from the matrix of your thoughts and emotions. In so doing you gain insight into consciousness.

The third secret of controlled thinking is not to confuse tangential thinking with the mode of return. This is a subtle point. When the mode of return arises, concentration has been mastered.

Mode of return implies all wandering and deviation from the object of concentration has ceased. As an example, if mode of return has arisen and you are concentrating on a cow, this may lead to thoughts of milk... babies... marriage... life... the beauty of life... the sacredness of life... the Hindu sacredness of the cow. You have deviated from the object of concentration, but that diversion has led you to return to the object of concentration. You have therefore completed a cycle. Your mode of return automatically returns you to the point at which you began. This completion of the cycle has deep symbolic significance. Not only has concentration been attained, but you have slipped over into the next stage of yoga called meditation. With a little practice, this mode of return can be induced at will.

SUPPORTS FOR CONCENTRATION

Concentration is supported when you adjust your daily lifestyle to sound yogic principles, removing all mental and physical imbalances in your life, and adding serenity of your mind. Here are a few more specific supports to help attain the goal of concentration.

1. As you begin serious concentration, your endeavor will be helped by curtailing your wants, needs, and desires. Not all your needs and wants ought to be discarded. Eliminate your superficial and extraneous wants and needs.
2. Limit your life activities to those most significant. This helps concentration, and improves your lifestyle. You become more efficient, and have more time. This reduces stress and gives longevity.
3. Throughout the day, not only when practicing concentration, induce a state of peacefulness and mental serenity.
4. Repeatedly, make an effort to be more cheerful and friendly.
5. In your everyday life, lessen the number of thoughts, by breathing more deeply.
6. During the practice of concentration, proceed in living your outer life, but devote more time and effort to introspection. Always be more mindful. This develops greater perception and greater intuition.

GUIDES TO PRACTICING CONCENTRATION

1. Find a place where you can sit quietly and concentrate daily, where you will not be disturbed or easily interrupted. If

possible, do not use the same area for yoga postures. The vibration set up by physical exercises is contradictory to the vibration needed for inturning.

2. Choose the best time for concentration, early or late in the day, when you will be least likely to be disturbed.

3. Place a small blanket on the floor which is used only for concentration and meditation. This is commonly called a meditation mat and is usually made of wool.

4. The general recommended procedure for beginning concentration is:

    a. Sit in any comfortable yoga meditation pose.
    b. Close the eyes and focus on the root of the nose at the eyebrows.
    c. Take a deep breath and relax.
    d. Chant OM aloud slowly 3 times.
    e. Practice any pranayama for a few moments.
    f. Proceed to focus on the object of concentration.

    These six steps will drive away the external force fields, and quiet the total mind and body.

5. Begin concentration on gross objects, and later concentrate on subtler objects. Regularity in concentration is more important than the choice of the object.

6. When in deep concentration there is no perception of body awareness, nor any perception of your external surroundings.

7. In the beginning practices you may have to coax your mind. Speak to your mind and give it direction.

    'Mind, settle down. Do not foolishly run this way nor that way. Look at this object of beauty. Here, in the inward state there is sustained quietude and happiness. Mind, be my friend and share with me this untold joy.'

8. Gently settle down, sit down, close the eyes, relax, concentrate, and be serene in your inturning; otherwise you will find no enjoyment in the technique. If you find no enjoyment your mind will not return to the practice of concentration.

9. Be sure the mind is not wildly jumping from one emotion to another, nor from one daydream to another. This can be checked with mindfulness, constant introspection, and self-analysis.

10. Most neophytes make the mistake of wrestling with their minds. As you are concentrating, and lose your concentra-

tion, gently, ever so gently return the mind to that object. Any forceful movement of the mind will destroy your concentration.

11. Many people, each time they begin concentration, need to urinate. This is caused by an irritation in the micturition center of the spinal cord. It means they need to relax more, and become calmer before starting concentration.

CONCENTRATION TECHNIQUES

CONCENTRATION GAZING

Concentration is defined as 'an intense, calm watching, accompanied by attention of the mind, without tension'. This definition will help understand the concept of gazing. There are two basic guidelines.

a. The eyes may be either opened or closed. However, it is recommended that the eyes be closed as this helps deeper inturning.

b. Historically, your attention is focused at one of four points:
-The root of the nose (sun center),
-The tip of the nose (venus center),
-The heart, or
-The length of the spinal column.

The sun center and then the venus center are the two most important.

However, practice focusing at each point, and determine which point is naturally suited to you. Then hold to that focal point. Do not change it. Carefully read the information given for each gaze, before determining which gaze is most suited to you.

1. FRONTAL GAZE

(Bhrumadhya-drishti)

In the frontal gaze the attention is focused at the single eye or sun center (ajna chakra). This is at the root of the nose between the eyebrows. Sit in the adept's pose or the lotus pose. Close the eyes and gently focus at the root of the nose. Do not stare! Just gently gaze. There is no violent effort involved in this procedure. Hold your attention from 32 to 72 seconds. Gradually increase the duration of concentration. The frontal gaze must always be performed with the eyes closed.

The frontal gaze is described in the Bhagavad Gita, chapter V. It is the concentration technique utilized by the philosophical yogis and some kriya yogis. It is recommended for students who are philosophically inclined. In this particular gaze, more so than the other gazes, the mind is easier to control.

2. NASAL GAZE
(Nasikagra-drishti)

As the name implies, nasal gaze is performed with the attention focused at the tip of the nose. Sit in the adept's pose or the lotus pose. The nasal gaze may be performed with the eyes either opened or partly closed. At first close the eyes to help concentration. Gaze gently, but fixedly at the tip of the nose. Having firmly fixed the eyes, do not become distracted by anything. Gaze from 32 to 72 seconds, gradually increasing the length of time.

Nasal gaze is, also, described in the Bhagavad Gita in chapter VI. It is sometimes utilized by the philosophical yogis and kriya yogis, as this practice rapidly steadies and develops the power of concentration.

3. HEART GAZE
(Anahata-drishti)

In the heart gaze, the attention is focused on the lotus of the venus center (anahata chakra). Sit in the adept's pose or any other meditative pose. Close the eyes and focus on the heart center. Hold the attention at this point from 32 to 72 seconds. Gradually, without strain, increase the duration. The heart gaze is utilized by devotional yogis. This point of focus is recommended to those students who are of a devotional nature.

4. SPINAL GAZE
(Sushumanic-drishti)

The spinal gaze focuses the attention on the entire length of the spinal column. Sit in the lotus pose. Close the eyes and focus the attention on the totality of your spinal column. In this technique you are to simultaneously see with your mind's eye, and to feel the entirety of the balanced center channel (sushumna). The attention is held from 32 to 72 seconds and the time is gradually increased. The spinal gaze is utilized by most hatha yogis, kundalini yogis, and some kriya yogis. A balanced state of consciousness evolves from this technique. The beginning student is cautioned that spinal gaze is an extremely difficult technique to perform properly. For beginners, success in concentration is more easily attained by focusing on a smaller area, like the sun center.

OTHER CONCENTRATION EXERCISES

Here are some simple concentration exercises that will greatly help you to concentrate. You can then move on to the more advanced stages of meditation and contemplation. The simplicity of these techniques cause some people to feel they are unimportant. They are extremely helpful and meaningful in developing a deep state of concentration.

AUDIO TECHNIQUES

1. THE TICKING EXERCISE

Sit in the adept's pose, or any comfortable meditative pose. Set a watch or clock about 6 inches from yourself. Close the eyes and perform frontal gaze, concentrating on the ticking sound. Hold to this sound to the exclusion of all other sounds, thoughts, or feelings. See how long your mind is able to remain fixed on this sound. Repeat daily.

2. WATER EXERCISE

If you are near a body of water: a river, lake, ocean, or waterfall, sit down, close the eyes and concentrate on the water's sound as long as you can, to the exclusion of all else. You can concentrate on the sound of rain in the same manner.

3. MUSIC EXERCISE

Turn on a favorite piece of music, playing it softly. Lie down wherever comfortable. Close the eyes. Lose yourself in the music. Do not daydream. Think only about the inspiration induced by the music. Forget all things internal and external, except the music. Repeat this process and go so deeply into the inspirational feeling that you lose even the awareness of the music itself.

VISUAL TECHNIQUES

1. FLOWER EXERCISE

Sit in the adept's pose. Close the eyes and perform frontal gaze. Visualize a flower, allowing your entire being to become engrossed in the flower. Forget everything else, thinking only of the flower: mentally sense it... smell it... feel it... see it... touch it... become totally absorbed in it. Once you have forgotten everything but the flower... then even forget the flower. Mentally dissolve the flower and become aware of your true self.

2. NUMBER DOUBLING EXERCISE

Sit in a comfortable meditative pose. Close the eyes and perform frontal gaze. Think of the number 3, double it to 6, and continue doubling it into infinity. As you double each number, try to visualize the numbers on the screen of your mind's eye. If you lose track of which number you are on, do not be disturbed. Gently draw the mind back to the number 3 and begin again. With each new number, draw into the mind more deeply.

3. READING COMPREHENSION EXERCISE

Read a page in any textbook or scripture. Then, close the book. Close your eyes and perform frontal gaze, abandoning all distracting thoughts. Draw your mind together and comprehend what you have just read. Associate, classify, group, combine, and pair the data you have just read. Use knowledge you have in that specific field as well as knowledge you have in other fields to do this classifying. The secret in this classification of information is to let go of all thoughts of the external world. When you finish your task, you will find you have been deeply inturned. There may even be a slight jerk of your body as your eyes open and you realize you have been deeply inside your mind (sometimes, for an extended period). Repeat the process, reading two pages. Repeat the process, reading three pages. Continue increasing the number of pages depending upon the amount of time available and your inclination.

4. MULTIPLICATION EXERCISE

Sit in a comfortable meditative pose. Close the eyes and perform frontal gaze. Pick any number and multiply it by 3. Multiply the new number by 3. Continue multiplying by 3, until you reach infinity or lose count. When you lose track, return to another number, without becoming upset with yourself. Again begin multiplying that new number by 3.

5. THE 'WHO AM I?' EXERCISE

It is very difficult for the average person to penetrate the inner mind... much less the origin of consciousness. However, we must start somewhere into this investigation of consciousness. The starting point is the exploration of the mind itself. During this exploration you realize, you are one thing and your mind another thing. Here is the greatest concentration techniques there is:

Form the adept's pose, utilizing frontal gaze, with eyes closed. Employ the seven rays of discernment and repeatedly keep asking yourself, 'Who am I...? What am I...? Where am I...? Why am I...? Which one am I...? When am I...? How am I...?' When you have finished the seven rays, return to them, asking the same, or a different set of questions. In the process you will attain deep concentration and, also, insight into your own nature.

Chapter 15

MANTRA AND MEDITATION
-FACT AND FANCY-

Some time ago, a national TV panel had a discussion regarding meditation and mantra. There were some misconceptions expressed. Some motion picture celebrities and political leaders gathered to discuss this deep subject. Their discussion on meditation and mantra was equivalent to grammar school students attempting to discuss a college curriculum. Due to the vast confusion existing today on the subject of meditation and mantra, it would be helpful to preface the chapter on meditation with some basic information. A few historical facts will remove the misunderstandings that often arise.

What is Mantra?

A mantra is a genuine sound vibration that exists in the causal and astral universes. These sounds are not nonsense syllables. They are well-known to all gurus. A mantric sound when properly given and utilized leads to stillness, and induces a state of meditation.

How Many Mantras Are There?

The Vedas point out there are an infinite number of mantras. However, only a few are genuinely suitable for meditation purposes. Mantras can run from 32 syllables down to a single syllable. Special, single syllable mantra is usually referred to as a seed-mantra or bija. Bijas contain great energies and are to be used only after a person has advanced in the study and practice of yoga.

Where Do Mantras Come From?

The great mantras come from ancient sages who have recorded them in the great texts. Mantras can also be composed especially for an individual, by wise souls who studied the hora-shastras. It takes from 12 to 24 years of study before one becomes a maker of mantras (mantra-kara). Although the science of composing and creating mantras contains many deep secrets, the sounds are all found in the ancient texts. Now, whether the mantra is given by a person who found it in a text, or by a guru who found it in the

Vedas, or by a sage who created it by discovering astral sounds, the importance of any mantra is whether it has adhi-kara.

What is Adhikara?

If a sage utilizes a mantra to attain illumination and then gives that particular mantra to another person, the mantra contains his vibration of illumination called adhikara. It contains the mind of the giver of the mantra (adhikara). It contains within it, his living consciousness which empowers the mantra (adhi-kara). In short, adhikara is the transference of the illuminative state from the giver of the mantra to its receiver. This illuminative state impinges itself into the mantra. Consequently, when a sage gives a mantra, the illuminative state is transferred into the consciousness of the receiver, awaiting a time when it will blossom forth. If there is no illuminative state in the consciousness of the giver, no transference can take place. There is no adhi-kara.

Who Can Initiate Mantra?

Only a spiritual guru can initiate mantra. That is, only a person who has reached the illuminative state can meaningfully give a mantra, whereby the adhikara is transferred to the receiver. Without the adhikara, the mantra has lost most of its mystical power. They still have some mental value.

It should be quite obvious, some people bestowing mantras do not have adhikara. They do not have the insight to determine which mantras are individually suitable for a particular student. They have not learned the horashastras. They have simply concocted nonsensical sounds, giving these sounds to specific sociological types, i.e., students, housewives, businessmen, etc. They are not specifically created for individuals.

Are Mantra and Meditation the Same as Relaxation?

Psychological experiments have shown that the repetition of any meaningless sounds will lower the breathing rate and blood pressure, and produce a state of relaxation. As a matter of fact, putting your attention on the ticking of a clock or on dripping water will produce the same results. However, the point is that relaxation is not meditation; nor is meditation a passive state. This was clearly shown many years ago when professor Einstein, along with a number of students, was placed on an electroencephalogram (yes, they had them way back then) in which brain wave activity was recorded. The students and Einstein were both induced into a relaxed state as shown by the alpha waves. But, when the students were given a simple problem to solve, the electronic instruments immediately reflected that their minds had moved out of the passive state. However, when Einstein was asked to solve the problem, he was able to remain in this passive state. In short, the students were in a relaxed state; Einstein was in a meditative state. They were in an inactive semiconscious state incapable of being utilized to solve problems. On the other hand, Einstein was in a true meditative state, capable of being utilized to solve problems. Have I communicated this important idea to you?

That which is only a process of relaxation, some people call meditation. Relaxation is relaxation, but meditation is meditation. Proponents of this type of relaxation, which they call meditation, talk about the benefits of its energization. They say people doing their 20-minute meditation technique come out of the state raring to go, rushing forth to accomplish their goals. This energization is angular (emotional) energy. Meditation is not a way of energizing your vehicle so you can get ahead in the world. Rather, it is a deep, mystical process by which you de-energize and balance the mind and desires. Meditation is a way of eliminating excessive energies. It is not a way of re-energizing your vehicle. It is usually this energization that enmeshes us in karma.

The oldest and most scientific method of meditation is that expounded by Patanjali, in his Kriya Yoga Sutras. This method is a steady, continuous discipline based upon creative thinking, proper physical exercise, proper breathing, proper sense-withdrawal, and concentration. These practices combined are the only means to produce the deep inturned state of meditation. Meditation produces a spiritual way of life that creates and generates an influx of wisdom, not relaxation and energization.

Transcendental Meditation

It should be pointed out that all meditation is transcendental, for in all meditation, the lower emotions are transcended and the meditator experiences a unity of self with life, thus, there is a transcendence of body consciousness.

Techniques of Meditation

Also, there are many types of meditation, each type leading to a different goal.
1. Some techniques lead only to mindfulness;
2. Other techniques lead to fuller consciousness;
3. Others reach one-pointedness;
4. Still others lead to ecstasy or bliss; and
5. A select few techniques lead all the way to the final 15th stage of samadhi: kaivalya or God-consciousness.

Chapter 16

MANTRA
-WHAT IS MANTRA?-

The word mantra is a composition of two Sanskrit root words: the first root 'man' means 'continual or constant thinking'. The second root 'tra' means 'free' or 'to be free'. Mantra is a process by which you free yourself from worries or doubts, but not from consciousness. In short, mantra is a means of transcending thought, and bringing consciousness to a much higher level of spiritual being. The root 'tri' also means 'to protect'. Thus, in India a great number of mantras are called protection mantras. True mantra is that which frees you from constrictive limitations of mind thought.

We live in the iron age (Kali yuga), and it is filled with martian forces which disturb and distract human consciousness. Mantra is a way of fixing the mind upon peace, tranquility, serenity, and equanimity, enabling you to reach deeper into consciousness.

A mantra is a mystical sound or a combination of sounds which were originally heard mystically by the sages in their deep states of samadhi. The sages passed on these powerful sounds to their disciples. As their disciples chanted the words, the power, the majesty and the magic of the mantra brought them into those higher states of consciousness experienced by their guru. Thus, it is important that a mantra given by a guru, be a mantra that he has used and experienced.

Mantra is a mystical formula, a metaphysical formula, utilized to induce certain spiritual states of consciousness, when intensely and devoutly chanted. The efficiency of the mantra is dependent upon both the spiritual awareness of the guru that gave the mantra, and the sound vibration innate within the mantra itself, and the student's ability to concentrate.

Each mantra has a particular intonation or sound pattern. The knowledge of the use of mantra (mantra-vidya), is one of the deepest secrets of yoga sciences.

The word mantra also means 'thought-form'. It is the science of thought forms and knowledge of how to crystallize those thought-forms in the physical world. Ultimately, all things in the universe are thought-forms from the consciousness of Reality.

273

For mantra to be effective, it is necessary for it to be combined with kriya and bhakti. These three are essential. Mantra is the activation of the thought-form; kriya is the mental and external action consistent with that thought-form; and bhakti is the proper attitude (devotion) with which to crystallize these events harmoniously into your life. It is not enough to merely bring things and events into life, they must be brought into life surely, swiftly, and most harmoniously.

There are four main types of mantra. These are,
1. Vedic mantras
2. Upanishadic mantras
3. Tantric mantras
4. Puranic mantras

Vedic mantras are mantras that are found within the Vedas, the basic ancient scriptures of India. Upanishadic mantras are found in the Upanishads. Tantric mantras are found in the Tantra texts, and the Puranic mantras are found in the Puranas. The Vedic mantras are considered to be the most sacred, while the Puranic mantras are considered to be least sacred. All mantras, however, are effective and efficient in producing their given results.

Each main division of mantra are divided into three subdivisions. These are 1) sattvic, 2) rajasic, and 3) tamasic.
1. Sattvic mantras have the innate power to produce wisdom, illumination, compassion, or any major attribute of God-consciousness.
2. Rajasic mantras are those chanted to produce children, wealth, worldly success, and the like.
3. Tamasic mantras are used to invoke lower forces from the astral planes. Tamasic mantras are like words-of-power used to invoke forces through ceremony.

Philosophically and psychologically speaking, you should practice only one mantra until the mantra releases its potency. The mantra should be given at the right moment, to the right person, with the right mental attitude, to produce the right spiritual effect. A mantra that is given in such a way is called a guru mantra, a mantra given by a spiritual preceptor.

The chanting of many different mantras at the same time can produce confusion. Therefore, if you do not have a guru mantra, it is suggested that you listen to a number of mantras and choose for yourself one which is most harmonious to your inner soul. Upon choosing that special mantra, chant it, and give it emphasis. This mantra is then called your ishta-mantra, or the mantra of your choice.

The best time to practice mantra is during the hours of 4:30 a.m. to 6:30 a.m. A quiet place of meditation is recommended. Flowers and incense are helpful in setting a good vibration. The room should be simple and clean. Before beginning the mantra, any pranayama that quiets the mind will be extremely helpful. Prior to pranayama, many teachers suggest quietly reading verses from the scriptures or inspirational writings to bring your consciousness to a higher vibration. When this is done, mantra will be even more effective.

Do not fix the number of mantras that you are going to do, for there will be days when you will not have the time. More important than the number done, is attitude. Be totally unrushed for those few minutes of time. In this way, you will have moved your mind from the surface world, recalling that there is an inner world. It is this inner world that is important. The formula consists in turning away from your surface mind to find the place where happiness truly lies... deep within you.

The beauty you see in a sunrise is not actually in the sunrise, it is within you. It is within your mind, and your heart.

The whole meaning of practicing mantra is to find some degree of peace. It is not what the mantra literally means, but what you feel from the mantra that is significant. Although every mantra does have a word meaning, it is the feeling evoked within you, by you, through the repetition of the mantra that is meaningful. Mantra can be compared to a beautiful song. Music is capable of producing a stirring within your soul. Mantra is the same. The stirring it produces may simply be a little spark, just a slight feeling, but this spark is all that is needed. It will bring forth a fire of positive creative feelings which will produce constructive thinking. Mantra is a process just like priming a pump.

1. AUM: THE BASIC HOLY MANTRA

The mother of all mantras, the first mantra, is the holy AUM. It is Romanized A-U-M but chanted as O-MMM. AUM is a three-syllable mantra. This Vedic mantra is the primal sound of creation. It is also the primal symbol of Wisdom, for it is the vibratory sound of Sri Brahman, The Reality. A-U-M symbolically stands for the three manifestations of Reality:

    a. The projecting force,

    b. The preserving force, and

c. The redissolving force.

Our universe projects out of the mind of Reality, is sustained by that Mind, and ultimately redissolves back into that Mind. Here you see the cycle of necessity or the cycle of birth-death-rebirth.

AUM stands for the harmonious interaction of the three modifications of nature (gunas), by which all is sustained in balance.

AUM also symbolizes our physical vehicle, our astral vehicle, and our causal vehicle. The silence that follows the AUM symbolizes Spirit (atma) itself, which is beyond the three bodies.

A symbolizes guttural sound. U symbolizes middle sound. M symbolizes labial sound. All manifested sounds utilize a guttural, middle, and/or labial character. In this way, AUM represents all that which is capable of being understood and spoken. It symbolizes supreme wisdom.

AUM is a seed-mantra (bija), a basic vibratory sound, and prefixes most mantras. This not only intensifies and brings the thought form of the mantra into crystallization on the physical plane, but also bestows wisdom regarding the mantra itself. This wisdom additionally brings forth a realization of the power of any thought you think, which is mantra itself.

Quiet the mind. Sit in a yoga posture. Close the eyes, and place them in frontal gaze. Enter into an inward state of meditation. Begin to slowly chant the mantra over and over and over again. It can be chanted either verbally or silently. Find deep quietude and serenity within yourself. Your entire mind should be drawn to the intonation of the sound and the beautiful ecstasy that it produces. Continue to chant the mantra. Each time the mind wanders, gently bring it back to the mantra (not harshly, but gently), until the mind settles itself upon the mantra and the mantra alone. Become absorbed in the vibrations of the mantra. When your consciousness is holding to the sound vibrations (nada), you can also meditate gently upon the light that exists at the sun center. This spiritual light (jyothi) helps to center the mind into your own consciousness and brings about rapid spiritual illumination.

2. HARI-OM

The second mantra is Hari-OM. The name Hari is one of the names of Vishnu, the principle of the preservation of the good. Hari is an internalized symbol which assists in removing all fear and all affliction from your being. It makes you courageous and fearless. It is a very powerful and meaningful mantra in today's world. Hari-OM is called the three-lettered mantra.

3. OM NAMA SHIVA YA

The third mantra is OM Nama Shiva Ya. This mantra is repeated by many yogis. Shiva is the divinity principle that dissolves away all imbalances. The mantra means, 'Oh Lord of Auspiciousness, to You my salutations again and yet again.' It is a powerful mantra utilized to experience God-consciousness. It is usually chanted 5 times. Inhale and chant the mantra 5 times before another breath is taken. If you have a very small lung capacity, you may have to chant a little faster. If you wish, however, you can take a deep breath and chant the mantra slowly, 1 time per breath.

Symbolically, Shiva is considered the god of death. He, thus, symbolizes the principle of destroying all the imbalances and negatives within life. When these imbalances are dissolved away, you become joyous over the changes which come into your life. This opens new doors, not only of adventure but for the fulfillment of karma. Consequently, this mantra should be chanted in a light, bubbly manner, not as a funeral dirge.

This mantra has locked into it a very deep secret of life, for as we evolve into beings with five senses, sentient life evolves. By performing this mantra, an understanding of the secret of human existence, as a sentient life-form with five senses, is attained.

4. OM SHANTI SHANTI SHANTIH

The fourth mantra is one of the most commonly used mantras. It is the seven-lettered mantra: OM shanti, shanti, shantih. It is a tranquility and peace mantra. It can be chanted silently or aloud to produce a quiescence of the mind. If you begin to become upset, chant this mantra silently. Or, if for some reason you are already upset, chant it aloud to resettle your mind.

Its simplest meaning is, 'Oh, Lord of life, of laughter, of love, reestablish in all the facets of Your being, tranquility, serenity, harmony, and peace'. The first shanti is chanted strongest and louder than the other two. The second is chanted more softly. The third is chanted softest of all. The first shanti symbolizes serenity and health of the physical body; the second symbolizes equanimity and peace of the mind; the third symbolizes balanced equanimity and joy of the spiritual vehicle. This mantra is often chanted at the conclusion of a yoga class.

5. OM NAMO NARAYANAYA

. The next mantra is the eight-lettered mantra. It includes the activation of the seven basic chakras within your inner universe including the thousand-petalled lotus. It is a most powerful mantra. It is chanted: 'OM Namo Naraya Naya'. Narayana is another name of Vishnu, the principle of preservation of the good, the preservation of self-conscious awareness. The surface meaning of the mantra is: 'O Infinite Lord, O Thou Indestructible Self-existent One, unto Thee do I make my obeisance'. The inner awareness of this mantra dissolves away the surface ephemeral ego, revealing the eternal reality within you (atma). This mantra, because of its eight syllables, will bestow upon you a blessing, (darshan), a vision of God.

6. OM SRI RAM, JAI RAM, JAI JAI RAM

The sixth mantra is a very famous one, chanted by almost everyone in India. It is:

> OM Sri Ram, Jai Ram, Jai Jai Ram
> OM Sri Ram, Jai Ram, Jai Jai Ram
> OM Sri Ram, Jai Ram, Jai Jai Ram

This is the twenty-four lettered mantra. You should not think of it as one line of eight letters, repeated 3 times. All three lines combined make up the entire mantra. The first line is chanted for the physical body; the second line is chanted for the mental vehicle; and the third line is chanted for the causal body. After chanting this mantra once, it should be repeated at least 12 times, completing 1 round. One to 12 rounds should be done at one sitting.

7. OM NAMO BHAGAVATE VASU DEVAYA

The last mantra is called the twelve-lettered mantra: 'OM Namo Bhagavate Vasu Devaya'. The surface meaning of this mantra is: 'Oh, Infinite Lord, Indweller in the hearts of all beings, unto You do I turn my consciousness'. According to yoga tradition, this is a very auspicious mantra, for it consists of twelve letters, corresponding to the measure of man. For this reason, it is called the maha-mantra. It is also called the kriya mantra, as it is the mantra that is given to kriya-jyothis (wisdom seekers) and kriya-bans (devotion seekers).

There are two ways this mantra is chanted. One is called the monosyllabic, monotone method:

OM-Na-Mo-Bha-Ga-Ba-Te-Ba-Su-De-Ba-Ya

The second is the classical method:

OM Namo Bhagavate Vasu Devaya

You will note that in the monosyllabic method, the V sound becomes a B sound. When chanted, this special mantra will reveal to you the universality of God-consciousness. In effect, you will see in everyone and everything the God within, the indwelling Reality called Vasu. According to yogic mystical symbolism, Sri Vasu has a symbolic relationship to Hanuman. Vasu is the Lord of Breath (prana), which creates the mind. Vasu is the father of Hanuman, the monkey god, who symbolizes the mind. In and through this kriya mantra you learn to control prana and create new states of mind that are young, vibrant, flexible, and constructive.

MANTRAS FOR
AFFECTING THE SPECIFIC CHAKRAS

1. Saturn -- OM Nama Shivaya
2. Jupiter -- OM Namo Narayanaya
3. Mars -- Hai Ram Jai Ram, Jai, Jai Ram
4. Venus -- OM Namo Bhagavate Vasu Devaya
5. Mercury -- OM Sri Hanuman Va Namah
6. Sun -- OM Bhur Bhuvah Svah
7. All -- OM Shanti, Shanti, Shantih

These mantras may also be utilized in the hold position for each appropriate group of asans.

A mantra tape giving the proper pronunciations and intonations of many yoga mantras is available from the Temple of Kriya Yoga.

Chapter 17

HONG-SAU KRIYA MEDITATION TECHNIQUE
-THE GANDER OF ACTION BREATH MEDITATION-

In Sanskrit, the word Hamsa (hong-sau) means wild gander, and has great symbolic significance. No matter how far the wild gander flies, at some point it remembers, and migrates back to its home, always at the proper season. In the same way, we as spiritual beings following a spiritual principle must, like the wild gander, remember, and migrate back to our spiritual home. The spiritual home is the inward state of samadhi. Our body is called the lower nest, wherein we are nestling. Through samadhi, we find our higher nest. Some people are comfortable within the lower nest, while others are not. Being uncomfortable, some people migrate back to the higher nest to be happier. Some people being comfortable in the lower nest, migrate back to the higher nest to attain samadhi. This migration is the spiritual principle of the hamsa.

The hong-sau kriya meditation is a key technique whereby you return to that higher nest. Meditation is a technique utilized to make the mind serene, tranquil, producing a state of spiritual receptivity. In most systems of meditation, there is a particular spiritual result that is sought. This may be trance, vision, or clairaudience. This is not, however, the end goal of kriya yoga. Religionists have learned how to induce receptivity to visions and voices. However, these are in accordance with their own religious beliefs. They bring to the surface of their minds and objectify that which is already embedded in the deepest substratum of their mind. There is nothing wrong with this, but you must remember, it remains subjective.

The yogi goes beyond religious concepts to a state of consciousness that is truly objective. It is not hallucinatory and thus contains noetic quality. It is knowledge-bearing. In yogic meditation, visions and voices do arise, but only as side products and certainly not as the main goal. Although these states can be helpful, they can, also, be a very great hindrance. The yogi ultimately seeks something more than objectification of a concept.

There is a higher meditation, in which you enter a state of consciousness with meaning beyond your own mind. In this state of meditation, you remove the illusions, delusions, cravings, loyalties, and prejudices. These states produce emotional ignorance within your everyday consciousness. When these states have been removed, you see the reality. You will understand reality in much the same way that a soul knowing a drop of water (two parts hydrogen, one part oxygen) understands all water, everywhere and anywhere. In the selfsame manner, to understand embodied consciousness, is to understand consciousness everywhere and anywhere.

Higher meditation produces a strength and an intensity of consciousness making you courageous and fearless. The most universally applicable method for developing meditation is attentiveness on the incoming and outgoing breath! This technique in no way interferes with the normal breathing pattern. It is used as a point of concentration. It is a pattern upon which the hong-sau meditation technique is based.

THE ESSENCE OF HONG-SAU KRIYA

The hong-sau technique is also known as the secondary kriya technique. The hong-sau kriya technique is really an extremely powerful, illuminative procedure. It is powerful because:

1. It utilizes yama.
2. It utilizes asan. `
3. It utilizes breath control, one of the greater mystical techniques.
4. It utilizes mantra.
5. It utilizes concentration on the breath.
6. It utilizes meditation.
7. Finally, it utilizes mindfulness on the self, which leads to the balanced awareness of samadhi.

In essence, in hong-sau kriya, seven techniques are blended into a natural, harmonious method for reaching samadhi. There is no disjunctive, artificial joining of techniques. According to the Kriya Lineage and the philosophy of kriya yoga, you can, through the hong-sau kriya technique, reach illumination within this very lifetime! However, it must be practiced each and every day. Moreover, technique alone is not enough. The practice of the hong-sau technique must be an adjunct to a sane, spiritual way of life.

In the beginning stages of hong-sau kriya, as in meditation, you should not be concerned about how rapidly you unfold. This will come later. Attempting too much will hinder, rather than help you. Do not meditate on hong-sau to accomplish anything. Meditate because meditation is the way of life. If you meditate to get something, you will soon become bored. When you meditate like that, you will meditate even though you seemingly do not achieve the results you think you should. If you breathe hong-sau for any length of time, you will associate the idea of peace and serenity with the hong-sau. In so doing, you add something to your meditative state, allowing rapid spiritual unfoldment.

At first, it may take several months before you can breathe one or two meditative hong-sau's without mental distraction. Some progress faster than others. It's most important to establish the technique properly. Take plenty of time to do this. Make sure you understand how it is performed. Spend plenty of time practicing hong-sau so it becomes automatic and habit-formed, effortlessly. In this way, a groove is formed within your mind. Although it is difficult to make kriya effortless, strive to do so. Turn the kriya into an effortless habit by enhancing the enjoyment of meditation. After all, meditation must be enjoyable, in order to be effortless. Remember: if it's effortful, it's not meditation. It's concentration. If it's effortless, you will automatically focus upon the object of meditation, rather than on the technique, itself. As long as your awareness is focused upon the technique, you are not meditating properly.

In the initial stages of meditation, people who ask questions like, 'Am I doing it right?' or 'Did the current go all the way down?' remain meditating 'with effort' upon the technique. If you are asking questions of this nature, it is a clear indication that you have not properly learned the technique. Your meditation is upon the technique rather than the effect. As long as your attention is focused only on the technique you will improve only the technique, rather than gaining the total results from the effect. When hong-sau is performed without thought of anything other than the feeling and the joy of meditation, it will then begin to produce the desired effects. This is the most important facet of meditation.

PRELIMINARY TECHNIQUES
TO HONG-SAU KRIYA

1. THE RESURRECTION BREATH

The resurrection breath is a ritual performed before the hong-sau. It is performed by turning your head to the left side and forcibly expelling the air through the mouth, in two short exhalations. By expelling the air in this direction, you are symbolically dying to the ego self. When you bring your head forward, the breath that flows in is known as the resurrection breath. In a symbolic way, this new breath is bringing in new life... a new spiritual life.

2. THE SIPPING BREATH

This is similar to sipping air through a straw. It is also similar to the cooling breath. However, unlike the cooling breath, the tongue remains in the mouth. Forcibly expel the air through the open mouth to your left and perform the resurrection breath. Bring your head forward. Pucker your lips as tightly as possible, allowing for a small opening in the puckered lips. Sip the air inward, in an unending stream, without any break in the breath. Sip strongly so you can hear the sound. However, sip softly so that it does not whistle. A whistling sound indicates you are being too forceful. The slower you go, the better. Do not sip so slowly that is a break occurs in the stream of air.

When the lungs are full, hold the breath for as long as comfortable. As soon as the slightest discomfort occurs, forcibly expel the air through the open mouth again, while the head is still facing forward. The resurrection breath is only performed once, at the very beginning. Draw out the breath as long as possible, but without strain. If discomfort arises, it indicates you are straining.

In the earlier stages, practice the sipping breath 3 to 5 minutes a day for a few weeks before practicing hong-sau. The key to this technique is that your body must be absolutely motionless. You must not wiggle. There must be stillness and an ease within that stillness. The sipping breath will reduce phlegm.

HONG-SAU KRIYA TECHNIQUE

It makes no difference whether you practice the hong-sau technique in the morning, afternoon, or evening... just practice it. Find a regular time in your schedule to do so. At whatever time you choose, practice it, daily, at the same time. Consistency is very important, for where and when are important to the subconscious mind.

1. Hong-sau kriya consists in concentrating on one spiritual principle. As mentioned in the Yoga Sutras of Patanjali, the holy breath is considered to be the one spiritual principle. Thus, hong-sau kriya consists of concentrating on the inhalation and exhalation. Or you can concentrate on the single principle of the mantra that is chanted during this pranayama. There is also the meditation during the still-point of the breath.

2. When you do the hong-sau kriya, you must hold the following awareness: Now the breath is flowing in... Now the breath is still. Now the breath is flowing out... Now the breath is still again... Now the breath is flowing in again. The stillness of the breath occurs at the point where the breath is held. This is not an intentional hold, but rather, it is something which occurs naturally as you breathe.

3. Hong-sau begins by turning your head to the left, not to the right. You turn your head to the left and exhale twice through the open mouth vigorously. When the breath is exhaled, close the mouth. Immediately turn your head forward and relax. As the breath flows in of its own nature, mentally chant Hong. (It's Hong as in Hong Kong). When the breath flows out of by its own nature, mentally chant Sau. (It's Sau as in seesaw).

4. There are no restrictions in breathing hong-sau kriya. The secret of the technique is allowing the breath to breathe you. Throughout, feel quietude, serenity, and peacefulness.

5. In breathing hong-sau, there can be no forceful inhalation or exhalation. There can be no stress or strain. You must allow the breath to naturally do its own thing. In short, the breath breathes you.

6. Pranayama-wise, hong-sau is a totally passive process. You merely watch the incoming and outgoing breath. But, with regards to the mantra, it's totally active.

7. Whenever the breath is at full chalice or empty chalice, you simply remain in silence and enjoy the meditative bliss of that breathless state.

8. The function and the purpose of hong-sau is to increase the interval of breath suspension. This naturally increased interval of breathlessness is what it is about. Your body weight, your diet, your sleeping, resting, laughing, playing, and working habits must be somewhat balanced.

9. In hong-sau, be continually aware whether you are breathing in or out. Be aware whether there is an empty chalice or full chalice.

10. While performing this technique, in no way, shape, or form should you attempt to regulate the breath. Do not try to chant in any given pattern or to any definite rhythm. The mental chanting must follow the exact natural pattern of your breathing. There is no mantra sound at the hold points.

11. At the automatic hold of the breath, meditate upon blissfulness. In no way should you force the extension of the breathless, blissful state.

12. By observing this breathless state, you mystically loosen identification with your body. You come to realize you are something other than the body. You come to know that your body is sustained by something other than physical breathing.

13. The breath and/or mantra is a mystical valve that ties consciousness to its body. This valve must be controlled, enabling you to release your mind's consciousness from body-consciousness. This is obtained by reaching the breathless stage. In this breathless stage, your mind meditates without distraction and perceives the Reality within you. By performing the hong-sau kriya technique, you transcend consciousness of bodily desire.

The hong-sau meditation is done not to attain anything, it is perforce to remove something: desire and craving. It is the desires and cravings that produce restlessness and body attachment.

Hong-sau is a regenerative technique. It is the only time you are pouring energy into your mind-body vehicle, rather than taking energy out of the vehicle.

RESULTS OF THE HONG-SAU:

1. The practice of hong-sau energizes your physical body and fills it with great peacefulness.

2. It activates and instills in the mind an enthusiasm, but not a restlessness.

3. It slows the heart action and gives vital rest to the inner organs.

4. It rests the catabolic process of the inner organs.

5. It is conducive to spiritual experiences that lead to wisdom.
6. Your humor will improve.
7. Your detachment, not indifference, will unfold.
8. You will become more mindful and more aware of what is happening in your mind, your external world, and the astral world.
9. You experience quietude and serenity. You see the unfoldment of consciousness within yourself, and the creation of events external to your body.

This section on hong-sau is concluded with an affirmation called The Infinite Lord of Stillness.

THE INFINITE LORD OF STILLNESS

Oh, Infinite Lord of Stillness,
May we approach Thee at the altar of stillness.
May we who gather here at this most holy altar, lay
    flowers of silence at Thy holy lotus feet.

Oh, Lord of Stillness, teach us to meditate with fervent,
    silent devotion.
Oh, Lord of Stillness, teach us to commune with Thee;
    teach us to contact Thee.
Oh, Infinite Lord of Stillness, teach us how to gently
    decree Thy holy presence.

Remove from us, Oh, Lord of Stillness, all mechanical
    meditation, all mechanical words, and offer at Thy
    altar of silence, our souls to Thee.

Teach us to gently and humbly request Thy presence.
    Take from us the veil of ignorance that we might not
    drown, but remain awake in Thee and Thy service.

Fill each cell of our being with Thy luminous light.
Fill each petal of our mind with Thy luminous love.
Fill our lives with Thy luminous wisdom.

Oh, Lord of Stillness, strengthen us that we might see the
    highway to heaven and thus find Thee.

Chapter 18

MEDITATION
(DHYANA)

-The Art of Self-Unfoldment-

Having covered the first two of the inner stages, sense-withdrawal and concentration, we now come to the seventh stage of yoga called meditation. Moving forward we must walk in one of four ways. There are four ways to evolve:

1. The social path whereby we learn to sympathize and love mankind by serving him.

2. The path of physical discipline whereby you learn to control our body.

3. The path of mental discipline whereby we learn philosophy which produces equanimity of mind and soul.

4. The inner path... the art and science of meditation.

This inner path of meditation necessitates learning:

a. How to switch from body consciousness, existing in the lower chakras of the cerebral-spinal column, to higher non-body states of consciousness, that exist in the higher chakras, and

b. How to take your consciousness out through the sun center, into the infinite, transcending the cerebral-spinal system. When you are able to sustain self-consciousness without the breath, you can then move beyond consciousness into balanced self-conscious awareness. At the end of this stage, you reach a level of non-confinement called illumination.

    In the yoga system, you are attempting to move from the outwardness of objects and penetrate into the inwardness of individuality. This is achieved through the art of meditation, which finds its fruition in samadhi and the nine stages of samadhi which lead to total enlightenment known as Freedom (kaivalya).

According to Patanjali, the goal of the yogi is to dissolve pain, resolve trouble, and attain samadhi. He elaborates on the impediments to the attainment of this tri-level goal. These impediments are also impediments to meditation.

1. Physical and/or mental sickness. Throughout this text, the importance of physical and mental well-being was emphasized. They are necessary to attain the goal.
2. Dullness, folly, ignorance, or being insensible and unfeeling. Unwise ideas and actions may often be foolish, leading to extreme folly.
3. Carelessness. Carelessness means being negligent, inattentive, and unconcerned about your internal or external life conditions.
4. Indecision or confusion. This means being unable to commit yourself because of a disorderly mind and life.
5. Laziness. This implies lack of any inclination to work. The mind and body are inactive.

Yoga beginning at the initial stages of yama-niyama through samadhi is a system to remove these obstacles. Move inward and totally immerse yourself in order to see the great Truth: 'I am not my body. I am spirit.' Meditation is not just a technique, but also a basic approach to life that becomes a foundation for living, loving, and laughing. Meditation removes strife on all levels of your being. Meditation is the ultimate psychology, the ultimate therapy for mankind. It is an ancient method of abstract concepts, but also the key to the core of your existence. But, before meditation can be practiced, you must, to some degree, master the earlier stages.

Meditation is a mental activity having nothing to do with words, but rather with a feeling. This feeling is an awareness of the Self. The whole meaning of life itself is a movement toward enlightenment. To touch the Self, the reality of life, is to become one with life. Touching the Self gives birth to by-products such as compassion, gentleness, insight, knowledge, and understanding. This touching opens you up to the music of the spheres. Herein you can hear the wisdom of silence which expresses all. It says, 'Know thyself'. Meditation is a movement to peace and serenity, to a galactic awareness of ever new, ever-changing bliss which cannot be expressed in words. However, it can be experienced. This Truth lies within each individual's consciousness.

It is restlessness of the mind and body that obstructs this vision of Truth. The mind is like a pond. It is only when the pond becomes stilled that both what exists within the pool, and the perfect reflection of the sun above it, can be perfectly seen. Meditation gives the ability to still that pond, to calm the mind, and to illumine it, that you may see deep within, finding Truth and joy. This experience of Truth is not an intellectual realization but a process of lifting your consciousness upward and holding it at that point where it receives the life-force... the eternal cosmic intelligent vibration. The experience of meditation is universal to all mankind. There is no human being on this earth plane who cannot meditate, regardless of how little or how completely his mind comprehends its purpose.

Because mankind does not understand that this Truth is near, mankind seeks it afar. We are as fish in the pond, crying for water, we are as the birds, crying for air. Meditate and hear the wordless voice of creation. Enter into the boundless realm of unfettered consciousness wherein shines the perfected moonlight of wisdom. Through this moonlight we realize this earth is the Garden of God, and this body is a Flower of Enlightenment.

MEDITATION:
A STAGE IN THE YOGA CONTINUUM

In the Yoga Sutras of Patanjali, meditation (dhyana) is the fourth state of consciousness in the movement toward cosmic consciousness. These stages are:

1. Waking consciousness (jagrat), which is everyday gross consciousness.
2. Sense-withdrawal (pratyahara), the ability to withdraw from the gross objects of everyday consciousness.
3. Concentration (dharana), which is holding, with effort, one subtle object.
4. Meditation (dhyana), which is holding, effortlessly, one subtle object, and
5. Calm, deep quietude of the mind (vritti-nirodha).

There are nine remaining stages. These are the levels of contemplation which will be discussed in a later chapter.

The calm serenity of the mind (vritti-nirodha) is so closely allied with the function and effect produced by meditation that it is difficult to separate them. Calmness of the mind is the link be-

tween meditation and contemplation wherein thought is transcended and you ascend toward spiritual consciousness.

Concentration, meditation, and contemplation always function
together to form a sequence. This continuous, single operation is
called samyama. Sense-withdrawal and concentration are related,
as they both necessitate a deliberate effort to diminish the impulses
streaming into the sense organs. Meditation, although it has many
points of similarity to sense-withdrawal and concentration, is technically a major step beyond. There are major differences between
concentration and meditation. Although these differences are subtle, an understanding of them will assist in comprehending meditation.

THE DIFFERENCES BETWEEN
CONCENTRATION AND MEDITATION

1. In concentration, the mind is restricted to one object, with
   effort, causing one-pointedness of attention. This introversion of one-pointedness is only a step toward achieving the
   later stage of meditation.

   Meditation is an enlarging of the field of concentration
   not by logic but by a subtler feeling state which reveals subtler relationships.

2. The following diagram reveals that in the first stage of concentration there is a steady stream of thoughts related to
   one object. These thoughts are linked to this single object,
   one following the other very rapidly. There is no distinction
   between one thought and the other.

   In the second stage of light meditation, the mind focuses
   upon the thought process. In this inturning toward thoughts,
   the meditator becomes aware that spaces exist between one
   thought and another. The spaces are called void (sunyata).
   This is called light meditation.

THE MOVEMENT FROM
CONCENTRATION TO MEDITATION

A. Concentration:
    (Thoughts appearing as a stream.)

                    ---------------------->
                    stream of thought

B. Light-meditation:
   The awareness that thinking is composed of individual thoughts having a beginning and an end. A beginning perception of a void or space between these individual thoughts.

| Thought | Thought | Thought |
| -------> | -------> | -------> |

C. Deep meditation:
   In deep meditation the center of awareness is more upon the spaces, than it is upon the thoughts. The space seems to be filled with feeling.

   -------> (f e e l i n g) ------->

3. As you develop depth and perception in this stage of meditation, there is an awareness beyond the thinking process, and therefore, beyond thought. This is called deep meditation. Transcending thought occurs by passing through that void (the spaces of non-thought). This void is not unconsciousness. It is not a lethargy. It is not an unawareness. On the contrary, the void is consciousness that is not constricted by concrete thought (of the concentration stage). Within this void exist feelings: The aura of thought. In short, feeling creates thought.

4. In concentration you are fixed to a thought which can be compared to a chunk of ice in a pond. Being water, it is actually part of the pond, yet it can be seen as distinct from it.
   In meditation you are looking effortlessly into a thought (symbolized by the chunk of ice). The thought then dissolves back into the pond, and you become aware that the substratum of thought is feeling. In meditation you are effortlessly fixed to a feeling, the precursor of thought. This is an expansion and not a contraction.
   In our everyday life, a thought, much like an aura, has a feeling contained in and surrounding it. In thought, however, the feeling is heavily limited, formed, and constricted. As we move into the meditation phase of a thought, we find a feeling, unconstricted, unbound, in its purest nature. In short, meditation reveals more clearly the feeling, rather than the logical thought. A thought is only thought and because of its limited nature can actually invoke no other thought. In sustained meditation, however, a feeling (a living creative force) can invoke new thoughts.

To illustrate this, when a writer is attempting to write, he may state he is holding to a thought. In truth, he is using the thought as an anchor of meditation to hold to a feeling of creativity. If he sustains the feeling, new thoughts will flow, thoughts which are related to his mental processes. When we think or concentrate upon a thought, the very nature of the concentration limits or makes us unaware of the feeling element, or of other thoughts. It is for this reason that we say concentration is a constriction of the mind. Thus, it is a necessity to move from concentration to meditation. You must master concentration before meditation is possible.

The problem with concentration is the inability to move beyond thought. Why? Because of hardened mental habits; habits which inhibit us from thinking creatively; habits which keep our minds in a continuous rut. The process of meditation assists in developing feeling awarenesses. This breaks the hardened habits of the past, on each and every level of your being. You must realign and become mindful of the feeling states that relate to objects, thoughts, and so forth. This is not an easy process and is the reason why meditation techniques constantly emphasize holding to a feeling.

Study the section on the object-of-beauty meditation technique which is a simple, yet meaningful, procedure wherein you focus upon the feeling in relation to the object of meditation.

Meditation is becoming aware of the feeling state. However, feelings should not be confused with emotions! They are different. This is a very important difference.

Emotions are heavy angular energies that propel us to do something physically or mentally.

A feeling, on the other hand, is an awareness that has no compulsion behind it.

In the initial stages of meditation, many beginners find a series of emotions and negativities within themselves that drive them away from practicing meditation. The observance of yama-niyama begins the process for removing these states. Also, the utilization of chants, mantras, and affirmations assists in creating or centering the mind into positive feelings rather than emotions. These practices will begin to direct the mind to a more positive acceptance of your life's image as well as a more positive acceptance of that which dwells within your consciousness.   This enables one to meditate more easily.

In meditation you are not thinking.   If you are thinking, you are concentrating.   People who sit and meditate for an hour or two cannot possibly be meditating.   The feeling state of meditation is difficult to sustain even for a few seconds, let alone minutes.   You can, however, concentrate for long periods of time.   Although meditation is a pure feeling state of non-thinking, it is not an unconscious state, nor is it an illogical state.   The thoughts in concentration are gross.   The feelings in meditation are subtle.   Beyond meditation exist the super-subtlety called samadhi... and Freedom.

5. The object of concentration may be either gross or subtle.   It is highly recommended that you begin your concentration with a gross/concrete object.

    In meditation the object is subtle or super-subtle.   It is linked to a feeling element; an abstract concept.

6. In concentration you gather all gross factors directly associated with that object of concentration.   If you are concentrating on a football, you would think about its unique shape, the skin substance, the unusual stitching, and so on.

    In meditation you extract from the mind all the subtle data related to that object of meditation.   If you are meditating on a football, you might meditate on the airflow over the football and thus the necessity of the spiral motion which keeps it moving in a straight line, on the need in mankind that created the game.

7. Concentration is concentric; that is to say, it turns back upon itself and holds to one object with effort.

    Meditation is not concentric; it is an effortless expansion; it lets consciousness expand beyond the object.

8. In concentration you conceptualize by using words.   In meditation you feel, rather than think with word-thoughts.

9. In meditation there is a definite feeling of bliss.   This bliss does not accompany any concentration stage.

MEDITATION IN ACTION

Meditation is not a condition within which you find yourself, but a function you perform.   Meditation can be compared to walking as opposed to a static state of sitting.   There are three important factors to explain the action of meditation:

1. Meditation is remaining totally still, physically and mentally. Gently and quietly center your awareness to a concept which is meaningful to you, and then move one step beyond that concept. Later move beyond truth to stand face to face with the beholder of truth: the Self. Meditation is not passivity, inertia, nor inactivity. It is, however, a stillness.

2. Although meditation is a process of driving gently, quietly, and serenely into your being, it is the opposite of going to sleep. In the normal sleep state there is unconsciousness; in meditation, consciousness is at a maximum, extending even beyond the normal waking state.

3. You cannot meditate unceasingly. The meditator must move from meditation to action. This requires an understanding of the purpose of earth existence, as well as the meaning of your individual life. You must take your meditation out of the meditation room, enabling you to effectively function on this earth plane.

   The action of meditation is a movement from the object of meditation to an objectless inwardness; from external consciousness to internal consciousness; from the ephemeral to the eternal.

   Meditation takes place within the following threefold process. These three, in combination, form the act of meditation. If one phase is missing, the meditation becomes incomplete. It is vitally important to understand these three distinct phases of meditation:

   i. Mindfulness. In the phase of mindfulness you are mindful of your mind. You have an awareness of everything within your mind as well as body. With this awareness you are able to observe your thoughts, mental images, and feelings, as well as the void between the thoughts.

   ii. Attentiveness. This is sometimes called one-pointedness and should not be confused with concentration. In this state there is an elimination of all that is irrelevant to the meditation. Here you key into or hold the object of meditation with a minimum amount of effort until the meditation is established, becoming totally effortless. This is the grip phase of meditation.

   iii. Wisdom. Here you center into the void, realizing the meditator. This is called the established phase of meditation.

This threefold process should be explored in greater detail.

Mindfulness

Within the beginning stages of meditation, the first thing perceived is mindfulness. If there is no mindfulness, there is no meditation; that soul is either asleep or unconscious. In the light stages of meditation, attentiveness and wisdom exist, yet the mind is more focused upon mindfulness.

When the body has been purified by posture, breathing techniques, sense-withdrawal, and so forth, there is a shift of attention from the sensory realm to the realm of the inner mind. The mind has three levels: the surface mind, the inner mind, and the depth mind. The surface mind is constantly changing and thus constantly disturbed. The inner mind is calm and quiet. The depth mind is eternally in samadhi. Karma, which consists of latent tendencies from previous lifetimes, basically affects the surface mind. Karma has a little effect upon the inner mind. Karma cannot ever effect the depth mind.

Regardless of how much the surface mind runs, rants, and raves, it hardly ever disturbs the inner mind. The surface mind does not and cannot affect the tranquility of the depth mind. This tranquil depth mind exists forever within everyone.

The turmoil of the surface mind is caused by five basic factors:
1. Activity of the mind,
2. Craving for sense objects,
3. Analytical, discursive thinking.
4. Desires and daydreams.
5. Special karmas of the past.

Through meditation you are attempting to attune to and become aware of the inner mind, and then the depth mind. As you draw closer to this depth mind, there is more awareness of cosmic peace and tranquility. As you begin to bring your life into a greater balance through yama-niyama, asan-pranayama, and pratyahara, meditation is established and it becomes easier and easier to be released from the thoughts and emotions of the day. Daily, you can reestablish yourself in a deep meditational feeling. Thus, you transcend your emotions and thoughts and lift your center of consciousness. This assists in rebuilding and rebalancing your earth life.

Pulling away from sense objects and the activities of the senses is a major step towards meditation. It is relatively easy to momentarily break away from the awareness of objects, to a feeling state. What is difficult is to hold that feeling state. This feeling of tranquility should accompany you as you move out of your meditation, back into the world carrying on life's duties, challenges, and joys. Meditation is a process that affects each and every level of your life. Take that meditational feeling into your everyday life to establish greater balance and earth wisdom.

In meditation, there is a shift of awareness from the surface mind to the depth mind. To withdraw meditatively from the surface mind does not produce a state of unconsciousness but rather a highly intensified state of awareness that reveals insight into life.

There are four degrees of mindfulness:

1. There is an increased introversion. A deeper interest in, attunement to, and awareness of what is happening inside your own mental mechanism.
2. There is a progressive diminishing impact of all external stimuli.
3. There is less interest in objects; there is a deeper interest in the inner values.
4. There is an increased interest in the reality behind objects.

The movement toward renunciation of objects does not cause you to get up in the morning and butter your book and read your toast. Meditation is not losing your awareness of the relationship of external objects, it is a technique whereby you gain the ability to understand that the shape and color of food is not what sustains life; that which sustains life is something beyond the externals.

Attentiveness

As you enter into the intermediate stage of meditation there develops attentiveness. If a person begins meditating on God and winds up meditating on something else, he has not sustained attentiveness. Attentiveness is a sustained state. In this phase of meditation although mindfulness and wisdom exist, the awareness is more intensely focused upon attentiveness. This stage of meditation is often called one-pointedness. It is unconditioned consciousness in which there is an elimination of everything that is unimportant to the meditator's mind.

If your attention is narrowed to one-pointedness because of some external force such as a blow on the head or the use of drugs, there will be no spiritual unfoldment. There will be no development toward meditation. These examples are not meditational experiences, for there is no mindful action involved. It is only through the development of mindful action that stability is given to the flux of consciousness. It is only through this single-minded intent that consciousness is capable of doing things more effectively.

As you move out of the concentration stage, there is an expanding of consciousness. However, as the mind is expanding, there is a tendency to lose the object of meditation. Thus, this phase of meditation is called the grip. In this early stage of meditation, you are gripping effortlessly to hold a feeling. In the grip stage, your mind is fixing to the object of meditation. Historically, the yogis refer to this fixed stage as being established in meditation. In the grip phase of meditation you lock into the meditation so your mind does not wander onto any other irrelevant factors.

Wisdom

The third phase of meditation is the wisdom phase. It is deep and intense meditation. Once you are established in meditation, you enter the grasp phase whereby you must now grasp the meaningfulness of what you have perceived in your meditation. To be aware of the knowledge of the object of meditation is one thing. To realize its full meaning is another. Though the other two factors of mindfulness and attentiveness exist in this phase of meditation, your awareness is fixed upon the wisdom factor. Wisdom is that function of the mind that penetrates into the darkness of delusion, permitting the meditator to see the world as it is. Wisdom concerns itself with:

1. The true reality.
2. The meaning of life,
3. The conduct of life,

Ultimately these three aspects of wisdom combine together into a total view of life. This total view is developed as the ability to reach samadhi is gained. Wisdom is the strength of the mind which permits contact with Reality. This phase of meditation is not abstract, it is a living experience in which the meditation and the act of meditation become one with the meditator. This action reveals the true Self. This may occur for only a milli-second of time, or for a few seconds.

This is known as the grasping phase of meditation. Once you have locked into the meditation, you must realize what is happening in consciousness and become mindful of the meaningfulness within that meditation. Through the faculty of wisdom, the meditator feels and comes to know the indwelling meditator. It is an unfoldment to dignity, maturity, compassion, and understanding. It is a movement in which ignorance is transcended.

MEDITATION
-A NOTE TO THE STUDENT-

The foundation principle of meditation states that what matters is not what you meditate upon, but that it produces a pleasant feeling. My guru's object for meditation is the feeling of unselfish love. This is the feeling you experience when you give without any thought of recompense. In the act of unselfish love, you give of yourself, of what you are, without any thought of what you are; without any thought of reward. This feeling of unselfish love is the feeling we strive for in our meditation. As you yourself meditate, focus and hold your mind to this feeling. Anything that evokes this feeling of contentment should be utilized as your object of meditation. If for even one second you can introduce the feeling of unselfish love into your meditation, your meditation will be a success and your life will be markedly improved.

Meditation is effortless control of the mind whereby you overcome its natural tendency to wander. The mistake made in meditational practice is to become upset when the mind wanders. This then causes more emotionality. This scatters the mind-energies more and more. The secret of meditation is not to become emotional when the mind wanders. Do not be concerned if you have to bring the mind back to the object of meditation five times or fifty times. Success in meditation comes in being able to gently refocus on the object without emotionality and without scattering the energies. Ultimately, your mind will remain on the object of meditation without deviation.

Training the mind effortlessly, without becoming emotional in the process, is the meditation which produces great inner discipline. When you have finished meditating, be very sure you reflect upon it and determine any causes of interference which made the mind wander. In this way, you release or neutralize the energy of the interference and prevent it from affecting your meditation in the future. When this occurs, feel that your object of meditation is more important than the interference which disrupts the meditation. This will allow you to overcome it.

The beginning student makes another mistake by attempting to sit too long. My guru states that it is far wiser to meditate a very short time in a joyous, comfortable state of being, than to try to meditate for an hour with effort. One hour of effort will not accomplish the purpose of meditation. Remember, if it is effortful, it is not meditation.

Slowly increase your meditation time. When it reaches its capacity you will notice your mind wandering as other thoughts begin to disturb the meditation. It is at this point that you must ever so gently return your mind to the object of meditation without becoming upset or scattering the mind-energies. This might be the time to stop your meditation, and practice it again later.

Meditation practice should become a habit. Only then will it be enjoyable. When something is a habit it is automatic and takes no effort, thus it remains pleasant and the mind can focus on the object, and not one the process. If there are days when your mind is particularly scattered, or your physical health is bad, it is suggested you maintain the practice of sitting in meditation during your regular designated time. Even if you are not meditating, the mere sitting holds you to the habit of meditation. Thus, the habit will not be broken. If you feel that just sitting is a waste of time, realize you have taken a giant step by not disrupting the consistent daily meditation pattern. Remember, 'Yard by yard, yoga's hard; inch by inch, it's a cinch'.

The beginner usually tries to do too much, too fast, and is overly concerned with how well he is doing. Many students pour needless energy into wondering: 'Am I doing it right? Did I really see the astral light? Am I gently bringing the mind back? Did I hold my body perfectly still? Were my hands in the right place?' Questions of this type reveal the student is concentrating on the technique rather than on the object of meditation. In the early stages of meditation you should not be concerned with the rapidity of your unfoldment. When you try to do too much at one time, you hinder rather than help yourself. Do not meditate to accomplish anything other than the enjoyment and feeling that meditation gives. The accomplishments will follow automatically, at a later time.

When you meditate with the proper attitude it produces rapid spiritual unfoldment. In the early stages of meditation it may take months before you are able to truly meditate. However, there are some individuals who can advance much more quickly. It is wisdom to move patiently and consistently, taking the time to properly grasp the meaning of the techniques and gain an understanding of each stage of meditation itself.

You will most likely be the last person to know the true depth of your meditation. The people around you will perceive your maturing and unfoldment, long before you do. It is always easier to observe changes in others than to see them in ourselves. Therefore, be patient with yourself and do not fret over how much or how little you have progressed. Find joy, feel unselfish love, and return again and again to your meditation. Be ever mindful that the search is inside the heart of a soul, beginning with a smile, moving through a chuckle, and ending in untold warmth and laughter.

Meditation is not like the togetherness of a hayride. It is a singular inwardness wherein reality is found. It is first, last, and always an inner solitaire, like a single pristine diamond set alone. Inward and alone we unfold. This aloneness, however, should not be confused with loneliness. If anything, as we draw into ourselves, our lives become richer and more rewarding.

There is a heaviness in this world that must be shaken off. Shake it off rapidly and surely. Mankind suffers because of not fully understanding the world of impermanence, in which all is changing. Despite this, you can move forward on the path with great success and with a gentle smile. May you, indeed, find your path. May you discover that meditation brings great laughter, great joy, great understanding, and above all, great wisdom.

GUIDE TO PRACTICING MEDITATION

Meditation Area

The place you set aside for meditation practice should have the following characteristics:

1. The room's furnishings should be as simple as possible, without cluttering.
2. The room should be beautiful to you. This will be most helpful.
3. External stimuli should be at a minimum and the noise level reduced as much as possible. Music should not be played during meditation!
4. The room should not be totally dark; there should be a grayish light, enough that you can distinguish various objects in the room.
5. The temperature of the room should be comfortable for you. Cold hands and feet are not conducive to meditation.
6. The room should not be stuffy, nor should it be drafty.
7. A lightly scented or sandalwood incense may be used, or a flower fragrance.
8. A wool blanket should be sat upon. This blanket should be used only for meditation.

9. If possible, your meditation should not be practiced where you do hatha yoga exercises, as the vibrations set up are often contradictory.

Posture

You may meditate in any meditative pose which you find comfortable. Whatever the posture, your spine should be erect, chin parallel to the floor, the shoulder blades brought together, and stomach and anus muscles pulled slightly in and up.

Eating

Meditation should not be practiced on a full stomach nor should it be done in a state of hunger. The stomach should be half full. You should usually wait about 2 to 4 hours after a full meal and an hour after a small repast before meditation is begun.

Clothing

During meditation you should wear clothing that does not constrict, or produce a feeling of inhibition.

Direction to Face

During the daylight hours you should meditate facing east, in the direction of the rising sun. After the sun has set, you should face north, in the direction of the pole star.

The Best Time to Meditate

According to yogic tradition there are three best times to meditate. Here they are listed in order of importance:

1. 4:30 a.m. to 6:00 a.m. Classically, this period is the best time for meditation, for at this time the balanced energies are strongest. The 48 minutes just before sunrise is the best time. The 7 to 12 minutes just before sunrise is the most auspicious time for meditation.

2. Sunset. This is the second best time to meditate. For contemporary westerners, however, this is often a difficult time since many social and family responsibilities occur at this time.

3. Anytime. If you cannot meditate at the above times, meditate at any time. Remember this most important rule: any-

time is a great time to meditate. The second most important rule: meditate every day.

Do make an effort to choose a time convenient, and least likely to be disturbed by others, or to disturb others. Most importantly, choose a time when you can consistently and regularly meditate. The habit of meditating each day, at the same time, in the same place, and in the same way is extremely valuable in establishing overall discipline and control of the pranic energy and thus your mind.

Eye Position

It is recommended that the eyes are held in frontal gaze during your meditation practice. In frontal gaze the eyes are closed and gently focused at the root of the nose between the eyebrows. It is extremely important not to stare. Gently gaze upward toward this point. There should be no violent effort involved in this procedure.

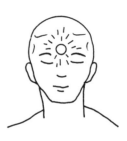

Beginning Meditation Practice

It is recommended that before meditating, you perform some very gentle exercise which will bring a sense of relaxation. Consequently, your body will be willing to sit motionless during the length of your meditation time. Having performed the gentle exercise, you are now ready to enter into meditation.

Entering Into Meditation

1. Sit in any comfortable meditative pose with your eyes closed and gently focused at the sun center, the root of the nose.
2. You should next offer a simple affirmation or dedication. This is a moment of devotion or communion.
3. Inhale slowly and fully, and relax the body.
4. Chant the OM-shanti mantra, relaxing the mind. Repeat 3 times if needed.
5. Refocus your attention at the sun center. Your attention should be focused at this point during the entire meditation.
6. You may proceed to whichever meditation technique you wish to practice.

The Golden Rules of Meditation

1. Meditation is an effortless movement of the mind. It is a function to be done without strain of the body or mind.

2. In meditation there needs to be attention to the mind without tension in the mind.
3. It does not matter how often the mind wanders during meditation, but how gently you bring it back to the object.
4. It does not matter how long you meditate, but how deeply you meditate.

MEDITATION TECHNIQUES

1. MINDFULNESS TECHNIQUE
(Thought-Watching)

Sit in a meditative pose. Take a few deep breaths. Relax and become mindful. Simply watch your mind continuously without judgment. Do not be concerned with whether a thought is positive or negative. Become as an onlooker sitting on a veranda, watching all the passing thoughts go by on the street below. Remember, you are attempting to establish clarity of your thoughts and emotions. This is a very important technique which will help you develop the deeper stages of meditation.

2. SOLAR-DISC AWARENESS TECHNIQUE

Sit in a comfortable meditative pose. Perceive the luminous (white, gold, or blue) sphere of light at the sun center. When it is seen, bring the light gently from the sun center down to the heart center. Visualize and feel it there for a few seconds and then bring it back up to the sun center. This will develop compassion and increase the depth of your meditation.

3. CENTERING TECHNIQUE

Sit in a meditative pose. Center yourself in the saturn center. Feel as well as visualize a straight ray of light moving up to the thousand-petalled lotus. Do this without any other thought. As you visualize the light moving up to the thousand-petalled lotus, do not allow the light to bow to either side. The light must only move in a straight line, upward. Now, return the light to the saturn chakra, in the same manner.

4. CHAKRA MEDITATION TECHNIQUE

Sit in a comfortable meditative pose. Center yourself at the saturn center and slowly feel, as well as mentally visualize, the life-energy slowly rising up the center sushumna channel. Let the mind rest a few seconds in the exact center of each chakra before ascending to the next one. Stop at the thousand-petalled lotus for a few extra moments. Now descend, stopping at each chakra in exactly the same way you ascended the spine. Repeat 3 to 7 times.

5. THE OBJECT-OF-BEAUTY TECHNIQUE

Sit in a meditative pose. Choose an object that is very beautiful to you. This object can be anything: the Grand Canyon, a sunset, a flower, an artifact, a piece of artwork, or any other object, subtle or gross. In the earlier stages of meditation, choose only concrete objects. The object-of-beauty can be anything that evokes in you a feeling of beauty. Focus at the sun center and visualize the object-of-beauty within your mind's eye. Mentally feel it, touch it, and perceive it totally. Each time the mind wanders from this object, gently refocus it on the object. After a while, your mind will hold to the object. Now, slowly and very gently shift your attention from the object to the feeling caused by that object. Become more aware of the feeling within you, than the object which evoked the feeling. You are now holding within yourself the pure feeling of beauty.

6. ADVANCED OBJECT-OF-BEAUTY TECHNIQUE

The same as above except with each inhalation, allow the feeling to saturate each cell of your being, and each petal of your mind. With each exhalation send the feeling of beauty out into the world. Create an even greater awareness that the object is a mirror which merely reflects that which already exists within you.

7. EXTENDED SOLAR-DISC MEDITATION TECHNIQUE

This practice is extremely significant in the study of meditation. Sit in a meditative pose, one which you find most comfortable. Use a woolen blanket to sit on. Rest the elbows on a table or stand that has been placed in front of you. Place the thumbs tightly on the tragus, closing the ears. Gently focus the closed eyes at the sun center and gently press the index fingers below the eyes to keep them from moving. It is important that the pressure not be too great, yet strong enough to hold the eyeballs still. Chant OM loudly. The chanting should be long and sounded from 10 to 30 seconds, whatever is comfortable to you.

After you have chanted, mentally listen for the OM sound; also look for the inner light, the solar disc which manifests as a gold disc, a blue disc, or an opaline blue disc. This is the third eye. Do not pay attention to any other lights seen other than this solar disc and what appears within it. While you are holding the attention at the sun center, breathe normally. If you notice the mind wandering, slowly and gently chant OM, one to three times and gently return your consciousness to the solar disc.

The solar disc meditation should be performed daily for a period of 5 to 15 minutes at each sitting. This meditation allows you to enter into your mind consciously and find the inner light that exists. Through this light, great knowledge regarding life and the universe can be gained. This light is the doorway to the infinite. Eventually this awareness is transcended into the attainment of samadhi. Seeing this light is an auspicious experience and an indication that you have achieved a great deal. Seek, therefore, and unfold unto this inner sun. Seek it while you are awake, while you are falling asleep, and after you are in the dream state. Seek it as soon as you awake. Look, therefore to the sun.

8. OM-MEDITATION TECHNIQUE

Sit in the lotus pose or the adept's pose, on a woolen blanket facing east. Close your eyes and perform yoni mudra, placing the thumbs on the ears, the index fingers on the eyes, the middle fingers on the nose, the ring fingers above the upper lip, and the little fingers under the lower lip. Use the index fingers to steady the eyes and fix the gaze at the sun center. The fingers should gently be applying light pressure to the eyes. Take a deep breath and hold, closing off the senses with the fingers as you draw inward.

After you have restricted the gross outer sounds and the inner biological sounds, release the middle fingers and make a short, full inhalation through the nose. Then mentally chant OM, listen for the ocean-like roar of the OMnic sound, and enter into the center of this sound. Secondly, listen for a subtler sound within this sound and enter into the center of that sound. Exhale and repeat. Chant for a length of time you find comfortable. If disquietude arises, stop the meditation.

9. OM-TRACKING TECHNIQUE

Repeat as above, but as you chant OM (silently or aloud), visualize it radiating from the sun center like a train running on a circular track, returning into the right ear. The actual chant runs only one-half the track. Chant OM only for as long as you visualize it moving to the half-way point around the track. Then listen for the mental sound of OM as it returns from the half-way point, into the right ear. This OM sound is the cosmic intelligent vibration within your own consciousness. As you center upon this sound-within-a-sound, you rise above the physical and astral sounds to experience the ultimate vibration of the universe. Gradually, your consciousness expands and you the meditator become one with the sound of OM. The eighth stage of yoga, contemplation, is then attained.

10. THE UNIVERSAL BLESSING

The universal blessing is a unique meditation wherein you attune to a oneness with the universe and radiate this feeling outward to all life-forms in the universe. Here are the steps in the technique:

a. Sit facing east and form a meditative pose with the eyes closed and focused at the sun center. Be motionless. Note that this meditation is only to be performed between 4:30 and 6:30 a.m.

b. Chant OM (OOOmmmm) deeply, concentrating at the solar plexus chakra. As you verbally chant, feel the OM vibration arise from this point in the spine and travel upward to the thousand-petalled lotus at the crown of the head. When the OM reaches the throat region, close the lips and continue with the sound trailing off: O-m-m-m-m-m. Finally, let the sound fade out as it reaches the crown of the head. Repeat the OM chant 3 to 7 times.

c. Tighten the throat slightly, which will allow the breath to be taken in more slowly. Observe the breath, being aware of it flowing into the body, stopping, and then flowing out.

d. Visualize a sacred image within your heart. Let it be alive, living, radiant, filling each cell of your being, each petal of your mind with its living sacredness.

e. Gradually let this image expand out through the pores of your vehicle, filling the entire room, ultimately the entire universe. At this point feel you are one with the universe. Feel that you are a part of, not apart from, divinity and goodness. Hold this feeling from 1 to 3 minutes.

f. Radiate this feeling, sending forth a blessing to all life-forms everywhere. Send forth vibrations of health, wealth, wisdom, and love.

g. Also, radiate this physical/spiritual blessing to the vehicle through which you express yourself; your own mind and your own body.

h. Sit quietly and peacefully for a few moments. Feel happiness, joy, and the beauty of your individual soul. Become absorbed in the simple tranquility of just existing.

i. Inhale one final time, taking in all the joy of existence. On exhaling, radiate this joy back out into the universe by chanting, 'OM, shanti, shanti, shanti.' Chant the mantra very slowly, gently, and softly, but with intense feeling.

j. Leave your meditation and return to your worldly obligations with joy.

11. THE 7 RAYS MEDITATION TECHNIQUE

The 7 rays meditation utilizes the 7 rays of discernment which were given to you in an earlier chapter on concentration. Take note of two additional points regarding the 7 rays, in order to assist in a proper and meaningful exercise. Remember in concentration, the object is gross and you are to utilize the 7 rays to extract all the concrete thought-word data that relates to the object of concentration. In meditation, however, the data received is subtle.

Secondly, before beginning the 7 rays meditation, remember that in meditation one is seeking feelings, not thoughts. The data being collected is in the form of feelings that are experienced. In this meditation wherein the 7 rays are utilized, you the meditator are to become aware of the feeling produced by each ray.

Through the 7 rays meditation technique, you can learn to extend your knowledge about anything you turn your mind toward. The object of meditation is placed before the mind and gently held there. It is then brought into conjunction with the feeling of each of the 7 word symbols: who? what? where? when? why? how? and which? The mind is gently held in a relaxed state as each word-symbol-feeling is brought into play. Throughout the meditation, the mind must remain relaxed. Remember, this meditation is a subtle, inner process and all the principles of meditation set forth in this chapter need to be exercised. Keep in mind these important factors.

a. Relax the mind and keep it balanced.

b. Ask only one question at a time.

c. Accept only one answer at a time.

d. Above all else, remember that meditation is the act of returning thoughts back toward feelings, the feelings that created the thought to begin with.

e. All the answers you receive will be experienced as feelings. The stage following the meditation must convert these subtle feelings back into words so the everyday mind can concretely comprehend and record them in your meditation journal.

12. CHAKRA MEDITATION TECHNIQUE

Sit in any comfortable meditative pose.   Make especially sure the head, neck, and spine are straight.   Be sure you are facing east, as this meditation is only to be performed in the early morning hours.   Close your eyes and meditate at the sun center.   With great joy take your consciousness from the sun center (third eye), down through the middle of the spine to the mercury chakra, holding and establishing a joyful feeling at this chakra.   Utilize the mantra, given at the end of this technique, for the mercury chakra.   Bring your consciousness back to the sun center and continue the meditation on the theme set forth in the mantra.   Reestablish a feeling of joy and serenity at the sun center and take your consciousness down to the venus center, utilizing the mantra for the venus center. Bring your consciousness back to the sun center.   Continue with the meditation, returning to the sun center after establishing a joyful feeling within each lower chakra.   Reestablish your consciousness at the sun center before proceeding further downward to the next chakra.   The meditation ends with your consciousness at the sun center.

This meditation takes you into the awareness of each of the chakras and leads to a fuller experiencing of consciousness within these different levels.   You are united with the energies within these chakras and ultimately united with the totality of the cosmic intelligent vibration.

The English mantra for each individual chakra is as follows:

Sun center:
'I am divine spirit. I am one with the radiant light of divine beauty, wisdom, and bliss.'
Mercury center:
'I am in conscious union with supreme knowledge... wisdom is flowing through me.'
Venus center:
'I am in conscious union with divine love. Beauty, joy, and unselfish love are within and around me.'
Mars center:
'I am in conscious union with supreme energy. I manifest spiritual strength.'

Jupiter center:
    'I am in conscious union with divine mind. I express bountiful happiness and divinity.'
Saturn center:
    'I am in conscious union with divine being. I materialize spiritual substance.'

The word 'I' here is used to express the atma; the word 'me' is used to express the instruments of the atma, the body and mind.

13. QUESTION MEDITATION

In seeking an answer to a question or in trying to solve a problem, the question meditation may be utilized with powerful results.

Begin in a meditative pose and perform the initial stages for entering into meditation. With the attention at the sun center, firmly fix the question in your mind, not so much with words, as with a feeling. Asking questions in meditation is a subtle process of internal consciousness and a mindful awareness of feeling. It is not creating an intellectual debate with yourself.

Still the mind. Then in the stillness of the full chalice draw in your senses and enter into the inner realm. Within this state of awareness, send forth the question by translating the sentence into a feeling. Direct your feelings toward the question. Answers will come forth in the form of various subtle feelings. Your ability to perceive these answers will depend upon your proficiency in stilling the mind and attuning to the meditative feelings. Whenever it becomes uncomfortable for you to retain the full chalice, begin to breathe normally. Do not concentrate on the breathing. In no way should your consciousness be interrupted.

Remember, your answers will come more as feelings than as concrete word-thought patterns. Through rigid discipline of the sense organs and devoted practice of yoga principles, the answers will come. Do not do yourself the injustice of allowing your emotionality or your ego craving to cloud the wisdom that lies within you. Above all else, be aware of when your emotionality is throwing you out of the meditation, down into the lower astral, affecting the answers you are receiving.

14. KRIYA KUNDALINI MEDITATIONS TECHNIQUE

Five meditations are used to awaken the latent kriya kundalini. These meditations are based on a Hindu system as it is set forth in

Yoga-tattva Upanishad. This system differs from the system we have previously used whereby the energy centers along the spinal column were related to various gross elements of nature. Here, in the Yoga-tattva system, these gross elements are related to regions of the human anatomy.

These meditations are performed in any comfortable meditation pose. You are to utilize the general procedures already pointed out for all meditation techniques. The meditations may be performed singly, or as a continual movement from the base of the spine to the sun center. This meditation is not for everyone.

Earth meditation
Meditate on:
the anatomical region from the feet to the knees.
Use the symbol:
yellow square.
Silently chant the seed-sound (bija): LAM.
Visualize your object of meditation:
a four-headed golden Brahma which is symbolic of the four realities, the four states of consciousness.
Attainment:
mastery over thought and the removal of dangers caused by the forces of saturn.

Water meditation
Meditate on:
the anatomical region from the knees to the anus.
Use the symbol:
white crescent.
Silently chant the seed-sound: VAM.
Visualize your object of meditation:
Narayana.
Attainment:
removes foolishness and helps to overcome karma; gives mastery over your emotions.

Fire meditation
Meditate on:
the anatomical region from the anus to the heart.
Use the symbol:
red triangle, pointing upwards.
Silently chant the seed-sound: RAM.
Visualize your object of meditation:

Rudra, with three eyes covered with the holy ash.   One
should beseech, "Rudra, please look."
Attainment:
>   produces freedom from dangers caused by impetuosity and
>   over-enthusiasm.

Air meditation
Meditate on:
>   the anatomical region from the heart to the sun center.

Use the symbol:
>   black hexagon.

Silently chant the seed-sound: YAM.
Visualize your object of meditation:
>   Ishvara, the omniscient one with faces on all sides.

Attainment:
>   gives mastery over the intellect.

Ether meditation
Meditate on:
>   the anatomical region from the sun center to the thousand-
>   petalled lotus.

Use the symbol:
>   smokey blue circle.

Silently chant the seed-sound: HAM.
Visualize your object of meditation:
>   sadashiva.

Attainment:
>   produces great occult abilities.

According to Hindu tradition, in order to attain the benefits of
these individual meditations, they are to be practiced for extended
periods of time.   Continual practice leads the yogi to proficiency in
overcoming unconsciousness in the dream state, as well as in the
states following the death of the physical body.   They are advanced
meditations to be used under the direction of a teacher.

15. KRIYA MEDITATION TECHNIQUE
It should be noted that this kriya meditation technique differs
from the hong-sau kriya technique given in another chapter.   In
this   kriya   meditation   technique,   the   following   E-E-E
mantra/pranayama is utilized.   It may be wise to begin by first
becoming familiar with it.

Preliminary to the kriya meditation technique:

E-E-E MANTRA/PRANAYAMA TECHNIQUE

The E-E-E pranayama is performed by inhaling through the open mouth as rapidly and as deeply as you can and without retaining the breath, exhaling the air while chanting out loud an E-E-E sound (e-e-e as in the word "bee"), while parting the mouth as in a smile. The E-E-E should be strong and forceful, but not violent. It can be at whatever pitch is most pleasing to you. Most importantly, there should be no trailing off or wavering of the sound. The ending should be decisive and definite. It is simply an audible expulsion of the breath. After the breath is expelled, the empty chalice is held as long as comfortable. This completes one E-E-E pranayama.

Now, to perform the kriya meditation, sit in any meditative pose that is comfortable to you. Close your eyes and bring your attention to the sun center. Having relaxed the mind and body, look for the inner sun according to the directions outlined in the solar disc meditation. Perform three E-E-E breaths in succession. After the third breath, hold the empty chalice and again look for the solar disc. When the breath can no longer be comfortably retained, begin breathing. Repeat the E-E-E breath 5 times in succession. After the fifth breath, hold the empty chalice and again look for the solar disc. When the breath can no longer be retained with comfort, begin breathing 7 E-E-E breaths in succession. After the seventh breath, hold the empty chalice and again look for the solar disc. Do not hold too long. Any strain will destroy the meditational benefits of this powerful technique.

At this point, relax into the feeling of joy that is radiating through your entire body/mind complex. Feel totally at peace. Feel the true meaning and purpose of meditation. Stay seated in the meditative pose for as long as you can sustain the meditative feeling you have just acquired. Gently arise, taking with you into the world, the peace and tranquility you have just experienced. Know that you have been regenerated and that you will radiate this energy out into the world, touching all that you shall meet.

It should be understood that in all these techniques the process of moving into the meditation occurs at the hold or still moment. In short, the meditation occurs during that short period of effortless full or empty chalice. All else is but a preparation to this moment of Truth!

Chapter 19

THE ETERNAL COSMIC VIBRATION

The deeper level truths in relationship to meditation reveal that,

Spirit is everywhere: it's ever conscious and ever new bliss.

And that creation is a multi-leveled, many faceted process. Spirit projects out of itself and first manifests as the cosmic intelligent vibration. The sincere meditator can tangibly contact this Spirit and experience the three materializations of the cosmic intelligence. These are:

1. BLISS

Bliss (ananda) is the cosmic consciousness of the material universe. It is the guiding force of all creation. It is the feeling-element. It is balanced self-conscious awareness radiating as bliss, joy, peace, tranquility, harmony, equanimity, and equipoise.

2. VISIBLE COSMIC ENERGY

Visible cosmic energy is the light of the sun center (ajna chakra) of all cerebral-spinal creatures. This light can be condensed at the sun center, and thus seen. Through the ages, this center has been called by many different names: the single eye, the third eye, the seat of wisdom, the spiritual eye, the cave of the ancients, and the pearl of great price. This energy radiates as three lights, which form the spiritual eye. These three lights include:

a. The golden ring,
b. The opaline blue disc,
c. The white, colorless star.

The Golden Ring

Within the golden ring you perceive the primal energies of physical creation, the substratum of gross form. As you penetrate the golden ring you experience the golden dawn of astral life and gain an understanding of the mystery of this golden ring. Consequently, you enter into the labyrinth of the garden of creation and come to understand the mystery of matter.

The Opaline Blue Disc

The opaline blue disc telescopes out into a tunnel. When you enter the blue disc, you experience an awareness called cosmic consciousness. Other names are Krishna consciousness or Buddhi-chit. It relates to consciousness existing in every unit of cosmic energy that is within each unit of matter (prakriti). Experiencing this light stills the mind, indicating your great success spiritually.

The Colorless 5-pointed Star

The colorless 5-pointed star is also called the silver star. It is a fluctuating 5-pointed body contained within the opaline blue disc. The star opens and closes.

You should know that,

The golden ring is the astral gate between the physical and astral worlds.

The opal blue disc is the causal gate between the astral and the causal worlds.

The colorless 5-pointed star gate opens to higher worlds.

Astral simply means those mental forces that precipitate and give form in and to the physical universe. The causal energies give form and impetus to the astral universe. The astral energies exist within an astral universe, while causal energies exist within a causal universe.

If you do not see the star, it is very difficult to find the entrance into the causal world. However, there are other entrances into the causal universe. The value of entering through the ajna chakra is that this entrance is easiest and the safest. If you enter through any other passage, you tend to become unconscious.

DIAGRAM OF THE
COSMIC INTELLIGENCE

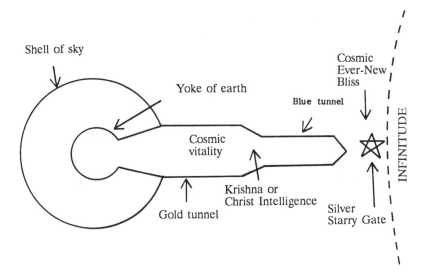

These three inner lights here are cosmic patterns, not hallucinations. This is an important point, for hallucinations and visions differ in that hallucinations always change. They come and go with your moods. They are not eternal; they are very temporal and transitory. They have no higher reality. In mystical symbolism: one day your mind may be affected by saturn conjunct the moon, and hallucinations seen or dreams dreamt may be from the pit of hell. A few months later your mind may be affected by jupiter conjunct the sun, and any hallucination or dreams will be on cloud nine. However, the third eye, no matter what aspect forms, is always seen as the same pattern. In short, the third eye is causal, not astral.

Thus, you may find yourself asking, 'What value is there on things that change? Should I place any value on visions'? The answer is, None. What is of value is your realization that you have moved into a higher, subtler realm.

The mathematics of consciousness reveal that all is transitory and ever changing. However, the inner lights remain unaffected by your changing moods or nature. Whether you have saturn conjunct the moon or jupiter conjunct the sun, the spiritual eye remains unchanging. It simply eternally exists. It is like a door that remains changeless, whether the sun shines or not.

After the third eye is perceived and your mind becomes fixed to it, it can be seen whether your eyes are opened or closed. It is only by recognizing it that you are able to consciously move through it. But, whether you recognize the eye or not, the entrance is always there. You should see and recognize it, just as you see and recognize your own home.

Going through the star is one of the end goals of yoga. This star is the way to God-consciousness. Although it is important to see this fluctuating star, it is essential that you hold the star steady and open. It is held open so that you can pass through the starry door and step into the realm of God-consciousness.

The visible cosmic energy manifests as lesser lights in the lower five chakras. As long as your mind is in gear and active, the star opens and closes. If your mind is stilled, however, the star will remain still. You then have to hold it open. All the lower stages have been utilized to enable you to do so. All that you have striven for, all your control over the prana, was to hold open and consciously walk through. Only if the star is open can you move to That which is beyond you.

3. OM, THE UNIVERSAL SOUND WHICH PERVADES EXISTENCE

OM is an audible manifestation of the cosmic intelligent vibration which exists along your spinal axis. The OM sound is a symphony of all other sounds. The following are specific astral sounds heard at each of the chakras:

a. The sun center at the root of the nose is the all-seeing single eye. The sound here is the pure OMnic vibration.

b. The moon center at the medulla oblongata is the mouth of God. As the life-energy enters the physical vehicle at this location, the sound here is also the pure OMnic vibration. This is so because the moon center is the feminine principle of the masculine sun center.

c. The mercury center, at the cervical plexus, symbolizes the ether element. The sound is like that of the ocean's roar.

d. The venus center, at the dorsal region, symbolizes the air element. The sound is like that of a gong, or bell.

e. The mars center, at the lumbar region, symbolizes the fire element. The sound is like that of a harp.

f. The jupiter center, at the sacral region, symbolizes the water element. The sound is like that of a flute.

g. The saturn center, at the coccyx region, symbolizes the earth element. The sound is like a humming of a bumble bee. It is often referred to as the baby-OM.

These sounds are most clearly perceived when the mind is calm and the breath has been stilled. Listening for these astral sounds is not to be confused with chanting. However after chanting a mantra for some time, the astral sounds of the chant can be heard mentally. With continual meditative practice, which may take months or years, the advanced student begins to attune to these astral lights and sounds at each of the chakras.

Misconceptions About the Chakras

There are two popular misconceptions regarding chakras. First, in some texts the chakras are not on the spinal axis. These texts derive their information from mystical studies, dealing with the symbolic interpretation of astral phenomena. In yoga, the chakras are always on the spinal axis.

Secondly, in contemporary books on meditation, there is a tendency to talk about meditating on the chakras. These books advise meditating on the saturn chakra first and then meditating on the other chakras. This is unwise because meditating on the saturn chakra could produce depression. You should not meditate on any chakra until you have reached a balanced state of consciousness. To meditate on the saturn chakra while in a balanced state of consciousness is to become aware of those balanced saturn objects--both mental and physical.

Spiritual Consciousness

There are several techniques and specific meditations which are given to assist you in attuning to the cosmic intelligent vibration. Meditation techniques consequently allow you to achieve God-consciousness. This leads to a progressively increased internal awareness. This occurs only after much practice. This internalized consciousness is called spiritual consciousness because it's balanced. Here the Self unfolds because of energies gathered into a fuller collectiveness of the mind.

To the degree you practice the art of meditation, and to the degree that you become established in internalized consciousness, the following effects manifest.

1. Self-conscious awareness:
   This can be defined as gaining increased awareness of what is going on in your mind, called mindfulness. Then there is

a lifting up beyond mindfulness to an awareness of Self. Mindfulness allows you to see within yourself, and to see internal emotional thought patterns. Seeing them you become aware that they can be overcome by new circumstances in your life. This can also be done by substituting negative thinking with positive affirmations.

2. Dissolving of the agitations:
   The ability to dissolve agitations in your mind and in your everyday life is the next effect of being established in internalized consciousness. This is best expressed as bliss, and the calm passivity of the mind. As you dive deeply into the ocean of meditation, the ocean of emotions is overcome and forgotten.

3. The more your consciousness expands and the more deeply you dive into your soul, the more will you experience a oneness with all life.

4. Meditation is relatively easy to establish, if you are a serious student. However, the length of time you can sustain that meditation is what becomes most meaningful. It is only when these meditative stages are sustained that you will be able to change your internal universe.

5. Attainment of truth:
   This is the final manifestation of internalized consciousness. There are three stages.

   a. Confused perception occurs when you first begin meditating. The individual memory of past experiences (whether in this life or previous existences) inaccurately colors the words, meanings, and objects upon which you are meditating.

   b. Acute perception refers to astral vision. These astral visions are nothing more than intense mental awareness of what exists in the subtler realms of your being.

   c. True perception occurs when you have advanced in the practice of meditation to the point that your mind is freed from individualized memory and devoid of its own nature. At this point, the mind is like a clear gem which truly experiences the object because it has become one with it.

      Just as you attain true perception of gross objects, you can accurately perceive true knowledge of subtle objects and subtle worlds as they exist on the astral plane. Just as you attain true perception of subtle objects, you can accurately perceive true knowledge of super-subtle objects and super-subtle worlds as they exist on the causal plane. This process progresses all the way to perception of the unmanifested.

True perception still contains the separateness between the individualized Self and the higher Self. Nevertheless, the attainment of Truth produced by the development of internalized consciousness is a continuation of the movement toward contemplation and the highest realm of creation: the ultimate unitive experience of God-consciousness.

Chapter 20

CONTEMPLATION
(SAMADHI)

The soul who has walked through the previous seven stages of yoga and who has entered into contemplation (samadhi) is no longer a student. He is now an initiate. This is not necessarily a person who has gained certain secrets but one who has ever so gently 'rent the veil of darkness,' and obtained direct experience of life-realization.

The yogi is a mystical scientist trying to understand the mystery of life. Samadhi reveals this mystery. What is this mystery? The mystery is that the most important purpose of existence is to understand life. It is a mystery because mankind does not realize that each and every moment of life is heaven and happiness. This very earth plane existence can be heaven.

This direct experience of life-realization reveals at least three great truths:

1. There is but one existence and within this existence lies the spiritual search as well as the everyday life. These two are not in conflict with each other.

2. The quest of yoga is not the attainment of a piece of data, a mathematical formula, or a secret mantra. It is the attainment of unalloyed bliss. Bliss is not a state of unconsciousness, unawareness, or irresponsibility but rather the feeling awareness of spiritual fullness. To give you an idea of what I am speaking of, let me ask you a few questions. Have you ever been sick? Do you remember the feeling you had the first day you became well? Do you remember how joyous your body life felt in being healthy again? In our everyday living patterns, it becomes very easy to forget and lose sight of this ever renewed health, this mini-bliss. Now, this joy multiplied seven trillionfold is the bliss of which the yogis speak.

3. You realize that you are immortal but not consciously immortal. The yogi strives to become conscious of his immortality. Man swims in the ocean of existence spending most of his earth life trying to determine whether he should swim in the Indian Ocean, the Adriatic Sea, the Mediterranean

Sea, or the Baltic Sea. Wherever you yourself swim, you must come to realize that you are a fish swimming in a variety of oceans at varying times in your existence. You must come to recognize that an ocean... is an ocean... is only an ocean. You should be striving to experience the blissful, joyous, harmonious waters of existence, in every moment of your life. This day, this very moment, is part of your immortality, it is not apart from that immortality. It should be lived as you would live in eternity.

Freedom (moksha) is the goal of every sentient life-form and it is through realization that each soul resolves and solves the mystery of life after death. You are a result of all you have thought. The habits you form are the result of your repeated actions over lifetimes of experience, be those actions wise or foolish. Once the habit is established, it requires a long, hard struggle to resolve, abandon, and transcend. It may take lifetimes to work through it. Your habits from this life and previous lives reside in the chakras of your spinal column which relate to the process of your spiritual evolution. We are on an evolutionary movement, from lifetime to lifetime, to resolve and transcend these hardened habits of the past. It is by their force that we are born again and again.

In the stages of our evolution, mankind generally lives in the saturn and jupiter states of consciousness, in which he has not as yet transcended his lower nature. He lives to eat rather than eats to live. His activities and drives (for the most part) are controlled within these two lower chakras. As he begins to spiritually ascend and completely breaks from saturn chakra states of consciousness, becoming firmly established in jupiter chakra states of consciousness, he rids himself of the basest segment of his animalistic nature. Thus he has begun his upward journey to Truth. Yet he truly has not yet transcended them until he overcomes the mars chakra states of consciousness. Here he escapes the pain of loss and gain. Finally, when he becomes established in heart chakra consciousness, there is no chance whatsoever of his reverting back to more primitive impulses.

Until then, his mind is enmeshed in the confining, constrictive forces of his lower nature. Samadhi breaks this imprisonment from lower forms and thus lower forms of consciousness. Through meditation and mantra, the mind becomes receptive to the inner levels of unlimited and unconstricted states of consciousness. In these inturning stages, the transitory mind dissolves away, and the eternal is revealed. The atman shines through the sattvic intellect, not changing the nature of the Self, merely revealing the Self.

When, through the practice and mastery of the eight stages of yoga, the mind ultimately stops all its wandering and fluctuations, the true Self (atma) is seen beyond the forms of thoughts and emotions.

I am thinking of a pond which is almost frozen over with chunks of ice, intermingled with twigs and leaves caught and enmeshed by freezing temperatures and winter winds. In a similar way, chitta or the mind-stuff, just as these chunks of ice, is attached with impurities... the twigs and leaves of thoughts and emotions. It appears that the true nature of the pond is frozen chunks of ice with impurities, just as it appears the true nature of the mind is twigs and leaves of thoughts and emotions. Surface perception does not reveal the true nature of the pond, which is water; in the same way, surface perception does not always reveal the true nature of the mind. But the pond, like the mind, beholding the radiant warmth of the sun: unselfish love, the ultimate discipline of yoga, changes form. The chunks of ice melt as the true nature of the pond is revealed; they again become formless. They become formless water which will take the shape of any container and yet is capable of becoming many other forms such as ice, snow, sleet, hail, raindrops, lakes, and rivers, even clouds.

Your mind, frozen with attached thought and emotion, is like the icy pond, unyielding and non-life bearing. Through the eight stages of yoga, the warmth of the soul, your own unselfish love, melts the icy pond and you again become the formless one: the waters of life, the atma... the life-bearing, uncontaminated, formless eternal being.

In Samadhi, you break the false awareness that the I (the atma) is a given transitory thought, feeling, ego state, mind or body; that it is a given condition or given reaction to stimuli. Rather, you become aware that the I is pure consciousness, which can take any transitory form. All forms are but variations of pure consciousness: formless consciousness. However, we confuse the form with the true reality. We are the waters of life and the goal is to perceive the true reality in its formless, pure state. This state is experienced through samadhi.

Samadhi is a soft, tranquil passivity which burns up our cravings for things. Samadhi, satori, and nirvana are called the cosmic flame that cremates karma. So you see, samadhi is neither a physical unconsciousness nor a lethargic state of nonexistence; rather, it is a state of the nonexistence of craving. Only in this state, the state of total wakeful consciousness, can the full truth be revealed. If this were not true, it would be meaningless for you to continually return to the earth plane. Samadhi is awakening to a way of life that is not a denial of life, but a movement toward living in simplicity, wherein you learn the following simple truth: heaven lies within. The lamp of truth, the lamp of understanding, is and has always been within your own mind. This lamp reveals to you that as you live, you become free. Freedom can be gained, however, only after your mind has become free. Your bondage is not external, it is internal. Bondage to destiny is in your mind. It is your mind that is binding you. The yogi and the scientist conceive the mind and consciousness differently. The yogi realizes the mind is the soul's instrument.

Philosophies, theologies, and religions differ. Their dogmas have never been, nor will they ever be, resolved through argumentation or lengthy discussion. It is only as the mystic, the initiate, obtains direct experience of divine illumination that his soul comes to know Truth.

Truth, the unitive, blissful state of being exists forever in the pericarp of the heart of each sentient life creature. It is a gift of God from eons past that no man, woman, God, or guru can give to you, nor take from you. It is, indeed, a gift from the eternal Lord. It is yours now and forever. It never has been, nor will it ever be a question of your worthiness or unworthiness to receive it, but rather, your willingness or unwillingness to ascend the mountain of Truth.

Truth is a circle; Truth has no beginning and it has no end. When you find it, you discover that it has always been there... both inside and outside of yourself. And it is you... and it was you. And it shall be you.

In all the universe, what is the greatest gift you can give anyone? The answer is, to give the waters of life and the bread of spiritual truth to those who hunger and thirst; to give them the lamp of understanding that they might see how to become free. This is the greatest gift. Through the lamp of understanding we come to realize that there is no need to remain a prisoner of poverty, ignorance, unhealth, or any other imbalance. There awakens a realization that each of us lives in our own personal hell (of our own making) and it is only when we decide that we no longer wish to remain there, or that we no longer deserve to be there, that we will crawl out of it.

Samadhi is not dependent upon externals. Samadhi has nothing to do with eating meat or being a vegetarian. It has nothing to do with being married or celibate. Samadhi is a realization of the valley of the unobstructed mind which dwells in the pericarp of the heart of each individual. It is there within you, awaiting your arrival. You alone are the adventurer who can break forth into that reality of truth. Your Shangri-la is, in truth, tucked warmly within that valley. The mountains that were so difficult to climb now protect and shelter you from the raging winds of emotion.

It truly is my dream, my hope, my constant meditation that you, that we, that every sentient being will find his Shangri-la.

THE UNIFICATION OF CONSCIOUSNESS

Contemplation is an extension of meditation, as well as a technique of yoga. It is not a condition or state in which you find yourself, but rather an action you perform, like walking. The techniques of yoga produce states of consciousness in the movement toward total liberation (kaivalya). To the degree you practice and experience these techniques, to that same degree will you approach the outer fringes of God-consciousness, the trans-human experience. Thus, yoga and life do not stop at meditation.

The Sanskrit word for contemplation is samadhi, which is composed of the following root words:

Sam-a-dhi

Combining these root words can be defined as complete and total intuition forever. It means illumination, or an eternal, complete manifestation of spiritual intuition.

The length of meditation or samadhi is not as important as their depth. Many teachers stress that the student should meditate 1 to 3 hours a day. Meditating for this length of time is impossible. For that matter, meditating for 20 minutes a day is impossible. Effortless holding of the mind can occur only for very short intervals. Depth rather than length of samadhi (or meditation) is what should be sought, for insight comes in a millisecond of time.

Here is a simple exercise to demonstrate this. Let us assume that I would have you close your eyes and as I hold up one finger, would ask you to open your eyes for 10 minutes and then close them. After this, I would ask you to tell me how many fingers you saw me holding up when your eyes were open. Then, let's assume I would have you close your eyes again. As I hold up one finger, again, I would ask you to open your eyes for a tenth of a second and immediately close them. Again, I would ask you how many fingers you saw me holding up. In both cases, you would see that I was holding up one finger. You see, the 10 minutes were not necessary. Truly, your perception was almost instantaneous. Similarly, in samadhi, the perception is almost instantaneous. Samadhi is measured in milli-seconds of time. All the techniques you have learned and disciplines you perform are but a preparation for the end goal: that instantaneous samadhi... that moment of illumination which may have taken years to prepare.

This simple moment, this one moment of samadhi, occurs when the mind becomes one with the object. When there is a oneness between the meditator, the object of meditation, and the act of meditation. At this point, you perceive directly with the all-seeing eye of life. The experience of this oneness, though it is ever present in your existence, is not normally part of your awareness. As long as the samadhi lasts you will have this heightened awareness of the eye of God. When the samadhi ends, it remains in the memory track of your being, never to be lost or forgotten.

The experience of samadhi is a unification of consciousness in which the mind is no longer separated into an internal thinking mechanism and an external universe. Some would say it is an experience whereby the individual consciousness is blended into the eternal consciousness, as expressed in this verse by Sir Edwin Arnold:

'The dew is on the lotus.
Rise great sun!
And lift my leaf and mix me with the wave.
Om Mani Padme Hum.
The sunrise comes... the dewdrop slips into the shining sea.'

The Trimurti

According to yoga, there are a number of ways in which the threefold nature of life (trimurti) manifests. This section will teach you some of the ways in which this occurs.

Some say the experience of samadhi is a blending of the individual consciousness into the eternal consciousness. I express it, saying the external universe is blended into and unified with the individual consciousness.

The unification of individual consciousness with external consciousness is a creation of the meditator. How does creation take place? If you were wishing to create something, and traveled to the higher planes to ask a celestial being (deva) what would be needed to do so, the answer would be vibration. There are three vibrations necessary for creation:

1. Heat, the lowest range of vibration, radiating out to produce the body (form).
2. Sound, the middle range of vibration, radiating out to produce the breath, and to give life to the body (form).
3. Light, the highest range of vibration, radiating out to give eternalness to that life.

Relating this trimurti to your movement through the eight stages of yoga, you have learned of:

1. The heat called kriya fire or the dumo fire,
2. The sound called mantra, and
3. The light known as jyothi.

In ascending to samadhi, you experience the trimurti through the following unification:

1. Mind and body. The unification of the mind and body produces the emanation of heat. This means the solar and lunar channels have been balanced, enabling you to move into the center channel of sushumna. This movement is done through the bindu points of the chakras. In this stage, the action of kriya produces the sensation of heat as the currents in the center channel begin to ascend. Through this channel you move toward total liberation (kaivalya), which is the balanced awareness state.
2. Mind and breath. The unification of the mind and breath produces the emanation of sound. In this stage there is no duality between mind and breath; you are so absorbed in the breathing process that there is no awareness of 'I am the body.' This second stage occurs after you experience the heat of the kriya energies in the spinal column quite often. At this stage you hear the inner astral OM sound. Often the heat and the OM sound are experienced together.
3. Mind and atma. The unification of the mind and atma produces the emanation of light. In this stage you realize there are three different things: you, your mind, and the thought process of the mind.

After the heat and OM sound are experienced, you generally begin to see the light at the single eye. Secondly, there is an awareness of the OM sound as an intense vibration. Thirdly, the light is very intense, flashing through you and sending you to the inner planes. This experience is one of a high degree of samadhi which technically refers to the bliss stages of samadhi. The stages of samadhi are discussed at the end of this chapter.

Once you experience this light, you may find you are no longer aware of the heat, but are still aware of the astral sound. But all three sensations are definitely present at this time, with the light being perceived the strongest.

These three phenomena of the samadhi experience can relate to the familiar yogic trimurti: sat-chit-ananda, which has the following meanings:

Sat is being, which to a greater degree pertains to the vehicle.
Chit is mind-stuff which pertains to the breath and mantra.
Ananda is the atma.

All three of these continually exist within your being but you are not consciously aware of them. Remember how good you felt the first day your body became healthy again after an illness? But you forgot that feeling shortly thereafter, didn't you? You became unaware of it. On a conscious level you felt a glow, but immediately lost the feeling because of your scattered life patterns. In the same way, though these three states of consciousness exist within you at all times, you have become unaware of them.

Just as salt dissolves and becomes one with water, through the experience of samadhi there is a union of man's mind with the universal mind, the atma. Man's mind dissolves into breath, and the breath subsides. Mind and body become united through the action of centering and moving through the sushumanic channel. The state of equilibrium is attained and the union of the individual soul partakes of the oversoul.

Transcending Time and Karma

The karma of a person is the natural result of his thoughts, speech, and actions, whether from three days ago or three lifetimes ago. This karma exists in the chakras of each individual's spinal column. The less controlled he is, the less control he has of his karma, either on the earth plane or astral plane. Thus, the more haphazard will be his existence. The state of samadhi is a state of consciousness established in unity and consequently neutralizes the effects of karma.

Karma is a time-conditioned factor. Samadhi is a state of being which is timeless. Since time does not exist in the state of samadhi, karma no longer reaches fruition. The concept of time as it relates to karma is as follows:

1. Time is a system of relationships between at least two events or thoughts based upon concepts of past, present, and future. In order to have time, there must therefore be motion. Now, when in samadhi, you close the thoughts down until you come to two remaining thoughts. Finally, you break that duality into one thought: pure concentration, pure meditation, pure samadhi. If there is only one thought (thing), what can you measure that one thought or one thing against? You can't. To measure time, there must be a duality enabling you to calculate the motion between the two things. Since this motion does not exist in samadhi, it is considered a timeless state. In this state of being, you have transcended time and are no longer relevant to the occurrence of the time phenomenon.

2. Karma, the law of reaction resulting from one's actions, exists only as long as a person is dependent upon the surface mind, or the astral vehicle. Once consciousness is established in samadhi, in the causal body, the astral vehicle is no longer utilized and consequently karma cannot crystallize. Karma exists in time, a reaction of the male/female principles, in a realm that is time-full. As soon as you move to a realm that is time-less, the seeds of karma cannot sprout.

   He who has attained samadhi has truly transcended time. He has not only broken the bonds of karma, but is beyond the bonds of unconsciousness. But remember, a single tasting of the nectar of samadhi does not produce eternal freedom (kaivalya). It is the repetitive experience of samadhi that ultimately produces absolute liberation (kaivalya), known as God-consciousness.

Samyama

In the chapter on concentration we talked briefly about samyama. Concentration, meditation, and contemplation always function together to form a sequence. This continuous, single operation is called samyama. In samyama, there is a combined action of concentration/meditation/contemplation with a dynamic thrust toward the exploration of inward consciousness. Samyama occurs when the concentrative, meditative, and contemplative (samadhi) stages merge together and are sustained.

Furthermore, these three stages of yoga, held in time, produce what is called the clear gem, often referred to as the jewel of wisdom. This jewel is achieved when the subtle principle of the mind crystallizes into a pure, clear, colorless light. Consequently, if this gem is set upon something it will take on the coloration of that upon which it is resting. If the crystal gem is set upon something red, it will appear red; if set upon a heavy object, it will take on the coloration of heaviness.

The technique of samyama consists of the following processes:

1. Taking the clear gem and setting it on any object, gross or subtle;
2. Perceiving the coloration of the gem;
3. Removing the gem and remembering the perception when the samyama has been concluded.

Perceiving is the key to knowledge; remembering is wisdom; and knowing the Knower (of knowledge) is God-consciousness. The technique of samyama is to be practiced as you would any other yoga technique. Having practiced it, you will gather great knowledge. Ultimately, you must set the clear gem upon yourself, so that the knower may become the known. What do you really know about yourself? Ultimately, it is not a matter of what you know, but a matter of realizing what exists within you. This knowledge is the basis of your wisdom that you might create for yourself an internal and external universe which brings you joy, eternally.

You create your own universe whether you are aware of it or not. The moods you experience set up a pattern that eventually manifests in your external universe. Samyama is a way of inducing balanced feeling which will crystallize harmonious events into your life. Through the practice of samyama, the creative process is as follows:

1. Yogic self-discipline creates balanced moods;
2. Balanced moods create feelings;
3. Feelings create thoughts;
4. Thoughts manifest action;
5. Actions bring objects into your universe;
6. Objects provide experience;
7. Experience produces knowledge;
8. Knowledge brings wisdom;
9. Wisdom results in the knower knowing the known;
10. Knowing the known, manifests happiness.

The key concept in relation to samyama is: Everything in this universe must be fed. Most assuredly, the dream of happiness must continuously be fed. It must be fed daily. If a dream is fed daily, at some point you will have poured enough energy, water, sunlight, and cultivation into it, that it blossoms forth: complete, total, and whole. Now, the dream is complete. But feeding and preserving that flower must be continued, for that which is born of this world contains within it the seeds of its dissolution. If it is not fed it will die. Your dreams, your life, your happiness, your wisdom, your samadhi must be fed, or they will die.

However, when God is known as Self (Atma), when Self is known as God (Brahman, the Reality), there is no birth, there is no death--of anything. There is only life, love, and laughter.

GUIDE TO ATTAINING SAMADHI

1. The most important factor regarding the attainment and practice of samadhi is this: It is the repetition of samadhi that produces God-consciousness! People forget that samadhi is a technique for achieving God-consciousness. Samadhi is not the end goal in itself. Samadhi is the procedure by which liberation is attained.

2. The movement toward samadhi is subtle. Some human beings are often unaware of their evolution as they move through the 15 stages to kaivalya. The average person enters samadhi very subtly and because of his unawareness may even taste this state two or three times before realizing he has experienced something out of the ordinary; as a matter of fact, something quite extraordinary. Rarely does a person move into samadhi in one full sweep.

   Because samadhi is so subtly attained, it is often equated with a person who wakes up in the morning and remembers having dreamt a dream but thinks little of it. Later in the day, however, he may stop in the middle of his tracks, realizing and thinking, 'Just a minute, that was no ordinary dream!' The subtle poignancy of an experience cannot always be immediately grasped.

3. In samadhi there is a non-movement of the vital organs. Because this deep state of relaxation occurs during samadhi, along with the cessation of certain bodily functions, the samadhi state has been called trance. This is partially true, but there are some major differences between samadhic trance, hypnosis, and the catatonic trance.

A catatonic trance which a medium may go into produces an extremely stiff and rigid body. It is more of a hypnotic state than anything else. The main difference between trance, hypnosis, and samadhi is that a person entranced is not aware, whereas in samadhi, his awareness is heightened. Going into hypnosis often produces an unconsciousness (of what took place when under the hypnosis). Along with this, there is no awareness of the inner realm. This unconsciousness is also very common in medium trances. Samadhi is not a state someone can put you into. It is a state of awareness, not unconsciousness. When a person enters a trance he returns unchanged, but when a person returns from samadhi, he is positively different. He is happier, wiser, and his personality is more mellow.

The word trance is used here to refer to samadhi only because in samadhi there is a heavy inturning. Along with this, it is 'transic' in that the senses are totally pulled away from this world.

4. Generally, when going into samadhi, all the energy is pulled out of the gross and subtle sense organs, yet, unconsciousness does not occur. Remember, when you are in samadhi no extraneous thought (external or internal) enters into your consciousness. Your mind remains in the pure consciousness. Any thought will immediately pull you out of samadhi, and cause you to return to lower states of consciousness.

5. There are several factors regarding astral experiences that need to be pointed out. When on the outer fringes of samadhi, the subtle sense organs, in some people, become active causing a great deal of visualization to take place, although these visions are not very common. For yet others, as they move toward samadhi their mind states are accompanied by hearing astral sounds (clairaudience), rather than clairvoyance, as a result of a greater sensitivity of the subtle organs of the ears. Consequently, many teachers refer to samadhi in relationship to clairvoyance (visional states) and clairaudience.

Some people, on the other hand, enter samadhi and never see a thing. Many pass through all the stages of samadhi, seeing nothing, hearing nothing, smelling nothing, yet they move into samadhi attaining the illuminative state. In short, as some people move toward samadhi their subtle organs become active, while in others they remain inactive.

The important point is that although visualization and clairaudience may occur on the outer fringes of samadhi, once samadhi is reached, these astral organs stop functioning.

Astral experiences of this nature usually are a hindrance to samadhi. Because many books refer to these experiences, the student often thinks he is not advancing unless they are occurring. As a rule, they hinder progress because they activate the mind. The great texts say, 'Be still and know....' It does not say, 'See and know.' These astral experiences transpire in the astral realm which is a lower realm, and a grosser realm. Samadhi happens in the higher causal realms.

Each person has a different subtle organ that is more easily stimulated or activated. This subtle organ can be determined by looking into the structure of his wheel of life (barva chakra). When studied by the guru it reveals these and other spiritual factors.

It is not uncommon for astral experiences to diminish or even completely discontinue as you move through yoga practice, reaching samadhi. After you begin balancing the currents and continue to do so, you will no longer have astral experiences and your mind will quiet down. It will be more receptive to the state of samadhi. Some people become irritable upon the loss of these astral states, but the lesser should be given up to attain the higher. This irritability produces a heavy angulation of energies which are detrimental to the search for two reasons:

a. First, because he uses astral visions as a criterion for unfoldment, he may tend to think he has lost his attainment.

b. Second, he may become so disturbed at losing these astral experiences that he will go to the extreme of leaving the samadhi path, seeking something more miraculous or sensational on the astral path.

The goal of yoga is not to titillate the inner sense organs, but to silence them, just as the outer sense organs have been stilled. The process of samadhi has to do with transcending the organs of the senses and seeing with the transcended mind.

6. If in your meditations you experience astral imagery and feel it is negative, you can simply tell it to leave in this way:

'Leave. Go in peace. Depart from whence thou came.' Simply dismiss the image. This experience is within your consciousness and you must be the master of your consciousness.

7. When you have entered samadhi, subtle personality changes begin to take place, which other people will perceive quite rapidly. If your nature is to be irritable, you will become less so. If your nature is to be fearful, you will become more courageous. These and other changes occur. In short, your personality begins to soften and your life takes on a more flowing attitude.

And these changes are yoga, for all yoga, particularly kriya yoga, states that if you balance your personality, you are unfolding and attaining. It is the personality that triggers karma. If you can truly balance your personality, your karma will not manifest as heavily, or not at all. This in turn enables you to enter faster and deeper into samadhi. In balancing your personality, you may tend to think you are only becoming nicer, lovelier, sweeter, and more mellow. Balancing your personality is everything.

8. The criterion for measuring success in samadhi. It is your degree of serenity, wisdom, and compassion. Remember, you must also be compassionate with your own mind-body complex. So don't get uptight about anything. When unwanted patterns manifest, simply recognize some added discipline is needed and move on.

9. Sooner or later someone will ask if there is a simple way to attain samadhi. There is. Here is the answer. While practicing the eight stages of yoga, hold in mind one basic thought. Feel it continuously. Go to sleep with it. Wake up with it. Remember it always, while eating, dreaming, working, playing, loving, meditating, living. What is that thought? It is holding to this one awareness:

I AM THE SELF-EXISTENT ONE.

Holding to this feeling, the feeling of being aware that you are self-awareness, will do more to bring about samadhi in this lifetime than any other single factor. Continually holding this awareness in conjunction with practice of the eight stages of yoga makes samadhi assured.

15 STEPS TO ILLUMINATION & 9 STAGES OF SAMADHI

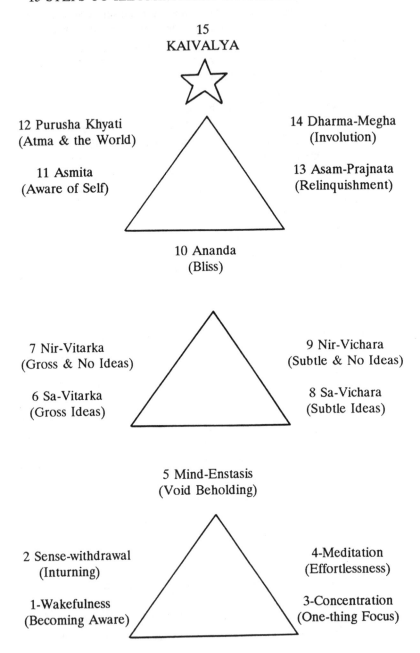

15
KAIVALYA

12 Purusha Khyati
(Atma & the World)

14 Dharma-Megha
(Involution)

11 Asmita
(Aware of Self)

13 Asam-Prajnata
(Relinquishment)

10 Ananda
(Bliss)

7 Nir-Vitarka
(Gross & No Ideas)

9 Nir-Vichara
(Subtle & No Ideas)

6 Sa-Vitarka
(Gross Ideas)

8 Sa-Vichara
(Subtle Ideas)

5 Mind-Enstasis
(Void Beholding)

2 Sense-withdrawal
(Inturning)

4-Meditation
(Effortlessness)

1-Wakefulness
(Becoming Aware)

3-Concentration
(One-thing Focus)

The nine stages of samadhi are included in the 15 steps to illumination, moving from everyday wakeful consciousness to total liberation. Before discussing these nine different samadhis, it will be helpful to recapitulate the first five grosser stages in order that you may grasp the movement away from everyday consciousness toward trans-human consciousness.

Step 1: WAKING CONSCIOUSNESS

This first stage is essential to kaivalya because it is within this stage of consciousness that you experience earth life. In these body-mind complex experiences you become aware that you do exist. The struggle within this existence makes you aware that you are alive. It is with this self-awareness that you turn toward consciously balancing your awareness and thus your universe.

Step 2: SENSE-WITHDRAWAL

This is the second necessary step to liberation. In the unfoldment of wanting to master yourself and your universe, you find that initially there is little that can be done to change the physical world. By withdrawing the senses you turn inward, and immediately move from the physical world into the inner mental world (referred to as the astral). It is only within this mental world that you can begin the self-mastery of your life, internal or external.

Step 3: CONCENTRATION

Within the mental realm you find that you are, and indeed ought be, the controller of your life. Here you utilize the technique of concentration. Of all the mental objects in your mental universe, you converge upon one object and focus on it. At this point you have taken three major advances in the movement toward self-mastery and liberation.

First, you have become aware that you exist.

Second, you have turned inward to the mental realm, thereby freeing your consciousness from the limitations of the gross, physical world.

Third, you have focused your mind on one mental object, thereby eliminating all the rest of your mental universe. With effort you hold to this one object of concentration, transcending the limitation of the inner mental realm, but not the limitation of the object of concentration.

Step 4: MEDITATION

Having dissolved from your consciousness everything except one mental object, you slowly begin to let go of this object. In this stage you do not dissolve the object, but rather, you hold to the object with less and less effort, until you can hold the object effortlessly. Thus, you are meditating on it. In short, meditation is a process whereby you are beginning to dissolve the object into your consciousness and your consciousness into the object. Yes, the meditator, the object of meditation, and the act of meditation become one.

Step 5: MIND ENSTASIS

(Vritti-nirodha)

You now come to the critical stage in the initial stages to God-consciousness. In Sanskrit, vritti means mind-activity, and nirodha means an enstasis: a stopping, a holding, or a restraining. This is the stage where you let go of, or drop, that final object in your mind. This fifth stage can be called the dumping stage. Having dropped the last object in your mind, you now have nothing to see, save the mind in its pure unformed state. This state is not a state of unconsciousness but a state of supra-consciousness. Symbolically, you have moved from cups, tureens, platters and plates, things of the mind, to amorphous clay, the mind itself. Individualized consciousness has become universal consciousness. In this state of pure consciousness without form, the mind perceives itself as the unformed, and as the all-forming substance. The Self beholds the Self, now knowing it is the reality-principle. In Sanskrit, this principle is expressed as: Aham-brahmas-mi. Translated, this means:

I AM THE CREATIVE PRINCIPLE.

At this point samadhi is attained and there is a transmutation of individual consciousness (with inherent limitations) into the unlimited being who now possesses omniscience, omnipotence, omnipresence, omni-love, and omni-bliss. This is why the Yoga Bhasya states: 'Yoga is samadhi.'

Samadhi is further divided into nine major stages, each stage being a progressive step toward God-realization.

THE 9 STAGES OF SAMADHI

Samadhi is classified according to the nature and content of super-conscious awareness. These nine stages begin with the sixth step toward kaivalya:

Sam-Prajna Classification

Step 6: SAMADHI-ONE
(Sa-Vitarka)

This samadhi relates to an enstasis directed toward a gross object as its basis. This state is also accompanied by supra-mental deliberation called vitarka. (Sa-vi-tarka means with deliberation). In this most basic form of samadhi there is, or occurs, an awareness of certain ideations but not thought. In this deliberation you have direct perception of the gross form of your object of samadhi. You will directly and instantaneously perceive the object as it was, as it is, and as it will be. Though this is the most basic stage of samadhi, you will nonetheless, by direct perception, perceive qualities of the object (unthought of), showing samadhi to be knowledge-bearing.

The word gross in the context used here relates to the elements: ether, air, fire, water, and earth.

Although this state of samadhi has a passing-into and passing-out-of samadhi (much like passing into and out of sleep), producing some form of deliberation, there is no possibility of conversation. There are no causal visions or causal auditions in this stage. If you practice entering into this stage of samadhi again and again, you begin to penetrate into the next stage.

Step 7: SAMADHI-TWO
(Nir-vitarka)

In this stage, the samadhi is directed toward a gross object as its basis. This state is not accompanied by supra-mental deliberation. Nir-vitarka means no deliberation. In this stage you find your consciousness no longer contains many of the awarenesses that exist in samadhi-one. The direct perception of a gross object is perceived as it is, as it was, and as it will be, but without ideation. The seventh stage has an admixture of astral and causal sounds, lights, and knowledge. By constantly returning to this stage, you will find yourself in the next stage.

Step 8: SAMADHI-THREE
(Vi-chara)

In this stage the enstasis has a subtle object as its support, however, the consciousness renews its supra-mental reflections of ideas, but not thought.

Step 9: SAMADHI-FOUR
(Nir-vichara)

This stage is the same as the above in which the enstasis still has a subtle object as its mainstay. The supra-mental ideation has totally ceased and the admixture of sounds, lights, and knowledge found in the last two stages gives way to transcendent knowledge. Thus samadhi-four is said to be clear and truth-bearing. It is at this stage that your inner journey comes to an end. You have now crossed the universe and ascended the mountain, traversing all the realms of your being. You have reached the cosmic ultimate ground of being. Now begin to move to the next stage.

Step 10: SAMADHI-FIVE
(Ananda)

In this stage you withdraw from all objective realities (note the plural). This is done because the reality (atma) cannot be found in matter (prakriti). It is found by penetrating into matter. This stage is an enstasis that is connected with the awareness of supreme bliss which breaks forth on the infinite shores of your being as soon as the supra-mental activities have been stilled. What remains is intense galactic supreme bliss.

Some people feel that having attained the bliss state, nothing else matters. All is complete in itself. There is still, however, something beyond bliss! You must even relinquish the attachment to bliss in order to find Truth.

These people cannot conceive of anything higher than bliss. They do not realize that the universe and the atma are distinct. They are called prakriti-layas. Their samadhi liberation is pseudo for they still (very, very, subconsciously) exist in a time realm and thus bear karma and karma's rebirth.

In this stage of samadhi, one has the choice of receiving the golden egg, or the goose that lays the golden eggs. Amazingly, most everyone chooses a single stage of consciousness (bliss, the golden egg), rather than the Reality principle (the goose or gander that lays the golden egg), which can produce any and all states of consciousness.

Once the bliss stage has been attained, the bliss is not lost in the remaining stages.

Step 11: SAMADHI-SIX
(Asmita)
In this samadhi there is an enstasis linked with the awareness or realization of yourself: the awareness of the atma. However, not the awareness of your atma, otherwise it would not be you. Within ananda and asmita samadhi, the crown of bliss and the scepter of being arise. In these stages you are on the outer fringes of God-consciousness. Asmita is the last of the samadhis classified as extroverted enstasis with supra-mental cognition of matter.

These outer stages make up what is often called sam-prajnata samadhi, meaning with transcendental knowledge. The sage Vyasa, in his commentaries expresses the samprajnata samadhi classification in the following fashion:

Stage 1 and 2:
 Sa- and nir-
 vitarka samadhi = vitarka + vichara + ananda + asmita

Stage 3 and 4:
 Sa- and nir-
 vitarka samadhi = vichara + ananda + asmita

Stage 5:
 ananda samadhi = ananda + asmita

Stage 6:
 asmita samadhi = asmita

The value of this table is that it points out the progressive unification of your consciousness in the practice of samadhi, within the states of samadhi itself.

Asam-Prajna Classification

Step 12: SAMADHI-SEVEN
(Purusha khyati)
This stage of samadhi is the total, complete, and uninterrupted discerning vision between the universe and the Self. Samadhi-seven has many other names.
 a. Viveka-khyati,
 b. Vivekaja-jnana,
 c. Taraka-jnana.

This seventh stage, as well as the eighth and ninth stages of samadhi, transcends supra-mental knowledge. They are therefore referred to as asam-prajnata.

Step 13: SAMADHI-EIGHT
(Asam-prajnata)

This stage of samadhi is the enstasis obtained by supreme renunciation of all worldly objects. This state is devoid of any conscious impressions with only subconscious impressions. These subconscious impressions (samskaras) are cremated by your repeated return to asam-prajnata samadhi.

Many teachers refer to only two states of samadhi:
a. Sam-prajna   meaning samadhi with seed.
b. Asam-prajna   meaning samadhi without seed.

Asam-prajna samadhi is samadhi without seed, meaning that in this samadhi, the subconscious impressions called samskaras or seed karmas (of future experiences and thus future births) are exhausted or cremated. In other words, in asam-prajna samadhi, you are in a state of consciousness beyond the ocean of this universe and thus all the seeds (of your karma) are extinguished. Although it is somewhat possible to convey an impression of the quintessence of the sam-prajnata samadhi, asam-prajnata samadhi impressions defy all and any description whatsoever. Few souls attain this state of asam-prajnata samadhi. But they all agree that the experience is beyond words. They also all agree that the experience is utterly Other Worldliness.

Step 14: SAMADHI-NINE
(Dharma-megha)

Dharma-megha samadhi is the enstasis producing an involution of the primary energies or qualities called gunas (tamas, rajas, sattva). This stage of samadhi consequently leads to liberation instantaneously. The fruits of karma and therefore the causes of bondage and limitation are dissolved. All fetters are removed and the long-sought goal is obtained. The Self (atma/purusha) shines forth in its radiant supreme splendor. You have safely crossed over the threshold of relative existence. You cross over, transported by your primordial wings of wisdom which have unfurled in the radiant sunlight of the springtime of your existence.

These nine stages of samadhi also have sub-stages. However, enough has been given to grasp an understanding of samadhi. You now know that samadhi is, to a greater or lesser degree, somewhat self-regulating. When the natural outturning tendency of the mind is stopped by your repeated effort of inturning, uplifting, and unifying your consciousness, you will be carried forth by the forceful life-current, from one stage to the next, sometimes quickly passing a stage or two and sometimes resting and balancing at a stage.

Step 15: EMANCIPATION (Kaivalya)

Liberation or emancipation will be dealt with in the next chapter. Whereas the nine steps to liberation are subtle techniques, this stage is the ultimate experience. It is sustained God-consciousness.

SAMADHI TECHNIQUES
-How To Know The Happy God-

Here is a series of techniques for perceiving and experiencing Reality. They suggest various processes for inturning and centering. Within each sentient being there lies a wondrous universe. We approach the wonder of this universe when we love. But something happens to our love. In our running, ranting, and raving to possess the beloved, we break the bond of love. In quietude we hold to that love.

We live in a wondrous wheel of existence, the bharva chakra, that constantly spins and changes. At the same time, our consciousness, our desires, and our vision of the world constantly change. This change, however, is not the cause of our problems. Life has less meaning for us because we live, for the most part, on the surface of our minds. We live on the periphery of our consciousness and therefore we do not really understand what is happening (in this world). When we become emotional, we do not touch or taste the Reality called bliss, joy, and happiness. Consequently, we must lift from negativity toward greater expectations, moving from pain to love, and from love to unselfish love and beauty. We must move from ignorance to knowledge.

Being aware is only the beginning, for once you attain greater awareness, you must then balance that self-awareness. Only balanced self-awareness can create a happy existence. There is a way, and there are indeed many pathways, by which you can fully, completely, and forever enter into this wild, wondrous universe called life. The techniques in this section are ways by which you can experience the reality of a joyous, blissful, harmonious existence.   You will find that each of them is a threefold procedure, the effects of which are inherent in the practice:

First, there is a quieting and stilling of your being, often referred to as purification.

Second, there is an inturning, often called a consecration to life.

Third, there is a balancing effort, which will allow you to see that you can change your life.   This balancing is called an illuminative experience: a satori, a nirvana, a samadhi.

Before beginning the techniques, two basic factors should be understood to assure their effectiveness.

1. The happiness factor.   In seeking out techniques of illumination, you should find one that is most meaningful to you. There should be something about it that gives to you a degree of pure pleasure or happiness.   You should sense in it something special.   In practicing the techniques you are actually coming closer to yourself.   Along with this, the nature of your individual personality, your hang-ups and your beauty, is revealed.

2. The naturalness factor.   With any technique, whether it is learning to ride a bicycle, or learning to find God, you pass through a fundamental training stage in which you are unfamiliar with the technique; thus it is uncomfortable and awkward.   This means to effectively perform a technique, you must practice it until it becomes automatic and has been saturated into your subconscious mind, locking into your spinal column.   According to the ancient yoga texts, when this happens you have mastered the technique because you are doing it naturally.   A typist can talk and type at the same time because she has learned typing with her cerebral-spinal column.   She has learned the skill with more than just her conscious mind.   In the same way, the techniques for reaching God offered here must become a part of you, as well as part of your cerebral-spinal axis.   When this occurs, you will realize you are a part of, not apart from, God.

Below you will find descriptions of the techniques to samadhi.

1. ABSORPTION-IN-OM TECHNIQUE

The first technique utilizes the intonation of the OM sound. As you audibly, but softly, chant OM, you are to enter fully into the sound and become one with the real you.   As Aristotle pointed out, 'To see a horse, in some sense, you must become the horse.'

If you are different from the horse, you cannot reach a point of communication, or awareness with it. Similarly, to reach a point of communication with yourself you must become one with your true self.

Simply close your eyes and chant Ooommm-m-m-m ... Ooommm-m-m-m ... Ooommm-m-m-m. The sound is gentle and slow, but totally full and strong. This sound quiets and stills the body and repetition of the sound will slowly draw you into yourself.

Secondly, try to center yourself by entering mentally into the fullness of the sound. The sound you are using here is not arbitrary, but a symbol of the Reality, the fullness of the universe. Thus you are able to attune to an awareness of galactic existence. In the fullness of this sound, the ego forgets itself and bliss freely breaks forth into your being. As your consciousness enters into the sound of OM and becomes centered within its fullness, with practice you will become that sound, and fullness. The secret is not in making the sound, but in taking your mind and entering into the fullness of the sound that you have created.

2. PERCEIVING THE LIGHT OF LIFE-FULLNESS TECHNIQUE

This technique is more complicated than the first yet can be extremely helpful to the restless soul who is trying to turn inward. Perceive yourself as the yoga spinal column, with a series of chakras one above the other. Perceive your chakric discs as rays of light. Move your awareness to the core of the ray, the center from which it emanates. Do not look at the ray. Go inside it. Next, try to feel that your real essence is light. With this perception of yourself, conceive rays of light emanating from within you. Feel this emanation at the base of the spinal column. Take this feeling of light, the essence of your being, to the center of the saturn chakra. Radiate it from the center of your spinal column, filling this chakra with rays of light. Lift through the center of the chakra by way of the sushumna channel filling the jupiter chakra, emanating rays from the essence of your being. Accumulate these rays of light, moving up the spinal column, from chakra to chakra. Do this until your consciousness is at the single eye. Take the light one step further to the thousand-petalled lotus. Having reached the thousand-petalled lotus, simply drop back to the base of the spine and re-ascend. This procedure can be performed any number of times: 3 to 108.

Simply gather your energy and lift it. As the light rays rise from the base of the spine to the crown chakra, so rises life-fullness itself. As the rays lift, the light becomes subtler, yet at the same time brighter. There is an awakening that has nothing to do with activity as we commonly know it, but rather with the dawn of illumination. This feeling of life-fullness produces a massive awareness of the Reality, since you are the Reality. Because we do not normally perceive this Truth, we are constantly drawn to things outside ourselves (persons, activities, objects). But as you center and lift, you become aware of life-fullness and the galactic amount of cosmic life within you; you become aware of the God within you. Your consciousness expands and you become aware of ever more joy, bliss, and ecstasy.

3. THE LOVING TECHNIQUE

This technique is done by loving, and then loving more, and then loving yet more. It is one of the most vital spiritual techniques. In loving you perceive something within yourself. Love is the mirror by which we come to know the reality of our body-mind complex. That which we love is a reflection of that which lies deep within us. As we learn how to love ourselves, and others, we learn to love all mankind and the universe.

The procedure, simply, is to love. Love as compassionately, fully, unselfishly and as totally as you possibly can. Who you are serving, what you are doing, who you are loving, is not as important as the resulting awareness within you that you can love.

The mystery is that to the lover, the world is the beloved. Everything in life is a mirror which reveals to you the beauty of your being. Remember, you are looking for inner beauty. The fruits of love are in this wondrous thing called love, as well as in the revelation of the following truth: the path to finding Reality--the meaning, purpose, and direction of life--leads to a life you will love, enjoy, and most fully understand.

Loving is not lying down and letting someone walk on you; nor is it an anguishing dark night of the soul in which you lose what you have loved. Rather, love speaks of detachment without indifference. You are not to become detached from loving, but from the attachment to the object of love, and the desire to possess the beloved. Detachment does not mean you are losing anything, it means you are gaining freedom from the pain that attachment brings.

Wherever there is life, there is love. Fear not to love, but also, do not grasp. Move through the world lovingly, finding beauty in life. Finding that beauty in life, realize you bring the beauty to the sunrise. If beauty were not already existent within you, you would not see it anywhere. The beauty of the sunrise is but the mirrored reflection of that which lies deep within you. Love, and find that which lies within. Find that which lies within and love. Love!

4. EXPERIENCING THE EXPERIENCER TECHNIQUE

This technique is a procedure for breaking into your inner consciousness by becoming aware of yourself rather than external phenomena.

Think of the word that has the most meaning in your life. It may be the word love; it may be the word wisdom; it may be the word God. As you close your eyes, try to mentally visualize this word written across your forehead. At first focus on the word, then focus on the individual letters.

Let us assume that you are using the word love. Now, look at the word, draw into the individual letters l-o-v-e, and then determine which letter is symbolic of the whole word. You may decide on the letter "l" because it stands for life. Or you may decide the most important letter is "o" because it is a circle, the symbol of eternity and the completeness of life. Whatever letter you choose, focus on it.

As you focus on the one single letter, become more and more aware of it. As you go deeper and deeper into yourself, think of the subtle sound of the letter. Enter into that sound. As you go into the subtleness of the sound, penetrate further into your consciousness to the feeling of the sound. There is nothing beyond feeling; therefore, set the feeling aside and become free.

This is an extremely powerful technique. It can be practiced as long as you are comfortable. The value of this technique is that you experience you. You reach a realization that you are the Reality. You are not the mind, the body, nor their experiences. But rather, you are you: the experiencer.

5. THE GURU-DISCIPLE RELATIONSHIP TECHNIQUE

This technique will help you to find God. The technique is to find a guru. When the disciple is ready, the guru will appear. The guru is drawn to you by your sincerity. Seek diligently and wisely for that person who will guide you on the path to finding happiness, joy, wisdom, and the ecstasy of life; even the very bliss of God. The guru does not choose the disciple, the disciple chooses the guru. Seek that soul who has attained what you are seeking.

You cannot see yourself without a mirror. The guru is the mirror which will assist you in the search along your path.

Once found, the guru is sustained by the disciple's mind and heart. Yet, it is the love you have for the Teaching, not the teacher, that frees you. This relationship is one of the most important adjuncts to achieving the goal. Although each of us must seek out our own illumination, the guru will assist your entering the path of enlightenment, safely, surely, and most harmoniously.

Chapter 21

GOD-CONSCIOUSNESS
(KAIVALYA)

Kaivalya is touching Ultimate Reality. It is becoming one with All-Life. Being one with God-consciousness, the yogi attains Kaivalya. This state of awareness can be symbolically compared to amorphous clay; clay which has no real form. Yet, if you add water to this clay, roll it, and work with it, you can transmute it into anything: a cup, a plate, a pitcher or a tureen, etc. Once the clay is formed, it is given a name, for it has been born. It has been created into form. It is at this stage that mankind becomes lost, because he looks at the form and sees only the form, its name and its function. In approaching God-consciousness, you are no longer concerned with form. You are only concerned with essence. Neither name nor function of clay is important, in the final analysis. The only thing important is the clay, itself.

All the stages of yoga have led to where you can take an object such as a sugar holder, and put it into an astral machine, press a button and disintegrate it back into amorphous clay. You can now reshape the clay into anything you wish. Thus the sugar holder can now become a vase. Similarly, God-consciousness can be compared to taking any creation, collapsing it back into itself, and projecting out from itself a new creation. The path to kaivalya, means your own creation, your own karmic condition, can be brought back into balance, after collapsing it. When this occurs, balance is attained, re-attained, and sustained. You are then freed of your human bondage, transcending humanness and attaining divinity.

Samadhi is the technique to become illumined so that you might attain kaivalya. Even if samadhi is attained for only a millionth of a second, it markedly improves and changes your existence. Samadhi reveals that you can obtain God-consciousness and transcend transitory human nature. It re-awakens a realization that life is to be lived on this earth plane, and that the things of the earth life are transitory and not to be possessed. It is said of old: 'He who would possess, will be possessed'.

Once reached, God-consciousness is forever in your memory. The experience may somewhat fade, but it remains forever in your consciousness. Each experience of God-consciousness makes your life less conditioned by human karma. In the words of my guru, 'God is ever new, ever changing, ever greater bliss. For were He not, He would surely become boring... and I assure you, God is not boring'.

In samadhi, God is seen differently at different times. How He is seen is determined by your karma. Your real karma is that which drives you to Him. This will determine how you see Him. Saying it another way, how you approach God is how He will reveal Himself to you. The yogi sitting in a cave in the Himalayas who has not seen a soul for years will experience God differently from the yogi studying and working in a modern city. Each person will experience God differently, for each individual's spiritual needs differ. All experiences of God are personal and intimate. Yet, each different experience of God is galactic and relates to the totality of life.

If a Himalayan yogi came out of his cave and began teaching, his awareness, the needs of his disciples, and God's approach to him would differ. His spiritual needs in the external world would greatly modify his vision. Knowing this, you will understand that God truly is the servant of mankind.

Not only does God appear according to your needs, but a most glorious thing also occurs. When He comes, He brings more than just one gift. He brings many gifts to help you balance your life. All the imbalances of a chakra disappear when God approaches. God-consciousness enters every cell of your being, according to your spiritual needs, and brings into your life, happiness, joy, contentment, bliss, and wisdom. Especially, He brings Wisdom. He does not judge, nor is He affected by your personality. He never leaves you with the feeling of the dark night of the soul. Only astral visions do that. He comes and improves your life. He is the light of life. He leaves you with your individuality to dream the dream you wish. This is the wondrous mystery.

The experience of God-consciousness is the experience of compassionate, unselfish love. The goal is not to run toward God, but rather to attune to His love and wisdom. The happiness of God-consciousness is not transitory. The expression of the spirit's soul is not temporal.

When you leave this physical plane, you take with you primarily one thing: the wisdom you have gained, and the love you have given and received. This wisdom-love bestows unto you the realization that you can manifest Spirit.

Spirit is the Lord of light. His light is intimate and unselfish Wisdom. The goal of God-consciousness is not to escape life, but to live life and manifest compassionate wisdom-love on this earth plane, and on all planes.

The yogi is not so much a theologian, a psychologist, or a philosopher. He is primarily a seeker. He is, in truth, a mystical scientist. He works with time and space in the laboratory of life and experience. To you, that soul who wishes to penetrate into the deeper meaning of life and reach a truer appreciation of it, life must not only be studied. You must also enter the inner temple of that laboratory.

Driving toward the mystical/metaphysical experience can only be truly understood by an examination of the ancient past. It is with the examination of that ancient past that the Golden Key to the future lies.

The very basis of yoga stems from the inborn human longing to cross the threshold of experience. To know the Knower, not knowledge. To see the Seer, not that which is seen. There are many souls who wish to taste the honey of existence. But, the yogi declares, 'I do not wish to taste honey, I want to become honey'. How impertinent he is to believe he can do this. Yet, all the ancient sages say it is possible.

The beginning point of yoga is quite different from Western psychology, psychiatry, or sociology. Its goal is even more dissimilar. Its goal is to bring about a re-realization of the answer to this question:

'Traveler, what do you seek here... since this
world is not your resting place?'

Chapter 22

EPILOGUE
-THE MOMENT OF ENLIGHTENMENT-

In conclusion, there is not much more that can be said. Men far wiser than I, souls more articulate than I, have said, 'Illumination is knowable, but inexpressible'. And yet I would like to give you some additional insights into the galactic feeling of God-Realization:

There is a moment of truth in each human being's life. It is a favorable moment. A moment in which you conceive of a word. That word is... enlightenment. This is the most auspicious moment in the evolution of your eternal existence. Some people never come to an awareness of the thought, 'enlightenment'. There are those, however, who find the auspicious moment and hear the word; they feel its feeling and know its meaning... and refuse to let go of it. This is called one-pointedness, or contemplative meditation. This moment is the beginning. It is the moment of the birth of the spiritual ecstasy of dignity, insight, joy, and understanding.

You are a result of all you have thought, and you will be tomorrow whatever form, whatever shape, whatever destiny, whatever karma, whatever dharma you have dreamt. Therefore, dream wisely. Today, at this moment, take hold of the awareness of enlightenment.

How easy it is to be distracted. How easy the memory of that auspicious moment when you realized this one word... enlightenment. Enlightenment is possible in this very lifetime. To attain this enlightenment, you must defeat the enemy. The enemy cannot be defeated with anger, with steel swords, or with lead bullets. The enemy is defeated with wisdom. The enemy is ignorance, is spiritual blindness, and must be defeated by your strength, your understanding, your insight, and your wisdom that we are all here to unfold.

It is not enough to simply be aware. Enlightenment reveals that you must gain awareness and then move forward. For Genghis Khan was surely aware of his power; Napoleon was surely aware of his power; Cardinal Richelieu was surely aware of his power. It is not enough to merely be aware. We must move beyond this to the realization that awareness and the power that comes from that awareness must also be BALANCED.

In the remembrance of the word, enlightenment, the power of your memory will continue to guide you to the end of the pathway, into the valley of the unobstructed mind. It is here that balanced awareness, illumination, insight, and enlightenment will enable you to walk this life fearlessly and courageously; with dignity, insight, inspiration, and compassion.

Through enlightenment you acquire a recognition of where you are in your existence. The most vital spiritual factor is to know that you exist. It is from here, and only from here, that you can unfold spiritually. Still, the mind will mind, the stomach will stomach, the body will body, the heart will heart, and the soul will soul. What, therefore, will you put emphasis on?

Enlightenment, through realization, makes your life aright so you are able to live it without guilt, without fear, without anguish, and without egotistical pride. You are able to see the order of your universe. Through this enlightenment, you realize that you are part of life, not apart from it. You will be amazed to find that as you organize your internal universe, your external universe becomes more orderly.

As a result of karma of the past, you dream a strange dream, in a strange land, in the form of people and things. They come running, ranting, and raving into your life to attack and ransack. But you alone are the guardian of the gate of your life. Though they may destroy your body, they can never destroy your memory track, nor the heart and feeling of the word, enlightenment. As seeds planted will sprout afresh, and as trees bear fruit again each year, so also will your dream bring forth the remembrance of the word, enlightenment.

The thought, enlightenment, seems so weak in a world so violent. Light seems so inaccessible in a world so dark. Wisdom seems so far away, in a world so close to foolishness and ignorance. It is not enough to turn inward and chant, nor to find what you think you have found within yourself. It is only if you move out into the world and take action, balancing your world, will you find your wisdom, your light, and your enlightenment.

Enlightenment brings about a discovery that you live in at least three worlds at the same moment. As you tend to one, you must not ignore the others. For to tend to one and to ignore the others will bring chaos and disharmony into your life. Yet the world thinks, 'I will love Mary Jane because Mary Jane is so beautiful'. It is easy to love Mary Jane because she is beautiful. But, can you love the unlovable? Can you be gracious to one who is ungracious? Can you be gentle to one who is violent? Can you do this, not because you are acquiring merits, but rather, because these poor souls are burning in their own personal hell, now. Compassion ought be the law of your life.

Unless you can reach out and touch gently the anguish in another, how can you touch and heal the anguish in your own being? Unless in some way you can comprehend, understand, and reach out and heal others, how can you inwardly touch that thought that flows through all minds, yet is perceived by few souls. The thought of enlightenment.

The essence of enlightenment is the idea of self-balancing. Lift your being up, through the realization that you must improve yourself. Not because you are in hell, but because of the realization that you must graduate from this kindergarten. This means that you must not be as concerned with the external chaos, as with the internal chaos.

Through illumination, you overpower the impetus of ignorance. This is done with wisdom and with gentleness. In the very gaining of enlightenment, in the very walking forth on the path of enlightenment, there must be gentle joy; there will be gentle understanding.

There is a strangeness in our lives. I call it the 'glu-i-ness' of the mind. We attempt to possess... we possess... somehow thinking that in possessing things we are going to enjoy them, and thus life. This cannot be. The attachment or possession of anything detracts from its joy. Shackles, fetters, and chains of gold will bind you as surely as those of iron. Possess no thing and you will not be possessed. Be free. But realize that while you possess no thing, you must of necessity care for the temple of your own being. I symbolically call it the Temple of Kriya Yoga, the temple of spiritual action.

Guard your thinking. Do not be fearful of the thoughts that enter your mind. But, be wise and enlightened in choosing that which you hold on to, that which you dismiss, that which you intensify, and that which you elevate and honor. That which you elevate and honor you will become.

You live in a realm of forms which blossom forth and decay. These forms are but mirrors to help give you direction, to help you to learn. To learn what? To remember what? To remember the Spirit within. This is not something to be remembered in another life. It is something for the here and now. It is not for tomorrow, nor for this evening. It's for now! It is not for some other place, but for here. There exists only the here and the now. Yesterday is but a memory, and tomorrow is but a hope. But, now is forever.

Can you remember when you first learned to ride a bicycle? This was a very spiritual action, for with this learning you were able to move faster than you had ever moved before. Swiftly, without effort. You were even able to coast as well as ride without your hands on the handle bars. The joy of learning to ride a bicycle (if you remember it) is absolutely nothing compared to the joy of soaring with your primordial wings of wisdom.

Life should be joyful. Why make it a battle? Why feel you must be oppressed? These are negativities. Listen to the ancient wisdom of the past: You have a spiritual birthright. The gift of life. It is Life who has given you this spiritual birthright. Once given, it can never be taken away. Wisdom reveals that life has given you life, love, and wisdom. These have been given to you in abundance. It is your consciousness which will determine whether life is meaningful or meaningless.

Joy is here in the now. It has always been here. Love is here in the now. It has always been here. With your primordial wings of wisdom you can soar and glide. You will glide and soar by letting go of your pain, by letting go of your ignorance which serves no purpose, except as a millstone around your physical, mental, sexual, economic, and spiritual life.

What is illumination? What is enlightenment? If it is anything, it is a lightness of your heart, now at this moment, which makes you aware that you are just a little happier, a little wiser, and a little calmer than you were a short while ago. Illumination is a realization that you can be happy now. Happiness is a completeness. It is a finality in much the same way that a circle is a circle and no circle is more circular than any other circle. If you have tasted of love, you know of love, for love is complete in and of itself. It looks for no thing beyond itself. Yet the miracle, the magic, and the mystery of love is that it continues to unfold and bring ever greater wonderment and fulfillment. So also with enlightenment. Thus, if you have had any enlightenment, you have enlightenment. Enlightenment is a completeness in and of itself. It is an awakening realization of where you will be tomorrow by simply looking backwards. Enlightenment is attuning to that which is positive, not to that which is negative. It is an awareness that if God dwells anywhere, He dwells within you.

Do you dare, or do you wish to awaken to the fullness of life, to the bliss, to the love, and to the wisdom of life? If you wish, then wish gently, swiftly, and harmoniously, without insisting that another find his bliss in the same way.

Wisdom is the key to enlightenment. Wisdom is gained not by merely reading books or by simply meditating. Meditation comes by revealing to you that which is within you; by your understanding this simple truth: aham brahmasmi. This can best be translated, 'you are the creative principle'. It is through the fullness, the gentleness, and the wisdom of love that the tree and the blossom of the tree allow the fruit to fructify. So it will be with your own being.

The world is in anguish because the mind of man is in anguish. With this understanding, do not say, 'When the minds of men are no longer in anguish, I will be at peace'. Be at peace now. In so doing, you will find that you have cosmically assisted in quieting the minds of all men. Similarly, do not say, 'When the world loves me, I will love the world'. Wisely love the world and you will find that you have helped the world to find love.

What else can I say? I have said that God loves you. He is not a jealous God. He is not an angry God. He is not a demerit-giver. God is not even a He. God is Life; the life that lives and flows through you.

Consume not life and be not consumed by it! Find within yourself, noble thoughts flowing to you from every side. Share these noble thoughts with your heart, with your mind, and with your soul. Become happy... now. Of course there are problems. But anguishing will not solve problems. The quietude, the serenity, and the peace, however, will give you insight to more quickly and more harmoniously solve problems.

Let me end this chapter with a short, meaningful meditation:

> Oh, Infinite Lord of the universe, who has a million forms, a million names, and a million faces;
> Oh, Wisdom that is one, but men make many;
> Touch the hearts, minds, and souls of all, enlivening each petal and each cell of our being, filling us with joy, love, bliss, harmony, happiness, equanimity, and Wisdom, which is enlightenment.
> Bring into our lives that which we need, swiftly, surely, and most harmoniously!

May both that which you feel you need and that which you need blend and merge into one.   May all that is benefic be yours. But above all else:

Seek out your own illumination with greater diligence.

INDEX

Book Releases
by Goswami Kriyananda

The Laws of Karma:
Deeper Insight to the Esoteric Teachings of Kriya Yoga

Goswami Kriyananda's text on karma clearly and simply explains the laws of cause and effect. This unique book contains many yogic techniques used throughout the ages to remove pain and suffering. It is a must for all who wish to move toward greater happiness in life.
8-1/2 X 5-1/2 , perfectbound, 183 pages. … $14.95

Intermediate Guide to Meditation

This book is a companion to Goswami Kriyananda's classic text, "Beginner's Guide to Meditation." It provides deep insights and techniques to expand your awareness and bring greater harmony and balance into your life through meditation practice. It is an easy to read text, excellent for the novice and advanced practitioner. *5-1-2 X 8-1/2, perfectbound, 145 pages … $13.95*

A Yoga Dictionary of Basic Sanskrit Terms

In this book, Goswami Kriyananda has taken a further step to include some major English mystical terms. He feels this basic dictionary will help the student of Yoga gain a deeper understanding of many Sanskrit terms, meeting the needs of the contemporary student, and being helpful to the general reader of yoga literature. He has taken the liberty of dividing the Sanskrit terms to make it easier for the student to pronounce them. *5-1/2 X 8-1/2, perfectbound, 112 pages … $8.95*

A Dictionary of Basic Astrological Terms

In this dictionary, Goswami Kriyananda has included the most basic astrological terms that will help the beginning or intermediate student gain a deeper insight into astrology. This book is a superb reference work. It is easy to read and one you should keep with you throughout your astrological studies. Goswami Kriyananda has taken complex astrological terms, not only simplifying them for easier understanding, but also adding deeper insight into their meaning.
5-1/2 X 8-1/2, perfectbound, 91 pages … $8.95

Pathway to God-Consciousness

Goswami Kriyananda first wrote Pathway to God-Consciousness as a home study course for his disciples living far from his ashram. It is composed of 16 lessons or chapters, each with self-help questions, and reveals much of the esoteric science of Kriya Yoga. It gives guidelines and Yogic techniques for the fundamentals of the mystical search: the evolution from Awareness to God-Consciousness or Balanced Self-Awareness. *5-1/2 X 8-1/2, perfectbound, 130 pages … $9.95*

Meditation
Books and Audiotapes by Goswami Kriyananda

The benefits of meditation are endless....Many of today's health and medical centers are suggesting meditation as a means to regain the ability to concentrate and reduce stress. Learn to improve your health and well-being, restore lost energies, and attain inner peace through meditation practice.

♦ *Beginner's Guide to Meditation* (Book)
This is Goswami Kriyananda's classic text on how, when and why to meditate. It is simple and clear and gives you a variety of meditation techniques to begin your own individual practice. It contains simple stories and analogies to bring ease and enjoyment to learning and practice.This book is an inspirational way to learn the joys and benefits of meditation. *5-1/2 X 8-1/2, perfectbound, 112 pages* .. *$13.95*

♦ *Beginner's Guide to Meditation - A Talking Book*
(**Audiotapes and book**) This talking book gives you the opportunity to listen to Goswami Kriyananda's recording of his classic text, *Beginner's Guide to Meditation*. It gives you the option to hear Goswami Kriyananda's voice as he teaches you a variety of simple and gentle meditation techniques. *Four 90-minute audiotapes (also includes the book).*
Introductory Offer ... $29.95

♦ *Beginner's Guide to Meditation - Book and 2-Audiotape Program*
This program gives you the *Beginner's Guide to Meditation* book and two audio tapes: *Meditation Techniques for Inner Peace* which contains five classical meditation techniques, and *Corridors of Stillness*, a gentle 30-minute guided meditation (recorded on both sides of the tapes).
Two 60-minute audiotapes and the book ... $22.95

♦ *Intermediate Guide to Meditation* (Book)
A continuation of *Beginner's Guide to Meditation*. This book includes added techniques and helps you train the mind to move from limited conceptualized thinking and negative emotions to more expanded awareness. It opens up practice to the deeper levels of inturning and meditation practice.
5-1/2 X 8-1/2 paperback, 151 pages ... $13.95

To order:
Outside Illinois: (800) 248-0024 - Inside Illinois (773) 342-4600
Fax: (773) 342-4608

 **SEMINARS ON AUDIOTAPE**

Karma, Causation and the Laws of Balance

The law of karma is the law of balance. Join Goswami Kriyananda as he shares his insights into a doctrine whose roots lie in antiquity. Gain a clearer understanding of your unconscious mental patterns. Master the deep-seated conditioning of your past. This program includes four 90-minute audio tapes along with Goswami Kriyananda's 183 page text: *The Laws of Karma: Deeper Insight to the Esoteric Teachings of Kriya Yoga*.

Highlights of the course include:

- ◆ The three types of karma
- ◆ Why your karma is the way it is
- ◆ Techniques to soften and dissolve karma
- ◆ Historical development of the theory of karma

This seminar is an opportunity to enrich your future by transforming your past.

Four 90-minute audiotapes and book ... $54.95

Dreams, Your Magic Mirror

Dreams reveal your future and illuminate your past. Dream symbols are the language of the soul, the means of communication between your subconscious, conscious and superconscious minds. In this seminar, Goswami Kriyananda reveals the deeper significance and function of your dreams.

Learn how to:

- ◆ Increase your dream awareness
- ◆ Understand the language of dreams
- ◆ Improve your life by improving your dreams
- ◆ Interpret dream symbols
- ◆ Keep a dream journal
- ◆ Develop conscious dreaming

To understand your dreams is to understand yourself. To master your dreams is to hold the key to personal transformation.

Three 90-minute audiotapes ... $39.95

To Order Call:
Outside Illinois: (800) 248-0024 - Inside Illinois: (773) 342-4600

The Chakras and Energy Transformation

Your chakras are energy converters which are unconsciously activating and controlling your body and mind. Goswami Kriyananda discusses the esoteric functions of the chakras and their activities, revealing techniques for utilizing and balancing chakric energy.

In this seminar you will discover:

◆ The anatomy of the chakric system
◆ The three worlds
◆ The dynamics of energy transformation
◆ The modifying principle of self-awareness

Learn to utilize the forces of your self-conscious awareness to speed up your spiritual unfoldment, soften your karma, and open hidden areas of your conciousnes

Three 90-minute audiotapes ... $39.95

Self-Improvement thru Self-Hypnosis

Self-hypnosis is a tool for releasing the creativity and hidden potential of your mind. Goswami Kriyananda will teach you safe and simple techniques designed to utilize the power of your mind to bring about permanent, positive changes in your life.

In this seminar you will learn how to:

◆ Remove unresolved conflicts
◆ Overcome self-imposed obstacles
◆ Eliminate negative habits
◆ Attain a deep, peaceful sleep state
◆ Gain self-knowledge to improve your life
◆ Increase your mind power
◆ Improve your attitudes and moods
◆ Overcome negative emotions

Through this seminar, you can learn to reprogram the negative mental patterns that block the fulfillment of your most cherished goals.

Four 90-minute audiotapes ... $54.95 (includes an accompanying 25-page booklet on self-hypnosis).

The Awakening of Your Serpent Power

Learn the concepts and obstacles to awakening the Kriya Kundalini Fire.

In this seminar Goswami Kriyananda answers such questions as: What is the Kriya-Kundalini? What does awakening the Kundalini mean? What should one know about Kundalini awakening? How does one know when the Kundalini has awakened?

This long-awaited seminar reveals the secrets associated with awakening your serpent power so that you can speed up your evolutionary unfoldment. Goswami Kriyananda discusses the methods, means and concepts dealing with the sacred art of wisely and sanely awakening and directing the Kriya-Kundalini. He explores the use and procedures for using the Kriya-Kundalini to neutralize negative pieces of karma and to help soften blockages so that you can move to higher transformative states. He also discusses the common misconceptions about the Kundalini and how these need to be overcome through higher spiritual knowledge.

Other Highlights of this program include:

◆ How to measure the Kundalini release
◆ Positive effects of Kundalini awakening
◆ The blessings of Yoga-siddhi; the dangers of Yoga siddhi
◆ The proper utilization of a sacred mantra
◆ The conversion of Kriya to Kundalini

Three 90-minute audiotapes $119

An Overview of the Kundalini Upanishad

Includes 3 Audiotapes and a 37-page Study Notebook

The Kundalini Upanishad is found in the Yajur-Veda. Although this Upanishad is classified as a minor Upanishad, it is of major importance to the yogi for it deals with the fundamental and esoteric subject of Kundalini awakening as well as directing that cosmic Life-Force. In this program, Goswami Kriyananda reads and gives an enlightening commentary to his newly edited edition of this most valuable text. The great secret of this Upanishad relates to the average Earthling's breathing pattern. Thus, Goswami Kriyananda will explain how the Kriya-Kundalini awakening can be accomplished by key yogic practices. This program is an excellent adjunct to 'The Awakening of Your Serpent Power' program listed above.

Three 90-minute audiotapes and a 37-page notebook which includes Goswami Kriyananda's edited version of the Kundalini Upanishad $99

Astral Projection Seminar

*(A New Expanded Seminar
Containing Added Data and Techniques)*

Astral Travel or "Out of Body Experience" is within your reach! Astral projection is the natural ability to withdraw your awareness from the outer universe into the inner universe, and then move from the lower inner universe, to the higher inner universe. It is natural to each one of us. Some find it easier than others, but everyone can accomplish this projection. All that is needed is a method and a great deal of practice.

This Astral Projection program is a unique opportunity to receive your training directly from Goswami Kriyananda. You, the mystical seeker, will find it of great value, for it will reveal the way that Life manifests from the invisible universes.

In this seminar you will learn about the four worlds and the seven planes, where, when and how to project, things that hinder projection, how to protect your physical and astral body while projecting, and how to create a safe platform in the astral for launching into Higher Planes of Consciousness.

Other Highlights of the course include:

◆ How to strengthen your aura
◆ The Ball of Light Projection technique
◆ The Mystical Sufi method of leaving your body
◆ Clues telling you which method is best for you
◆ The best method for "contacting" departed souls
◆ How your fears reveal what you need to overcome in order to project
◆ How to give greater elasticity to the Silver Cord
◆ How to tell the difference between a "thought-form" and a living entity

This extraordinary program gives you the opportunity to learn the ancient secrets which can give you freedom from the boundaries of your physical body!

8 hours of taped material (six 90-minute audiotapes) ... $249
Also available on videotape (four 120-minute tapes) ... $329

Home Study Programs

(Each program includes audiotapes and a full notebook with lessons to support
tapes. Each notebook contains self-help study questions at the end of the chapters
help you learn and retain the concepts.)

The Sacred Apprenticeship--the Guru Disciple Relationship

In this home study program, Goswami Kriyananda elaborates on the bond of t
Guru-disciple relationship which is deeply spiritual and personal. He answe
many asked questions about the Guru-disciple kinship: What is a true Gur
What is initiation? How does one prepare for initiation? What is the role of t
Guru ... of the disciple? He discusses obstacles on the Path, the 12 blessings of t
Guru, how to know if you are ready for discipleship, and many other integr
concepts related to the Guru-disciple kinship.

Six 60-minute audiotapes and a 151-page notebook: $49.75

The Philosophy and Methodology of Kriya Yoga

This program contains 25 lessons on Kriya Yoga. Goswami Kriyananda talks in
mately about some of his own experiences and elaborates on karma: the ultima
foundation of Kriya Yoga. He gives the basic concepts of Kriya Yoga including t
Sankya Yoga Philosophy, practices and techniques for accelerating progress wh
walking the Path, the history of Kriya Yoga, discussion of the chakras, and tec
niques for awakening the Kriya kundalini.

Six 60-minute audiotapes and a 143-page notebook: $49.75

Establishing a Firm Foundation on the Spiritual Path

Goswami Kriyananda takes the fundamental concepts of Kriya Yoga and sho
you how you can establish firm footing on the spiritual path. He stresses ho
person's individuality plays a key role for attaining spiritual progress on the Pa
You will hear many teaching stories and analogies which help give a better und
standing and memorization of the concepts. This program emphasizes the impc
tance of living a more balanced lifestyle--so you can more easily inturn to atta
deeper states of spiritual consciousness. It includes techniques such as "keyin
mantra, and the AUM mudra. You will learn the five truths of Kriya Yoga a
mystical methods for bringing "fragmented" consciousness into a unified whole.
is an inspiration for attaining personal happiness, a key ingredient for spiritu
success and Enlightenment.

Seven 60-minute audiotapes and a 179-page notebook: $59.95

To Order Call: (800) 248-0024 -- Inside Illinois: (773) 342

The Yoga Sutras of Patanjali
The Science of Enlightenment
A course on how to attain Samadhi in this very lifetime.

Goswami Kriyananda has said that this is a basic and essential course for anyone seeking to understand and attain higher states of consciousness. It is a vital course for anyone not having a Guru. If one has a Guru, it is the Guru's textbook for teaching Yoga, and guiding souls upon the sacred Path.

Sri Patanjali in his four books entitled, "*The Kriya Yoga Sutras*," gives the basics of all spiritual psychology. He shows the path for overcoming negative karma and for attaining happiness. In them he speaks of the causes of negative habits which lead to confinement, along with the methods to cure this confinement and thus attain Enlightenment. The emphasis in these great texts is the total step by step method for attaining Samadhi.

This home study course gives a detailed, step by step plan for moving from everyday earth consciousness to spiritual Enlightenment. It is a rare chance to tap the oral tradition of yoga. Goswami Kriyananda gives a new, deeper esoteric interpretation of each and every Sutra in the four books. He gives added insights into the more important Sutras and how to use them in your daily life to attain Samadhi.

Highlights of the program include:

- The nature and purpose of Kriya Yoga
- The key yogic techniques to overcome obstacles so that you can attain Samadhi and Enlightenment
- An exploration of the nature of karma and the things to do to avoid your karma from manifesting
- The means by which a dedicated soul can open the eye of wisdom and obtain, first hand, the occult, mystical secrets of the universe

This is truly a course which will guide you during your entire life. Each of the four books are conveniently divided into three parts for easier learning and remembering. Goswami Kriyananda lists each Sutra in the book, along with his deeper interpretation of its meaning.

This home study course contains fifteen 90-minute audiotapes, a 280-page notebook of printed text of the Sutras, along with Goswami Kriyananda's interpretation of them. It includes study questions to help you learn and retain the concepts and information.

Introductory offer ... $149

The Temple of Kriya Yoga's
Seminary Without Walls

*"Give a man a fish, he will eat for a day;
teach him to fish, he will eat forever."*

♦ Become an ordained Swami in just 18 months
  while studying at home.

♦ Gain a wealth of Wisdom and Esoteric Knowledge.

♦ Discover the answers to Life's deeper problems.

♦ Learn how to improve other people's lives through Spiritual
  Teaching.

♦ Find satisfaction in guiding others through Spiritual Counseling.

♦ Learn how to apply the Teachings of the ancient Seers to attain
  earth happiness and Enlightenment.

One of the basic building blocks of Kriya Yoga is the understanding that
each of us has the ability to be happy and fulfilled in this lifetime. One of
the best means of achieving this is to share our wisdom and compassion
with the world. The Seminary Without Walls is designed to provide you
with methods and techniques that will guide you in this effort.

The Seminary Without Walls was created for seekers unable to attend in
person. It is an 18-month audiotape program for those wishing to become an ordained swami. It is taught primarily by Goswami Kriyananda,
and supplemented with lectures by other swamis. It can also be audited
to learn more of the mystical Truths and Teachings.

It is not necessary to have prior experience in yoga or metaphysics in
order to enroll. It IS necessary to be dedicated to the awakening of your
own spiritual potential and the impetus to sincerely help others along
the path to greater earth happiness and Enlightenment.

Some of the subjects taught in the course include: Karma and Causation,
Meditation, Mantra, Pranayama, Bhagavad Gita, the Kriya Yoga Sutras of
Patanjali, Eastern Thought, Mystical Views of World Religions, and other
subjects to give you a well-rounded understanding of other spiritual traditions and the spiritual life.

For more information and an application, write or call the Temple.

Outside Illinois: (800) 248-0024 - Inside Illinois: (773) 342-4600

Kriya Samadhi Workshop

Learn the Science of Kriya Yoga from a living Guru of the Kriya Lineage....

Now you can learn how to transcend your earth existence, loosen the bonds of your karma, and attain the spiritual consciousness of Samadhi through the Science of Kriya Yoga.

The techniques and concepts covered in this very special course were originally given to Goswami Kriyananda's closest students and disciples and are presented in three parts:

Highlights include:

◆ **Your Spiritual Preparation**
Occult anatomy of man
Breathing techniques
The talases
Diet and cleansing techniques
Mantra and meditation

◆ **The Understanding and Softening of Karma**
The meaning and purpose of karma
Three types of karma
How to soften and dissolve your karma
How to know when karma will manifest
The Mystical formula for freedom

◆ **Kriya Projection: The Pathway to Heaven**
How to cultivate a thought to leave cyclic existence
The worlds and planes of consciousness
Transferring your consciousness to higher planes
Removing the obstacles to reaching the higher planes
Kriya techniques for God-Consciousness

Partake of the knowledge, wisdom and spiritual insight Goswami Kriyananda has attained that he might share these with you. Receive the blessing and Flame of Kriya into your life.

Complete course: 37 audiotapes (90 minutes each) and study guides ... $395

Learn Astrology....
The Language of the Soul

Goswami Kriyananda offers books and home study courses that explore Astrology from both the practical and spiritual levels. By understanding Astrology and learning to read charts, you can help yourself and others. Through Astrology you can learn the art of timing events--when and when not to begin them. Astrology is one of the finest tools for life-guidance and skillful living. By learning Astrology you can gain greater contol of your life.

Beginner's Guide to Natal Astrology
Home Study Program
Four audiotapes and an 84-page notebook

Learn the fascinating science of Natal Astrology. "Natal Astrology is the science and the key to character." To understand a person's character is to understand his destiny. This introductory Astrology program by Goswami Kriyananda takes you through the fundamentals of understanding and interpreting the natal chart. It includes lessons in the signs, houses, planets, aspects, and then how to blend these to meaningfully interpret any chart including your own.

This home study course includes four 60-minute audiotapes accompanied by an 84-page notebook which supports the tapes. It includes a set of flashcards, study guides, and study questions.

$64.95 (One-half of the cost of this program can later be applied to the Practicing Astrologer Course.)

Wisdom and Way of Astrology (Book)

Astrology is the language of the soul, a doorway to Self-Revelation. In this book, Goswami Kriyananda returns Astrology to its primary role as the mother science of the spiritual search. It is the science of proper timing, a tool for personal transformation, and a method for understanding oneself and the world.

The clear and understandable presentation of the signs, planets, houses, aspects and philosophy of chart interpretation makes this an excellent study guide for the beginner. It also includes an abundance of deeper mystical information for the more advanced astrologer. (*The Wisdom and Way of Astrology* is included free with the Practicing Astrologer Course.)

8-1/2 X 5-1/2, perfectbound, 420 pages....$17.95

To Order:
Outside Illinois: (800) 248-0024 - Inside Illinois: (773) 342-4600
Fax: (773) 342-4608

Become a
Practicing Astrologer
In 14 months or less

Through the study and practice of Astrology you can reap innumerable benefits in your life socially, financially and spiritually. Astrology reveals where your strengths and weaknesses exist, and how to use them so they work for you. Astrology affirms your ability to use free will and thus helps you to more comfortably manage your life-patterns. It helps you to recognize ways for achieving greater success and happiness in your life and how to share these with others.

Whether you are new to Astrology or have studied it for years, our extensive at-home course can provide you with the special knowledge, training and understanding needed to practice Astrology professionally. Learn how to give astrological readings with depth and skill! In this 14-month all encompassing program, Goswami Kriyananda begins with a thorough study of the basics of Astrology, and then continues with how to interpret a chart. He includes esoteric studies and gives you all the information needed to start your own practice.

The Practicing Astrologer program includes extensive study of the signs, houses, aspects, natal astrology, transits, progressions, spiritual and past-life astrology, and more. Goswami Kriyananda puts into this course the best of his 50 years of teaching and counseling in Astrology. He blends simplicity with depth.

The complete course includes more than 120 audiotapes (60-90 minutes in length), and three large volumes of printed astrology lessons which support these tapes, including study guides and transcripts. It also includes flashcards, self-help tests, and other essential books and information necessary to construct a chart and delineate it. We even provide the pencils and pens! It also includes a free copy of Goswami Kriyananda's 420-page classic text: *The Wisdom and Way of Astrology*.

The Practicing Astrologer home study program is divided into 3 individual parts at $550 each. (Or it can be purchased in its entirety for $1485 which includes a 10% discount). To order this all-encompassing program, complete and mail the order form on the final page, or write or call the Temple for more information.

To Order Call:
Outside Illinois: (800) 248-0024 - Inside Illinois: (773) 342-4600
FAX: (773) 342-4608

Attaining Conscious Immortality
(The Art of Dying Consciously)
Formerly called "Death, Dying & Rebirth"

According to yoga philosophy, death is a great spiritual opportunity, an auspicious moment for the enlightenment of the soul, the time to release the energies needed for a positive rebirth.

- ♦What do people experience during the death process?
- ♦What becomes of the soul after the body dies?
- ♦How can you overcome your fear of death?
- ♦How can you help a dying friend or family member?
- ♦How can you prepare for your next incarnation?

These are a few of the questions that are explored by Goswami Kriyananda and a team of health and counseling professionals in one of the finest courses ever offered by the Temple. Learn techniques from the Yogic, Tibetan and Egyptian traditions to insure a positive death experience for yourself and those you help in transition.

Highlights of the course include:

- ♦ Misconceptions about death and dying
- ♦ The effects of psychological attitudes about death
- ♦ The physical process of dying
- ♦ Mystical indications that death is near
- ♦ Acting as a guide and counselor for the dying
- ♦ The spiritual purpose of death
- ♦ The Bardo experience
- ♦ Guardians of the gates of death
- ♦ The planes of existence
- ♦ The theory of reincarnation
- ♦ A cross-cultural comparison of ideas about death

This course is a genuine help to all, layman and professional, who want to be better equipped to deal with death in a constructive way.

Twenty eight 90-minute audiotapes and study guides: $295

Goswami Kriyananda's
'How To'
Audiotape Series

This series of audiotapes will enable you to take a life improving concept and apply it positively to your life. Find new ways to solve many of the most common problems that we often face. Open your life to new ideas and new possibilities for success. Listed below are just a few audio tapes from this series:

How to Decide What You Want Out of Life gives you a step by step method to gain insights into your life and develop your goals.

How to Improve Your Life With Creative Visualization maps out an easy and systematic approach to materialize your dreams, plans and wishes, and transform your negative thoughts and emotions.

How Your Thoughts Materialize Into the Earth Plane defines what thought is, and how thoughts magnetize powerful astral forms that flow into your unconscious and manifest as your reality.

How to Understand the Yoga Diet teaches you that what you eat and the way you eat influences your mind, body and soul. A great tape filled with practical tips to help keep you healthy, peaceful, and focused on your life's goals.

How to Overcome Depression discusses the ingredients responsible for depression, the symptoms, and tools to overcome depression. You can attain a new life of happiness by refocusing the mind.

Other "How To" Tapes in the Series:
How to Attain a Peaceful Mind
How to Turn Your Obstacles Into Miracles
How to Manage Your Moods
How to Discover True Wealth
How to be Happy While Walking the Spiritual Path
How to Improve Self-Confidence
How to Understand Shamanism
How to Understand the Mystical Path
How to Become Aware of the Divinity in You and Be Happy Now
How to Begin to Recognize and Attain Your Spiritual Goals
How to Understand Yourself and Your Universe
How to Love, Remember and Serve
How to Solve All Your Problems
How to Understand Asceticism
How to Come Alive

60 minute audiotapes
Single tape: $8.95
Any three: $19.95

Chakras:
The Garden of God

Goswami Kriyananda's Comprehensive Audio Tape Home Study Course With Text

The Complete Set Contains:

- **15 Ninety Minute Audio Cassettes**

- **620 Page Text and Study Guide**

- **12 Full Color Illustrations**

- **Tape Case and 3 Ring Binder**

This extensive home study program is the most comprehensive course you can find on the esoteric philosophy of the Chakras. It contains a variety of very special mystical techniques given by Goswami Kriyananda for awakening and balancing the Chakras and bringing about higher states of consciousness. Kriyananda utilizes the Chakric Tree of Life to reveal the numerous ways in which we climb towards the apex of our spiritual maturity.

This program provides you with answers and insights into many of the most frequently asked questions about the Chakras, including:

- What are the Chakras?
- How do they affect your life?
- What is the value of this knowledge?
- How do you utilize them toward Enlightenment?
- How do you activate the Kriya currents within you?

- How do the Chakras relate to awakening Kundalini?
- What are some of the misconceptions about its awakening?
- What is the difference between Shakti, Kundalini and Kriya?

Chakras: The Garden of God

You know that your physical body has a highly organized, elegantly designed anatomy. In this course you learn to understand and explore the equally wondrous anatomy of your subtle or astral body. The key structures of the subtle anatomy are the Chakras. These creative centers of consciousness are the inner keys to transforming and recreating your life at every level. A clear understanding of the Chakric system provides you with a map for understanding how you have created your current life conditions and how you can recreate those conditions in a more balanced, joyful, and harmonious form.

Goswami Kriyananda presents teachings that cannot be found in any other text. These are the techniques and insights that, in the past, were only transmitted orally from teacher to student.

You Will Discover:

- How you can tap into the tremendous energy and creative potential stored in the Chakras

- How Chakric energies manifest as health or disease

- The relationship of breath to awakening the Chakras

- The difference between balanced and unbalanced energy in the subtle body

- How to awaken kundalini without pain or emotionality

- How Chakric energy manifests in our relationships

Complete set including 15 audio tapes, text and study guide $169.00

◆ NOTES ◆

◆ NOTES ◆

◆ NOTES ◆

◆ NOTES ◆

◆ NOTES ◆

◆ NOTES ◆

◆ NOTES ◆

◆ NOTES ◆

◆ NOTES ◆

◆ NOTES ◆

◆ NOTES ◆